Legal Entanglements

Legal Entanglements
Law, Rights and the Battle for Legitimacy in Divided Germany, 1945–1989

Sebastian Gehrig

berghahn
NEW YORK • OXFORD
www.berghahnbooks.com

First published in 2021 by
Berghahn Books
www.berghahnbooks.com

© 2021, 2026 Sebastian Gehrig
First paperback edition published in 2026

Every reasonable effort has been made to supply complete and correct credits for images inside this book. If there are errors or omissions, please contact the publisher so that corrections can be addressed in any subsequent edition.

All rights reserved. Except for the quotation of short passages for the purposes of criticism and review, no part of this book may be reproduced in any form or by any means, electronic or mechanical, including photocopying, recording, or any information storage and retrieval system now known or to be invented, without written permission of the publisher.

Library of Congress Cataloging-in-Publication Data
Names: Gehrig, Sebastian, author.
Title: Legal entanglements : law, rights and the battle for legitimacy in divided Germany, 1945–1989 / Sebastian Gehrig.
Description: New York : Berghahn Books, 2021. | Includes bibliographical references and index.
Identifiers: LCCN 2020051919 (print) | LCCN 2020051920 (ebook) | ISBN 9781800730830 (hardback) | ISBN 9781800730847 (ebook)
Subjects: LCSH: Law—Germany—History—1945–1990
Classification: LCC KK190 .G44 2021 (print) | LCC KK190 (ebook) | DDC 349.4309/045—dc23
LC record available at https://lccn.loc.gov/2020051919
LC ebook record available at https://lccn.loc.gov/2020051920

British Library Cataloguing in Publication Data
A catalogue record for this book is available from the British Library

EU GPSR Authorized Representative
LOGOS EUROPE, 9 rue Nicolas Poussin, 17000, LA ROCHELLE, France
Email: Contact@logoseurope.eu

ISBN 978-1-80073-083-0 hardback
ISBN 978-1-83695-391-3 paperback
ISBN 978-1-80758-745-1 epub
ISBN 978-1-80073-084-7 web pdf

https://doi.org/10.3167/9781800730830

Contents

List of Illustrations   vii

Acknowledgements   viii

List of Abbreviations   xii

Introduction   1

Part I. Trenches

Chapter 1
Legal Rubble   29

Chapter 2
Old and New Law   68

Part II. Internationalization

Chapter 3
The Clash of Legal Universes   105

Chapter 4
Entangled Citizenships   142

Part III. Universalisms

Chapter 5
International Networking   183

Chapter 6
Separated by Law   220

Conclusion. License to Legislate   259

Bibliography 275
Index 316

Illustrations

Figure 0.1.	Chancellor Konrad Adenauer standing on the corner of the carpet addressing the Allied High Commissioners, Petersberg, Bonn, 1949.	2
Figure 1.1.	Federal President Theodor Heuss viewing 'Divided Germany' at the West German Pavilion, World Fair, Brussels, 1958.	30
Figure 1.2.	Josef Henselmann, 'Divided Germany', Brussels 1958 in: *Werk und Zeit* 7(6) (1958), 5.	31
Figure 1.3.	ARD Weather Forecast Map, 1960.	31
Figure 1.4.	Remastered ARD Weather Forecast Map, 1960s.	32
Figure 1.5.	Election poster, 1947.	35
Figure 1.6.	Draft of the GDR constitution, 19 March 1949.	39
Figure 5.1.	The Rising Man, sculpture, Northern Gardens, UN Headquarters, New York City, 1975.	184
Figure 5.2.	The Quiet Room, Security Council, UN Headquarters, New York City, 1978.	185
Figure 5.3.	Cartoon, 'TV-Wetterkarte: Lästige Gemüter', *Der Spiegel* 7 (1970), 39.	188

Acknowledgements

It is a great pleasure to thank all the institutions and people who have contributed to writing this book. The many trips to gather sources for this book would not have been possible without the generous financial support of the Karl-Jaspers Centre for Advanced Transcultural Studies at Heidelberg and the German Research Foundation, the Fritz-Thyssen Foundation, the John-Fell-Fund Oxford, the German Academic Exchange Service (DAAD) and the British Academy/Leverhulme Trust Small Grant 'Divided Germany's Legal Cold War and the United Nations, 1945–73' (SG141620). I would like to thank especially all the friendly and helpful archivists in German, British, American and Swiss archives who patiently helped me identify materials in their collections. Aspects of Chapters 1 and 4 are explored in more detail in articles published in the *Journal of Contemporary History* and *Historische Zeitschrift*.

At Heidelberg, Edgar Wolfrum gave me the freedom to develop first ideas on a history of law during the Cold War as a doctoral student. Cord Arendes, Cordia Baumann, Marcel Berlinghoff, Kathrin Hammerstein, Angela Siebold, Martin Stallmann and Cathrin Weykopf discussed my ideas with me during many enjoyable evenings after research seminars at the Orange. Barbara Mittler invited me to join her reading group at the Institute of Chinese Studies and supported me throughout the work on my dissertation and after. Encouraged by Barbara Mittler, the doctoral research group 'Rethinking Trends' generously funded by the Karl-Jaspers Centre allowed me to work together with Laila Abu-Er-Rub, Jennifer Altehenger, Nora Frisch, Lena Henningsen, Annika Jöst, Cora Jungbluth, Jennifer May, Petra Thiel, Sun Liying and Huang Xuelei for three years. The exposure to Asian history and culture during this time expanded my horizons and was instrumental in helping me situate my own work in broader historical contexts.

At UCL, Mark Hewitson showed me the ropes of what it means to teach at university and let me take over his office for a year. The warm and collegiate atmosphere at the German Department made the transition into British academia a real pleasure. My thanks go to Judith Beniston, Stephanie Bird, Seb Coxon, Mererid Puw Davies, Mary Fulbrook, Geraldine Horan, Susanne Kord and Martin Liebscher for including me as one of their own.

At Oxford, Jane Garnett and Matthew Kempshall made Wadham College feel like more than a workplace. Together with George Southcombe, they taught me how to become a better teacher, for which I am very grateful. Paul Betts and Nick Stargardt welcomed me as co-convenor into the Modern German History Research Seminar. They both taught me a great deal on how to 'do' history – and German history more specifically – and gave me unwavering support in developing the framework for this book. In doing so, they have transformed how I think about the history of Germany in its European and global contexts. I will always be grateful for their mentorship and friendship. The unique environment at the Faculty of History inspired and enriched many aspects of the manuscript. I very much benefitted from the expertise and comments of Jakub Benes, Tom Buchanan, Patricia Clavin, Martin Conway, Robert Gildea, Ruth Harris, David Hopkin, Rana Mitter, Hartmut Pogge-Strandmann, Sian Pooley, David Priestland, Peter Pulzer, Anna Ross, Stephen A. Smith and Jonathan Wright. The Fritz-Thyssen Foundation and the Oxford Fell-Fund allowed me to co-organize a conference on 'Law, (Inter-)Nationalism and the Global Cold War, 1945–89' at the Oxford China Centre in 2015. Over two days, the wonderful papers and discussions inspired a lot of ideas for this book. Through the annual meetings at Cumberland Lodge during my time as DAAD-Fachlektor at Oxford, I also had the good fortune to meet Tim Buchen, Udo Grashoff, Henning Grunwald, Kathrin Hamenstädt, Rike Krämer, Nina Lück, Jochen Müller, Barbara Nastoll, Julia Partheymüller, Björn Siegel, Daniel Siemens and Kim Wünschmann. I have fond memories of the ritual of our annual meetings at the end of busy autumn terms and discussions around the fireplace at the lodge's bar.

Living between London and Oxford for the last couple of years has allowed me to discuss my work with Arnd Baurkämper, Martin H. Geyer, Birthe Kundrus, Johannes Paulmann, Andreas Rödder and Willibald Steinmetz when they spent time as visiting professors in the UK. The German History Institute London and the Institute of Historical Research provide wonderful nodes for exchanges between historians of Germany. I want to thank Tobias Becker, Jim Björk, Jeff Bowersox, Alexander Clarkson, Chris Dillon, Andreas Gestrich, Christina von Hodenberg, Valeska Huber, David Motadel, Felix Römer, Michael Rowe, Katrin Schreiter, Martina Steber and Astrid Swenson for the many chats between panels or after lectures over dinner from which I have always benefitted.

Since joining Roehampton, my colleagues Michael Brown, Michael P. Cullinane, Lewis Darwen, Trevor Dean, Sylvia Ellis, Iain Johnston-White, Suzannah Lipscomb, Glyn Parry, Yolana Pringle, Krisztina Robert, Katharina Rowold, Caroline Sharples, John Tosh, Edward Vallance, Andrew Wareham and Zbigniew Wojnowski have made work a real pleasure. Discussions with them in our departmental research seminar and the Research Group for Contemporary History accompanied the last stretch of work on the manuscript. I am grateful for the collegiate atmosphere that they provide as the history team at Roehampton.

Over the last years that I have worked on this book, conversations during and after conference panels and workshops as well as invitations to give papers on various aspects of the book have helped me to clarify my ideas. For their helpful feedback and comments along the way or their own papers for panels and workshops I participated in, I would like to thank Melinda Banerjee, Richard Bessel, Svenja Bethke, Frank Biess, Brandon Bloch, Bill Bowring, Thomas Brodie, Hubertus Büschel, Justin Collings, Jan Eckel, Mark Cornwall, Rogier Cremers, Barnaby Crowcroft, Rohit De, Celia Donert, Geoff Eley, Dina Fainberg, Moritz Föllmer, Sheldon Garon, Michael Geyer, Jens Gieseke, Bernhard Gißibl, Anna von der Goltz, Rüdiger Graf, William G. Gray, Raluca Grosescu, Steven L.B. Jensen, Rachel Johnston-White, Fabian Klose, Katharina Kunter, Barak Kushner, Sonja Levsen, Kerstin von Lingen, Stephen Lovell, Tehyun Ma, Aline-Florence Manet, James Mark, Elidor Mehili, Christina Morina, A. Dirk Moses, Dina Moyal, Alanna O'Malley, Nikolaos Papadogiannis, Valentyna Polunina, Aribert Reimann, Jessica Reinisch, Daniel Leese, Ned Richardson-Little, Dominik Rigoll, Ivan Sablin, Andrew Sartori, Alexander Semyonov, Sarah Shortall, Mira Siegelberg, Joseph R. Slaughter, Quinn Slobodian, Phillip Stern, Lauren Stokes, Glenn Tiffert, Heidi Tworek, Marc Volovici, Annette Weinke, Roni Weinstein, Bernd Weisbord, Natasha Wheatley and Benjamin Ziemann. Their formal and informal comments and advice certainly made this a better book. Dieter Grimm, Achim Krämer and Bernhard Altehenger provided their legal expertise in extended conversations and helped me to understand better the perspective of judges and lawyers. I will inevitably have forgotten to mention colleagues who also helped with their expertise, for which I apologize in advance. At Berghahn Books, Chris Chappell, Mykelin Higham and Caroline Kuhtz took wonderful care of the production of the book. Despite all the valuable comments I have received while writing the book, all omissions and mistakes of course remain mine alone.

Without the support of friends and family, this book would not have been written. Karl Gerth at important moments reminded me of the importance of work-life balance when things got too stressful. Over the years, Nicolas Büchse, Felix Böcking, Louis Goldmann, Johannes Jung, Sebastian Neuhäuser, Anna Ross and Felix Stolterfoth have been good friends. I grew up in a family that lived German division. Being among grandparents and great uncles and aunts who had lived through the division of the country and saw their families divided as well as witnessed its unification has shaped my work in many ways. My parents Ute and Klaus have always given me encouragement and support. Without them, I would have not embarked on a history degree and doctorate. My aunt and uncle Margit and Frieder have supported me every step of the way all my life. My in-laws Sherida and Bernhard helped in many ways and took us on lovely holidays in Britain to give us time away from the bustling life in London when we needed it. Together with my sister Katharina and brother-in-law Tobias and their children, my family has always provided a home. This book would not exist without Jennifer. Her energy, enthusiasm and support give me joy every day. This book is dedicated to her.

Abbreviations

ARD	Arbeitsgemeinschaft der öffentlich-rechtlichen Rundfunkanstalten der Bundesrepublik Deutschland
ASJ	Arbeitsgemeinschaft Sozialdemokratischer Juristinnen und Juristen
ATO	Allied Travel Office (West Berlin)
BACDJ	Bundesarbeitskreis Christlich Demokratischer Juristen
BdV	Bund der Vertriebenen
BGH	Bundesgerichtshof
BVerfG	Bundesverfassungsgericht
BVerfGG	Bundesverfassungsgerichtsgesetz
CDU	Christlich Demokratische Union Deutschlands
CSSR	Czechoslovak Socialist Republic
CSU	Christlich Soziale Union Deutschlands
ECA	United Nations Economic Commission for Africa
ECE	United Nations Economic Commission for Europe
ECHR	European Convention on Human Rights
ECSC	European Coal and Steel Community
EDC	European Defence Community
FAO	Food and Agriculture Organization of the United Nations
FAZ	Frankfurter Allgemeine Zeitung

FDP	Freie Demokratische Partei
FRG	Federal Republic of Germany
GDR	German Democratic Republic
IAEA	International Atomic Energy Agency
IMCO	Inter-Governmental Maritime Consultative Organization
IOC	International Olympic Committee
ITU	International Telecommunication Union
KPD	Kommunistische Partei Deutschlands
NATO	North Atlantic Treaty Organization
NSDAP	Nationalsozialistische Deutsche Arbeiterpartei
POW	Prisoner of War
PRC	People's Republic of China
ROC	Republic of China
SBZ	Sowjetische Besatzungszone
SED	Sozialistische Einheitspartei Deutschlands
SPD	Sozialdemokratische Partei Deutschlands
SRP	Sozialistische Reichspartei
TTD	Temporary Travel Document
UDHR	Universal Declaration of Human Rights
UfJ	Untersuchungsausschuß Freiheitlicher Juristen
UN	United Nations
UNDP	United Nations Development Programme
UNESCO	United Nations Educational, Scientific and Cultural Organization
USSR	Union of Soviet Socialist Republics
WHO	World Health Organization
WMO	World Meteorological Organization

Introduction

Small steps can be highly symbolic in the world of international diplomacy. On 21 September 1949, the first chancellor of the Federal Republic of Germany (FRG) Konrad Adenauer (1876–1967) took such a step. On this rainy day in Bonn, Adenauer went to see the Allied High Commissioners at the grand hotel on the Petersberg to receive the Occupation Statute. This document was meant to return some sovereign powers to the newly formed first West German government. Protocol demanded that Adenauer stop in the main hall in front of a carpet on which the three Western commissioners were waiting. It was here that he would be handed the legal document that validated and authorized his new government. Yet the symbolic politics carefully embedded in the protocol failed. When the French commissioner André Francois-Poncet (1887–1978) offered Adenauer his hand as a welcome, the West German chancellor seized the moment and stepped onto the carpet with the Allied representatives. With this small gesture, Adenauer had clearly signalled his intention to reclaim German sovereignty and meet the Allied powers on an equal footing.

Captured in a famous photograph (Figure 0.1), it was a historic moment. The statute returned legislative, judicial and executive powers to the new West German government.[1] It was also a crucial episode in an emerging legal confrontation between two nascent German states that would shape German history until 1989 and beyond. Less than a month later, on 7 October 1949, the German Democratic Republic (GDR) was established from what had been the Soviet Occupation Zone. In the years between the unconditional surrender of the Third Reich on 8 May 1945 and the founding of these two German states, in the midst of the first rudimentary reconstruction of housing, economic, social and political life, legal scholars and politicians in all four Allied occupation zones had formulated different legal frameworks for Germany's future. Rather than helping to give birth

---

Notes for this chapter begin on page 18.

Figure 0.1. Chancellor Konrad Adenauer standing on the corner of the carpet addressing the Allied High Commissioners, Petersberg, Bonn, 1949. Photo: © Berto-Verlag, Bonn.

to two separate states, however, they entangled the constitutional laws governing postwar Germany and the rights of Germans in an ideological struggle over German sovereignty, law and rights.[2]

After the unification of Germany on 3 October 1990, attention for the entanglements of German legal frameworks, laws and rights and the legal Cold War to which they gave rise was superseded by controversies within and beyond the legal profession on the nature of the GDR's legal system. Transitional justice trials against former GDR political and military leaders as well as border guards epitomized the GDR's *Unrechtsstaat* (unlawful state).[3] After 1990, the East German socialist state, propped up by the Stasi's – its secret police – mass surveillance and intimidation of political opponents, stood in stark contrast to the rule of law and legal security that the West German *Rechtsstaat* had developed after 1949 once Third Reich legacies in the legal sphere had been overcome.[4] With such post-unification comparisons of the East and West German legal systems, the parallel existence of two separate German states that had been based on ideologically competing and separate legal systems came to dominate public and scholarly perspectives on the history of law and rights during national division.[5]

However, this was not the perspective Adenauer took when he felt emboldened to take his symbolic step onto the carpet. Under his leadership, the Bonn government would exercise legal sovereignty over the whole of Germany, represent all Germans, and rebuild the *Rechtsstaat*. It was a legal vision that connected pre- and postwar Germany. The GDR, by contrast, was built on a different legal framework, one that emphasized a thorough break with the past. It nonetheless also laid claim to speaking for the whole of Germany. An anti-fascist Germany, the GDR's founders proclaimed, would emerge under their ideological leadership, protected by a people's constitution that secured the freedom and rights of its citizens, social and economic justice, and peace and friendship with all peoples. During the first decades of its existence, the GDR government declared that this legal vision was designed to lead the masses in the FRG to the revolution and secure the victory of socialism for all Germans.[6]

The two legal frameworks could not co-exist because each was premised on the demise of the other. Both the legal orders of the FRG and the GDR were constructed on the tenet that there was only one postwar German state, and that this one state would claim legal authority for the whole of Germany and all Germans. In this they agreed.[7] Yet government leaders in Bonn and East Berlin fundamentally disagreed over the legal mechanisms and sources of legitimacy that would enable them to represent Germany internationally and domestically. This would have a crucial impact on visions of law and actual rights granted to Germans east and west of the border. Both governments also disputed the territorial shape of this postwar Germany. Leading West German legal scholars argued that the Bonn government embodied the legal persona of the German Reich 'in its borders of 1937'. This formula postulated the prewar territorial shape of the German Reich as a starting point for legal reconstruction but excluded the period of the Third Reich's territorial expansion when the Nazis annexed Austria and the Sudetenland in 1938 before the outbreak of war in 1939. This strategic date retained claims to German territory, but complicated the condemnation of Nazi rule between 1933 and 1937.[8] In contrast, the GDR government accepted Germany's territorial losses in the East that the Allies had specified in the Potsdam Agreement. The East

German state was designed as the successor state of the German Reich that gained its legitimacy from the anti-fascist credentials of the socialist movement in Germany and socialist legality.[9] The two German states were thus at loggerheads over the very nature of law, the rights of Germans and the territorial shape of German sovereignty from their foundations in 1949 onwards.

Law and rights formed a crucial element of the global Cold War battle for legitimacy between the two German states as it played out in divided Germany, Europe and internationally.[10] At stake were the very foundations of rights and law. Until 1989, ideological conflicts over sovereignty, national self-determination, citizenship, basic rights and human rights frequently escalated between the two German governments. This book traces, first of all, how competing ideologies of law gave these legal terms different meanings and how conflicts between the two German states changed their meaning over time. As two German states claimed the same legal rights – yet based in fundamentally contradictory ideologies of law – for only one people, the competition over the legitimacy of different forms of law in divided Germany inevitably remained intertwined in a constant conflict over the question of which state could provide rights more legitimately. Beyond that, the book explores how the simultaneous existence of two German legal systems challenged the postwar international legal order, premised as it was on the assumption that one nation-state would represent one nationality, and how global conflicts over sovereignty and the right of self-determination of peoples in turn shaped ideas of rights and legal realities in the divided Germany.

The fortunes of the two German states in their legal confrontations rose and fell with the global struggles over legitimate claims to national self-determination, the impact of international law on nation-states, and the confrontations over competing ideological visions of universal human rights. Eric D. Weitz has argued that the struggles over individual and collective human rights cannot be disentangled from histories of the nation-state and citizenship. And that the same is true in reverse.[11] Both German governments therefore had to contend with the increasing impact of legal forces stemming from decolonization and the ideological struggle between Western legal traditions and socialist legality over human rights on their national legal frameworks after 1945.[12] Diplomatic histories on East and West German foreign policy have shown how both German governments vied for influence around the globe to bolster their legitimacy at home and against the other Germany.[13] This book expands this scholarship by asking how decolonization and the transition to an international system of nation-states during the Cold War impacted on German concepts of law, rights and statehood.

To examine divided Germany's legal history as an element of the Cold War opens up at least four analytical perspectives on the rise of law, rights concepts and legalist language in the international arena after 1945. First, it shows how the legal transition out of the Second World War and into the Cold War signalled a *Verrechtlichung von Politik*, in which law simultaneously became an object of the political conflict between the FRG and GDR and the means by which the two governments conducted their ideological struggle.[14] Second, we can trace how framing political demands in legal language allowed both German states in different moments not only to attack each other, but also to push back against the Allied powers and achieve more political leeway for independent policies. Third, it puts the puzzle piece of the competition between the two German states into the wider puzzle that was the transition from 'closed' sovereign states to more porous legal systems that reshaped national legal systems and the rights of citizens after 1945. Fourth, it demonstrates how the ideological battle over law and legality triggered the rise of human rights language and norms in divided Germany and connected the German conflicts over law to global rights debates.

By expanding the perspective from domestic and German-German frameworks to an entangled history of the two Germanys that also pays attention to their involvement in global rights debates, this book shows that both German states could no longer contain the evolution of foundational concepts of law and rights, law making, and the actual rights of Germans within closed domestic legal systems. Scholarship has illuminated how the governments in Bonn and East Berlin blamed each other for rights violations, shortcomings in prosecuting Nazi perpetrators, and used human rights language to discredit the other Germany.[15] These works have shown how rights activists and dissidents pushed for the translation of constitutional and human rights norms into everyday legal realities and how this activism had important consequences for domestic legal reform and jurisprudence.[16] Building on this scholarship, this book provides an entangled history of both German states and their relations with the wider world within and beyond their ideological alliances. It reveals how global currents of human rights and international law played a crucial role in the making of laws, rights and ideologies of law in divided Germany.

The Cold War in Germany was also made by laws and made law. Domestic and international law making produced legal structures that followed their own inherent logics within and beyond the divided Germany when the global ideological war over words turned into a war over legal concepts after 1945.[17] If we study the history of law and rights in divided Germany as the double dialectic between German-German conflicts over the transformation of German law after National Socialism and the simultaneous involvement of both German societies in the global conflicts between socialist legality and Western concepts of law that played out in confrontations over self-determination, sovereignty and human rights, we discover that the constant interplay between clashes within and between the two German states and their engagement with international politics had a crucial impact on legal policies, conceptual debates on law, and actual rights of Germans in both German states between 1949 and 1989.[18]

Out of War, Into War

To understand how Germany's legal Cold War began, we need to look at the doctrine dominating German legal debates on sovereignty before the Second World War. Legal scholars who were trained in the interwar period connected the postwar situation firmly to Germany's legal heritage, reaching back into the decades after the unification of the German Empire. Yet the existence of two German states questioned precisely this German tradition of thinking about the legal and temporal nature of the state and rights at its core. National division confounded the trinity of *Staatsgewalt* (state power), *Staatsgebiet* (territory) and *Staatsvolk* (people belonging to the state) that Georg Jellinek (1851–1911) had famously put forward as the remits of sovereignty in German *Staatsrecht* in 1895. Building on the work of the constitutionalists Friedrich Gerber (1823–1891) and Paul Laband (1838–1918), who had argued for a purely legal definition of the state, Jellinek divorced the social existence of the state from its legal perception and decisively shaped German legal thought for the following century.[19] In the twentieth-century, *Staatsrecht* became the supreme field in German legal scholarship as it dealt with the organization of the state and its institutions as well as basic rights of individuals.

Jellinek's doctrine made the legal survival of the state beyond catastrophic events such as Germany's defeat in the First World War and the foundation of the Weimar Republic possible. The Weimar Constitution of 1919 emphasized that it was the state that was sovereign to move beyond the tension between princely and popular sovereignty of the imperial era.[20] Throughout the Weimar period, influential legal scholars such as Hans Kelsen (1881–1973), Hermann Heller (1891–1933), Hans Nawiasky (1880–1961), Karl Loewenstein (1891–1973) and Carl Schmitt (1888–1985) argued over the legal nature of government, the legal safeguards of the political system, and the very nature of law.[21] While academic conflicts between proponents of natural law and advocates of a positivist approach to law raged until 1933 when the Nazis seized power, Jellinek's trinity defining German statehood remained unchallenged in German postwar debates on legal reconstruction.²² When the two German states were founded in 1949, legal scholars in the Western occupation zones had already prepared the grounds for the Bonn government to promote the assumption that the German Reich's state sovereignty had survived the end of the war in international law.²³ The judiciaries in both countries based their development of distinct legal systems – despite best attempts to conceal unwanted continuities from the Third Reich into the postwar era within both states – on this shared tradition of German legal doctrine to take on the mantle of Germany's legal existence.²⁴

The resurrection of German legal sovereignty took place in an era of international rights languages and growing legal entanglements. The doctrinal connection of prewar, wartime and postwar Germany through law based on Jellinek's doctrine made divided Germany part of international legal conundrums that also haunted many other international debates surrounding decolonization.²⁵ How should the demise of empires and states be treated under international and domestic law? Could states exist outside of time and against territorial realities? And who could legitimately claim sovereignty after the downfall of a state? While many legal experts and officials at the UN fought hard to shape universal legal standards of international governance against the unequal legal heritage of the League of Nations, legal experts in both nascent German states initially joined colonial powers in rejecting the idea of new universal international legal norms. Instead, only established German legal traditions should structure Germany's legal reconstruction. Yet divided Germany soon marked the European Cold War front line of the fight between two legal universalisms: socialist legality and the rule of law.²⁶ This meant that before long both German governments had to position themselves towards global rights conflicts.

Strong continuities in legal careers from the Third Reich into the FRG ensured that the West German legalist language of political transition was formidable. Legal elites, strong in numbers and confident in their understanding of the mid-century international legal world, in which German lawyers had once before made bids for the recognition of sovereignty in the 1920s within the League of Nations, discovered the power of law as part of the Cold War long before their East German counterparts.²⁷ When the Western Allies handed denazification and democratization efforts to West German authorities in the late 1940s, civil servants and scholars quickly re-established their own traditions and emphasized continuity in German legal codes, judicial practice and administrative regulations beyond the new Basic Law and the most audacious Nazi laws that the Allied Control Council struck from German legal codes before cooperation between the four Allies broke down in 1947.²⁸ While legal and historical studies have uncovered how the judiciary as a profession managed the transition into the FRG almost unscathed, many questions remain about the role these jurists and government officials played in maintaining many prewar and wartime legal policies and regulations.[29] Due to this continuity in doctrine and personnel, West German legal scholars were able to persist in their traditional approach to statehood and legal frameworks of sovereignty after 1945 and inscribed them into international legal debates.[30]

Unlike in West Germany, legal experts played no major role in the foundation of the new socialist state. Small in numbers, many of the scholars tasked with setting up the GDR's legal framework had specialized in other areas of law such as civil and public law before 1945.[31] But law was by no means unimportant in the early GDR, even if the leadership of the Sozialistische Einheitspartei Deutschlands (SED, Socialist Unity Party) had major reservations about the German legal tradition.[32] During the early 1950s, Hilde Benjamin (1902–1989) and other party leaders cleansed much of the legal elite of the new socialist state. This was done in the name and spirit of 'revolutionary legality', a process many East German communist exiles had experienced first-hand during the 1930s and 1940s in Moscow when numerous German communists who did not wholeheartedly support the Soviet party line fell victim to the Soviet secret police's paranoia.[33] At the same time, the SED leadership distanced itself from any responsibility for the crimes of the Third Reich by insisting on its anti-fascist heritage. Communist resistance to the Nazi regime turned into a fig leaf, which was meant to exculpate the GDR's whole society from any association with the Third Reich.[34] It was an important ideological argument that meant that SED leaders relinquished any political and legal responsibilities for the atrocities committed under the Nazi regime.[35] Yet this ideological separation from Third Reich legacies put the SED in an increasingly difficult political but also legal position: insisting on a fundamental break with the German fascist past in other areas of law made it much more difficult for the SED to legitimize its simultaneous claim of rightfully representing German sovereignty and citizenship in the succession of the German Reich. With the exodus of more and more East Germans to the West, SED legal scholars began to prepare the GDR's new legal foundations as a sovereign socialist state that drew on the rights language of anti-colonial movements to legitimize this new East German right of self-determination.[36]

Legal Sovereignty Contested

With the SED leadership's push to sever all legal ties to the German Reich's state sovereignty, the UN became an important legal battleground for the two German states. By the 1960s, two fundamental shifts in international politics opened up a space for establishing independent GDR sovereignty. On the one hand, Western international relations scholars – chiefly Leo Gross (1903–1990) – established sovereign equality of states as the new basis for international politics. Facing growing pressure from anti-colonial movements to end the colonial era, Western scholars established the 'Westphalian myth', claiming that ever since the Peace Treaties of 1648, European states had developed a state system based on the equality of sovereign states.[37] Such a narrative that disguised hierarchy within the international system fit the American Cold War cause. But it was immediately condemned by a growing number of Third World liberation leaders attacking the unequal standards within the UN that colonial powers intended to uphold.[38]

On the other hand, the acceleration of decolonization made the human right of self-determination the rallying cry of independence movements in Africa and Asia. The UN emerged in a world of international law conflicts in which the addressees of human rights – individuals or collective groups – and the question of whether rights originated with peoples or states were hotly contested. These global confrontations over human rights after 1945 allowed the GDR government to exploit the ambiguities of what a 'people' actually constituted under international law.[39] While the Bonn government insisted on the representation of state sovereignty in continuity with the Reich, the SED leadership now put the East German people at the heart of their legal agenda. The Final Communiqué of the Asian-African Conference of Bandung in 1955 had reinforced demands for independence and the recognition of territorial integrity of former colonies. From the mid-1960s, the SED leadership changed course in its international rights campaigning and demanded a right of self-determination for the East German people. This effort built on party-state initiatives to create a cultural sense of East German statehood to separate the GDR from West Germany.[40] As a de-facto sovereign state, the GDR government demanded the recognition of its sovereign equality and an end to the FRG's non-recognition policy that threatened third-party states with the immediate end of economic and diplomatic relations if they chose to recognize the GDR as a sovereign state.[41] East German diplomats and government-funded rights groups such as the League for Human Rights promoted the SED's support for UN racial anti-discrimination conventions to garner support among Third World liberation movements. In turn, the SED leadership hoped that newly decolonized states ascending to UN membership would support the GDR's claim to national independence.[42]

This East German shift in defining claims to national sovereignty in the rights language of Third World liberation challenged German philosophical and legal traditions of state sovereignty and continuity that dominated West German legal discourse.[43] The GDR government could refer to a long tradition within the communist movement to advocate for a right of self-determination of the East German people. From its origins in the thought of Immanuel Kant (1724–1804) and Johann Gottlieb Fichte (1762–1814), self-determination left an imprint on Karl Marx's (1818–1883) ideas on the overcoming of the alienation of the individual. Via leading socialists of the epoch, among them Ferdinand Lassalle (1825–1864) and Jean Jaurès (1859–1914), self-determination took on a predominantly collective meaning until the Socialist International included an article on the 'self-determination for all peoples' in its programme in 1896.[44] Vladimir Lenin (1870–1924), influenced by Otto Bauer (1881–1938) and other Austro-Marxist thinkers, supported the principle of self-determination as a road to independence and sovereignty at the outbreak of the First World War.[45] When the Second World War ended, traditional Western concepts of sovereignty and rights as outlined by Lassa Oppenheim (1858–1919), Jellinek and others at the turn of the century had long come under pressure from anti-colonial movements and revolutionary socialist constitutionalism advocated by leading Soviet scholars such as Evgeny A. Korovin (1892–1964), Evgeny Pashukanis (1891–1937) and Andrey Vyshinsky (1883–1954) at the Soviet Institute of State and Law in the interwar period.[46] After 1945, anti-colonial leaders pushed for the transformation of the principle of self-determination into a human right that was finally implemented into the two UN human rights covenants from 1966.[47] This Third World pressure on international law presented the SED leadership with an alternative rights language to secure independence and territorial integrity against West German legal *Staatsrecht* frameworks.

The Legal Division of a People

After the building of the Berlin Wall in 1961, the SED leadership put ideology and socialist legality at the core of a new vision of an East German right of self-determination. The GDR government now finally fully embraced the Soviet-led return to socialist legality as a stabilizing tool of governance to manage de-Stalinization.[48] This went fundamentally against West German debates shaped by natural law and legal positivist traditions that saw codified law and rights rooted in ethical, moral and religious norms outside state institutions.[49] Socialist legality denoted a new system built on Marxist-Leninist ideology in which rights exclusively flew from the existence of the socialist state that safeguarded legality based on East Germans' duty to uphold and build socialist society in turn. Law at once should serve as a set of clearly enumerated rights and duties and allow for the primacy of the party in transforming society.[50]

This shift put people at the heart of German-German legal entanglements. Since the turn of the century, nationality had formed the core of sovereignty and tied Germans to the German Reich as their state. When the SED leadership moved towards rights guaranteed through the existence of the socialist state as the new core for claims to self-determination, the nexus between nationality and sovereignty as the basis for claims to independence imploded in East German legal thinking. Until 1945, *Staatsrecht* doctrine had assumed that Germans belonged to the state and gained rights through ethnic belonging. This was expressed most clearly in the term *Staatsangehörigkeit* (belonging to the state) to denote legal citizenship. In 1949, both German governments had decreed that the Reich and Citizenship Law from 1913 that had first given legal language to German citizenship remained in force and struggled over the lawful representation of German *Staatsangehörigkeit*.[51] In 1967, an independent GDR citizenship law, pitting a new form of *DDR-Staatsbürgerschaft* (GDR citizenship) against German *Staatsangehörigkeit*, turned East Germans legally into GDR citizens. The term *Staatsbürgerschaft* emphasized active socialist rights of the citizen against the passive belonging to the state encapsulated in the term *Staatsangehörigkeit* that remained in use in the FRG. In turn, East Germans had a legal duty to engage in building socialism.[52] One year later, SED leaders commanded their citizens to discuss a new constitution in 1968, which eventually led to the proclamation of a socialist constitution in 1974 after the constitution of 1968 was once again amended.[53] East Germans had now been legally transformed into an independent people and their government renamed them *DDR-Bürger* (citizens of the GDR).

With the proclamation of the GDR citizenship law, SED leaders made the legal Cold War officially about people. Underneath this terminological shift that signalled more rights for the individual and was soon linked to human rights, however, East German law also remained a 'weapon' of political re-education as well as a tool to pressure the FRG into accepting the territorial integrity of the GDR. In the first half of the twentieth century, international lawyers had grappled with the dangers of statelessness for the individual.[54] The Nazi persecution of the European Jews had shown the global public to catastrophic ends that individuals needed a right to citizenship. In 1967, the GDR government reversed the danger of statelessness into a threat of forced naturalization.[55] The SED leadership did so by blurring the lines of what Dieter Gosewinkel has termed the 'outer' and 'inner dimension' of citizenship.[56] The new citizenship law backdated the emergence of a GDR citizenship to the foundation of the GDR in 1949. Release from citizenship could only be granted by the East German state.

This meant that Germans who had fled the GDR after 1949 and even their children born outside the GDR lived under the threat of being extradited to the GDR when they travelled within the Eastern bloc.[57] This regulation also applied even if they had become naturalized West Germans or citizens of another state. West German newspapers raged against this legal 'weapon' until the SED dismantled it again after the conclusion of Ostpolitik negotiations in 1972. When the two German states moved to détente, the German people were also legally divided.

The East German turn to anti-colonial rights rhetoric forced West German legal scholars, ministerial officials and diplomats to contemplate the relationship between international and domestic law. Viewed from a perspective of German-German conflicts over law, there was much more at stake in Ostpolitik negotiations than the recalibration of German-German diplomatic relations. West German chancellor Willy Brandt's (1913–1992) Ostpolitik has often rightly been described as a bold political agenda that forced West German society to confront the consequences of National Socialism and acknowledge the loss of territory in the East as a result of the Second World War. The East German push for new legal foundations of GDR sovereignty, however, also turned German-German diplomatic negotiations into a legal issue for the international community that intensified the global reverberations of Ostpolitik.[58] In the eyes of many international legal experts interested in preserving the nexus of nationality and sovereignty, the Bonn government openly contradicted established international legal standards by ratifying treaties with the Soviet, Polish and GDR governments. Many within the West German legal elite also fiercely pushed back against Ostpolitik to preserve *Staatsrecht* traditions and the formula of the 'German Reich in its borders of 1937' on which the FRG's legal foundations had been built since 1949.[59] What had begun as a legal competition over the question of which German state rightfully represented German sovereignty and citizenship in 1949 now turned into a complicated legal issue not just for the two German states and the four Allied powers, but for the international community at large.

The GDR government's assault on established concepts of international sovereignty tied the German-German struggle over law and rights to the fate of other 'divided nations' such as China, Korea and Vietnam (from decolonization until unification on 2 July 1976) in UN politics. The GDR's new legal foundations set up from 1967 to 1974 upset the legal norms produced by the UN. In turn, the UN legal bureaucracy fiercely defended the nexus of nationality and international sovereignty as the bedrock of the international system.[60] After 1945, UN representation of sovereignty still centred on 'nationality' in the tradition of the League of Nations as the core element of a right to national self-determination.[61] UN legal officials such as Secretary-General Thant's (1909–1974) legal counsel Konstantinos A. Stavropoulos (1905–1984) despaired over the GDR leadership's attack on UN procedural rules and regulations by pushing their way into UN politics when the FRG, which had acquired official UN observer status in 1952, still exclusively represented German nationality within UN affairs.[62] Yet Stavropoulos could do little about the appeal of the GDR's usage of legal rhetoric of self-determination as a human right to many African and Asian delegations at the time.[63]

The SED's turn to a new definition of independent GDR statehood rooted in the right of self-determination, socialist legality and human rights language prompted a wider fundamental question for UN legal experts and international law scholars as part of Ostpolitik that could no longer be avoided: could state sovereignty legitimately be divided? Especially the governments of other 'divided nations' therefore watched German-German negotiations with much unease.[64] When SED leaders suddenly claimed by the mid-1960s that they represented an 'East German people', Stavropoulos found an unlikely ally in the communist government in Beijing, which ardently pushed back against the GDR as it saw its own 'one China' policy threatened both by Brandt's rhetoric of 'two states in one nation' and the East German claim to the representation of a 'GDR nation'.[65] Soon after, US rapprochement with the People's Republic of China (PRC) and the shifting voting balance within the General Assembly towards a majority of Eastern bloc states and the Afro-Asian bloc caused the change in Chinese UN representation and reinforced the 'one China' paradigm when the PRC replaced the Republic of China (ROC) on Taiwan in 1971 within the UN.[66] This shift put pressure on the West German government to come to a new agreement with the GDR before the General Assembly might unilaterally acknowledge East German sovereignty.

After 1973, a new German legal exceptionalism formed when the UN admitted both German states simultaneously as full UN member states. The accession of both German states became possible after UN legal experts acknowledged that the different historical trajectories that had led to German and Chinese division in 1949 should form the basis for the UN's unequal legal treatment of divided Germany and China. While Germany was divided after a lost war and occupation, China ended up separated after years of civil war. In accepting Beijing's 'one China' paradigm and still permitting membership of both German states, the UN quietly and without an official discussion gave silent consent to the GDR's legal concept of sovereignty that replaced nationality with ideology as the basis for a legitimate claim to self-determination. Until 1989, the two German states thus remained the only officially recognized sovereign states that had originated from a 'divided nation' in UN legal affairs.

Separated Rights Universes

The separation of German legal sovereignty and citizenship until 1974 when the GDR proclaimed a new socialist constitution formed part of major shifts in international law and rights debates of the postwar era. The ability of states to brush aside international legal standards decreased from the 1960s onwards. This also had to do with the rise of international courts, but was driven by fundamental ideological disagreements over the nature of law and the impact of decolonization.[67] From the 1970s onwards, international politics of law forced legal experts both in West and East Germany to contemplate the relationship of international law and domestic legal systems anew. In the legal entanglements between the two German states, as in many other legal spheres around the world, international rights norms now entered national jurisprudence and law making and transformed the rights of citizens.

East German legal concepts of self-determination framed as a human right accelerated the pressure on West German jurists to engage with new international legal norms growing out of the decolonization process and UN legal disputes. If we see the rise of new international rights languages in the context of the legal Cold War, we discover that German jurists and governmental legal officials could no longer contain their legal struggle in a German-German framework by the 1960s. This book contributes to the vibrant field of human rights historiography by emphasizing the wider Cold War logics in which the rise of human rights both as a political language and law took place.[68]

When the SED leadership detached the East German legal sphere from the FRG both in bilateral as well as international relations between 1967 and 1974, SED ideologues confidently deployed their new legal vision of socialist legality to contest the basic rights-centred West German legal system and introduced UN human rights norms to East German law making.[69] Soon after the conclusion of Ostpolitik, the Helsinki Accords of 1975 affirmed East German sovereignty, territorial integrity and the existence of GDR citizenship both as political and legal categories in the new Cold War security architecture. In the eyes of SED leaders, the turn to socialist law and international rights languages played a major role in this success. The inclusion of human rights in the Helsinki Accords occurred at a time of heightened legal reform across the socialist bloc, culminating in the new Soviet constitution of 1977. Party leaderships staged rights talk campaigns and let their citizens debate their new constitutions in countless town hall meetings.[70] The GDR leadership took part in these legal education efforts across the Eastern bloc and confidently equipped its population with knowledge about socialist law and human rights as the territorial integrity of the GDR finally seemed secured in the Helsinki agreement.[71]

Yet socialist constitutionalism could only claim legitimacy in the logics of party doctrine if it appeared to be grounded in popular consent of the masses.[72] If we take the SED's efforts to build socialist legality seriously, despite its heavy emphasis on social control within the GDR and pushback against human rights norms within state institutions from the late 1970s onwards, we see that the adoption of human rights language in the GDR – also by dissidents – first happened not as a post-Helsinki Western import but in the remits of a language provided by the state itself.[73] Socialist legality promoted a 'rules consciousness' rooted in social and economic rights and in what T.H. Marshall called 'social citizenship'.[74] 'Rights consciousness' of civil and political rights in the GDR first also developed in a preconfigured legal universe shaped by socialist law.[75] Only when the economic crisis of the GDR worsened in the early 1980s, dissidents were able to subvert this state-endorsed language of constitutionalism, citizenship and human rights and the SED returned to strengthening political justice and domestic criminal law against the state's own human rights rhetoric.[76]

In contrast, West German courts, government officials and legal scholars grappled with the inclusion of international rights norms in their basic rights framework for a long time.[77] Against collective human rights norms emanating from the Eastern bloc and Global South, the US administration under Jimmy Carter (b. 1924) eventually promoted individual human rights rooted in liberal thought. This was in many ways a response to socialist and Third World advances in global human rights and international legal politics.[78] In the course of this shift, the Bonn government at first had great difficulty in capitalizing on the new American emphasis on human rights. When the Helsinki Accords were signed in 1975, there certainly was no immediate 'Helsinki effect' reshaping the German-German legal conflict.[79] The West German legal sphere held onto its initial legal frameworks rooted in German concepts of state sovereignty, citizenship and basic rights for as long as possible as it guaranteed East German refugees immediate access to West German citizenship if they managed to escape the GDR.[80]

Rights of citizens and their foundation in competing ideologies of law now overtook the issue of sovereignty in the clashes between the two German states. This occurred at a time when domestic debates on new forms of state–society relations and citizens' rights captivated West German confrontations over the reform of legal codes and calls for less rigid social norms.[81] Following student protests raging in West German streets around 1968, tectonic shifts in state–society relations crystallized in West German politics of law when the social-liberal coalition under Brandt accelerated the reform of West German legal codes in 1969.[82] This domestic focus on legal policies led to the professionalization of legal politics within the major West German political parties from the 1970s onwards. Older ideas of government, centred on a strong state bureaucracy, now came under political pressure.[83] Brandt's vision of 'daring more democracy' that headlined his first address as chancellor in the West German parliament in 1969 captured this demand amidst radical left-wing opposition to the West German state.[84] Calls for more legal rights of the *mündige Bürger* (mature citizen), especially for women, encapsulated many demands for reform that shaped domestic politics of law in the 1970s and 1980s and promoted human rights norms within the West German public.[85]

Ostpolitik gave rise to the acknowledgement of the evolution of a distinctly West German legal culture after 1949. West German society began to debate new notions of the West German state after the international recognition of the GDR's sovereignty had discredited the idea that the German Reich 'in its borders of 1937' continued to exist under international law.[86] Acknowledging the existence of the two separate German legal systems, Dolf Sternberger's (1907–1989) notion of constitutional patriotism, first noticed by a wider public in 1979, gave language to a focus on constitutional rights within West German politics of law in the 1980s. Constitutional patriotism, a concept later driven by Jürgen Habermas (b. 1929), marked a departure from legal principles and frameworks that had negated German national division after 1949.[87] A new generation of high court judges, governmental legal officials and legal scholars now finally departed from the complicated heritage of the immediate postwar period and concentrated firmly on the West German legal system. In the 1980s, both German states therefore largely accepted the existence of the other state's legal system as part of the separate ideological universes of the Cold War.

Organization of the Book

This book traces German-German legal entanglements during the Cold War by connecting files from the UN archives, the archive of the Academy for State and Legal Sciences in Babelsberg, the Foreign Office Archives, the archives of West German political parties, as well as archival holdings detailing SED legal policies and the role of the GDR High Court from the German federal archives and the Berlin-Brandenburg Academy of Science. West German Cold War legal policies are recorded in the files of governmental ministries, court verdicts and private papers of leading judges, as well as archival materials of the West German constitutional court. These documents permit fresh insights into seemingly familiar episodes such as *Deutschlandpolitik* and Ostpolitik. But their relevance only becomes fully apparent when they are connected to the court cases of ordinary Germans which, though equally remarkable and influential, have gone unnoticed even though these individuals became embroiled in larger debates they could barely understand at the time and that sometimes even had ramifications beyond German-German borders. The work of government officials at local, regional and national levels as well as diplomats working in embassies around the world or lobbying in UN corridors were the glue between high-level national and international politics and district court cases, in which the lives of ordinary Germans were directly affected by the fallout of the legal Cold War. Taken together, these materials show how ideas of law and rights shifted in both German states under the ideological pressures of the Cold War and decolonization and created the legal worlds on which the contemporary Germany is built.

The book consists of three parts, each of which approaches German-German legal entanglements from a different perspective. Part I concentrates on the legal transition from the Second World War to the Cold War and the establishment of two competing legal systems from the mid-1940s to the late 1950s in a shared framework of German sovereignty. Chapter 1 analyses the politics of sovereignty that laid the groundwork for Cold War confrontations over law. Chapter 2 focuses on the ensuing ideological struggle over rights of Germans in both states. Part II explores how the German states took their legal battle into the international arena in the 1960s and 1970s. Chapter 3 focuses on the legal struggle at the UN and explores how the GDR government employed human rights language from the mid-1960s onwards to garner support for an East German right of self-determination. Chapter 4 shifts perspective and traces how the GDR's legal policies of separating the East German legal system from all-German frameworks of sovereignty turned into a struggle over people and citizenship. Part III analyses the evolution of two separated legal universes that shaped new domestic legal cultures in the 1970s and 1980s: West Germany's *Rechtsstaat* with its emphasis on basic rights, and socialist constitutionalism in the GDR. Chapter 5 traces how the separation of German legal spheres forced legal experts of both states into the international arena to strengthen transnational legal cooperation. Chapter 6 turns to the development of new domestic legal cultures in both German states and shows how in the 1980s both German legal systems finally departed from the prewar and wartime legal frameworks that once had inevitably intertwined them and forced them into a Cold War over law.

The book's three parts operate on a parallel temporal register.[88] The chapters of each part are designed to show how German-German legal entanglements played out simultaneously in domestic East and West German contexts, German-German confrontations, and in international affairs. The chapters of each part thus trace developments that happened alongside each other in many different legal arenas, sometimes directly affecting each other, sometimes influencing each other more indirectly and over time. Yet it is this complexity of the German-German struggle over law, rights and legitimacy and how it played out at the same time in courtrooms, ministerial offices, the UN and other international networks that allows us more insight into the interplay of international legal norms, new rights languages, and how they were appropriated by two ideologically competing states. It was this complex web of legal interactions that fundamentally transformed a once unified legal system into two separate legal cultures. Ultimately, this book shows how law as politics – or in Dieter Grimm's words as *geronnene Politik* – shaped concepts of law and actual rights of Germans in both German states during a time when rights languages became a central part and mode of international politics at large.[89]

Notes

1. Benz, *Auftrag Demokratie*, 465.
2. Rückert, 'Die Beseitigung des Deutschen Reiches'; Diestelkamp, *Rechtsgeschichte als Zeitgeschichte*, 25–84; Hacker, *Der Rechtsstatus Deutschlands*, 78–115.
3. Research so far estimates 140 deaths of people killed at the German-German border. See: Hertle and Nooke, *Die Todesopfer an der Berliner Mauer*.
4. For Nazi legacies and the SED's consolidation of power, see: Müller, *Furchtbare Juristen*; Perels, *Das juristische Erbe des 'Dritten Reiches'*; von Miquel, *Ahnden oder amnestieren?*; Friedrich, *Freispruch für die Nazi-Justiz*; Friedrich, *Die kalte Amnestie*; Rottleuthner, *Karrieren und Kontinuitäten*; Günther, 'Vom "Rising Star" zum Sündenbock'; Görtemaker and Safferling, *Die Akte Rosenburg*; Frei, *Vergangenheitspolitik*; Frei, *Karrieren im Zwielicht*; Stolleis, *The Law under the Swastika*; Requate, *Der Kampf um die Demokratisierung*.
5. Most studies published after 1990 remained restricted to comparative perspectives rather than focusing on entanglements and legal competition between the two German states. This is also the case in the path-breaking studies on postwar legal history by Diestelkamp and Stolleis. See: Diestelkamp, *Rechtsgeschichte als Zeitgeschichte*; Stolleis, *Geschichte des Öffentlichen Rechts in Deutschland, Bd. 4*. For recent conceptual debates within legal scholarship on entangled history, see: Duve, *Entanglements in Legal History*. There exist comparative studies such as Markovits, 'Socialist vs. Bourgeois Rights' or Hacker, *Der Rechtsstatus Deutschlands* conducted during the Cold War that pointed to legal connections, but entangled legal histories of the divided Germany have been largely absent from historical scholarship since German unification in 1990. In the aftermath of unification, scholars argued over the question of whether the GDR should be labelled an *Unrechtsstaat* (unlawful state) and represented a totalitarian system. Some critics suggested that such frameworks unjustly equated the GDR with the Third Reich, while oth-

ers supported these analytical concepts and frameworks. For the controversy over the issue of the *Unrechtsstaat* after German unification in 1990, see: Schöneburg, 'Recht im nazifaschistischen und im "realsozialistischen" deutschen Staat'; Müller, 'Die DDR – ein Unrechtsstaat?'; Joseph, 'Der "DDR-Unrechtsstaat"'; Rottleuthner, 'Das Ende der Fassadenforschung'; Sendler, 'Die DDR – ein Unrechtsstaat'. The politically charged debates of the immediate phase after German unification have in the meantime given way to a more nuanced treatment of GDR legal history. While the GDR government had little regard for civil law and the protection of individual rights against the state, it was not a 'lawless' state. For a more nuanced treatment of GDR legal history and a call for social and cultural perspectives, see: Markovits, *Justice in Lüritz*; Betts, 'Property, Peace and Honour'; Betts, 'Socialism, Social Rights, Human Rights'; Westen and Schleider, *Zivilrecht im Systemvergleich*; Göhring, 'Ohne pauschale Verdammnis und Nostalgie'; Westen, 'Das Menschenbild der ZGB der DDR'; Schröter, *Ostdeutsche Ehen vor Gericht*; Günther, 'Autonomie im Recht der DDR'; and Schneider, 'Kommentar zu Frieder Günther'.

6. For the drafting of the GDR constitution, see: Amos, *Die Entstehung der Verfassung*.
7. The prefaces to both constitutions embodied these legal visions. The 1949 GDR constitution opened with the following preface: 'The German People, imbued with the desire to safeguard human liberty and rights, to reshape collective and economic life in accordance with the principles of social justice, to serve social progress, and to promote a secure peace and amity with all peoples, have adopted this Constitution'. The Basic Law preface stated: 'Conscious of its responsibility before God and mankind, filled with the resolve to preserve its national and political unity and to serve world peace as an equal partner in a united Europe, the German people in the Länder Baden, Bavaria, Bremen, Hamburg, Hesse, Lower Saxony, North Rhine-Westphalia, Rhineland-Palatinate, Schleswig-Holstein, Württemberg-Baden and Württemberg-Hohenzollern has, by virtue of its constituent power, enacted this Basic Law of the Federal Republic of Germany to give a new order to political life for a transitional period'.
8. Gehrig, 'Recht im Kalten Krieg', 66–70. For West German perspectives on Germany's postwar legal status, see: Rückert, 'Die Beseitigung des Deutschen Reiches'; Diestelkamp, *Rechtsgeschichte als Zeitgeschichte*, 25–84.
9. For a summary of GDR legal debates on the legal nature and impact of the Potsdam Agreement on both German states, see: Hacker, *Der Rechtsstatus Deutschlands*, 284–91. Hacker's conclusions are coloured by the ongoing Cold War confrontation between the two German states at the time of publication in 1974. For the Soviet roots of socialist legality, see: Newton, *Law and the Making of the Soviet World*.
10. There exists a wealth of studies on the ideological dimensions of German division and the formation of ideological alliances as part of the Cold War. For some of the leading paradigms of postwar German history, see: Jarausch and Siegrist, *Amerikanisierung und Sowjetisierung in Deutschland*; Doering-Manteuffel, *Wie westlich sind die Deutschen?*; Herbert, 'Liberalisierung als Lernprozess'; Schildt, *Zwischen Abendland und Amerika*; Gassert, 'Amerikanismus, Antiamerikanismus, Amerikanisierung'; Bauerkämper, Jarausch and Payk, *Demokratiewunder*. These studies used comparative or entangled approaches to investigate social, cultural and political change after 1945. For debates on methodologies, see: Kleßmann, 'Verflechtung und Abgrenzung'; Bauerkämper, Sabrow and Stöver, 'Die doppelte deutsche Zeitgeschichte'; Jarausch, 'Divided, Yet Reunited'; Wengst and Wentker, 'Einleitung'; Möller and Mählert, *Abgrenzung und Verflechtung*; Doering-Manteuffel, 'Die deutsche Geschichte in den Zeitbögen des 20. Jahrhunderts'. Scholarship has concentrated on the transformations of the notion of the German nation in the attempt to regain postwar political legitimacy. For some instructive examples, see: Roth, *Die Idee der Nation im politischen Diskurs*; Hacke, *Die Bundesrepublik als Idee*; Müller, *Verfassungspatriotismus*; Kronenberg, *Patriotismus in Deutschland*; Bergem, *Identitätsformationen in Deutschland*; Moses, *German Intellectuals and the Nazi Past*; Langguth, *Die Intellektuellen*

und die nationale Frage; Geppert and Hacke, *Streit um den Staat*; Hacke, *Philosophie der Bürgerlichkeit*; Müller, *Another Country*; Müller, *German Ideologies since 1945*; Nolte, *Die Ordnung der deutschen Gesellschaft*; Loth, 'Die Deutschen und die Deutsche Frage'; Jarausch, *After Hitler*; Jarausch, *After Unity*; Jarausch, 'Die Postnationale Nation'. For comparative studies, see: Herf, *Divided Memory*; Fulbrook, *German National Identity after the Holocaust*.

11. Weitz, *A World Divided*, 5; see also Weitz, 'Self-Determination'. For the impact of human rights on European concepts of citizenship, see: Gosewinkel, *Schutz und Freiheit*, 346–518. Weitz's argument echoes Hannah Arendt's claim that people needed the 'right to have rights' and thus the UDHR's claim to universality failed to account for the need of people to belong to a political community that secured their rights. See: Arendt, 'Rights of Man', 37. For a recent summary of trends in human rights history that highlights the importance of studying competing visions of human rights that rivalled for hegemony rather than following an evolutionary narrative of human rights, see: Burke, Duranti and Moses, 'Introduction: Human Rights, Empire, and After'.

12. There exist studies on the history of human rights in either West or East Germany, but no entangled history of the Cold War competition over human rights. See: Wildenthal, *The Language of Human Rights*; Richardson-Little, *The Human Rights Dictatorship*.

13. So far, scholarship has mostly concentrated on only one German state and its international relations. For leading accounts, see: Wentker, *Außenpolitik in engen Grenzen*; Kilian, *Die Hallstein-Doktrin*; Fink and Schaefer, *Ostpolitik 1969–1974*; Gray, *Germany's Cold War*; Sarotte, *Dealing with the Devil*. For a rare exception of a study on German-German diplomacy at the UN, see: Stein, *Der Konflikt um die Alleinvertretung*.

14. Bernhard Diestelkamp has used this concept to describe the political usage of law by West German politicians and legal scholars to carve out agency for the developing FRG against the occupation powers until 1949. See: Diestelkamp, *Rechtsgeschichte als Zeitgeschichte*, 49. German lawyers and diplomats had already once before tried to lobby the international legal world for the reinstatement of the German Reich's sovereign rights after they had been curtailed in the Versailles Treaty. See: Pederson, *The Guardians*, 195–204.

15. Weinke, *Die Verfolgung von NS-Tätern im geteilten Deutschland*; Wildenthal, *The Language of Human Rights*, 45–62; Gehrig, 'Reaching Out to the Third World'.

16. Betts, 'Socialism, Social Rights, Human Rights'; Richardson-Little, *The Human Rights Dictatorship*, 138–221; Wildenthal, *The Language of Human Rights*, 61–166. For a broader perspective of the impact of a socialist framework of human rights on global politics, see: Betts, 'Socialism, Solidarity and Decolonization'.

17. Legal language became another form of political languages in the postwar era. See: Steinmetz, 'New Perspectives'.

18. Despite the fact that recent historiography, especially on the formation of the German-German border, has challenged writing German postwar history as the parallel history of two states in the tradition of Christoph Kleßmann's call for writing German postwar history highlighting entanglements and delineations, legal histories of the two German states have remained focused on the FRG and GDR as closed legal entities. For the debate on how to write postwar German history, see: Kleßmann, 'Verflechtung und Abgrenzung'; Kleßmann, *Die doppelte Staatsgründung*; Kleßmann, *Zwei Staaten, eine Nation*. Konrad Jarausch has called for putting this agenda into practice in Jarausch, 'Divided, Yet Reunited'. See also: Möller and Mählert, *Abgrenzung und Verflechtung*; Hochscherf, Laucht and Plowman, *Divided, But Not Disconnected*. Edith Sheffer's social history of the German border paved the way for putting Kleßmann's call for German-German histories into practice. See: Sheffer, *Burned Bridge*. In Frank Bösch's recent volume on German-German history since the 1970s, law as a theme is still largely absent. See: Bösch, *A History Shared and Divided*. The recent history of the East and West German Ministries of the Interior makes a first foray into entangled institutional histories of postwar Germany. See: Bösch and Wirsching, *Hüter der Ordnung*. Older accounts such as Peter Graf Kiel-

mansegg's *Das geteilte Land* also write in a German-German perspective, though Kielmansegg does not consider the GDR a valuable political alternative in German history. Others have described postwar Germany in parallel histories, e.g. Bender, *Deutschlands Wiederkehr*. For broader European perspectives integrating East and West, see: Major and Mitter, *Across the Blocs*; Vowinckel, Payk and Lindenberger, *Cold War Cultures*; Mikkonen and Koivunen, *Beyond the Divide*.
19. Jellinek, *Allgemeine Staatslehre*. For a concise overview of the European genealogy of the idea of sovereignty with a special emphasis on the holistic, indivisible nature of ideas of sovereignty, see: Bartelson, 'On the Indivisibility of Sovereignty'.
20. Stolleis, *Geschichte des Öffentlichen Rechts in Deutschland, Bd. 3*, 77–79.
21. For a recent history of the Weimar constitutional crisis and its impact on postwar West German constitutional consensus, see: Strote, *Lions and Lambs*, 23–45 and 151–74.
22. For Weimar-era intellectual debates on law, the legal system and *streitbare Demokratie*, see Greenberg, *Weimar Century*; Strote, *Lion and Lambs*. For Schmitt's intellectual trajectory, see: Müller, *A Dangerous Mind*. Jellinek's hegemonic view was also not challenged when Kelsen introduced a temporal dimension into his thinking about the state and proclaimed the primacy of international law in thinking about the state and sovereignty. Kelsen developed this view after being the prime drafter of the Austrian post-First World War constitution to explain and account for the legal demise of the Austrian-Hungarian Empire and the transition into the interwar order. See: Kelsen, *Das Problem der Souveränität und die Theorie des Völkerrechts* and *Allgemeine Staatslehre*. Natasha Wheatley's work on legal debates around the demise of the Austrian-Hungarian Empire promises to shed further light on Kelsen's impact on international legal debates.
23. Diestelkamp, *Rechtsgeschichte als Zeitgeschichte*, 25–84.
24. This becomes especially apparent in the continuous use of legal codes despite changes in political systems in 1918/19, 1933 and 1945/49. Legal codes such as the Civil Code, Criminal Code and Family Code as well as the citizenship law remained in use since their development from the late nineteenth century onwards. For their nineteenth-century origins, see: Crosby, *The Making of a German Constitution*.
25. Frieder Günther has shown how interwar legal concepts of statehood and governance survived into the 1960s in the FRG. See: Günther, 'Ordnen, gestalten, bewahren'; Günther, *Denken vom Staat her*; Günther, 'Vom "Rising Star" zum Sündenbock'; see also: Stolleis, *Geschichte des Öffentlichen Rechts, Bd. 4*, 76–82 and 82–87; Diestelkamp, *Rechtsgeschichte als Zeitgeschichte*, 25–66.
26. There exists a wealth of studies on various aspects of postwar legal history. For a comparative landmark study of the GDR and FRG, see: Stolleis, *Geschichte des Öffentlichen Rechts, Bd. 4*. On the development of legal thought in the FRG, see: Günther, *Denken vom Staat her*. For a perspective spanning from the Weimar period into the early FRG, see: Kutscher, *Politisierung oder Verrechtlichung?* For scholarship on the GDR and socialist legality, see: Mollnau, 'Sozialistische Gesetzlichkeit in der DDR'; Heuer, *Die Rechtsordnung der DDR*, 42–58; Dreier et al., *Rechtswissenschaft in der DDR 1949–1971*; Engelmann and Vollnhals, *Justiz im Dienste der Parteiherrschaft*; Stolleis, *Sozialistische Gesetzlichkeit*; Sieveking, *Die Entwicklung des sozialistischen Rechtsstaatsbegriffs in der DDR*; Glaeßner, *Herrschaft durch Kader*; Mohnhaupt, 'Europäische Rechtsgeschichte als Zeitgeschichte'; Mollnau, 'Die staatsanwaltliche Gesetzlichkeitsaufsicht in der DDR'; Schröder, 'Die Juristenausbildung in der DDR'; Mollnau, *Deutsche Demokratische Republik (1958-1989)*, 2 vols; Sperlich, *The East German Social Courts*; Schröder, *Zivilrechtskultur der DDR*, 4 vols. For the SED's takeover of the legal profession, see: Güpping, *Die Bedeutung der 'Babelsberger Konferenz'*; Eckart, *Die Babelsberger Konferenz vom 2./3. April 1958*. For the use of political criminal justice under the early SED government, see: Fricke and Engelmann, 'Konzentrierte Schläge'. For studies on transitional justice, see: Priemel, *The Betrayal*; Weinke, *Gewalt, Geschichte, Gerechtigkeit*; Weckel and Wolfrum, *'Bestien' und 'Befehlsemp-*

fänger'; von Lingen, 'Defining Crimes against Humanity'. For a landmark legal study discussing Ostpolitik, see: Grigoleit, *Bundesverfassungsgericht und deutsche Frage*.
27. See: Pederson, *The Guardians*, 195–204.
28. Etzel, *Die Aufhebung von nationalsozialistischen Gesetzen*. The conflicts between the West German Parliamentary Council and the Western Allies over the wording of the Basic Law's preface showcased Allied concerns over the West German legal framework. See: Benz, *Auftrag Demokratie*, 325–419.
29. See: Hirsch, Majer and Meinck, *Recht, Verwaltung und Justiz im Nationalsozialismus*; Görtemaker and Safferling, *Die Akte Rosenburg*. Michael Stolleis estimates that 80–90 per cent of all local judges in the early FRG had been members of the Nazi Party. See: Stolleis, *Law under the Swastika*, 176. The continued influence of Hitler's 'crown jurist' Carl Schmitt on intellectual and legal life in the FRG is well established. See: Müller, *A Dangerous Mind*; van Laak, *Gespräche in der Sicherheit des Schweigens*; Günther, *Denken vom Staat her*.
30. Diestelkamp, *Rechtsgeschichte als Zeitgeschichte*, 25–66.
31. See: Hacker, *Der Rechtsstatus Deutschlands*, 78–104; Stolleis, *Geschichte des Öffentlichen Rechts in Deutschland, Bd. 4*, 96–114.
32. Peter C. Caldwell has highlighted the conflicts over law in the context of state planning in the 1950s. See: Caldwell, *Dictatorship, State Planning, and Social Theory*, 57–96.
33. Benjamin recalled years later how this cleansing of judicial elites and the change of the entire curriculum at law faculties also drove away many aspiring law students who 'ended up in the camp of the class enemy'. See: Benjamin, *Zur Geschichte der Rechtspflege*, 127.
34. For the developing East German memory culture after 1945, see: Herf, *Divided Memory*; Fulbrook, *German National Identity after the Holocaust*.
35. One of the SED's aims was disassociating their state from any compensation claims by victims of the Nazi regime. See: Meining, 'Zwischen Nichtbeziehung, Feindschaft und später Annäherung', 176; Goschler, *Schuld und Schulden*, 361–411.
36. Hacker, *Der Rechtsstatus Deutschlands*, 116–53; Gehrig, 'Reaching Out to the Third World'.
37. See: Osiander, 'Sovereignty, International Relations, and the Westphalian Myth'; Stirk, 'The Westphalian Model and Sovereign Equality'.
38. Getachew, *Worldmaking after Empire*, 98–99. For the unequal institutional make-up of the UN, see: Mazower, *No Enchanted Palace*.
39. For the ambiguity of 'people' as a category of international law, see: Fisch, *The Right of Self-Determination*. For ideological clashes over the nature of the new international system of governance, see: Mazower, *Governing the World*, 191–405; Normand and Zaidi, *Human Rights at the UN*. For Western dominance in international law making until the mid-twentieth century, see: Koskenniemi, *The Gentle Civilizer of Nations*. For alternative visions for modes of global governance originating in Africa in the 1960s, see: Getachew, *Worldmaking after Empire*. For the Soviet influence on international law, see: Quigley, *Soviet Legal Innovation*.
40. Palmowski, *Inventing a Socialist Nation*; Palmowski, 'Citizenship, Identity, and Community'.
41. For the West German foreign policy campaign of non-recognition, see: Kilian, *Die Hallstein-Doktrin*.
42. Gehrig, 'Reaching Out to the Third World'; Horn, 'Die Deutsche Liga für die Vereinten Nationen (LVN) in der WFUNA'; Richardson-Little, *The Human Rights Dictatorship*, 97–137.
43. For West German conflicts over the legal nature of the state after 1949, see: Günther, *Denken vom Staat her*.
44. Weitz, 'Self-Determination', 469f. and 482.
45. Lenin, 'The Right of Nations to Self-Determination'. Woodrow Wilson only reacted to Lenin's advocacy at the end of the First World War. See: Fisch, *The Right of Self-Determination*, 129–37.

46. Oppenheim described sovereignty of states as legal personas under international law as follows: 'Sovereignty is supreme authority, an authority that is independent of any other earthly authority. Sovereignty in the strict and narrowest sense of the term includes, therefore, independence all around, within and without the borders of the country'. Oppenheim, *International Law*, 101. For Oppenheim's approach to international law and its lasting impact over the last century, see: Kinsbury, 'Legal Positivism as Normative Politics'; Schmoeckel, 'The Story of Success'. The Soviet Union offered an alternative legal universe of rights after the revolution in 1917; see: Weitz, *A World Divided*, 281–319; Newton, *Law and the Making of the Soviet World*. For the impact of Soviet legal theory on international law, see: Quigley, *Soviet Legal Innovation*.
47. For anti-colonial mobilization around self-determination, see: Manela, *The Wilsonian Moment*; Fisch, *The Right of Self-Determination*, 190–217; Getachew, *Worldmaking after Empire*, 71–106.
48. For the Soviet return to socialist legality, see: Moyal, 'Did Law Matter?'. See also: Heuer, *Die Rechtsordnung der DDR*, 58–71. For the SED's attack on the legal sphere at the Babelsberg Conference in 1958, see: Güpping, *Die Bedeutung der 'Babelsberger Konferenz'*; and Caldwell, *Dictatorship, State Planning, and Social Theory*, 57–96.
49. See: Requate, *Der Kampf um die Demokratisierung*, 43–55.
50. For Soviet legal origins, see: Newton, *Law and the Making of the Soviet World*. For the organization of East German legal scholarship, research institutions and legal training, see: Stolleis, *Sozialistische Gesetzlichkeit*.
51. For the origins of the 1913 law, see: Sargent, 'Diasporic Citizens'.
52. This shift had been prepared for a long time with new ideological patterns explaining the social and political role of GDR citizens in a socialist society. See: Palmowski, 'Citizenship, Identity, and Community'; Betts, 'Socialism, Social Rights, Human Rights'.
53. Richardson-Little, 'Erkämpft das Menschenrecht'. This campaign was based in Soviet traditions of rights talk. See: Nathans, 'Soviet Rights-Talk in the Post-Stalin Era'.
54. See: Siegelberg, *Statelessness*.
55. The Soviet legal system had pioneered such a state-controlled system of citizenship since the October Revolution. See: Lohr, *Russian Citizenship*, 132–76.
56. Gosewinkel distinguishes between an 'outer dimension' (the membership of a state that includes citizens and excludes foreigners from rights) and an 'inner dimension' (the rights of citizens within the state). See: Gosewinkel, *Schutz und Freiheit?*, 12–30.
57. After the SED had ordered targeted kidnappings of former Nazis and opponents of the East German state in the late 1940s and early 1950s, the GDR government 'legalized' threats to former citizens in the 1960s. See: Gehrig, 'Cold War Identities'.
58. Fink and Schaefer, *Ostpolitik 1969–1974*; von Dannenberg, *The Foundations of Ostpolitik*; Sarotte, *Dealing with the Devil*. This fundamental shift in West German politics is underlined by conservative pushback against Ostpolitik. See: Grau, *Gegen den Strom*. Klaus Grigoleit has provided a fascinating and detailed legal study of Ostpolitik's implications for West German jurisprudence, but has not placed the legal transformations that accompanied Ostpolitik in their German-German and international legal contexts. See: Grigoleit, *Das Bundesverfassungsgericht und deutsche Frage*, 271–89.
59. Grigoleit, *Das Bundesverfassungsgericht und deutsche Frage*, 180–301.
60. Even anti-colonial assaults on colonial powers using the right of self-determination operated in the logics of dominant ethnic groups as deciding factors for nationality after independence. See: Fisch, *The Right of Self-Determination*, 190–217.
61. Against 'nationality' as the dominant legal norm, the League of Nations set out to protect minority rights, but was repeatedly curtailed by its member states. For the German interwar context, see: Salzborn, '"Volksgruppenrecht"'.
62. International law scholars firmly believed in the indivisibility of sovereignty in the international arena at the end of the Second World War. When the UN was born in the

mid-century disjuncture of 1945, the basic mantra of international representation became 'one nation, one seat' when the founding members took their seats in the General Assembly. This remained the case despite the fact that the Soviet Union undermined this principle from the outset by managing to increase its UN representation against a Western voting majority to three votes by seating the Soviet Republics of Belarus and Ukraine as independent UN delegations within the General Assembly. For a leading American scholarly voice of the immediate postwar years, see: Morgenthau, 'The Problem of Sovereignty Reconsidered', 344. For a contemporary perspective, see: Zürn and Deitelhoff, 'Internationalization and the State', 193–217. See also: Sheehan, 'The Problem of Sovereignty in European History'.

63. Gehrig, 'Reaching Out to the Third World'. For GDR foreign policy and exchange programmes with African states, see: Winrow, *The Foreign Policy of the GDR in Africa*; van der Heyden, *GDR Development Policy in Africa*; Stevens, 'Bloke Modisane in East Germany'. This diplomatic race for support from Afro-Asian states was underpinned by a growing involvement of both German governments in development aid initiatives. See: Büschel, *Hilfe zur Selbsthilfe*; and Hong, *Cold War Germany*. Until this point, the FRG was able to defend its position, but the period between 1968 and 1971 saw an upsurge of support for the GDR among the Afro-Asian bloc in the UN. See: Gray, *Germany's Cold War*. This race was accompanied by media diplomacy of both states. See: Gißibl, 'Deutsch-deutsche Nachrichtenwelten'. For a conceptual approach to cultural diplomacy of the two German states, see: Paulmann, 'Auswärtige Repräsentation nach 1945'.

64. For a diplomatic history of German-German UN politics until 1973, see: Stein, *Der Konflikt um die Alleinvertretung*.

65. See: Chiang, *The One-China Policy*; Forster, 'Threatened by Peace'. Bernd Schaefer has shown the PRC's diplomatic manoeuvring to upset Ostpolitik negotiations. See: Schaefer, 'Ostpolitik, "Fernostpolitik," and Sino-Soviet Rivalry'. There is a wealth of scholarship on the Hallstein-Doctrine. The campaigns of both German states to maintain or break the West German isolation of the GDR focused on Africa and Asia by the 1960s. See: Gray, *Germany's Cold War*; Stein, *Der Konflikt um Alleinvertretung*; Das Gupta, Handel, *Hilfe, Hallstein-Doktrin*; Engel and Schleicher, *Die beiden deutschen Staaten in Afrika*; Troche, *Ulbricht und die Dritte Welt*; Döring, *'Es geht um unsere Existenz'*; Hein, *Die Westdeutschen und die Dritte Welt*; Jetzlsperger, 'Die Emanzipation der Entwicklungspolitik von der Hallstein-Doktrin'. Earlier scholarship had explored Ostpolitik in the framework of the two German states and the four Allied powers.

66. For the PRC UN campaign, see: Forster, 'Threatened by Peace'.

67. Antony Anghie has argued that the origins of international law and 'sovereignty doctrine' can only be understood if we acknowledge its roots as 'the attempt to create a legal system that could account for relations between Europeans and non-European worlds in the colonial confrontation'. See: Anghie, *Imperialism, Sovereignty, and the Making of International Law*, 3. Decolonizing states' attack on this unequal system created the pressure at the UN and elsewhere to reconfigure concepts of sovereignty that also impacted the German-German legal battle after 1949. See: Pahuja, *Decolonising International Law*; Normand and Zaidi, *Human Rights at the UN*, 243–315.

68. Starting with Samuel Moyn's landmark study on human rights, a vibrant debate within human rights historiography has emerged over the historical moment of a 'human rights revolution' and its intellectual and ideological nature. See: Moyn, *The Last Utopia*; Hoffmann, *Human Rights in the Twentieth Century*; Eckel, *Die Ambivalenz des Guten*. Against Moyn's argument of a human rights revolution taking place in the late 1970s, others have pointed to the importance of Third World legal campaigns during the 1960s. See: Burke, *Decolonization and the Evolution of International Human Rights*; Jensen, *The Making of International Human Rights*; Thompson, 'Tehran 1968 and Reform of the UN Human Rights System'. See also: Eslava, Fakhri and Nesiah, *Bandung, Global History, and International*

Law. After a prolonged debate on the periodization of a human rights 'breakthrough', recent scholarship called attention to the competition between different visions of human rights. See the exchange between Stefan-Ludwig Hoffmann, Samuel Moyn and Lynn Hunt in *Past & Present* 232, 2 (2016) 233, 1 (2016); Burke, Duranti and Moses, 'Introduction: Human Rights, Empire, and After'. Samuel Moyn's recent return to a focus on inequality and social and economic human rights also does not engage more deeply with socialist legal traditions as an important driver of Cold War debate about human rights and the law. See: Moyn, *Not Enough*. Scholars such as Roland Burke and recently Steven L.B. Jensen have argued for the Third World origins of human rights. See: Burke, *Decolonization and the Evolution of International Human Rights*; Jensen, *The Making of International Human Rights*. Lydia Liu meanwhile has questioned the exclusively Western origins of the Universal Declaration of Human Rights, while Paul Betts has drawn out the importance of the early Cold War's ideological and religious battle for the framing of the European Convention on Human Rights. See: Liu, 'Shadows of Universalism'; Betts, 'Religion, Science, and Cold War Anticommunism'.

69. The socialist bloc's contribution has remained largely absent from these debates on the history of human rights. Rare exceptions for the GDR context are: Betts, 'Socialism, Social Rights, Human Rights'; Gehrig, 'Reaching Out to the Third World'; Richardson-Little, *The Human Rights Dictatorship*. For a broader perspective, see: Betts, 'Socialism, Solidarity and Decolonization'.
70. Benjamin Nathans has traced the evolution of state-sponsored rights talk in the Soviet Union from the 1930s onwards. See: Nathans, 'Soviet Rights-Talk in the Post-Stalin Era'.
71. Jennifer Altehenger has reflected on this necessity for legal education and law propaganda under socialism from the state's perspective in the case of the PRC and exposed its unintended consequences for the CCP government. See: Altehenger, *Legal Lessons*.
72. It was this facade of socialist law that Charter 77 called 'virtual apartheid' in 1977 and Vaclav Havel attacked in 1978 usurping the language provided by socialist legality. In Havel's attack on the legal systems under socialist governance, he concentrates on the socialist legal system's deficiencies using the terminology of the state to undermine the authority of socialist legality. See: Havel, 'The Power of the Powerless'.
73. Markovits, 'Law or Order', 525–30; Gehrig, 'Reaching Out to the Third World'; Richardson-Little, *The Human Rights Dictatorship*.
74. See: Marshall, *Citizenship and Social Class and Other Essays*. Scholars of late socialism and popular protest under communist governments such as Paul Betts and Elizabeth Perry have cautioned against interpretations of direct imports of Western rights understandings into socialist contexts during the late Cold War. Rights protests that spread across the socialist bloc in the late 1980s first developed very much 'with the state'. See: Betts, 'Property, Peace and Honour', 252. Elizabeth Perry has argued that in the specific case of the PRC, popular protests are framed in a century-old cultural tradition of the responsibility of the ruler or the state to provide for the economic needs of the Chinese people. See: Perry, 'Chinese Conceptions of "Rights"', 45–47. Beyond her analysis of the particular Chinese cultural and political traditions, her notion of 'rules consciousness' sharpens the analysis of legal cultures in socialist states in Eastern Europe.
75. For a broader perspective on alternative socialist geographies of human rights, see: Betts, 'Socialism, Solidarity and Decolonization'.
76. The shift in popular understandings of rights and citizens' active attempts to claim rights became visible by the early 1980s. See: Markovits, 'Socialist vs. Bourgeois Rights', 635f.; Betts, 'Property, Peace and Honour'; Richardson-Little, *The Human Rights Dictatorship*, 180–221.
77. Lora Wildenthal has shown various forms of human rights activism in the FRG ranging from calls for a right to homeland to humanist initiatives and Amnesty International as

well as women's activism. See: Wildenthal, *The Language of Human Rights*. These initiatives had only limited effects on law making and jurisprudence until the 1970s.
78. The historical significance and role of the American turn to human rights in the 1970s has resulted in much conflict within human rights historiography. For the different positions, see: Moyn, *The Last Utopia*; Keys, *Reclaiming American Virtue*; Bradley, *The World Reimagined*; Snyder, *Human Rights Activism and the End of the Cold War*; Slaughter, 'Hijacking Human Rights'; Franczak, 'Human Rights and Basic Needs'.
79. Thomas, *The Helsinki Effect*. See also: Romano, *From Détente in Europe to European Détente*; Bange and Neidhardt, *Helsinki 1975 and the Transformation of Europe*. Sarah Snyder has argued for the direct transformative role of the Helsinki Final Act through the coordinated work of rights activist groups across the Iron Curtain. See: Snyder, *Human Rights Activism and the End of the Cold War*.
80. In the late 1940s and 1950s, lawyer associations that served as Cold War front organizations to attack rights violations of the other Germany first used the language of human rights. See: Heitzer, *Die Kampfgruppe gegen Unmenschlichkeit*; Stöver, 'Politik der Befreiung?'; Fricke and Engelmann, *'Konzentrierte Schläge'*. Yet, beyond this early Cold War propaganda rhetoric, human rights remained on the margins of legal and public debate for a long time. See: Wildenthal, *The Language of Human Rights*; and Richardson-Little, *The Human Rights Dictatorship*.
81. Liberalization of legal practice took root within West German jurisprudence during the 1960s, but also met with resistance and returned the question of the function of law for social transformation and the provision of welfare rights to West German legal debates in the 1970s; see Chapter 5 of this book. For the 1950s West German intellectual and judicial controversies over welfare rights and provisions for citizens, see: Caldwell, *Democracy, Capitalism, and the Welfare State*, 46–70. For the conflicts over a democratization of the judiciary that went alongside these debates in the 1960s and 1970s, see: Requate, *Der Kampf um die Demokratisierung*.
82. Pekelder, 'Towards Another Concept of the State'; Friedrich-Ebert-Stiftung, *Archiv für Sozialgeschichte*, Bd. 44. For studies highlighting the broader historical shifts of the 1970s, see: Ferguson et al., *The Shock of the Global*; Raphael and Doering-Manteuffel, *Nach dem Boom*; Jarausch, *Das Ende der Zuversicht*. For shifts in understandings of citizenship, see: Gosewinkel, *Schutz und Freiheit?*, 346–518.
83. Günther, *Denken vom Staat her*.
84. There is a wealth of literature on '1968' protests in the FRG. I only cite the recent study by Timothy Brown that has tied together the results of previous scholarship and expanded them in a global framework. See: Brown, *West Germany and the Global Sixties*.
85. See: Knoch, '"Mündige Bürger"'.
86. The 1970s saw a mobilization of conservative milieus against the social-liberal reform agenda. See: Schildt, '"Die Kräfte der Gegenreform sind auf breiter Front angetreten"'; Wehrs, *Protest der Professoren*; Koischwitz, *Der Bund Freiheit der Wissenschaften*; Geyer, 'War Over Words' and 'Die Gegenwart der Vergangenheit'.
87. Constitutional patriotism remains a contested focus of German debates on national identity. See: Müller, *Verfassungspatriotismus*. See also: Bergem, *Identitätsformationen in Deutschland*, 155–75; Kronenberg, *Patriotismus in Deutschland*, 182–206; Hacke, *Die Bundesrepublik als Idee*.
88. I take inspiration for this term from Joachim Häberlen's phrase 'consciously dissonant temporal registers'. See: Häberlen, *The Emotional Politics of the Alternative Left*, 33.
89. Dieter Grimm famously highlighted the political nature of law in the context of debates over a liberalization of West German legal codes in the late 1960s by labelling it *geronnene Politik*. See: Grimm, 'Recht und Politik'.

Part I
TRENCHES

Chapter 1

Legal Rubble

When the Brussels World Fair of 1958 opened, architects and designers praised the modern 'non-ideological' architecture of the West German pavilion. Yet this international acclaim was not matched with approval by West German mainstream media.[1] Journalists from left-wing papers such as *Vorwärts!* (Forward!) to conservative tabloids like *Bild* and *Quick* lamented that the display of West Germany was not 'nationalist' enough and 'the terrible effect of our home country's partition upon the German people is forgotten'.[2] The majority of the West German public thought that national division had not received enough attention in the curation of the exhibits and design of the pavilion.[3] The art centrepiece of the West German pavilion belied this controversy. It stood in sharp contrast to the modernist architecture and allegations of an apolitical, industrial exhibition. Using a branding iron, the artist Josef Henselmann (1898–1987) had engraved the shape of the German Reich in its borders of 1937 on raw wood panels. The piece was titled 'Divided Germany' and carried the slogan, branded across the map, 'The heartbeat of a people goes through a divided country' (Figures 1.1 and 1.2).

By 1958, legal scholars, politicians and high court judges had achieved an almost impossible feat. In the first decade after the end of the war, they had managed to persuade domestic and international publics of a tripartite division of Germany after 1945 under international law.[4] This partition consisted of the FRG, the GDR and former Eastern territories that now formed parts of Poland and the Soviet Union. The legal construct of the 'German Reich in its borders of 1937' proved so successful that West Germans took it as an expression of reality by the late 1950s rather than a framework born in the early years of the Cold War. In 1958, it was an

---

Notes for this chapter begin on page 62.

Figure 1.1. Federal President Theodor Heuss viewing 'Divided Germany' at the West German Pavilion, World Fair, Brussels, 1958. Source: Collection Expo 58, dept. Architecture & Urban Planning, Ghent University.

imagined reality that West Germans thought was only prevented by the Cold War military standoff on German soil. The fact that the victorious Allies had agreed at the Potsdam Conference in 1945 that Germany was to lose territory as a result of the war had long been brushed aside in West German public debates.[5] From 1960 onwards, the eight o'clock news programme *Tagesschau* broadcast by the Arbeitsgemeinschaft der öffentlich-rechtlichen Rundfunkanstalten der Bundesrepublik Deutschland (ARD) even used maps of the German Reich in its borders of 1937 for the daily weather forecast (Figures 1.3 and 1.4). This daily representation of the lost

Figure 1.2. Josef Henselmann, 'Divided Germany', Brussels 1958 in: *Werk und Zeit* 7(6) (1958), 5. Photo: © Expo-Photo-Service.

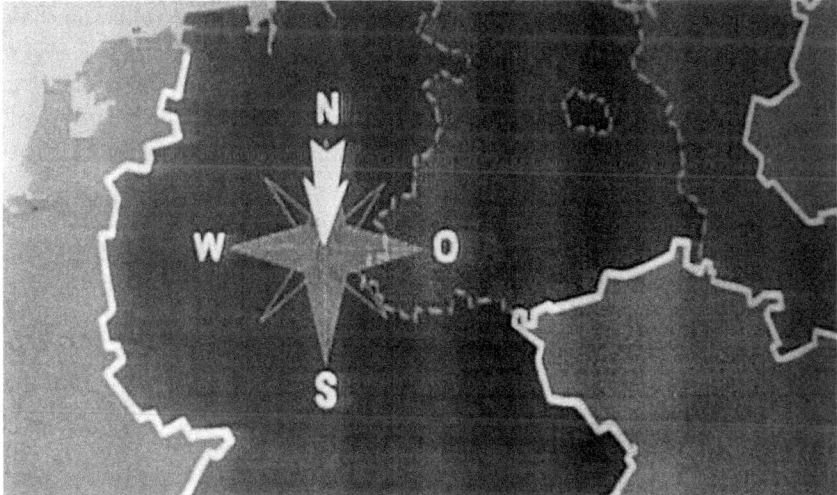

Figure 1.3. ARD Weather Forecast Map, 1960. Photo: © Studio Hamburg (ARD), used with permission.

Figure 1.4. Remastered ARD Weather Forecast Map, 1960s. Photo: © Studio Hamburg (ARD), used with permission.

nation-state engraved the prominence of the trope of a 'still existing German Reich' into everyday consciousness.

The mid-century's strict separation between international law as rules that governed legal affairs between countries, on the one hand, and sovereign domestic legal systems, on the other hand, gave West German jurists the necessary room for manoeuvre to attack the Allies' postwar settlement. Confrontations over the kind of human rights the UN should codify between the US and Soviet Union in the late 1940s and the superpowers' simultaneous declaration that such rights should have no impact on established sovereign states reinforced this doctrine. In the wake of colonial powers' attempt to re-establish unequal legal standards at the UN, West German legal experts promoted the argument that the Bonn government now represented German nationality and the German Reich's sovereignty in its prewar borders. In the tradition of German nationality politics of the interwar period, the Bonn government pushed back at decolonized states such as India and asserted that the right of self-determination should not just apply for peoples under colonial rule, but all peoples – including Germans.[6] They connected this claim to the rules of representation in international affairs. In the UN's own logic of membership, one nation was represented with one seat. If the US, Britain and France wanted to support Bonn's claim against the socialist East that the FRG represented the only legitimate German government, which they did by permitting the Bonn government official observer status at the UN in 1952, West German jurists and government officials intended to tie this international sovereignty to their *Staatsrecht* vision of postwar state sovereignty. In the eyes of the West German legal elite, this sovereignty inevitably took territorial shape in the German Reich prior to Nazi expansion.[7]

Under the cover of US rhetoric of a 'roll back' of communism, West German politicians thus disputed the postwar Allied settlement and the legal legitimacy of the GDR.[8] Soon, the government also secretly financed rights activists to promote a human right to homeland to reclaim the territory lost in the Potsdam Agreement.[9] Legal experts manoeuvred between international and domestic legal spheres, but hoped to keep them theoretically strictly separated in their legal arguments.[10] They did so in the hope of keeping their East German counterparts out of the international law world as only one state could legitimately represent 'Germany' in the logics of postwar international law doctrine. The SED leadership meanwhile observed these developments from the sidelines. The Soviet Union's temporary withdrawal from the UN in 1949 – following the frustration caused by the relegation of social and economic rights to secondary importance within UN politics and the accession of the ROC to the UN to represent China – left the GDR without access to international legal arenas outside the Eastern bloc after 1949.[11] The GDR government thus first concentrated on the German-German legal contexts. The SED leadership chose the only immediate avenue available to attack and contest West German legal frameworks and instructed communist lawyers to make the case for the SED in front of West German high courts in trials against communists.

Managing Transition

At the end of the Second World War, the Allied powers shied away from decisively assuming full sovereign governmental powers in Germany. The Allies stated their intent to take over sovereign tasks in the Berlin Declaration of 5 June 1945 to begin their agenda of denazification but stopped short of annexation and taking over all governmental powers within Germany. Instead, they opted for occupation. This decision opened up room for competing legal interpretations of the status of German sovereignty and the rights of Germans.[12] It was not an entirely unexpected situation. Already in 1944, there had been warning voices. The most prominent belonged to Hans Kelsen (1881–1973), the giant of interwar Austrian

Staatsrechtslehre, who had urged the Allies to clarify the legal status of a defeated Germany. In 1945, he reiterated his warning when the Allied Control Council declared a mere belligerent occupation under international law. Occupation made it possible to treat German soldiers as POWs and prosecute the Nazi elite for their crimes and the Holocaust. Yet this Allied reluctance to take the necessary legal steps to create a firm new beginning of German statehood would result in complicated, incoherent and contested interpretations of Germany's legal status.[13] In the summer of 1945, Kelsen made a last attempt to warn the Allies: 'No German puppet government should be allowed to operate under the control of the only true government, that is, the military government of the occupant powers. For any German government operating under the control of the occupant powers might be inclined to resort to sabotage'.[14]

New Cold War legal alliances formed. Between 1947 and 1949, the re-founded German Society for International Law passed several motions that reaffirmed the continued existence of Germany under international law.[15] The German-Jewish émigré Francis A. Mann (1907–1991), member of the Legal Division of the Allied Control Council, aided the society by stating in the association's journal that 'Germany has ceased to be an independent sovereign state in the sense of international law, but continues to be a state'.[16] Satisfying Allied demands for wide-ranging occupation powers, statements such as those by Mann paved the way for rhetoric that allowed for the claim that the German Reich's state sovereignty had survived the unconditional surrender following Jellinek's *Staatsrecht* dictum that separated the state's legal existence from its social existence. The Berlin Blockade of 1948–49 helped West German legal experts to silence and shut out Kelsen's position from German debates.[17]

Kelsen's warnings went unheard. He only had a few supporters, including fellow legal scholar Hans Nawiasky (1880–1961), who returned to Germany in 1946 and introduced the basic rights catalogue to the draft of the Basic Law in 1948. Indeed, the majority of German legal scholars fiercely resisted Kelsen's calls for a firm end date of the German Reich's existence and the subsequent new emergence of German statehood.[18] There were many reasons to favour a continued existence of the German Reich's sovereignty under occupation. Millions of Germans were on the move or interned in POW camps. Reference to a sovereign state provided legal shelter of citizenship for those Germans, even if occupation suspended the sovereign powers of this state.[19] It prevented Germans across the world from potentially becoming stateless. Such sentiments, however, could also be used in calls for a reversal of the Allied territorial settlement, which election campaigns of the immediate postwar years showed (Figure 1.5).

Figure 1.5. Election poster, 1947. Source: Archiv für Christlich-Demokratische Politik (ACDP), Plakatsammlung, 10-009-21.

As Bernhard Diestelkamp has highlighted, most German legal experts hoped to rescue as much of prewar Germany as possible in the years until 1949 and the instrumentalization of legal language seemed the most promising way of pressuring the Allies into agreement in an atmosphere of international rights codification between 1945 and 1948 when the UN proclaimed the UDHR.[20]

West German legal experts were not alone in their rejection of Kelsen's viewpoint. Scholars in the emerging GDR also opposed his argument, yet for different reasons. In East Germany, nascent theories of sovereignty focused on people's sovereignty. Peter Alfons Steiniger (1904–1980), professor of public law at the Humboldt University Berlin, articulated one of the first legal arguments along these lines for the SED in 1947. Together with Karl Polak (1905–1963), who went on to become the doyen of GDR law until his death in 1963, the SED tasked Steiniger to head a constitutional committee and find answers to the legal questions of national self-determination and state succession. Steiniger firmly rejected the argument that the loss of sovereignty under Allied occupation equalled a *Staatsuntergang* (demise of the German Reich's statehood). But he grounded this assumption in the existence of the German people, not including territory and state power as most West German scholars did. Following Soviet demands, East German legal scholars omitted territorial references in their deliberations on Germany's postwar legal status.[21] Steiniger and Polak nonetheless entered the legal confrontation with their Western counterparts based on the assumption that German sovereignty continued to exist. Their goal was to formulate a new constitution based on people's sovereignty that should enable the building of socialism across all four occupation zones. The aim of building socialism, rather than the restoration of the prewar territorial status quo, guided Polak and Steiniger's legal theories. The premises of legal reconstruction thus differed markedly in the two nascent states from the very beginning.

Unheeded Warning

If legal scholars in both nascent states fundamentally disagreed on legal strategies, many of them worked towards the same goal: to claim the German Reich's sovereignty. Because the Allies had not decisively declared the end of German state sovereignty in 1945, West German politicians and legal experts began their legal reconstruction work based on their preferred assumption that no new sovereign had emerged after 8 May 1945.[22] This implied that no second German government could legitimately exist if one followed the letter of *Staatsrecht* definitions, as following West German logics, territory, statehood and people were firmly linked. The Parliamentary Council, formed by representatives of the Western occupation zones in 1948, decided to work towards a new constitution based on the assumption that the Reich's state sovereignty still existed. There was no legal 'zero hour'.[23] When the West German constitutional assembly claimed the Reich's sovereignty in deliberations lasting until 1949, it immediately included claims to the German Reich's former territory. With a view to reunite the prewar nation-state, the Parliamentary Council labelled its constitutional draft a mere 'Grundgesetz' (Basic Law) rather than a new constitution.[24] Social democrats such as Carlo Schmid (1896–1979) knew that emphasizing international legal continuity risked inviting former Third Reich bureaucrats to exploit this formula to retain politically tainted laws and regulations in the domestic legal sphere. But they were prepared to take this risk because it fermented their opposition against the SED's state socialist agenda. Under their leader Kurt Schumacher (1895–1952), the Sozialdemokratische Partei Deutschlands (SPD, Social Democratic Party) adopted a national rhetoric to fend off interwar conservative and right-wing stereotypes that social democrats had never truly backed the nation-state.[25] As a result, there emerged a broad coalition supporting legal state continuity.

The Western Allies criticized the West Germans for trying to evade their command to draft a fully-fledged democratic constitution. West German politicians defended themselves with the intricacies of translation. The term Basic Law was much more precisely translated as 'basic constitutional law'.[26] While the Berlin airlift was in full swing in 1948–49, West German legal experts concentrated on the international assertion of German statehood to regain governmental agency. By 1949, debates within the Parliamentary Council on the legal foundations of Germany focused on the right of self-determination and a new democratic government for the Western zones, the continuity of the 'old Reich', the transitory character of the new legal order of the Basic Law in temporal and territorial questions, and the demand for the unification of *Gesamtdeutschland* (the whole of Germany).[27] US political advisors with intimate knowledge of German politics, such as Carl J. Friedrich (1901–1984), repeatedly criticized this strategy. In Friedrich's view, the legal contestation of an East German state through an emphasis on continuity in German sovereignty was too ambiguous politically.[28]

Yet the outbreak of Cold War confrontations in Berlin brushed aside such concerns. In 1949, the Western Allied powers grudgingly allowed language of a 'provisional' legal reorganization of the FRG under the Basic Law until unification, but insisted on a clear break with the Nazi past and a turn to democracy in domestic West German politics.[29] Following accepted international law doctrine of the time, this decoupling of domestic and international legal spheres posed no major theoretical obstacles. But it provided grounds for future legal conflicts between the two German governments.[30]

This explicit West German embrace of legal continuity in international affairs set the two German constitutions of 1949 distinctly apart.[31] Against West German claims to the prewar territory of Germany, the GDR constitution's preface omitted any reference to national division or territorial aspects and focused on the road ahead. This was in line with Soviet demands for territorial reorganization of Central Europe and a legal and political break with the Nazi past.[32] With Cold War tensions mounting, Steiniger's original deliberations on the legal continuity of German sovereignty soon faded.[33] When the emerging GDR government circulated a draft of the new constitution in spring 1949, the authorities made sure to print a map of what they thought postwar Germany was on the cover. This map only showed the territory of the four occupation zones (Figure 1.6). After his election as the first GDR president, Wilhelm Pieck (1876–1960) declared on 11 October 1949 that 'we will not rest until the unlawfully detached parts of Germany that are now subjugated to the Occupation Statute are unified with the German *Kerngebiet* (core area) [he meant the GDR here] in a unified and democratic Germany'.[34] The 'parts of Germany' that were now governed by the Occupation Statute were the three Western occupation zones. Pieck thus only laid claim to the territory occupied by the four Allied powers following the Potsdam Agreement.

Legal Continuity in the Face of the Nazi Past

The West German government instantly faced domestic problems after 1949 due to the territorial claims wrapped up in the claims to the German Reich's sovereignty. For the Bonn government, the transition away from the Third Reich was complicated. The notion of a continued existence of the German Reich's sovereignty in its borders of 1937 may have served as a mobilizing force against the GDR government, but it also provided supporters of National Socialism with an excuse to attack the political order of the new republic. If the Reich still existed under international law, how could the FRG claim any political legitimacy and legality? Members of the Sozialistische Reichspartei (SRP, Socialist Reich's Party), the Nazi successor party, mocked the new formula of the 'German Reich in its borders of 1937'. The territory Germans had to reclaim 'was not determined by an artificially chosen year'. 'What only matters is the German claim to the *Reichsraum* (realm of the Reich) based on history, human rights, and

Figure 1.6. Draft of the GDR constitution, 19 March 1949. Source: VEB Staatsverlag der DDR. Wikimedia Commons, public domain.

international law'.³⁵ The SRP demanded a return to Third Reich demands on uniting all territories in which Germans lived, which the party at times wrapped up in the language of a human right to homeland.³⁶ Facing such right-wing activism, the federal government resorted to legal measures. The resurgence of former Nazi Party members in local elections, especially in northern Germany in 1951, posed a serious danger to the young republic. After 1945, desecrations of Jewish cemeteries continued. By 1950, two hundred of the five hundred Jewish cemeteries across the FRG had been violated.³⁷ In light of these continued antisemitic attacks, the rise of the SRP was not a problem that ministries in Bonn could ignore for long. In November 1951, only weeks after the Federal Constitutional Court had taken up work at Karlsruhe, the government called on the judges to declare the SRP unconstitutional.³⁸

The swift trial against the SRP before the constitutional court in 1952 exposed the difficulties for the government in keeping international law and *Staatsrecht* interpretations of the continuity between the German Reich's sovereignty and the FRG separate. The SRP's attorneys concentrated on the question of the legal nature of the unconditional surrender in 1945 in their defence. The party leaders Fritz Dorls (1910–1995) and Otto Ernst Remer (1912–1997) claimed that the unconditional surrender of 8 May 1945 had been a military surrender with no implications for the Reich government's existence. Hitler had decreed before his suicide that Karl Dönitz (1891–1980) should assume governmental leadership after his death. Remer had played a role in preventing the plot against Hitler on 20 July 1944. He used this to boost his popularity in Nazi circles in the late 1940s. Only the armed forces had surrendered, Dorls and Remer claimed, as they went around the country agitating in front of crowds. While the armed forces had surrendered, the German Reich's governmental powers had only been suspended. With the end of occupation, these governmental powers had again come back into effect.³⁹ In other words, the SRP rallied people to believe that the German Reich and its government still existed. For Remer and Dorls, then, the Bonn government was suppressing the resurrection of the Reich's governmental powers.⁴⁰

In its agitations, the SRP could rely on the intimate legal knowledge of Wilhelm Stuckart (1902–1953).⁴¹ Now a prominent SRP member, Stuckart had supplied the last German military government under Dönitz with legal expertise. Stuckart had made a career in service of the Third Reich, beginning as a legal adviser of the party in the mid-1920s. In 1935, he was appointed head of Section 1 of the Interior Ministry dealing with constitutional legal questions. Stuckart later participated in the drafting of the Nuremberg Laws, attended the Wannsee Conference in 1942, and, on 3 May 1945, became acting Minister of the Interior and Education.⁴² Stuckart carried out one of the Dönitz government's last administrative actions when he wrote a memorandum dated 22 May 1945 on the legal status of the German Reich after its surrender. In this legal brief for Dönitz, Stuckart opposed British voices he had heard on the radio arguing for the end of the German Reich's statehood after the unconditional surrender on 8 May 1945. The next day, British troops arrested him together with the remaining members of the Dönitz government in Flensburg.[43]

During the SRP trial in 1952, the FRG still scrambled to secure its territorial integrity and sovereignty against both the GDR and Soviet Union as well as the three Western Allies. The Saarland was still internationalized under French control and the occupation powers held onto essential governmental prerogatives. In the SRP verdict, the constitutional judges thus trod carefully and avoided saying anything they may later regret about the nature of German sovereignty. They avoided a lengthy engagement with the question of state continuity. For now, the court ruled that as the Dönitz government at no point held legitimate governing powers, it therefore could not have survived the unconditional German surrender.[44] To defuse the idea that the Dönitz government was merely suspended, but had not been dissolved after 8 May 1945, the court distinguished between the issue of state continuity and the legitimacy of the Dönitz government. The court argued that, 'apart from all doubts whether Hitler as the Führer represented all powers he claimed for his position, he certainly could not simply decide on a successor by way of a simple decree'.[45] The judges concluded that the last Reich government, which Dönitz had convened at Flensburg after Hitler's suicide on the Führer's command, had never legitimately represented German sovereignty. The court opened up a dangerous road with this argument. It suggested that the Dönitz government had never lawfully governed. At the same time, it said very little about the legal nature of the Third Reich under Hitler.[46] With the verdict, the nature of the transition in state sovereignty from the Reich to postwar Germany thus remained opaque.

Instead, the judges placed the basic rights catalogue of the Basic Law at the core of their arguments in the fight against the resurgence of National Socialism. They outlined their view of the guiding legal principle of the *freiheitlich-demokratische Grundordnung* (free and democratic basic political order) of the young republic.

> The *freiheitlich-demokratische Grundordnung* is defined as an order that represents, by banning all forms of rule through violence or despotism, a *rechtsstaatliche Herrschaftsordnung* (legal form of governance) that secures based on the self-determination of the people the will of the majority in freedom and equality. The foundational principles of this order include at the very least: adherence to the human rights enshrined in the Basic Law, especially the right of the

individual to life and expression of self, people's sovereignty, the separation of powers, responsible government, a lawful bureaucracy, independence of the courts, a multi-party system and equal opportunities of all parties as well as the constitutional right to form an effective political opposition.[47]

The SRP verdict turned this ethos of governance instantly into the guiding political-legal principle on which the defence of the West German state against radical tendencies was built until 1989 and beyond.[48] Any political organization that denied or violated these central rights and values was now defined as unconstitutional. These central passages of the SRP verdict allowed for a value-driven interpretation of the Basic Law, which gave democratic parties their institutional place in the political arena.[49] Through the centrality of basic rights in defining the new political system, the judges began to promote the Basic Law as a fully-fledged constitution that should guide political life in postwar Germany.

The SRP trial paved the way for a new legal understanding of political conflict, in which the legal system played a central role. The internal nature of the SRP's leadership, modelled after the NSDAP's *Führerprinzip* (leadership by the Fuhrer), marked the party as undemocratic. Yet the SRP tried to disguise this dangerous form of political organization. This made it harder for state institutions to defend themselves. 'Modern revolution', the judges declared, originated in the middle of society.[50] This rendered the political contest between different ideas and ideologies into a process that affected all parts of social and political life. Small instances of insubordination occurring in different places and social arenas taken together might amount to a serious threat to national security. The SRP had just showcased such a subversive revolutionary agenda. In the mask of a legitimate party, former National Socialists had attempted to undermine the political order.[51] Yet the constitutional court saw the SRP case not as an isolated incident. The Cold War had transformed political conflict into an often-clandestine struggle. The court argued that:

> Within the modern constitutional state, power struggles with the goal of destroying the existing order are less and less fought with open violence, but rather increasingly with the means of stealthy attrition. The unconstitutional goals are only implemented with open violence once political power has already been secured.[52]

Political subversion, the debates surrounding the SRP trial suggested, was the upcoming central threat to the stability of the young republic. Most observers within the FRG saw this threat originating on the political left. After the SRP ban, many thought that the legal system had to be immunized against the communist threat. But first the government planned to secure the FRG's territorial integrity and its claims to the German Reich's sovereignty against domestic West German opposition and GDR interference.

The End of German Sovereignty?

The first direct legal confrontation between the GDR and the Bonn government broke out over the question of West German rearmament. After the FRG's foundation, the Adenauer government began talks with France and the Benelux countries over the formation of an integrated Western European army. Accompanied by a large-scale media campaign, which included the clandestine financing of film screening vans that transported the government's message to the remotest rural areas, the government hoped to convince West Germans that a Western military alliance against the Soviet bloc was needed. These efforts would eventually end in the FRG joining NATO in 1955.[53] In the early 1950s, the Soviet Union and the SED leadership fervently opposed plans for a West German army and its integration into the Western military alliance.[54] GDR pamphlets pointed to potential breaches of the Basic Law by the West German government. The SED party leader Walter Ulbricht (1893–1973) declared that 'the Basis Law doesn't know a *Wehrverfassung* (defence constitution). This [rearmament] is something foreign to the Basic Law that had been explicitly rejected in the domestic and foreign policy deliberations of the Parliamentary Council'.[55] The GDR government's peace campaign that targeted Bonn's plans for rearmament was part of the Soviet Union's global campaign against nuclear armament that peaked in the Stockholm Appeal of 1950.[56] Even if the first Soviet nuclear bomb test in 1949 had already discredited this international propaganda campaign, the argument for a ban on German rearmament after two world wars carried much weight within divided Germany.[57] GDR legal experts outlined that the threat of military aggression against the people's democracies of Eastern Europe made the resistance of West Germans against the European Defence Community (EDC) treaty a legitimate right under the Basic Law.[58] This was a problematic move as the Basic Law had not codified a right of resistance. It would only be added to the basic rights catalogue in the context of the introduction of Emergency Laws in 1968. The SED nonetheless encouraged members of the West German communist party to make this case to workers and take it onto West German streets.

To stop the Adenauer government from pushing through its agenda, the West German opposition soon also turned to the new constitutional court in Karlsruhe. The formation of a West German army was highly controversial and also strongly opposed by many within the conservative party.[59] Even so, the attempt to build a majority in parliament against rearmament failed. Encouraged by its leading legal expert Adolf Arndt (1904–1974), the SPD took to the constitutional court to continue fighting rearmament.[60] This was not an unusual move by this point. In the early 1950s, Arndt also represented the SPD in the cases against Western political integration and the internationalization of the Saarland that are discussed later in this chapter. Legal politics thus dominated many of the key decisions on West Germany's future during the early Cold War.[61]

The social democrats made the legal status of the FRG a central component of their case against rearmament. In his second legal brief on behalf of the SPD, Arndt dismantled the government's view of German sovereignty. In its defence, the government relied on the so-called *Kernstaatstheorie* (core state theory) in explaining the status of German sovereignty. Ulrich Scheuner (1903–1981), professor at the University of Bonn and the government's leading legal expert in the EDC case, developed new distinctions between the legal nature of the 'Federal Republic' and the 'Federal Republic of Germany'. To Arndt, this was all about semantics rather than proper legal theory. Scheuner introduced distinctions between the sovereignty of the Reich and FRG to allow for the Bonn government's claim to the German Reich's sovereignty on the one hand and at the same time he made a case for the Federal Republic's independent statehood that would allow the government to enter into a defence community with other Western European states on the other hand. Scheuner referred to the 'Federal Republic of Germany' when he spoke of the German Reich's sovereignty. In contrast, Scheuner's argument went, the 'Federal Republic' without the addition 'of Germany' represented a different kind of sovereignty. Scheuner saw in the 'Federal Republic' the 'free core of German statehood' (*freier Kern dieses Staatswesens*) that he encapsulated in the term 'Federal Republic of Germany'.[62]

In court, Arndt had only mockery for Scheuner's argument of a parallel existence of the international sovereignty of the Reich – Scheuner's 'Federal Republic of Germany' – that encapsulated West German sovereignty. Arndt and many other legal experts argued that the EDC undermined Bonn's legal front against the GDR. Arndt characterized the European army as a sign of a developing European federal state. Already the agreement to form the European Coal and Steel Community (ECSC) signed on 18 April 1951 had hinted at ambitions to form a federal economic union in the future. Western European leaders had also begun negotiations over the drafting of a European constitution alongside the first steps of economic integration. In this climate, Arndt argued, the establishment of a

European army for at least fifty years would result in the entry of the FRG into an 'undissolvable unit of a supranational nature with other peoples'.[63] The German people were 'no longer in its entirety free to give itself a constitution valid for the whole [German] state'.[64] Arndt contended that robbing Germans of this option meant a violation of the Basic Law's purpose to serve as a provisional constitutional law until German unity was achieved once more. Any agreement to join a European military union of a federal character, Arndt went on, would result in the permanent exclusion of the Saarland, Berlin and the 'supposedly existing German Democratic Republic'. The 'federal regime' in Bonn, he continued, had no authority to make such agreements, which concerned the German people as a whole. The 'speculation of a core state theory' ignored the still existing legal unity of Germany, which structured the national situation of Germany in international law.[65]

This was a persuasive argument for many West Germans at the time. In 1952, rumours began to spread in Karlsruhe and Bonn that the court leaned towards the SPD's position. The government grew increasingly nervous as the entire project of Western integration potentially hinged upon the outcome of the court case.[66] As Western integration hung in the balance and amidst constant propaganda attacks from East Berlin, Chancellor Adenauer and the Federal Minister of Justice Thomas Dehler (1897–1967) assaulted the court's institutional independence and the judges' political conviction to defend the young republic.[67] In response to this attack, the judges closed ranks against the government. By summer 1952, this confrontation had turned so public that the press spoke of a 'constitutional crisis', a showdown between the court and the government.[68] Indeed, it was a conflict over the court's powers that threatened to overshadow some of the other political questions the judges had before them at the time, many of which concerned the establishment of a Cold War legal position of the FRG.[69]

The constitutional court had been in a difficult position since its foundation. It had been conceived as an entirely new kind of high court. When the court took up work in 1951, however, the position of the constitutional judges within the FRG's judicial and political system had not been clearly defined.[70] Part of the problem was that there was no precedent in German constitutional history. The judges themselves saw their court as an independent institution equal to the government, the office of the federal president, and parliament in its constitutional standing.[71] Gerhard Leibholz (1901–1982) was one of the constitutional judges who advocated for the expansion of constitutional jurisprudence's reach against government attacks. For him, the US Supreme Court was the model to aspire to. The new constitutional court, he believed, dealt with 'matters of the political itself' and its central function was to navigate the contradiction between 'the nature of the political and the nature of the law'. In short, as Leibholz summarized, the judges' 'great task is one of statesmanship'.[72] The government was outraged. Dehler, known for his temperament, provocatively suggested that the judges had violated the 'spirit of the constitution'. But Dehler's fervent public attack had gone too far. In December 1952, the standing committee of the Deutsche Juristentag (German Lawyers' Association) issued a public statement condemning the government's attacks.[73] Dehler had crossed a political line, an action that ultimately cost him his position as Minister of Justice. After the general election campaign in 1953, Adenauer did not again offer him a ministerial post.

Once the government had backed down and the court's position was secured, the controversy over rearmament returned with full force. While the SED supported West German communist organizations that called for active resistance at public rallies against rearmament, the court proceedings also bore the imprint of early Cold War anti-communist policies.[74] Dehler's attacks on the court always suggested that the judges would aid the communist cause if rearmament were to be blocked. Foreign legal experts involved in the EDC case, too, were deeply worried by the anti-communist tide sweeping across Western states. The émigré legal scholar Karl Loewenstein, for example, feared that his assistance to the SPD's lead lawyer Arndt and Arndt's assistant Horst Ehmke (1927–2017) could render him 'an agent of a foreign principal' in the eyes of the US Department of Justice.[75] Loewenstein made sure to disclose his advisory role in the SPD's case to the Department of Justice. Transnational legal aid in the early Cold War still fell under the US Foreign Agents Registration Act of 1938.[76] In light of Adenauer and Dehler's attacks on the constitutional judges, Loewenstein feared that he could become a subject of the vicious campaigning of Senator Joseph McCarthy (1908–1957). Questions of German sovereignty and rearmament formed an integral part of building Cold War front lines in Europe, and legal experts in the FRG and abroad felt considerable political pressure if they opposed Western Cold War politics.

The solution to the EDC controversy ultimately came from outside of Germany when the French parliament stopped the EDC plans. The constitutional court was thus relieved of the burden of finding legal answers to this highly divisive issue.[77] Yet the case had shown that the government and its legal experts struggled to find a comprehensive strategy that accounted for the continuity between the German Reich and the FRG's statehood when they tried to account for Western political, economic and military integration, and combative legal positions against the GDR. In short, the EDC case revealed the fact that the realities of German division and the formula of the 'German Reich in its borders of 1937' collided from the very beginning in West German jurisprudence.

Setbacks

The West German government's legal positions were inconsistent during the early 1950s. This inconsistency became especially problematic when courts started to rule on cases that affected the interests of the Western occupation powers directly. West German legal experts were fighting a two-front battle in defending West German claims to the German Reich's prewar territory. In the early 1950s, the GDR was not the most immediate legal threat to a further disintegration of former German territory. A far more dangerous situation, in the eyes of many West German politicians, was developing in the Saarland.[78] The internationalization of the Saarland under French control and the threat of a permanent loss of the Saarland had to be opposed at all cost. In the tradition of French policies following the First World War, the French government had demanded the internationalization of the Saarland in return for the release of the FRG from direct Allied occupation. Adenauer negotiated an agreement with the French government, the Saar Statute, that confirmed the separation of the Saarland from the FRG on 24 September 1954 but allowed for a later plebiscite on a return to West Germany. Adenauer's government claimed that a later referendum on the Saarland's future would satisfy the Basic Law's demand to work for unification.

Not everyone, however, readily accepted this logic. Some critics worried that the Saarland issue threatened the legal position against the GDR. They believed that the claim to the German Reich's continued legal sovereignty demanded stern opposition to any separation of territory from German governmental control. When it came to the Saarland, many legal experts saw no difference to the issue of former Eastern territories and the refusal to accept GDR statehood. In this climate, it came as no surprise that the SPD put the question to the constitutional judges of whether the government had the authority to agree to an internationalization of the Saarland.[79]

While the SPD disputed the government's foreign policy in the Saarland question in court, the conflict with the French government also affected the rights of ordinary Germans. In a second parallel case, the constitutional court was asked to decide if extraditions to the Saarland were constitutional. Just how much the Saarland's internationalization affected West Germany's approach to law as part of the Cold War can be gauged from this second case over citizenship rights. On 14 January 1955, the

Saarland's attorney general demanded the extradition of a Jewish German citizen charged with false testimony, illegal use of a doctoral title and the falsification of legal documents.[80] The state prosecutor in Frankfurt am Main, where the man now resided, suddenly had to deal with a legal problem that had wide-ranging ramifications. Following the law on mutual legal aid between the FRG and the Saarland from 2 May 1953, the case seemed straightforward: the defendant had to be transferred to Saarbrücken. Yet the international status of the Saarland complicated matters. The defendant was German, so did the West German state not have the duty to protect German citizens from foreign jurisprudence and insist on them being tried before a German court?

The Higher State Court in Frankfurt ruled that the extradition was legal as the Saarland was part of the still existing German Reich. The court thus opposed French demands for a clear separation and internationalization of the Saarland, but it did so to allow itself a legal route to satisfy French demands of extradition. If the man was a German citizen and the Saarland was treated as a part of Germany, there existed no legal extradition issue as the man would simply be transported from one part of Germany (Frankfurt) to another (Saarbrücken). The state prosecutor, who had to deal with the request for extradition of the Saarland authorities, set the extradition in motion based on this verdict. After the High State Court's criminal senate had reaffirmed the verdict, the extradition date was set for 11 March 1955.

The defence attorney now changed strategy and built his new argument on the constitutional right of every German citizen to be tried in a German court. Given French insistence that the Saarland was independent of the FRG, the defence claimed that the law regulating legal aid between West Germany and the Saarland from 1953 was unconstitutional. The argument that the Saarland should still be seen as a part of the German Reich's sovereignty, an opinion endorsed by the majority of West German international law experts, courts and the federal government, was not enough in the eyes of the defence lawyer. The territory that actually belonged to the FRG had to be determined based on 'the current actual situation of sovereignty', not following 'the hopes and wishes of the Federal Republic'.[81] The defence attorney called out the constitutional court and the federal government either to defy the French government and declare the Saarland a part of Germany or reverse the verdict against his client.

As an expert in these kinds of legal questions, the president of the constitutional court Josef Wintrich (1891–1958) immediately realized the potential ramifications of the case. Since his days at the Bavarian Constitutional Court, Wintrich had dealt with basic rights issues and the question of what kind of legal avenues individual citizens had available to them to claim such rights.[82] Wintrich realized that this extradition case was directly linked to the question of whether the Saarland was treated as a foreign country. It thus impacted in crucial ways on the second case between the SPD and the government over the Saarland's territorial status that the court had to decide at the same time. The court had to take a position on the question of the man's citizenship status as his extradition was imminent. Yet Article 11 of the Saarland constitution defined its citizens as 'Saarländers', not Germans. If the court accepted a separate citizenship of the Saarland, the legal position against the GDR was seriously endangered.[83] In the fight against the GDR government, it was vital to insist on a shared citizenship of all Germans – the German *Staatsvolk* in Jellinek's doctrinal *Staatsrecht* terminology – as part of the claim to German sovereignty under international law.[84]

Given these political stakes, the Frankfurt authorities tried to avoid further escalation and looked for an administrative solution to defuse the situation. While the constitutional court deliberated the facts of the case, the Frankfurt state prosecutor contacted the attorney general in Saarbrücken in spring 1955 to ask if the man's prosecution for false testimony in the Saarland could be transferred to the Frankfurt district court. This administrative solution would have avoided all questions over extradition and still secured the man's legal prosecution. Yet the Saarbrücken prosecutor refused. At this point, the Federal Ministry of Justice got involved and evaluated the case given its diplomatic ramifications.

In May 1955, ministerial officials in Bonn hoped to navigate the case to safe ground. They approached the issue by first accepting the defendant's German citizenship following the Basic Law's Article 116(2), which demanded the restoration of citizenship of Jewish Germans that the Third Reich had revoked based on the Nuremberg Laws.[85] Following this decision, the ministry was left with contesting the Saarland's status as a foreign country as the only way to find a resolution for the man's extradition case. The legal experts argued that the Bonn government had not officially acknowledged the exclusion of the Saarland from German state sovereignty. Given the existing treaties with the French state, this assumption was not entirely accurate. Yet, if accepted, West German courts could treat the Saarland as part of the German Reich 'outside of the Federal Republic'.[86] The law regulating extradition then would not apply because moving the man from Frankfurt to Saarbrücken could no longer be an international extradition. West German ministries would then just classify this as a transfer within German lands. Following the initial logic of the Frankfurt district court, the ministerial officials suggested that the sentence of the Saarbrücken court that had set the extradition request in motion should be treated as a 'domestic verdict'. The Ministry of Justice hoped that this explanation allowed for the extradition without diminishing the West German territorial claim to the German Reich's state sovereignty.[87] Most importantly, the Bonn officials hoped to keep the case quiet.

The constitutional court meanwhile played for time in the extradition case. The French occupation authorities demanded a decision in the high-profile case between the SPD and the government over the Saarland's status that was before the court at the same time. The court thus put the extradition case on hold and returned to the case on the legal status of the Saarland. The French occupation authority demanded that the constitutional court clarify how to interpret the treaty between the FRG and France. In May 1955, it remained uncertain if Saarländers would vote for a return to West Germany or a continued internationalization under French control. The French state insisted on a clear-cut separation under international law. The court had to accept that a former German territory was legally separated from German sovereignty. The idea of a temporal suspension of the Basic Law's validity in the Saarland, in other words the projection of German sovereignty onto a separated area as in the case of the GDR or the former Eastern territories, was no option for the court. The French government forcefully rejected such legal constructs.[88] The judges therefore endorsed yet another new legal theory to keep a door open for the return of the Saarland and to sustain the government's Saarland policy. In their verdict on 4 May 1955, they stipulated that the Saar Statute and the scheduled plebiscite at least positioned the Saarland 'closer to the Basic Law'. This so-called *Annäherungstheorie* (proximity theory) in theory allowed for the acceptance of French demands while still upholding the claim to the German Reich's sovereignty.[89] Not many outside of West German jurisprudence followed this logic.

The court only returned to the extradition matter at a time when opinion polls showed that Saarländers would most likely vote to return to the FRG. The judges confirmed the extradition on 6 October 1955. By this time, the plebiscite had been scheduled for 23 October 1955 and the Saarland's return seemed in reach. This emboldened the court. The judges returned to the protocols of the Parliamentary Council from 1948 to make their case. In negotiations over the wording of the extradition article of the Basic Law, the framers of the constitution had introduced a crucial semantic shift when they changed the wording from banning extradition to a 'foreign government' to banning extradition to a 'foreign power'. In early drafts of the extradition article, 'foreign power' denoted 'no German country'. In the final version of the Basic Law, the phrase was amended to *'an das Ausland'* (foreign territories). At the time of writing the Basic Law, this decision had had a specific goal. As the delegate Hermann von Mangoldt (1895–1953) explained to his colleague Hans-Christoph Seebohm

(1903–1967) in a meeting of the drafting commission on 19 January 1949, the phrase allowed for exchanges of persons with the 'Eastern Zone'. The framers of the Basic Law wanted to allow for legal aid across occupation zone borders. The Saarland was of less concern at the time.[90] Yet it was a phrase that served the purpose of the constitutional court well several years later in 1955. By labelling Saarland courts 'non foreign', the court reaffirmed the existence of the German Reich's sovereignty in territorial terms. However, by asserting a West German claim on the courts and territory of the Saarland, the judges actually went against some of their own conclusions they had reached in the Saar Statute verdict only months earlier in May 1955.

The conflict over the Saarland illustrated the importance of the right to self-determination of people expressed through referenda. Referencing the opportunity of Saarländers to exercise their right of self-determination in 1955, the court temporarily retreated from extreme positions of direct legal continuity between the German Reich and the FRG in the verdict on the Saarland's international status. In deflecting from the issue of state continuity, the judges concentrated on the Basic Law's demands for German unification in freedom and democracy. The court now relegated the provisional character of the Basic Law that West German politicians had stressed in the years up to 1949 to secondary importance. In defining the constitutional standard in their verdict, to which the Saarland should return, the court postulated the Basic Law as guiding constitutional authority. The judges promoted the 'order of the Basic Law' as the normative framework into which the Saarland should be incorporated. The verdict therefore represented the first step to elevate the Basic Law's provisional nature to a higher plane of constitutional legitimacy.[91] These cases were therefore the starting point of a process that, over time, led the majority of West German legal scholars to accept the Basic Law as the framework for unification rather than a 'provisional' constitutional text.[92]

In 1956, preparations for the Saarland's return to the FRG highlighted the difficulties of integrating territory into an existing state. The Ministry of Justice quickly recognized that a comprehensive integration of the Saarland into the FRG in one legal act seemed impossible. The legal unity between the Saarland and the FRG had ceased to exist after years of French administration.[93] The ministry therefore treated the inclusion of the Saarland as a change in sovereignty to allow for an organized reintegration. Government officials in Bonn decided that there should be no automatic introduction of federal law and a slow coordinated expansion of the Basic Law to the Saarland.[94] This was of course an administrative irony. The practicalities of the Saarland's reintegration defied all theoretical legal claims that West German politicians, high court judges and legal scholars had previously made when they disputed the Saarland's legal separation from German sovereignty.

The dynamics of the early Cold War, mirrored in the Saarland cases, illustrate how West German high courts, ministries and legal scholars shifted their emphasis on the three constitutive elements of sovereignty following Jellinek – *Staatsgewalt, Staatsgebiet, Staatsvolk* – flexibly depending on the legal issue at hand. This produced at times contradictory interpretations and opened the West German legal sphere to future East German law propaganda attacks.[95] Once the Western Allies handed back sovereign governmental powers to the Bonn government in 1955, and after the Saarland joined the FRG on 1 January 1957, the constitutional court moved to a more open endorsement of the *Kontinuitätstheorie* (continuity theory), stating that the German Reich's sovereignty in its borders of 1937 still existed unqualified in international law.[96] Yet anyone who had followed West German constitutional jurisprudence in the 1950s could see how strategic the courts had been in their interpretation of Germany's postwar legal situation.

The First Major Battle

The SED leadership understood early on the potential for disruption of West German legal affairs. East German interventions into legal disputes over West German rearmament and against the anti-communist mobilization within the FRG since 1949 were designed to attack the West German legal Cold War front at home. This strategy of subversion was in many ways a sign of diminished communist influence on international law debates at the time. The Soviet support for anti-imperialist movements and endorsement of the right of self-determination had garnered the interest of anti-colonial thinkers. Yet the Soviet challenge to the Western-dominated international law world and the development of socialist legality and socialist human rights norms first failed to shape postwar international politics. The Soviet Union and its allies remained isolated within the UN in the late 1940s. While legal concepts of sovereignty as outlined by Soviet legal minds thus had a significant propaganda impact on Third World movements at the time, the GDR government could not capitalize on Soviet backing in the immediate phase after the foundation of the East German state as the SED leadership remained shut out from UN politics. The Western grip on international law remained too strong until decolonization transformed international politics in the 1960s.[97]

Barred from international law politics, the SED began to attack the Bonn government's legal positions within West German courts. This attack began when the West German government and constitutional court fought the occupation powers over the FRG's territorial integrity and the Saarland's status while the SPD appealed against the legal validity of Western military integration. The Kommunistische Partei Deutschlands (KPD, Communist Party of Germany) had fallen fully under the SED's spell and command in the late 1940s.[98] SED organizations such as the Freie Deutsche Jugend (FdJ/Free German Youth) co-organized peace rallies against rearmament in West Germany in the early 1950s. Together with other organizations, the FdJ became a mobilizing factor in workers' protests against the Bonn government.[99] In response, the government submitted a case to ban the KPD as early as 1951, yet it would take the constitutional court until 1956 to reach a verdict. The complicated international situation, the uprising in East Germany on 17 June 1953, and Stalin's death dramatically altered the political circumstances in which this first direct legal battle between the two states was fought.[100]

The GDR's turn to subvert the Bonn government in West German courtrooms was also a response to activities of West German Cold War front organizations and rights groups such as the Kampfgruppe gegen Unmenschlichkeit (KgU, Combat Group Against Inhumanity), the Untersuchungsausschuß Freiheitlicher Juristen (UfJ, Investigation Committee of Free Jurists) and the Deutsche Liga für Menschenrechte (German League for Human Rights) in the GDR. These organizations tried to expose rights violations and instigate revolt against the SED leadership in the early 1950s. This legal aid work attracted cross-partisan support in the FRG. Some West Germans were making genuine efforts to help Germans in the GDR while others saw these organizations as a gateway for covert actions against the East German state.[101]

Mutual interference through rights activism quickly escalated. The GDR secret police hunted East Germans who had escaped to West Berlin as well as Nazi perpetrators and returned them to the East.[102] One famous case was the abduction of the acting president of the UfJ, Walter Linse (1903–1953), which happened days before the first International Congress of Jurists took place in Berlin from 25 July to 1 August 1952. Linse had organized the 'Aryanization' of Jewish companies in Chemnitz during the Third Reich. Like him, many UfJ and KgU activists were former Nazis driven by their anti-Bolshevik beliefs that the Third Reich had propagated. Linse was brought to Moscow and executed for espionage one year later. His kidnapping propelled the congress to the headlines of the international press. Chiefly prepared by Linse's organization, the congress promised to give the 'global public reliable insights into the development of law and its application behind the Iron Curtain'.[103] The meeting resulted in the formation of the International Commission of Jurists (ICJ), whose members observe court trials around the globe and report on their compliance with international law until today.

The SED needed to find answers to what the party leadership perceived as West German political sabotage. A stream of East Germans had consulted the UfJ in legal matters since 1949. The organization claimed that it answered five thousand inquiries monthly. 'There is no institution [in the GDR] in which there would not be a secret member' of the UfJ, the organizers of the 1952 congress claimed.[104] During the meeting, delegates had a chance to consult 'original files' from GDR authorities that UfJ members had smuggled to the West. UfJ members saw themselves as subversive anti-communist activists whose work was more espionage than rights activism in their minds.[105] In conjunction with the German League for Human Rights and other groups, the UfJ collected evidence against the GDR government.[106] Rhetoric of 'serving justice' underpinned all these West German activities against the Cold War enemy, which contributed to intense policing of the inner-German border from both sides.[107]

The SED sought ways to counter this West German rights activism. The trial against the KPD provided the opportunity for a sustained campaign against the Bonn government. Recent scholarship has highlighted that the constitutional court and West German government agencies breached the constitutional rights of KPD members in combating this East German influence through the West German communist party.[108] The KPD case centred on the question of how anti-democratic parties should be treated in a democratic society. This focus continued the court's work in the SRP verdict from 1952. The KPD trial was therefore a seminal moment in the development of West German legal norms and judicial practice, but it also became the first major direct legal confrontation between the Bonn government and the East German government.[109]

One remarkable feature of the KPD trial was the SED's decision to send East German lawyers to represent their comrades, who were now defendants, before the constitutional court in Karlsruhe. These East German lawyers, and their direct links to the SED party apparatus, informed the strategy of the KPD's legal team, which also included West German lawyers. The East Berlin lawyer Friedrich Kaul (1906–1981) and the law professor Herbert Kröger (1913–1989), director of the Institute for State and Administrative Law at Humboldt University, spearheaded the KPD's defence team. Letter exchanges and records show how closely Kaul and Kröger coordinated their court statements with GDR ministries. The SED bureaucracy even prepared parts of the defence strategy by outlining the line of argument the legal team should take in courtroom proceedings. The defence centred on the question of sovereignty and German unity. With East and West German lawyers in situ, the courtroom in Karlsruhe became the first legal space in which the two German governments contended over interpretations of law.

That the trial had a distinct and contentious political dimension was clear from the outset. The KPD's East German lawyers tried to turn court proceedings into political performances whenever they could. From the early days of the trial in 1952, they politicized the atmosphere in the courtroom by accusing the court and government of 'fascist bias', stalled legal procedures, and propagated German unification in military neutrality. The trial thus dragged on.[110] The GDR government seized the opportunity and incorporated the trial into its referendum campaign on German unity that began in 1952. That year, Stalin famously pretended to offer the unification of Germany if the country would remain neutral in the Cold War.[111] These East German advances into West German domestic politics worried the West German government.[112] To combat such SED interference in West German political life, the Western occupation forces instituted comprehensive secret surveillance of all mail and phone contacts between the GDR and FRG.[113] While effective, these were clandestine secret police solutions. Finding a legal strategy against the GDR's propaganda of national unity remained a much harder task. But a legal strategy was essential because the federal government could not allow the East Germans to make inroads into West German political debates via high court trials.

Yet the SED at first successfully managed to use West German legal channels to do exactly that. For one, the KPD defence attorneys knew how to exploit legal language for their cause. Max Reimann (1898–1977), the KPD chairman, for example, called on all West Germans to resist their government.[114] The KPD aimed at the government's plans for rearmament, which the party saw as a breach of constitutional law that demanded resistance. In the brief before the court, the KPD reiterated these calls.

> The call of the KPD for 'national resistance' is not unconstitutional, but an appeal to the masses of the German people to unite against the federal government's continued breaches of the constitution. . . . This 'national resistance' is nothing other than the resistance of all democratic and patriotic forces of the German people against a government policy that has left the grounds of law and order a long time ago.[115]

Resistance was justified, Reimann argued, even though the Basic Law had not codified a right of resistance in 1949. The Adenauer government would pursue national division when it promoted rearmament and the integration of the FRG into the Western military alliance. As evidence, Reimann pointed to the provisional nature of the West German state that, he made sure to note, the Bonn government freely admitted.[116] To underline his defence, Reimann had carefully selected quotations from Adenauer's public statements. He mentioned, for example, that Adenauer himself had said that 'it remained the national right and national duty of all German patriots' to demand national unity. Banning the KPD and founding a Western European army, according to Reimann, were contrary to any plans for a quick unification of Germany. Instead, Germans should be allowed a vote in free self-determination on the future of the nation.

Ritter von Lex (1893–1970), the West German government's representative at Karlsruhe, tried to rebut Reimann's testimony and attempted to contextualize Adenauer's statements. National unity, Lex explained, was only possible in the presence of freedom and liberty, and these could exclusively be guaranteed by the FRG's free and democratic basic political order. German unity, in other words, could only be reached on West German constitutional terms.[117] If the new legal order of the Basic Law had originally been presented as temporary, this was another example of how the government and high court jurisprudence transformed its ethos step by step to a permanent legal order. From the perspective of the Bonn government, the restricted territorial reach of the new West German state represented the provisional aspect of the Basic Law, not the constitution's framework of the new West German political system.

While the Bonn government desperately tried to contain the case in the domestic context, international jurisprudence was of major importance in the defence mounted by the KPD's team of lawyers. The East German government constantly supplied the KPD defence with new material from other countries to undermine the federal government's position. For example, they emphasized the Australian High Court's 1951 verdict against the Australian government's ban of the communist party. In 1954, when the case moved to trial in open court, the West German KPD lead defence lawyer Böhmer presented the Karlsruhe court with a physical copy in one of the court sessions. In a letter that Böhmer later submitted to the court, he highlighted selected paragraphs that directly related to trial proceedings of the West German case. His intention was clear. The Australian case suggested that the Karlsruhe court had no choice but to rule in favour of the communist party.[118]

In response, the court also began to play politics openly. The court's president Wintrich countered this political manoeuvring with a public note to the UfJ in October 1954 congratulating the organization on five years of successful work uncovering human rights violations in the GDR. The KPD's lawyers swiftly responded by demanding the removal of Wintrich from the bench.[119] The UfJ, the KPD lawyer Wessig argued, represented an organization tasked with the 'instigation, preparation and execution of espionage'. Wintrich's support for such an anti-communist front organization that included many supporters of the National Socialist regime could only be seen as political bias. 'By congratulating such an organization that . . . engages in criminal activates within our own country, the president [Wintrich] . . . has objectively documented his bias'.[120] It was constant political infighting such as this that kept prolonging the case.

As the trial went on, the West German police, security service and courts did not wait for the constitutional court's decision but actively prosecuted communists.[121] Shortly after the government had submitted its case to the constitutional court in 1951, the Sixth Criminal Senate of the Bundesgerichtshof (BGH, Federal Court of Justice) had begun to restrict the KPD's activities. The sixth senate, renamed the Third Criminal Senate in 1956, exclusively prosecuted political justice cases and had the power to federalize cases immediately if national security seemed endangered.[122] The senate's judges classified any distribution of party publications and leaflets as aid to 'a traitorous plot'.[123] The police put out warrants for party leaders and leading KPD lawyers.[124] The sixth senate justified this crackdown on known communists under the treason act by citing security service reports.[125] By 1954, when the constitutional court moved to trial in open court, key party members such as Reimann could no longer move freely in the FRG. The authorities had issued warrants that led many leading KPD members to leave for the GDR. When the constitutional court scheduled further court days for summer 1954, Reimann and other leading party members could only attend court sessions after the BGH had granted them free passage to Karlsruhe for court days but restricted their freedom of movement without arrest to the immediate local area.[126]

In turn, the KPD defence team attacked the legitimacy of the trial by pointing to Nazi legacies that shaped the national security framework in the early FRG. Kaul declared in front of the constitutional court that the prosecution of communists defied the West German *Rechtsstaat*'s own constitutional standards. Such arguments, the government feared, threatened to turn the KPD trial into a media disaster.[127] The Federal Press Office tried to convince the editors-in-chief of leading radio and regional TV stations to send more reporters. Trials against communists were meriting more public attention than West German media had expected. Viewed from Karlsruhe, the situation worsened by the month. The government sent Hanns Küffner of the Federal Press Office as a permanent observer to the trial. It was Küffner who alarmed Hans Globke (1898–1973), the head of the chancellery who later became the target of a GDR campaign exposing his Nazi past, with news of the sloppy preparation of governmental experts who were meant to testify for the prosecution during court days in 1954 and 1955. Küffner's criticism also befell the court's judges. According to Küffner, the reporting judge for the KPD case, Erwin Stein (1903–1992), was making crucial mistakes in the preparation of court sessions.[128] All in all, the GDR government suddenly seemed much better prepared for the propaganda war over law than the FRG.

Küffner called for 'necessary counter-propaganda' and he proceeded to oversee the compilation of brochures to explain the KPD trial for domestic and international audiences.[129] Küffner felt that these measures were necessary, as the court's president Wintrich had no experience in criminal cases and his performance in court weakened the court's public performance.[130] As the West German government was getting more manifestly worried about the trial, SED cadres felt emboldened and convinced that their legal rhetoric of national unity could pose a serious challenge to the Bonn government.[131] The defence now called for a complete suspension of the trial until an all-German referendum on national unity had been held, stressing the right of self-determination of Germans.[132] The SED's confidence was misguided, however. Since the East German uprising in June 1953, the KPD had rapidly dropped in public appeal and only attracted 2.2 per cent of votes in the general elections in autumn 1953, the last that the party was allowed to participate in. The restrictive anti-communist legislation and police work as well as Soviet tanks had succeeded in squashing support for the communist party within West Germany.[133] Wintrich now tried to convince Adenauer that a KPD ban was no longer necessary. It was difficult to legitimize a verdict and the trial's integrity had suffered from the government and court's frequent breaches of the law.[134] The judges hoped to be spared from having to find a convincing legal argument to ban the KPD.

Adenauer would not have it. He refused to listen to Wintrich's concerns and pressured the court to rule against the communist party.[135] On 17 August 1956, the court released a verdict more than three hundred pages long – the judges had had to go to great textual lengths to rebut East German arguments. The verdict was an important milestone for several reasons. As Manfred Doering-Manteuffel, Uwe Wesel, Justin Collings and Peter C. Caldwell have argued, it contributed to developing core legal principles of West German jurisprudence in the field of *streitbare Demokratie* (militant democracy) and the welfare state. The judges further elaborated on their view of the free and democratic basic political order, the role of political parties in a democracy and militant democracy.[136]

Yet the judges also had to touch on the national question as it formed the central argument of the defence lawyers. As such, the verdict marked a remarkable transition in the court's view on German unification.[137] The 1955 Saar referendum had concluded the territorial consolidation of the FRG, and the court no longer had to pay attention to French demands in the definition of German sovereignty. The time had therefore come to transform the call for national unity from a political to a legal claim in response to the SED's law propaganda. The Basic Law's preface, the verdict outlined, represented a 'political vow, a sacred call on the German people to support an All-German agenda, which at its core is aimed at the achievement of German unity in free self-determination'.[138] This call, the judges continued, was not restricted to certain legal implications for the interpretation of the Basic Law. 'In fact, the preface represents a legal imperative for all political organs of state of the Federal Republic to strive with all powers at their disposal for Germany's unity . . .'.[139] With this sentence, the Basic Law's preface acquired legal meaning. This was a direct rebuttal of arguments presented in court by the KPD defence team. The KPD's lawyers had argued their case precisely on this argument, with Stalin's offer of unity in military neutrality in mind. Beyond this German-German conflict, the verdict again raised the question of which unification was meant here as most West German legal scholars would have read this sentence in the context of the claim to the German Reich's sovereignty in its borders of 1937 at the time.

The KPD ban did not end the legal action against communists.[140] Many West German judges and lawyers had long tried to get rid of the kind of political heckling from the East that had been showcased during the trial, and they continued to do so after the trial.[141] The example of Friedrich Kaul, the East Berlin lawyer on the KPD defence team, shows how the West German government's all-German legal frameworks allowed East German lawyers access to the West German court system. Legislation on Berlin's legal status from 1952 had foregrounded the unity of the city under Allied extraterritorial control and it also allowed Kaul access to the West Berlin legal sector. Kaul had been admitted to the West Berlin Higher State Court before the East and West Berlin legal spheres were separated in the early 1950s. His access to West Berlin court files made him a thorn in the side of West German jurisprudence. Kaul's bar membership granted him access to West German court and police files that 'the Stasi has enormous interest in'.[142] In the heated months around the East German uprising in June 1953, the West Berlin general prosecutor first moved to get rid of Kaul and, trying to provide supporting evidence, the bar association cited his book titled *The Defendant as Prosecutor*, his frequent articles in the GDR press, and radio addresses on GDR channels as evidence.[143]

Kaul had made savvy use of a specific historical moment in Berlin to further his activities. To exclude him from the bar, the legislation that organized Berlin courts from 1952 had to be declared unconstitutional. His personal ties to Hilde Benjamin, the infamous second GDR Minister of Justice, and his loyalty to the SED were well known by 1953. But getting rid of him remained difficult. In the middle of the KPD trial, Kaul's case reached the constitutional court. The West Berlin bar association wanted to see Article 2 of its own regulations declared unconstitutional to remove Kaul as a member. Judge Martin Drath (1902–1976) advised that the case could not be admitted. In a draft decision on the matter for his fellow judges, he named two reasons 'after cursory reading' of the case details. First, the constitutional court had no jurisdiction in West Berlin due to its extraterritorial status under Allied control. In 1945, the four Allied powers had reserved special rights for themselves in the control of the capital city. Second, the West Berlin bar's court of honour did not constitute a proper court following Article 100 of the Basic Law. There was no legal basis to submit the case to the court at Karlsruhe. Drath urged all involved ministries not to publicize the first reason. The judges could not afford to weaken their position in the ongoing case against the communist party even further by admitting the restricted powers of their own court.[144] The Allied status of Berlin thus saved Kaul, who continued to practise law in West German courts.[145] It also showed once more how much the rhetoric of the FRG's direct succession in the German Reich's state sovereignty diverged from Cold War realities.

Conclusion: Settling In

West German legal frameworks of sovereignty rooted in *Staatsrecht* traditions of the mid-century dominated the early years of the legal Cold War between the two German states. In the many parallel legal battles of the late 1940s and early 1950s, West German high court jurisprudence split the legal claim to the sovereignty of the 'German Reich in its borders of 1937' that the Parliamentary Council had established until the foundation of two German states in 1949 into many and sometimes contradictory legal interpretations. Only when the territorial integrity of the FRG was secured at the Western border in 1957 with the return of the Saarland, West German high courts moved to a direct endorsement of the continued existence of the Reich's sovereignty within its prewar territory. As a result, the trope of the sovereignty of the 'German Reich in its borders of 1937' became the dominant legal framework in which the West German public debated German division by the late 1950s, when Henselmann's artwork formed the core of FRG representation at the Brussels World Fair.

The international law debates on international sovereignty made this West German manoeuvring possible. While the superpowers clashed over human rights at the UN in the preparation of the UDHR, both superpowers defended the legal sovereignty of nation-states.[146] The Bonn government could develop a set of domestic arguments on German sovereignty that could be treated as detached from Germany's international sovereignty.

To make this possible, legal scholars and high courts shifted emphasis between Jellinek's three core components that made up sovereignty in his definition – *Staatsgewalt, Staatsvolk, Staatsgebiet* – to arrive at legal reasonings and resolve political key issues in negotiating West German legal sovereignty in the rapidly shifting position of the FRG during the early Cold War. The effects of East German attacks on these shifting positions in front of West German courts remained limited despite the fact that they exposed inconsistencies and contradictions in West German Cold War legal positions as the international law world saw them as not directly related to claims to sovereignty under international law. In the end, the SED's strategy proved unsuccessful. West German jurists held the upper hand by definition in the unequal struggle over legal Cold War frameworks when confronted with communist lawyers in their own courts.

More importantly for the SED leadership perhaps, these German-German legal battles postponed the SED's official shift to new foundations of its state rooted in socialist legality. With the official announcement of the building of socialism in the GDR in 1952, the SED party leadership turned to legal arguments of discontinuity in the existence of German statehood in an atmosphere of 'revolutionary justice' and political cleansing within the GDR.[147] After the East German uprising in June 1953, securing the socialist revolution at home became ever more important.[148] By the mid-1950s, the East German leadership and leading legal scholars started to develop a new legal position that endorsed the existence of two separate sovereign German successor states of the German Reich. Yet the KPD trial was one important battleground that postponed the official announcement of this fundamental shift in the GDR's legal foundations as the defence team promoted German legal unity in the KPD's defence. By 1956, when the KPD had been banned in the FRG and the SED was once again rattled by the Hungarian Uprising, the GDR leadership would direct its legal experts to double their efforts to develop frameworks of German division that advocated the existence of two sovereign German states to secure SED rule.[149]

Underneath these legal clashes over sovereignty, basic rights and freedom of movement, as the next chapter shows, the politics of law centred on the nature of domestic legal systems in the context of establishing political legitimacy through rights and law at home and abroad. With every sign of East German retreat from a direct legal competition over the representation of the German Reich's sovereignty, West German legal scholars would push for further implementation of judicial regulations, which underscored the argument that the FRG embodied the statehood of the German Reich. This strategy had several advantages in the eyes of the vast majority of West German jurists and politicians. It enabled the FRG to offer a safe haven to all German refugees from the East. But above all, politics through law allowed the Bonn government to frame territorial demands for a return of former Eastern territories in a seemingly neutral legal language. The claim to the exclusive representation of German sovereignty and citizenship, which high court jurisprudence had upheld through complicated legal constructions until the mid-1950s, helped to pave the way for the diplomatic isolation campaign of the Bonn government against the GDR through the so-called Hallstein Doctrine from the mid-1950s onwards.[150] The Bonn government now threatened third-party states with revoking economic and diplomatic relations if they acknowledged the GDR as a sovereign state. This policy rested on the legal claim that the Bonn government alone represented 'Germany' and Germans in international affairs.

Notes

1. Polcuch, 'Was fehlt in Brüssel?'.
2. Cited in: Betts, *The Authority of Everyday Objects*, 196.
3. Ibid.
4. Diestelkamp, *Rechtsgeschichte als Zeitgeschichte*, 32–55, 61–64.
5. Benz, *Auftrag Demokratie*, 29–65.
6. Normand and Zaidi, *Human Rights at the UN*, 223.
7. Diestelkamp, *Rechtsgeschichte als Zeitgeschichte*, 25–67.
8. Stöver, *Die Befreiung vom Kommunismus*; Benz, *Auftrag Demokratie*, 29–45.
9. For the roots of the right to homeland in the work of the Austrian-German-born Hamburg law professor Rudolf Laun (1882–1975), see: Wildenthal, *The Language of Human Rights*, 45–62.
10. This approach built on the separation of international law from domestic legal systems since the late nineteenth century. See: Koskenniemi, *The Gentle Civilizer of Nations*.
11. Mazower, *Governing the World*, 214–43.
12. Diestelkamp, *Rechtsgeschichte als Zeitgeschichte*, 29.
13. For a summary of this legal and political conundrum, see: Rückert, 'Die Beseitigung des Deutschen Reiches'. US political and legal advisors such as Carl J. Friedrich (1901–1984) opposed the idea to make German occupation and the problem of resurrecting German sovereignty a matter for the UN and relinquish Allied control over the process. HUGFP 17.39, Papers of Carl J. Friedrich, folder 'Secret Activities', confidential letter exchange between Carl J. Friedrich and Edward Litchfield (Civil Administration Division, US Military Government), 7 October 1948.
14. Kelsen, 'The Legal Status of Germany', 526. See also: Kelsen, 'The International Legal Status of Germany'.
15. Wildenthal, *The Language of Human Rights*, 60.
16. Mann, 'The Present Legal State of Germany', 42.
17. Diestelkamp shows this closing of ranks against Kelsen. See: Diestelkamp, *Rechtsgeschichte als Zeitgeschichte*, 67–84.

18. Ibid., 42. For Nawiasky's work on the federal state, constitutionalism and basic rights, see: Staatsarchiv St. Gallen, Nachlass Nawiasky, HSGN 008-009 and 008-012. Nawiasky was instrumental in drafting the Bavarian constitution and attended the Herrenchiemsee meeting in preparation for the Parliamentary Council's work on the drafting of the Basic Law. Facing massive public opposition, he returned to Switzerland after only a few years, where he had spent the wartime years.
19. Diestelkamp, *Rechtsgeschichte als Zeitgeschichte*, 25–67.
20. Ibid.
21. Hacker, *Der Rechtsstatus Deutschlands*, 81–90 and 98–99; Amos, *Die Entstehung der Verfassung*, 153–97.
22. Diestelkamp, *Rechtsgeschichte als Zeitgeschichte*, 32–55. There is a wealth of legal literature on the nature of the state and sovereignty in the German legal tradition. A concise summary of the postwar debates on these issues can be found in: Stolleis, *Geschichte des Öffentlichen Rechts in Deutschland, Bd. 4,* 32–37.
23. This agenda of a 'provisional' legal reorganization caused friction with the Western Allied powers; see: Benz, *Auftrag Demokratie,* 325–419.
24. The double-bind between legal continuities and a new constitutional beginning led to many draft versions of the Basic Law's preface. The preface was meant to give the new Basic Law political purpose and interpretation. The twofold political message of the new constitution was extremely controversial among delegates, but eventually won over the majority. See: Leibholz and von Mangoldt, *Jahrbuch des Öffentlichen Rechts der Gegenwart, Bd. 1,* 20ff.
25. This was also a strategy to win over German expellees for the SPD; see: Müller, *Die SPD und die Vertriebenenverbände,* 33–35.
26. Leibholz and von Mangoldt, *Jahrbuch des Öffentlichen Rechts der Gegenwart, Bd. 1,* 14f.
27. BArch, Z5/127.
28. See Friedrich's correspondence with Lucius Clay in his capacity as political advisor to the US Occupation Forces: HUGFP 17.39, Papers of Carl J. Friedrich, Box 1, Folder M.G. Constitution, 'Memorandum concerning governmental developments in Germany leading up to the convening of the constitutional convention', 11 October 1948.
29. For the impact of the accelerating Cold War confrontation in Germany on the drafting process from the Frankfurt Documents outlining Allied demands for a new constitution to the proclamation of the Basic Law, see: Benz, *Auftrag Demokratie,* 325–419.
30. See Benz, *Auftrag Demokratie,* 325–419 and the documentation on the drafting of the Basic Law's preface in: Leibholz and von Mangoldt, *Jahrbuch des Öffentlichen Rechts der Gegenwart, Bd. 1,* 20ff.
31. The prefaces of the two German constitutions embodied this difference in approach to legal continuity. See note 7 in the Introduction to this volume.
32. One of the SED's aims was to disassociate their state from any compensation claims by victims of the Nazi regime. See: Meining, 'Zwischen Nichtbeziehung, Feindschaft und später Annäherung', 176; Goschler, *Schuld und Schulden,* 361–411. For the developing of an East German memory culture after 1945 that advocated a clean break with the past, see: Herf, *Divided Memory;* Fulbrook, *German National Identity after the Holocaust.*
33. During the Cold War, Jens Hacker has pointed to the complications inherent in early East German positions on German sovereignty, which led the SED leadership to quickly abandon a focus on arguments of legal continuity. See: Hacker, *Der Rechtsstatus Deutschlands,* 105–15.
34. Cited in: Hacker, *Der Rechtsstatus Deutschlands,* 108.
35. BVerfGE 2, 1 (56).
36. For the concept of a human right to homeland, see: Wildenthal, *The Language of Human Rights,* 45-62.

37. Foschepoth, 'Das Kreuz mit dem Davidstern', 237. For the resurgence of National Socialists and their demands for a 'Fourth Reich', see: Rosenfeld, *The Fourth Reich*, 106–57.
38. Collings, *Democracy's Guardians*, 38–40.
39. For the SRP's legal defence, see: BVerfGE 2, 1 (56).
40. BArch, B237/215.602.
41. Jasch, 'Civil Service Lawyers and the Holocaust'.
42. See: BArch, N1292, Nachlass Stuckart. See also: Jasch, 'Civil Service Lawyers and the Holocaust'.
43. Diestelkamp, *Rechtsgeschichte als Zeitgeschichte*, 33.
44. See: Menzel, 'Vergangenheitsbewältigung in der frühen Judikatur des Bundesverfassungsgerichts'.
45. BVerfGE 2, 1 (56).
46. The infamous case of pension claims by civil servants who had served under the Nazi regime and claimed benefits for their service would provide a chance to condemn Hitler's regime much more thoroughly in 1954. Grigoleit, *Bundesverfassungsgericht und deutsche Frage*, 189–92.
47. BVerfGE 2, 1, Leitsatz 2.
48. For a historical perspective, see: Doering-Manteuffel, 'Freiheitliche demokratische Grundordnung und Gewaltdiskurs'.
49. BVerfGE 2, 1 (10). Gerhard Leibholz orchestrated this strengthening of political parties within the court. See: BArch, N1334/28, manuscript Gerhard Leibholz, 'Die kritischen Punkte des Grundgesetzes', radio broadcast, 29 May 1957. For Leibholz's ideas of the relationship between political parties and the state, see: Kaiser, *Der Parteienstaat*.
50. BVerfGE 2, 1 (20f.).
51. Ibid.
52. Ibid.
53. Uelzmann, 'Building Domestic Support'.
54. Large, *Germans to the Front*, 31–61.
55. 'Die Stunde der Verantwortung ist gekommen', *Neues Deutschland* 6, 105 (10 May 1951): 5.
56. Harrison, 'Popular Responses to the Atomic Bomb in China'.
57. Large, *Germans to the Front*, 31–61.
58. BArch, DY30/IV2/13/487.
59. For the conflicts surrounding Western integration within the CDU, see: Geiger, *Atlantiker gegen Gaullisten*; and Large, *Germans to the Front*. CDU members also became targets of legal action by the government and had their freedom of movement curtailed to stop them advocating against rearmament. See: Rojahn, 'Elfes'.
60. Gosewinkel, *Adolf Arndt*, 280–348.
61. BVerfGE 1, 372; Grigoleit, *Bundesverfassungsgericht und deutsche Frage*, 228–33.
62. BArch, B136/999.
63. For Arndt's brief, see: BArch, B136/999.
64. Ibid.
65. Ibid.
66. Wesel, *Der Gang nach Karlsruhe*, 54–82.
67. Gehrig, 'Recht im Kalten Krieg', 77–81.
68. For a short summary of the confrontation between government and the court, see: Requate, *Der Kampf um die Demokratisierung*, 39–43; Wesel, *Der Gang nach Karlsruhe*, 54–82.
69. Radkau, *Theodor Heuss*, 353–59.
70. Collings, 'Gerhard Leibholz und der Status des Bundesverfassungsgerichts'; Gehrig, 'Recht im Kalten Krieg', 77.
71. For the court's early development, see: Collings, *Democracy's Guardians*, 1–62; and Dreier, 'Das Bundesministerium der Justiz', 93–95.
72. For all citations from the *Statuschrift*, see: BArch, B122/2168.

73. BArch, B136/4436.
74. See: Harms and Popp, *Westarbeit der FdJ*.
75. See: Amherst College Archives, The Karl Loewenstein Papers, Series: Karl Loewenstein, Subseries C: Policy Advising and Research, Constitutional Law Advisor (1952–1955), EDC Controversy, Rechtsgutachten 1952, Box 48, Folder 10. Loewenstein had an intimate knowledge of the German legal sphere and witnessed the failure of US denazification attempts in Bavaria in 1945–46. See: Kostal, 'The Alchemy of Occupation'.
76. Amherst College Archives, The Karl Loewenstein Papers, Series: Karl Loewenstein, Subseries C: Policy Advising and Research, Constitutional Law Advisor (1952–1955), EDC Controversy, Correspondence and Enclosures, Feb 1954–May 1955, Box 48, Folder 20.
77. Gosewinkel, *Adolf Arndt*, 247–348.
78. For a comprehensive history of the separation of the Saarland, see: Elzer, *Konrad Adenauer*.
79. Grigoleit, *Bundesverfassungsgericht und deutsche Frage*, 233–41.
80. BArch, B136/39, appeal to the constitutional court in case 1 BvR 85/55, 7 March 1955 (BVerfGE 4, 299). The man, a Jewish lawyer from Berlin, had lost his German citizenship under the Third Reich, spent the war in France and returned to the Saarland after 1945. In 1948, he acquired Saar citizenship. The authorities wanted him for the illegal use of a doctoral title, false testimony and the falsification of legal documents.
81. Ibid.
82. See memoranda and notes for public lectures and radio broadcasts in: BayHStA, NL Josef Wintrich, Dienstlich, Karton 1.
83. BArch, B136/39, letter Wintrich to federal ministries, 17 March 1955.
84. The preservation of a united German citizenship against the Allied powers and the emerging GDR government was an early priority among West German legal experts. The Deutsches Büro für Friedensfragen (German Office for Questions of Peace), a fact-finding division of the federal states Bavaria, Hesse and Württemberg-Baden, already pressed for a binding legal answer to the problem posed by Saar citizenship before the official foundation of the FRG in 1949. The bureau's archival collection later formed part of the Foreign Office's archive on legal issues, territorial questions, economic and financial matters, and de-militarization and denazification policies connected to a peace settlement. Under the guidance of the office's head Fritz Eberhard, former career civil servants and proponents of the Nazi regime such as Eugen Feihl, Günther Harkort, Margarete Hütter, Klaus Mehnert, Ernst-Günther Mohr, Karl Mommer and Peter-Heinz Seraphim worked for the resurrection of the German Reich's sovereignty. See: BArch, Z21/1248, 'Aufzeichnung: Betr.: Saarländisches Staatsangehörgkeitsgesetz', 3 March 1949.
85. BArch, B136/39, letter Ministry of Justice to Foreign Office and Ministry of the Interior, 20 May 1955. Jannis Panagiotidis has shown the frequent conflicts around the legal recognition of Jewish immigrants as Germans in the local administration of citizenship after 1945. See: Panagiotidis, 'The Oberkreisdirektor Decides Who Is German'.
86. BArch, B136/39, letter Ministry of Justice, 20 May 1955.
87. Ibid.
88. The French government managed to gain American approval to separate the Saarland from all Allied debates on the future of Germany, which complicated the Bonn government's position on the issue. See: Thoß, 'Die Lösung der Saarfrage'.
89. Grigoleit, *Bundesverfassungsgericht und deutsche Frage*, 237.
90. See: BVerfGE 4, 299.
91. Grigoleit, *Bundesverfassungsgericht und deutsche Frage*, 238ff.
92. This process resulted in public support from the majority of West Germans for the preservation of their constitutional order in 1990. See: Detjen, Detjen and Steinbeis, *Die Deutschen und das Grundgesetz*.
93. BArch, B141/59160, report of meeting in Ministry of Justice, Saarbrücken, 21 July 1956.
94. See: BArch, B141/280.

95. For this East German propaganda and West German counter-measures, see: Creuzberger and Hoffmann, *'Geistige Gefahr' und 'Immunisierung der Gesellschaft'*.
96. The case of the validity of the *Reichskonkordat*, the treaty signed by the Nazi regime and the Vatican on 20 July 1933 guaranteeing the rights of the Catholic Church under the Third Reich, demanded an answer to the question of whether treaties signed by the German Reich continued to hold legal validity. The Holy See intervened against the new school law passed by the state government of Lower Saxony on religious lessons. The court acknowledged that the *Reichskonkordat* remained in force as both treaty parties – the Holy See and the German Reich – still existed as sovereign subjects in international law. See: BVerfGE 6, 309.
97. For Soviet isolation in UN politics, see: Normand and Zaidi, *Human Rights at the UN*, 197–212; and Mazower, *Governing the World*, 214–49. For the Soviet challenge to the Western legal world, see: Weitz, *A World Divided*, 281–319; Newton, *Law and the Making of the Soviet World*. For the impact of decolonization on concepts of sovereignty and self-determination, see: Getachew, *Worldmaking after Empire*, 71–106.
98. For the transformation of the KPD from 1945 into the early 1950s, see: Kössler, *Abschied von der Revolution*; Foschepoth, *Verfassungswidrig!*, 21–50.
99. Gustav Heinemann's entry into the SPD over the issue of rearmament is the most prominent case of defiance of Adenauer's policies in his own coalition. For the protest against rearmament, see: Large, *Germans to the Front*, 62–82.
100. Foschepoth, *Verfassungswidrig!*, 21–82.
101. See: Heitzer, *Die Kampfgruppe gegen Unmenschlichkeit (KgU)*; Wildenthal, *The Language of Human Rights*, 17–44.
102. See: Smith, *Kidnap City*.
103. AdsD, 1/MHAC01431, International Congress of Jurists, 25 July–1 August 1952, West Berlin.
104. Ibid.
105. Heitzer, *Die Kampfgruppe gegen Unmenschlichkeit (KgU)*.
106. See: Wildenthal, *The Language of Human Rights*, 17–62.
107. A day after Linse's death in 1953, a large crowd of West Berliners protested and appealed to the international public. Linse's abduction in the boot of a car triggered the closure of streets between East and West Berlin with the exception of a few checkpoints. See: Mühle, *Auftrag: Menschenraub*, 133–51; Fricke and Engelmann, 'Konzentrierte Schläge', 95; Bauernfeind, *Menschenraub im Kalten Krieg*, 88–135.
108. For a recent summary of the trial and its importance for the history of the constitutional court, see: Collings, *Democracy's Guardians*, 40–45; Foschepoth, *Verfassungswidrig!*.
109. For public security frameworks set up in this context and the building of a political justice apparatus in the early years of the FRG, see: Jaschke, *Streitbare Demokratie und Innere Sicherheit*, 141–63; and Rigoll, *Staatsschutz in Westdeutschland*, 33–140.
110. Gehrig, 'Recht im Kalten Krieg'; Foschepoth, *Verfassungswidrig!*, 235–78.
111. For the larger Cold War context and Stalin's offer of unification in 1952, see: Wettig, *Stalin and the Cold War in Europe*.
112. Gehrig, 'Recht im Kalten Krieg', 81–90.
113. West German authorities would later carry out such work as well. See: Foschepoth, *Überwachtes Deutschland*, 19–118.
114. For a legal discussion of the right to resistance in the context of the KPD verdict, see: Johst, *Begrenzung des Rechtsgehorsams*, 204–12.
115. BArch, B237/215.651–654, legal brief KPD defence, 23.
116. The 'provisional' nature of the Basic Law formed the core of West German debates on the foundation of the Federal Republic. See: Benz, *Auftrag Demokratie*, 325–419.
117. BArch, B237/215.651–654.
118. Ibid.

119. Ibid.
120. BArch, BY1/1793.
121. Foschepoth, *Verfassungswidrig!*, 83–105.
122. For the BGH's internal organization, see: President of the BGH, *The Federal Court of Justice*, 10–23.
123. BArch, B237/215.655–658.
124. Ibid.
125. BArch, B237/681–685.
126. BArch, B237/651–654.
127. See governmental reactions to the trial in: BArch, B136/4434; BArch, BY1/1793.
128. BArch, B145/3392. See also: Gehrig, 'Recht im Kalten Krieg', 81–90; Foschepoth, *Verfassungswidrig!*, 138–234.
129. BArch, B145/3392 and 1860.
130. BArch, B145/3392.
131. BArch, BY1/1892.
132. BArch, BY1/1793.
133. Rigoll, *Staatsschutz in Westdeutschland*, 94–140.
134. Foschepoth, *Verfassungswidrig!*, 235–78.
135. Wesel, *Der Gang nach Karlsruhe*, 90f. In a last desperate attempt, the KPD defence team drew attention to a recent decision in favour of a communist newspaper editor. The district court in Cologne had not followed many other district courts' compliance with anti-communist governmental legislation. The Cologne court refused to apply the treason paragraph. The court did not view working for a communist newspaper as a direct danger to national security and high treason. GDR legal experts now expected even more political pressure on the constitutional court to rule on the party ban. See: BArch, DY30/IV2/13/487. See also: Dreier, 'Das Bundesministerium der Justiz', 104f.
136. Doering-Manteuffel, 'Freiheitliche demokratische Grundordnung und Gewaltdiskurs'; Collings, *Democracy's Guardians*, 38–49; Wesel, *Der Gang nach Karlsruhe*, 83–96; Caldwell, *Democracy, Capitalism, and the Welfare State*, 68–70. See also: Jaschke, *Streitbare Demokratie und Innere Sicherheit*. For some of the intellectual roots of *streitbare Demokratie* in the Weimar era, see: Greenberg, *Weimar Century*, 169–81; Strote, *Lions and Lambs*.
137. Grigoleit, *Bundesverfassungsgericht und deutsche Frage*, 244ff; Gehrig, 'Recht im Kalten Krieg'.
138. BVerfGE 5, 85, 127.
139. Ibid.
140. Foschepoth, *Verfassungswidrig!*, 279–353.
141. The SED continued its propaganda campaign after the KPD verdict. See: BArch, DY30/IV2/13/487 and BArch, BY1/1896.
142. BArch, B237/97038, memorandum, 21 January 1954.
143. BArch, B237/97038, bill of indictment, 1 June 1953.
144. BArch, B237/97038, memorandum, 21 January 1954.
145. BArch, B237/97039, verdict Court of Honour Berlin, 13 May 1957; AdsD 1/MHAC01198A, 'Pressedienst: Weiter im Dienste Pankows', 20 January 1958.
146. Normand and Zaidi, *Human Rights at the UN*, 102–5, 190–91.
147. Hacker, *Der Rechtsstatus Deutschlands*, 133–48.
148. Engelmann and Vollnhals, *Justiz im Dienste der Parteiherrschaft*; Fricke and Engelmann, 'Konzentrierte Schläge'.
149. West German scholars later traced the resulting inconsistencies in the GDR government's official legal position on sovereignty before a two-state position was proclaimed. See: Hacker, *Der Rechtsstatus Deutschlands*, 116–53.
150. See: Kilian, *Die Hallstein-Doktrin*.

Chapter 2

Old and New Law

On 29 May 1961, Karl A. Mollnau (b. 1933), a leading East German legal scholar and philosopher of law, argued at a meeting of the Commission for West German State and Legal Questions convening at the German Academy of State and Legal Science at Babelsberg:[1]

> Just as the development of a socialist theory of the state was only possible in the struggle against legal positivism, the creation of a socialist legal theory and a socialist idea of law is only achievable if the positivist idea of law is overcome once and for all. The abstract approach of bourgeois law, its theory, and idea of society and its history have to be completely abolished and society itself, its law and logics of development, have to form the core of socialist law and the socialist concept of law [*sozialistischer Rechtsbegriff*].[2]

Mollnau touted the party line spearheaded by the doyen of GDR law Karl Polak that socialist legality remained tied up in the conflict with the FRG and this had to be changed.[3] Unlike some of his colleagues, Mollnau insisted that both German states continued to be intrinsically linked in a national *Entwicklungsgesetzmäßigkeit* (uniform principle of development).[4] The West German 'imperial legal doctrine' based on legal positivism, as Mollnau, Polak and other party faithfuls believed, thus had to be fought with all means available to GDR legal scholars as it was rooted in German religious and ethical traditions. The shared legal tradition, Mollnau pointed out at the meeting, could only be left behind by renewed efforts to implement a socialist approach to law rooted in Marxism-Leninism. While the battle over legal frameworks of German sovereignty had demanded much of the SED's attention until the late 1950s, the ideological differences in how law and rights were generated and guaranteed under the competing German legal systems now moved to the forefront.

Notes for this chapter begin on page 98.

In blaming legal positivism, Mollnau reaffirmed the SED leader Walter Ulbricht's command to turn the legal sciences finally into a 'practice-oriented' field of scholarship in service of the party-state.[5] More than a decade after the foundation of two German states in 1949, the GDR legal field still clung to many established Central European legal practices and traditions despite the adoption of Soviet law propaganda language. Three months later, in August 1961, the Berlin Wall was to become the physical manifestation of the GDR's separation from the West German legal sphere. GDR legal experts now felt the leadership's overwhelming pressure to move to socialist law and legality in clear separation from German legal tradition ever more keenly. Addressing an elite group of legal experts, Mollnau gave voice to the urgency of this agenda.

Law was seen to play a crucial role in delineating socialist society from the FRG from the early 1960s onwards. In 1958, Ulbricht had called for redoubling efforts in the legal struggle. Legal scholars were crucial in 'ripping away the veil of the state and constitution of the Federal Republic' and exposing its true authoritarian nature. At the same time, they had to develop an independent socialist legal universe, a fact that Mollnau reminded his colleagues of in 1961.[6] This chapter examines how the SED leadership arrived at this conclusion in the late 1950s in response to ever increasing West German legal pressures. Until then, West German government officials had turned old Third Reich citizenship legislation into new laws. Shielded by the legalist language of sovereignty frameworks set up by the constitutional court, discussed in the previous chapter, government ministries resurrected expansionist Third Reich rights policies for the Cold War cause in the 1950s. In tune with the anti-communist mobilization of West German courts, local and ministerial bureaucracies, too, used all means at their disposal to attack the communist enemy. West German local and national administrations not only contested the GDR government's right to represent its own citizenry and administer citizenship by the mid-1950s, but also advanced the legal rights framework of 'Germanness' against the resurrected Austrian state after both German states were released from direct Allied occupation in 1954–55.[7] To facilitate this aggressive use of rights frameworks, that clearly went against Allied demands, federal ministries outsourced the most outrageous legal claims to research centres such as the Research Centre for Self-Determination and Nationality Policies in Lüneburg when international pressure mounted to retreat from Third Reich-inspired legislation.

It was this intrusion into GDR sovereignty through citizenship rights frameworks that played an important role in Ulbricht's urgent demand to thoroughly sever all ties to German legal tradition.[8] In reaction to ever more aggressive West German rights policies, the East German leadership decided to depart entirely from the competition over whether there was still a unified German sovereignty and citizenship as well as who was its legitimate representative.[9] The never-ending exodus of East Germans to the West in the 1950s increased the social and economic pressure for the SED to invent a new socialist national identity and wall off their state against the FRG.[10] As part of this process, and underneath the conflict over the international representation of German sovereignty, the division of a once united legal tradition took hold in the competition over citizenship rights in the two German states until the early 1960s and ended in open calls such as Mollnau's in 1961 for a departure towards a new socialist law and legality.

Original Sin: The West German Resurrection of Wartime Rights

The long retreat of the SED leadership from contesting West German dominance over *Staatsrecht* and the German legal tradition more broadly had already begun in the early 1950s. The more the GDR government and its legal experts retreated to the domestic project of building socialist legality after the East German Uprising in 1953, the more West German officials felt emboldened.[11] GDR lawyers and East German law propaganda may have constantly tried to disrupt West German high court trials in the 1950s, but citizenship legislation quickly provided West German ministries with an effective legal tool to retaliate. The citizenship law from 1913 had remained in force after 1945. As this law included no provisions to regulate the loss or maintenance of German citizenship in the case of territorial changes to the German state, ministerial officials had scope to develop a new standing institutional practice to fill this void. Against Rogers Brubaker's argument of a long-standing focus on ethnic cultural idioms in German citizenship law, Andreas Fahrmeir, Eli Nathans and Dieter Gosewinkel have shown how only in the Weimar Republic and the Third Reich did German citizenship acquire a decisive ethnic and racial bend.[12] By regulating citizenship after 1949, ministerial officials translated expansive nationality policy logics of the interwar period and the Third Reich into the West German framework of the continuation of the German Reich's sovereignty in the name of disputing the GDR's sovereign right to regulate citizenship within its own borders.

To continue citizenship administration in the tradition of the Third Reich meant to dispute the existence of more than one state bureaucracy being responsible for former citizens of the Reich, which had included Austrians, German minorities in annexed territories, and foreign soldiers fighting in the Wehrmacht who had been naturalized by decree during the war.¹³ This agenda raised many questions among West German judges and officials about how they could actually claim to administer citizenship rights of 'all Germans' in practice. The most important question of course remained how to deal with the GDR. Should the West German judiciary insist on undivided sovereignty and citizenship, but accept the realities of a shared administration of citizenship with the East German government? Or should West German ministries dispute the legitimacy of the GDR administration altogether?

Local officials and state-level ministries first operated in the dark and determined actual policy out of necessity and case by case. In 1951, for example, legal experts of the Hessian Ministry of the Interior informed the federal government that they had decided to acknowledge naturalizations of foreigners that had been processed by GDR authorities as long as they followed the 1913 law.¹⁴ The issue reached the Ministry of the Interior in Bonn in December 1951. Four months later, Deputy Assistant Under-Secretary Ernst-August Kleberg convened state-level experts at a meeting in Bad Homburg to discuss this question because the federal government had no ready answer. The group decided that any administrative action taken by GDR authorities should be subject to West German judicial review. It was the same approach that had been established for East German court decisions which also had to be checked by West German courts before they could be validated. Yet Kleberg urged the group to keep their decision confidential. The ministerial bureaucracy in Bonn worked on strategic regulations that accounted for different groups of former German citizens and hoped to preserve their rights even if the postwar situation had excluded them from the German citizenry. Federal ministries, for example, Kleberg explained, were in the middle of preparing legislation to repatriate German women who had married Austrians between 1938 and 1945 and their children. They had lost their German citizenship after the resurrection of the Austrian state. This legislation, Kleberg pointed out, was part of a comprehensive draft of changes to citizenship regulations, and it would also touch on the issue of collective naturalizations carried out by the Third Reich.¹⁵ As long as no new federal legislation to amend the citizenship law had been passed in parliament, Kleberg did not want to attract undue East German attention and propaganda attacks.

Back in Bonn, Kleberg radicalized his position. He now pushed for a general non-recognition of naturalizations carried out by GDR authorities and no longer advocated a mere judicial review by West German authorities. This went against the recommendations of state-level officials whom he had met with in Bad Homburg and who had to deal with this issue in practice. Kleberg inquired with the Königstein Circle, a group of lawyers and legal experts who had migrated from the GDR to the FRG and had intimate knowledge of ongoing East German legal reform efforts, and the UfJ about GDR naturalization practices, but received no definite recommendations on how to proceed. The general mood within the Federal Ministry of the Interior was for a strict non-recognition policy. Kleberg was sure to find allies in the Federal Ministry for All-German Affairs. Yet, even if these two ministries agreed, the politicking in Bonn divided ministries on how to deal with the GDR. When Kleberg sent a report about the citizenship issue to the Foreign Office, he carefully deleted any mention of the unease about the complete rejection of the legal validity of GDR administrative acts expressed by the state-level experts he had met at Bad Homburg. The diplomats traditionally opposed any unnecessary radicalization of legal politics as it put them in a more difficult position in negotiations with the Allied powers. The document the Foreign Office received was therefore merely a notice of a new standing practice of double-checking all East German naturalizations.[16]

Although the Ministry of the Interior internally drove plans for the radicalization of rights administration in this period, it did not seem to possess detailed knowledge of the actual East German administrative practice. Kleberg, for instance, presumed that only 'socially progressive' persons were naturalized in the GDR.[17] In other words, convinced communists. Yet it was quite presumptuous to think that all Germans and foreigners who arrived in the GDR from Eastern Europe were socialists.[18] Kleberg thought that one could not risk communist subversion of West German society by integrating naturalized Germans coming from the GDR without any checks. Such persons would then enjoy all citizen rights, especially the right to vote. This was the decision Kleberg filtered back to the Hessian state-level ministry, where the query had originated. Naturalizations granted by GDR authorities should not be declared void without any legal evaluation, but they posed a serious risk to national security. Kleberg pointed out that 'it has to be prevented at all costs that the Soviet zone endangers important interests of the Federal Republic in employing citizenship law along communist ideology'.[19] At this point, the trial against the KPD was still underway, and in his letter Kleberg expressed the fears of his superiors that the GDR might send convinced communists disguised as expellees to West Germany.[20] The BGH's Third Criminal Senate would eventually reinforce that GDR naturalizations had to be checked. Simply handing in a 'Soviet-zonal German passport' in exchange for a West German one was insufficient as it undermined national security.[21] The Hessian ministry fell in line and advised all local offices to 'inconspicuously' investigate the background of persons who applied for West German passports.[22] Local administration became the first line of defence against communist subversion.

This first line of defence had to be bolstered constantly by evidence that confirmed the reality of the communist threat and the subversion it was meant to prevent. Only a day after the Hessian ministry confirmed the new guidelines, the Königstein Circle reported the case of a man on 19 June 1952 who had served in the Polish army before becoming stateless, but had gained German citizenship when 'serving' in the KPD after 1945. He immigrated to the FRG and now claimed to have fled the GDR for political reasons. This case, the Königstein Circle concluded, pointed to the dangers of accepting East German administrative power over German citizenship.[23] By the summer of 1952, the situation had escalated. Anti-communist suspicions promoted through such individual cases supported Kleberg and the Federal Ministry of the Interior's agenda to disregard any GDR legal action or administration of citizenship rights. However, while the policy Kleberg had helped to outline was being implemented in administrative practice, his department had to concede to the Foreign Office when the diplomats inquired about the reason for this shift that there was little to no information about actual East German legal practice.[24]

Still, this concession mattered little. By March 1953, local and federal administrations across the FRG had adopted the new guidelines. With the question of naturalization covered, officials turned their attention to expellees and *Aussiedler*. Many *Aussiedler* – after unification called *Spätaussiedler* – came from German families who had lived for decades as minority groups in the East and their ethnic status as Germans remained in question.[25] The German administration in the Soviet zone had granted citizenship to *Aussiedler* on their arrival in 1946. Kleberg was of the opinion that they had no legal authority to do so because only West German authorities had legitimate legal powers to administer citizenship. In 1953, Kleberg's department instead confirmed the collective naturalizations that had been conducted by the Third Reich. This also applied to the directive from 14 October 1941, the interior ministry stated in the language of the Third Reich, which had naturalized Germans in 'Under-Styria, Carinthia, and Carniola'. In other words, they considered these *Aussiedler* as already being German. This directive was also transferred into West German drafts of citizenship amendments. Yet, by request of the Federal Minister for All-German Affairs Jakob Kaiser (1888–1961), it was kept confidential. Made public, as ministry officials explained in a meeting at the Ministry of the Interior in March 1953, it could 'endanger bilateral negotiations over this group of persons'. The Italian and Austrian governments claimed these *Aussiedler* and property that was seized from them at the end of the war for their states. If word got out, the Italians and Austrians were likely to see this amendment as an infringement on their sovereignty.[26]

West German citizenship policies revealed a prevailing expansionist ethnic agenda towards the East. Already in 1952, officials within the Ministries of the Interior and Justice as well as the Foreign Office first pondered the drafting of a new citizenship law.[27] Yet German expellees from former Eastern territories had already formed powerful associations that defeated these initial plans to implement large-scale changes in citizenship law. Because GDR propaganda might have branded a new citizenship law as a signal of the end of German statehood in 1945, expellee organizations demanded that citizenship rights of the Reich had to be preserved in conjunction with the claim to the German Reich's sovereignty in its borders of 1937. From 1952 to 1953, officials backed down in the face of public pressure of expellee organizations and instead turned to amendments of the existing law. The 1913 law therefore remained in force and the Federal Law on Expellees and Exiles passed in 1953 guaranteed the rights of German refugees – now also legally called *Heimatvertriebene* – as German citizens if they had resided in the 'borders of 1937' before 1945.[28]

This focus on continuity in citizenship rights legislation opened an important door for administrative radicalization in the following years as many local and federal officials silently moved beyond the threshold of the year 1937 in the application of law. First drafts of amendments to citizenship law from 1953 incorporated all changes instituted by the Third Reich during the Second World War. It was such an open legislative continuity with the Nazi regime that sparked social democrats' fears for the democratic new beginning. Given such developments, the SPD's lawyers association began to monitor signs of a return of National Socialist legal traditions across the entire legal field in the early 1950s.[29]

The more governmental powers the Allied powers returned to West German ministries in the early 1950s, the more ministerial officials felt emboldened to return to their old ways. Against initial US demands to ignore all Third Reich naturalizations carried out after 31 December 1937, West German ministries step-by-step re-established wartime citizenship regulations. They had support from leading legal scholars. Consider the case of Walter Schätzel (1890–1961), a professor of law at the University of Bonn, who in 1954 explained to a scholarly audience in the yearbook *Ostdeutsche Wissenschaft* the legal reach of the term *volksdeutsch* that the Nazis had introduced to denote Germans living outside of the German Reich and Austrian borders.[30] Next to German citizens, Schätzel argued, *volksdeutsch* was an 'ethnographic term' that 'incorporates all persons – regardless of their citizenship – who pledge allegiance to German *Volkstum*'. Schätzel claimed that *Volksdeutsche* mainly lived in Hungary and Romania, but he argued that the term was also applied to German refugees in Austria on decree of the Reichsminister of the Interior from 23 May

1944. Heinrich Himmler (1900–1945), the SS leader, had held this post at the time, a name Schätzel conveniently chose to omit in his legal opinion. Back in 1944, with German casualties mounting, Himmler had extended the definition of persons who could claim to be '*deutschstämmig*' (of ethnic German descent). Rather than having to prove descent from two German grandparents, applicants could now be counted as German 'if the person in question is seen as being German in the eyes of the German part of the population in his homeland'. Himmler had qualified this extension by adding that descendants from two German grandparents remained excluded if they 'had been assimilated in foreign *Volkstum*' or counted as 'second-grade *Mischlinge*' following the Nuremberg Laws.[31] Quietly, Schätzel was endorsing the continued use of Himmler's regulations. It was this widespread attitude within West German bureaucracy and academia to continue in the spirit and language of wartime regulations that led to Jewish Germans who returned to the FRG from Eastern Europe, often via Israel, suffering under the power of local officials. Depending on the local official they had to deal with, applications to have their citizenship rights reinstated were often refused or unnecessarily complicated as they were still judged by the racial and antisemitic standards of the Third Reich.[32]

Schätzel published several articles on this topic that were seen as major contributions to the scholarly debates on the planned amendments of the citizenship law in 1954. His stance was in line with Cold War legal politics: he conflated the definition of Germanness with the issue of German sovereign territory. Based on Himmler's definition, which, as he wrote in 1954, 'could still give a certain amount of guidance today', there existed 'more definitive factors'.[33] Schätzel alluded here to the ethnic and racial definitions of citizenship that had been shaped during the Third Reich. At the same time, Schätzel exercised some care in his choice of argumentation. He referred to the various relocation treaties that the German Reich had signed during the war. The legal term *volksdeutsch* as stipulated in the Basic Law, he declared in his piece in *Ostdeutsche Wissenschaft* erroneously in confusing it with the term German *Volkszugehörigkeit* used in Article 116 to define access criteria to citizenship, was no longer entirely identical to Himmler's definition. There had been some adjustment in legal interpretation since 1945. The legal term now only encompassed persons who had entered the territory of the German Reich in its borders of 1937 as refugees or as part of forced relocations. This included *volksdeutsche* refugees in the Soviet occupation zone, the Saarland, and in areas east of the Oder-Neiße line, as the GDR-Polish border was called in the FRG. To comply with Western demands, Schätzel had to exclude German refugees currently living in Austria, Switzerland or overseas. For him, the decisive criterion to acquire rights was expulsion: persons who had to leave their place of residence due to their ethnic German background were to acquire citizenship automatically. This included Germans coming from the East as well as from the Netherlands, Belgium and Alsace-Lorraine.[34] This argument became policy. German bureaucrats, moreover, also granted citizenship rights to war children of German soldiers and their mothers from countries under German occupation during the war.[35]

Austrians, or no Austrians?

West German bureaucrats soon went even further. If German citizenship could be granted along Third Reich logics, why stop at German minorities who had come under Nazi rule after the outbreak of the war? Why not also open a door for Austrians who wanted to retain their German citizenship that they had acquired after the *Anschluss* in 1938? The absence of specific citizenship regulations in international law allowed room for political manoeuvre. At the UN, the colonial powers still tried to defend the League of Nations' unequal rights regime and blocked Third World initiatives to transform claims to self-determination into a reform of international law to overcome the nexus of nationality and sovereignty that European powers had established to defend their dominance over colonies after the First World War.[36] West German lawmakers and federal ministries took this situation as an opportunity to maintain the expansive ethnic nationality policies that had fuelled German demands for a return of lost territory first after the First World War and again after 1945.

On 30 October 1954, the Federal Administrative Court's first senate caused national and international outcry when it ruled that Austrians remained German citizens if they had lived within German borders on the date of the Austrian state's resurrection in 1945. A woman had filed a case to retain her German citizenship, which she had gained in 1938.[37] However, this verdict stood in explicit conflict with an earlier constitutional court ruling from 1951 on the extradition of Austrians who claimed German citizenship based on naturalizations carried out between 1938 and 1945.[38] Here the court had stopped an extradition to Austria, but argued that the person in question could credibly argue that he would suffer at the hands of the Soviet occupiers. Now the Federal Administrative Court argued on the basis of citizenship claims.

Administrative practice had long treated Austrians as Germans. Already in the late 1940s, before the FRG's foundation, civil servants of the Rechtsamt der Verwaltung des Vereinigten Wirtschaftsgebietes (Legal Office of the United Economic Area) had advised former Austrian citizens that administrative offices in the Western zones would acknowledge their

German citizenship despite obvious pending legal questions. One case of a former Austrian military officer, who had requested his return to active duty in the Wehrmacht in 1939 and rose through the ranks from major to colonel by the end of the war, was indicative of this practice. Officials told the man and his wife, also born in Austria, that they had an unchallenged claim to German citizenship 'if they claim their German citizenship within Germany'.[39] This administrative practice also gave Austrians who had served in positions of power during the Third Reich or were implicated in war crimes or the Holocaust a route to legal protection in the emerging FRG.

The Federal Administrative Court's 1954 verdict had far-reaching implications. In a review in the *Juristenzeitung*, Alexander Makarov (1888–1973) levelled a damning critique against the court's judges. Makarov, born in Zarskoje Selo/Russia in 1888, had settled in Germany in the interwar years and became one of the foremost experts in citizenship questions and international law in the postwar years. He heavily criticized the court for overruling preceding verdicts of lower courts in the case of the naturalized Austrian woman who filed a complaint against the withholding of a German passport. The woman had become German through the collective naturalization of Austrians in 1938. She now lived in West Germany. Makarov argued that the Federal Administrative Court's first senate had excluded her from the Austrian state's *Wohnbevölkerung* (inhabitant population) as they saw her as German. For Makarov, the judges had taken a dangerous route to reach their conclusion because they implied that their reasoning could potentially be applied to all Austrians living in the resurrected Austrian state.[40]

High court jurisprudence now revealed this clear political bias. It mattered where people came from who hoped to retain their German citizenship. In the case of one former Czechoslovakian citizen who belonged to the German minority living in Bohemia-Moravia, for example, the constitutional court upheld his citizenship rights because the judges chose to delink the question of territory from the issue of rights. In this case, they argued that the CSSR had released all former citizens of German and Hungarian descent from their citizenship in 1945. What the judges meant was that Germans who had been forcibly expelled from Czechoslovakia needed the protection of West German citizenship. For Bavarian lower and appeal courts, the protection from statelessness for such persons had not merited the granting of German citizenship. When the plaintiff appealed to the constitutional court, the Bavarian Minister of Justice Josef Müller (1898–1979) represented the Munich higher state court at Karlsruhe. Müller argued that citizenship claims in this case rested on the illegal annexation of Czechoslovakian territory in 1938. The constitutional court in turn stressed that all Germans who had lost Czechoslovakian citizenship in 1945 had claims to German citizenship to avoid statelessness. This did not impede the condemnation of Third Reich territorial expansion. The protection of people's rights simply had to take precedence.[41]

The case of Austrians, however, was entirely different. The Austrian state had no intention to relinquish the sovereign representation of its citizenry.[42] Yet, contrary to the Austrian opinion, West German ministries and the Federal Administrative Court in its 1954 verdict believed that the absence of international law regulations and domestic legislation provided scope for interpretation. The Allied powers had only declared the annexation of Austria by the Third Reich illegal. Citizenship questions had not been explicitly regulated. While the Allies unanimously condemned the territorial expansions of the German Reich, many legal experts and judges refused to conclude that naturalizations conducted as part of Third Reich annexations had to be declared void as well.[43] Against their reluctance when it came to naturalizations of foreigners, West German officials pushed hard for legal continuity in the rights of Germans based on prewar and wartime regulations.

On 22 February 1955, parliament passed the Law for the Regulation of Questions of Citizenship. While the law remained silent on the Austrian issue, officials in the Ministries of the Interior and Justice managed to introduce many wartime treaties and regulations into the new legislation and made them officially government policy. The 1955 law reaffirmed the treaties between the German Reich and Czechoslovakia from 1938 and with Lithuania from 1939 as well as the regulations granting German citizenship to Germans living in Bohemia-Moravia from 1939, naturalizations in 'Eastern territories included into the Reich' in 1941 and 1942, the naturalization of Germans in Under-Styria, Carinthia and Carniola, and the naturalization of Germans in the Ukraine in 1943. All persons affected by these treaties and regulations remained German citizens if they had not 'explicitly declared' their will to be released from citizenship. The new legal amendments to the exiting citizenship law pertained exclusively to people and avoided any mention of territorial shifts in the course of the war that had structured these collective naturalizations of *Volksdeutsche*.[44] This omission of a nexus between territory and people should mask the adoption of Third Reich decrees and regulation in the new law.

The legal categories of *deutsche Volkszugehörige*, *Volksdeutsche* and *deutsche Staatsangehörige* enabled this inclusive ethnic approach without direct references to territorial sovereignty. *Volkszugehörigkeit*, the belonging to the German people, now encompassed persons who had 'in their homelands shown allegiance to German *Volkstum*'. This allegiance could be proven by descent, language, education and culture.[45] References to racial categories, on which these definitions had been based during the Third Reich, were now simply omitted when citing legislation originating between 1933 and 1945. Yet their logics were retained.

In November 1955, the constitutional court retaliated when the judges used a criminal case to make a stand against the BGH, Federal Administrative Court and ministerial officials. In this particular case, the Austrian government demanded the extradition of a man wanted for theft. The man himself had appealed to the court to evade prosecution in Austria. His attorney argued that his client's German citizenship protected him from extradition. In its verdict, the court adopted large parts of Makarov's criticism. The judges concluded that the naturalization of Austrians as part of the *Anschluss* in 1938 had only temporarily granted them German citizenship. With the enactment of the Austrian citizenship law at the end of the war, the period of German citizenship of Austrians had ended. This decision highlighted the many layers in the politics of citizenship and needs to be read in conjunction with the Saarland case about territorial sovereignty discussed in Chapter 1. While the court defended West German claims to German sovereignty in the Saarland case, here the judges demarcated the legal reach of German citizenship towards Austria. Cold War politics much more than universal application of the law underpinned these rulings.

The guiding role of Cold War politics was not disguised in this verdict. The constitutional judges themselves acknowledged it. As they stated in their ruling from November 1955, an 'appreciation of the political and historical circumstances' was determining their legal reasoning.[46] In other words, when it came to Austrian citizens, the nature and outcome of war demanded a retreat from Third Reich territorial expansionism, but this was different from other cases. The verdict was an open pushback against the legislation that had just passed through parliament. Against their own earlier decisions, the constitutional court now argued on the basis of transfers of sovereignty and, at least in this case, saw territorial shifts and citizenship as intrinsically linked: the *Anschluss* had incorporated Austrian sovereignty into the German Reich. The de-annexation of Austria in 1945 consequently returned Austrian citizenship to all persons who had possessed it in 1938.[47] The court's decision made automatic naturalization of Austrians impossible and instituted a clearly regulated immigration process for anyone who wished to acquire German citizenship. In the case of Austrians, the court therefore removed the rights of individuals to choose between citizenships that they had possessed at different moments in time. After the verdict, parliament had no choice but to amend legislation accordingly.[48] This curtailed the politicking of local officials and courts when it came to giving Austrians shelter in the FRG based on their Third Reich rights status.

After the international uproar in 1955 over the status of Austrians in the first amendment of German citizenship law after the war, West German ministries now had to support the legal position that Austrians had not legitimately become Germans in 1938. The controversy over the citizenship of Austrians was an example of bureaucracy overstepping the mark. International pressure and dissenting voices within the scholarly community demanded a retreat from initial expansive definitions of German citizenship after 1955. This, together with the constitutional court's verdict from November 1955, showed effect. When an Austrian man applied to become a German citizen again in 1960, the Foreign Office immediately determined that there existed no legitimate legal claims for such a change in nationality.[49] This decision, however, by no means meant that federal ministries stopped working for inclusive regulations.

Outsourcing Legal Revanchism

West German legal frameworks and administrative practice came under pressure from the mid-1950s onwards. Lora Wildenthal has shown how legal scholars such as Rudolf Laun (1882–1975), professor of law at the University of Hamburg and president of the *Staatsgerichtshof* (state constitutional court) in Bremen, became an embarrassment for his academic colleagues in the 1950s.[50] Laun had impeccable credentials when it came to his opposition to the Third Reich. This opposition catapulted him into leading positions in his university and made him the first president of the re-founded German Society for International Law from 1946 to 1953. In the interwar period, Laun had introduced progressive ideas of rights of the individual under international law to German debates. After 1945, he advocated a 'right to *Heimat*' (homeland), framed as a human right and rooted in the concept of self-determination, for Germans expelled from the East. Driven by his own background as an ethnic German who had grown up in Bohemia and witnessed how Germans had lost their rights when the Austrian-Hungarian Empire collapsed, he now promoted arguments for a new right under international law that should guarantee people a right to their specific homeland.[51]

Laun's new rights language and his personal background gave cover for ministerial officials who searched for arguments not just to restore the prewar German territory but to engage in expansionist ideology to unite all Germans in Central Europe in one nation-state. While Laun saw a right to homeland rooted in the self-determination of ethnic groups, he opposed the idea to link such a right to state sovereignty.[52] His legal distinctions, however, did little to discourage expellee organizations and ministerial officials from making precisely this connection. When expellee organizations appropriated human rights language and called for a right to homeland in the 1950s, officials in Bonn realized the revanchist potential of such a right of self-determination.[53] This did not mean that they had any intention to transform *Staatsrecht* traditions and domestic legal frameworks of sovereignty. Instead, high-ranking federal officials planned to advance the language of self-determination in international affairs. Yet, after the public outcry over the first citizenship law amendment and the inclusive approach to the rights of Austrians to German citizenship, this expansionist rights rhetoric came under public pressure.

Arguments based on Third Reich legislation and expansionist ideology, that ministries such as the Federal Ministry for All-German Affairs had made openly in the early 1950s, now had to be outsourced to distance the government officially from such ideas.[54] By 1955, the ministry approached an external expert to do its public bidding. Günter Decker (d. 1958) had made a name for himself as a freelance publicist researching questions of self-determination and nationality. Decker's legal career had begun with a doctorate in international law that he submitted in 1944. After the war, he worked as an independent publicist writing for several newspapers. He travelled extensively as part of this work and visited both the Middle East and the US in the early 1950s. During this time, he came into contact with the Ministry for All-German Affairs and submitted two internal expert opinions on 'The Solution of the European Nationality Problem' and 'The Right of Self-Determination of Peoples' in 1955. The ministerial experts were impressed by his work, not least because he articulated what many of them might have privately thought. They saw Decker as the perfect match to promote their aggressive agenda of uniting all Germans. With the ministry being curtailed in its public statements after the citizenship law controversy, Decker's expertise appeared so valuable that the ministry granted funding for the Research Centre for Self-Determination and Nationality Policies that opened in Lüneburg on 1 July 1955 with Decker as its head. The federal government had effectively outsourced public advocacy of its aggressive legal rhetoric that ministries could no longer be seen to support directly.[55]

Decker did his bit to make the centre instantly known. In his public statement for the opening of his centre, he promised the press that he would discuss the 'hot irons' of the time. He emphasized the political significance of independence movements across the globe for international legal debates and stated that he aimed to build legitimacy for West German territorial claims from decolonization movements. In his view, such claims had flourished after '700 million people had been released into independence since 1945'.[56] Ethnic tensions in Cyprus as well as racial conflict in the US and South Africa, in particular, prompted the question of how the right of self-determination related to nationality or ethnicity. Decker clearly sensed that a new global political language was on the rise, and he saw himself as the right man to exploit it for the Bonn government.

Decker argued that self-determination was about to unfold its full force as an international law principle.[57] He thus saw the work of his new centre secured.[58] He also did not avoid harsh criticism of the West German legal establishment. Their focus on *Staatsrecht*, in his view, had largely ignored self-determination as a potent international legal concept since it rose to prominence in the early decades of the twentieth century. As expected, Decker quickly delivered by advocating outrageous legal positions that a governmental ministry could no longer possibly have voiced. One of his internal opinions, the ministry decided, should become a book. The manuscript titled 'The Solution to the European Nationality Problem' went into review in 1956. The Ministry for All-German Affairs selected Herbert Kraus (1884–1965) as a reviewer, a retired professor of international public law and former head of the Institute for International Law at Göttingen.[59] Besides criticizing Decker's prose as 'inaccessible', Kraus questioned central arguments of Decker's book.[60] He doubted Decker's view that a future government of a united Germany could legally demand the return of all German territories that had been part of the Third Reich in 1939. This included not just the territorial expansion laid down in the Munich Agreement in 1938, that the Allies had declared void, but also the inclusion of Austria into the German Reich. While he disagreed with Decker's territorial conclusions, Kraus did not dismiss Decker's work on self-determination entirely.

The Ministry for All-German Affairs thought Kraus's evaluation was good enough to proceed with the publication of Decker's book. Yet ministerial officials insisted that no part of the book or its marketing should make any connection to the ministry. In the current political situation, the demand to return to the German borders of 1939 was 'not a tenable demand' for the government.[61] This was putting it mildly. Leading ministerial officials were more candid in internal communications when they argued that Decker's 'planned book can become the most important book for German foreign policy making since (without any judgement!) *Volk und Raum, Mein Kampf,* and *Zwischeneuropa'.*[62] Suddenly, Decker was placed in linage with the novelist Hans Grimm (1875–1959), Adolf Hitler, and the former Sicherheitsdienst des Reichsführers SS (SD) member and now editor-in-chief of the weekly newspaper *Christ und Welt*, Giselher Wirsing (1907–1975). The agenda of recovering German territory even beyond the borders in 1937 was clearly not dead within the ministry.

Decker may have been highly controversial, but he did accurately foresee the importance of international public opinion for upholding a claim to German unity based on legal arguments.[63] Following such ministerial praise, albeit of a dubious kind, Decker schemed to become the hegemonic public voice on German self-determination. Decker thought the Bonn government should make more effective use of developing UN norms and international law in the quest for unifying all Germans in one state based on self-determination claims.[64] In the future, he predicted in view of the right to homeland in 1956, the FRG might be forced to 'call on the *Rechtsgefühl der Völker* (sense of justice of peoples)' in its striving for national unity instead of pointing to concepts of state continuity.[65] He approached the UN in Geneva and New York to keep up with their most recent publications on the right of self-determination. To establish his credibility, he was much more indiscriminate than in domestic contexts, pointing to the Ministry for All-German Affairs to accredit his work.[66] In 1957, Decker was appointed as foreign policy adviser to the newly founded Bund der Vertriebenen (BdV/Association of Expellees), the new federal association of German expellees. He used this appointment to question the location of his centre. Lüneburg provided insufficient library provisions and minimal contact to other researchers. Bonn or Berlin seemed to be much more suitable places from which to promote his agenda.

Yet Decker, backed by secret government funding, had fallen prey to his own revanchist interpretation of self-determination as a tool to demand a renewed German territorial expansion in Central Europe in the late 1950s. Self-determination no longer attracted international appeal as a means to justify territorial unification of ethnic groups. Instead, it turned into the cipher for decolonization.[67] The growing tide of decolonization had already put the FRG on the wrong side of nascent new legal languages of self-determination and human rights. At the recent Asia-African Solidarity Conference in Cairo from 26 December 1957 to 1 January 1958, delegations labelled the FRG an 'imperialist state' for the first time. African and Asian states showed next to no interest in the question of German unification based in claims on the sovereignty of the German Reich.

Decker unexpectedly died in the summer of 1958, but the report that turned out to become his last one was in some sense prophetic. He argued that the rhetoric of self-determination was an ideal vehicle to connect to these regions of the world and garner additional support for West German legal policies. Yet time was of the essence. In vain, Decker warned his ministerial contacts that the West German government did not pay enough attention to Third World liberation movements. The 'world-wide self-determination movement', as Decker called it, would only grow in strength in the coming years. He already saw signs that GDR legal scholars might engage in similar research to his own. Time was running out to solidify the West German advantage in this field of expertise.[68] He urged the Minister for All-German Affairs Jakob Kaiser to increase the funding for his centre dramatically. Decker argued that the centre's focus on the right of self-determination gave the West German government a unique advantage over the GDR. There was no other institution similar to his centre anywhere in the world, or at least that was what he claimed. He had already scouted for potential German and foreign employees to expand his work. Decker foresaw the turning tides in international politics of law that decolonization began to produce in the 1950s.[69] He warned that the FRG could not continue to focus on state sovereignty rooted in *Staatsrecht* alone. Claims to the representation of Germany urgently needed to be reframed in a language of human rights and self-determination. Yet his warning went unheard.

Disputing East German Administrative Authority

Despite pressure from expellee organizations to continue to uphold collective naturalizations conducted before 1945 as symbolic gestures, West German ministries had to retreat step-by-step from direct legal continuities with Third Reich legislation in the late 1950s.[70] The treatment of Austrians had dragged administrative practice and the adoption of expansionist wartime traditions into the open. The constitutional court may have insisted on a territorial limitation of rights politics to the formula of the 'German Reich in its borders of 1937' against voices such as Decker's in verdicts between 1951 and 1955, but the judges left the issue of shared administration of German citizenship with GDR authorities unresolved. By the late 1950s, an increasing number of international inquiries in the administration of German citizenship rights demanded an answer to this question.[71]

Administrative practice and scholarly constructs kept colliding with everyday legal realities. The Ministry of the Interior continued to push for a complete non-recognition of East German administration, something Kleberg had already advocated in 1952. In no uncertain terms, Deputy Assistant Under-Secretary Erna Dlugosch pointed out in 1959 that the Ministry of the Interior now supported the view that only a legitimate state could grant naturalization and full citizenship rights. There was only one legitimate sovereign German state: the FRG. Consequently, administrative action by GDR authorities could at best represent, as she explained, the granting of 'certain rights and duties within the territory of the SBZ'.[72] Yet administrative practice complicated this radical view. While making her claim, Dlugosch had to acknowledge that several state-level ministries still accepted East German administrative acts. More importantly, Ulrich Scheuner, acting as the government's official academic adviser on the matter, explicitly endorsed the view in a memorandum that a unified German citizenship could only be upheld if West Germany accepted naturalizations by GDR authorities, exactly the problem that had plagued Kleberg in the early 1950s. If the federal ministries argued that citizenship administration and rights diverged in East and West, so Scheuner's logic went, the Bonn government would automatically acknowledge the East German government's sovereign power to naturalize individuals on its own terms by granting a separate GDR citizenship. Dlugosch, however, questioned Scheuner's conclusions, characterizing his reasoning as a 'quite messy argument'.[73] How could the FRG acknowledge GDR administrative acts, but not treat those acts as legally binding and conducted by a separate sovereign state administration? Dlugosch did not understand how such a partial acknowledgement of East German legal authority ought to be administered in practice.

At the time, antisemitic undertones still reigned strongly in the administration of citizenship matters. State and local officials dominated everyday legal realities. That old racial norms prevailed becomes evident in the documents of a meeting of the Federal Office for Administrative Matters in 1959. In this meeting, leading state and federal officials took stock of standing practices. They discussed the naturalization process for Jewish Germans who wanted to immigrate to the FRG. This process should commence not on application but only once the state of Israel had officially released citizens from their citizenship. Jewish immigrants from Eastern Europe were treated with even more suspicion, as the notes of the meeting illustrate. Bavarian officials, for example, had as recently as 1959 enlisted the help of the Eastern European Institute in Munich to revoke an expellee ID card of a Jewish applicant. The man, they argued, did not qualify as a *Volksdeutscher* because of his Jewish descent. The group of officials debated whether this incident could be treated as a model case. This implied that based on Third Reich exclusionary racist citizenship regulations, Jewish German immigrants from Eastern Europe should be blocked from immediate access to citizenship without a full application for citizenship as foreigners. Children of German mothers and foreign fathers should also have no automatic claims to German citizenship. Families needed to prove that such children were raised 'German'. The officials assessing such cases effectively could now decide what qualified as German child-rearing.[74]

From 1957 onwards, the GDR government further complicated West German legal positions by centralizing naturalizations. The East German government issued a new regulation, which transferred all naturalization requests from local authorities (as in West German practice) to the GDR Minister of the Interior. This centralization was a first step by the GDR government away from shared citizenship frameworks. After the building of the Berlin Wall in August 1961, the Federal Ministry of the Interior called for an emergency meeting on the issue in 1962.[75] As so often before, differences in state-level and federal administration had surfaced that this meeting hoped to address. In West Berlin, local officials actually accepted naturalizations conducted on the authority of the GDR Minister of the Interior. Their colleagues from federal ministries had to oppose this practice for obvious reasons. As they pushed for the recognition of West German governmental powers against Allied extraterritorial rights in Berlin, the ministry hoped to adjust administrative practice in West Berlin to the guidelines used in the FRG.

To solve this new dilemma of East German centralized naturalization regulations versus local West German practice, federal officials once more reverted to Third Reich regulations. At first, they believed to have found a suitable legal precedent in a directive from 5 February 1934 that had stipulated a *Zustimmungsbefugnis* (right of approval) of the Reich's Ministry of the Interior to acts of naturalization granted by state-level administrations. If the West German government treated the GDR government as an equivalent to a state-level government, a right for judicial review by the federal ministry could be constructed following the 1934 guidelines. The Bonn officials had no qualms with the fact that this directive had formed part of the Nazis' centralization of legal powers in preparation of the Nuremberg Laws that had policed the Third Reich's racial and antisemitic citizenship framework from 1935 onwards. In the end, experts from federal and state-level ministries agreed that 'routine' acts of sovereignty carried out by GDR authorities could be accepted as legitimate. This referred to everyday matters such as passing a test for a driver's licence to other administrative acts of registration. The radical demands, expressed by Kleberg and others in the early 1950s, of a complete non-recognition of GDR administrative powers could not be upheld in practice. Administrative acts with 'political implications', such as naturalization and citizenship regulations, however, had to be treated with more caution. There had to be some sort of informal West German check if people who had been naturalized in East Germany immigrated from the GDR to the FRG.[76]

The muddling through to avoid acknowledging GDR sovereign governmental powers to grant rights thus continued. Trying to delay the inevitable and simply acknowledge the GDR's independent state administration, officials from the Ministries of the Interior, All-German Affairs, Justice, and the Foreign Office under consultation with Ulrich Scheuner introduced another fine legal distinction in 1962: administrative acts by

GDR authorities, which potentially validated GDR sovereignty, were to be diminished by labelling them mere administrative acts in contrast to sovereign legal decisions.[77] Yet more than a decade of GDR legislative action began to show. While West German bureaucrats were still playing semantic games, the existence of two separate rights regimes was all too obvious after the building of the Berlin Wall.

A Waning Bourgeois Science?

In the late 1950s, the GDR government realized that it needed to build an entirely separate legal universe to end West German dominance in rights politics both at home and abroad. The SED leadership began to overhaul its legal system drastically while West German government officials radicalized administrative practice and citizenship regulations. West German ministries in their approach to citizenship administration largely pretended that they could ignore the entire GDR legal sector. By the mid-1950s, the East Berlin government realized that GDR institutions mostly reacted to Bonn's Cold War legal politics and seldom shaped the terms of the confrontation. This was supposed to stop. Ulbricht felt strongly that turning the tables on the FRG could only be achieved by establishing the primacy of the party in all fields of policy.[78] Law finally had to become a 'strong weapon' in the struggle against the FRG, and this could not happen on the basis of faithful adherence to German legal tradition.[79]

Yet there was a fundamental problem. In the aftermath of the East German Uprising in 1953, ministerial cadres such as Heinrich Toeplitz (1914–1998), at the time state secretary in the Ministry of Justice and member of the East German CDU, as well as leading academics privately acknowledged that they had no clear vision of how the theory and practice of law under socialism related to each other. As a result, the transformation of the legal system from its traditional 'bourgeois' roots to socialist legality stagnated after 1949. Toeplitz criticized legal scholars for their failure to draft appropriate curricula for the training of socialist legal cadres. In a confidential letter to Horst Büttner, the deputy director of the German Institute for Legal Science, Toeplitz complained that he thought academic work since 1949 had been too theoretical. The practical application of new socialist-inspired law was still lacking.[80]

Over the next years, also due to constant West German infringements on the legitimacy of the GDR legal sector through rights frameworks, party ideologues grew increasingly impatient with their legal scholars and the legal sector more generally because it seemed they constantly lagged behind other areas of governance in effecting the turn towards socialism.

One of the problems, the SED leadership finally acknowledged, was that the party had from the start lacked qualified personnel to push for legal transformation at home. In the early 1950s, legal scholars, judges and lawyers had fled the GDR in scores.[81] Karl Polak and other émigré scholars who returned from Moscow to the GDR had attempted to forge a new legal elite in crash courses in the early 1950s, but since then no uniform cohort of party faithfuls had emerged to take the fight to their West German counterparts in the international arena. Young legal scholars such as Rainer Arlt (1928–1997), Karl Bönninger (1925–2000), Hermann Klenner (b. 1926), John Lekschas (1925–1999) and Karl-Heinz Schöneburg (1928–2013) had still been schooled in a mixed tradition of the Soviet Vyshinsky School and German legal traditions.[82] This hybrid training led to a long period of internal struggles over the correct approach to law until the early 1960s.

The turn to Soviet legal traditions thus was in no way straightforward.[83] Peter Alfons Steiniger, one of the drafters of the GDR constitution and professor at Humboldt University, wanted to move away from Soviet legal orthodoxy in the mid-1950s. Rejecting the Soviet legal theorist Andrey Vyshinsky's claim that law had ideological authority independent of the party-state, Steiniger outlined that legal scholarship and the court system had to adopt the ideological line of the party-state. Soviet legal scholars such as Vyshinsky and V.A. Tarchov had claimed that law as 'a superstructure category cannot be explained by another superstructure category'.[84] By this definition, law was a political category in its own right next to the party's authority. The Stalin Constitution of 1936 had affirmed this separate quality of law. Vyshinsky and Tarchov had successfully argued against 'nihilists' like Evgeny Pashukanis, who believed that law was no longer necessary given the expected 'withering away' of the state and the coming of communism. Steiniger now openly disagreed with the prevailing doctrine in Vyshinsky's tradition that shaped Khrushchev's return to socialist legality as part of de-Stalinization. Law, in Steiniger's view, only represented a 'secondary superstructure category' in service of the state and the party.[85] With this shift, Steiniger anticipated Ulbricht's attack on the legal field to establish the primacy of the party over law.[86]

The ensuing scholarly disputes revealed a basic theoretical problem in conceptualizing socialist law. Peter C. Caldwell has shown in the context of the idea of the 'plan' under socialism that GDR scholars struggled to answer the question of how laws as 'general and stable legal forms' related to 'the prerogative of state and party administrators' to shape social and economic policy.[87] This problem persisted in the transformation of law towards socialist legality. Many of Steiniger's colleagues did not fall in line so easily when he developed his new ideas in 1955. Hans Nathan (1900–1971), professor at Humboldt University and legal advisor to the government, used proposed new legislation governing the court system that brought courts under party supervision to object. He defended the traditional organization of the legal system that was based on constitutional law and legal codes, not the primacy of the party. Toeplitz, meanwhile, criticized the fact that Steiniger had not situated Vyshinsky's arguments in their historical context of the Stalin Constitution. Had he done this, Vyshinsky's elevation of law as a superstructure could not have been brushed away so easily. Steiniger's defence illustrates how complex the departure from existing *Staatsrecht* to socialist legality was. He started with the constitution and laws with 'constitutional character'. *Staatsrecht*, he continued, regulated the 'conditions, which materially secure the building of socialism'.[88] This called for a subjugation of law and the legal system under the will of the party. How this subjugation should be organized, however, remained controversial. Horst Büttner, the head of the SED's Section State and Legal Theory, had planned to endorse Steiniger's argument and announce 'a new chapter' in the legal work. But after Steiniger's arguments met heavy criticism, he took no decisive stand to support him.[89]

The party leadership reacted to this academic infighting by restructuring academic working groups to achieve the desired scholarly push towards a new vision for a party-led legal system. The German Academy of Science invited a select group to the first meeting of its Section for Legal Science, a new subgroup within the academy. On 12 October 1955, the founding members met with the explicit agenda to provide 'a lively connection between academia and practice'. The first head of the new section became the president of the German Academy for State and Legal Sciences, Arthur Baumgarten (1884–1966). Hilde Benjamin as Minister of Justice and the State Prosecutor Ernst Melsheimer (1897–1960) represented legal 'practitioners'. Both Benjamin and Melsheimer supported a close connection of state power and party control over law and the legal sector.[90] Yet their paths to this conclusion could not have been more different, showing that the GDR also grappled with personal continuities from the Third Reich. Benjamin had risen through the communist ranks after being barred from practising law in the Third Reich. Melsheimer in turn looked back on a fast career under the Nazi regime, which reached its peak with his nomination to become a Reichsgerichtsrat – an associate judge – at the Supreme Court of the Reich in 1944. Unlike as the pair may have been, they both met in their belief in strict party control of courts and the primacy of party leadership in the field of law.[91] The new section's political role was to serve as a think tank.[92] Polak was made the secretary of the new group of nine legal experts. Next to the organization of conferences and the republication of 'progressive legal scholars', the section's aim was 'to engage with bourgeois legal science and develop a clear position towards it'.[93] In other words, the group was tasked with crushing the continued internal resistance of many legal scholars to fall in line with the new party line.

There were thus several debates underway at the same time. One was the debate about how to break away from German sovereignty and traditional legal codes. Another was the debate about the party's control of the legal sector. After the West German KPD ban in 1956, East German legal scholars stopped trying to debunk the legal validity of West German frameworks on the level of arguing about the correct understanding of German legal tradition, as this strategy clearly had proven futile. By 1957, West German observers realized that the GDR was then about to undergo a complete and official turnaround in international and German-German Cold War legal politics. The party apparatus now publicly propagated the legal downfall of the German Reich in 1945 and the emergence of two independent German states.[94] This impending turnaround was already heralded in a meeting of the Section for Legal Science on 15 April 1957, and the discussions at the meeting are worth examining in detail as they show that GDR legal experts began to realize the importance of international law for their quest.[95]

During this meeting, the working group discussed the development of a new position on the status of the GDR in international law. It was not a regular meeting from the outset, as the group had guests that day in Dzhangir A. Kerimov (1923–2015), who was a visiting professor from Leningrad at the German Academy for State and Legal Sciences 'Walter Ulbricht', and Michael Lakatos, a member of the Legal Institute of the Academy of Science of the CSSR. When Joachim Peck (1915–1979) introduced the topic of how to break West German legal dominance, the pressure from Ulbricht and the party leadership to develop an alternative rights universe became evident to their foreign guests. If there had been a short period of a more open debate on domestic and international aspects of socialist legality after Khrushchev's secret speech, it had ended abruptly with the Hungarian Uprising in 1956.[96]

To secure territorial integrity and sovereignty, Peck stressed, GDR legal experts had to turn to international law. He believed the GDR needed a new legal strategy that explained German division in international contexts. As one important example, Peck highlighted the fact that the United Kingdom had recently acknowledged the PRC and opened diplomatic relations. With this, the British government had confirmed the PRC's national sovereignty. East German legal scholars, in Peck's opinion, should now concentrate on convincing international audiences that the GDR's situation mapped onto the PRC's position in international affairs. After all, Chinese and German division after the Second World War would present the same legal challenges under international law. This legalist argument, coupled with a socialist interpretation of sovereignty and constitutionalism, Peck argued, was a promising strategy to secure the GDR's international status as a sovereign state and push back against West German rights infringements.[97]

Others argued that the nature of rights under socialism should form the basis for claims to international sovereignty, not comparative arguments with other divided nations. The president of the German Academy for State and Legal Sciences, Arthur Baumgarten, for example, rebutted Peck's argument because he thought ideology and not universal international law norms underpinned the GDR's sovereignty. Only states that respected the 'true interests of the people', by which Baumgarten meant socialist societies, could be attributed with legitimate legality. This version of people's sovereignty in a new disguise, Baumgarten stressed, had to be contrasted with recent US scholarship to highlight the moral superiority of socialist law. The new realist approach promoted in American international law circles at the time focused exclusively on power and power relations. This shift, according to Baumgarten, had to be exploited in legal propaganda. Such propaganda should make clear that the socialist camp was the bloc of 'ideas' that was fighting a militant Western camp, which in turn only used 'money and violent measures' to pursue their international interests.[98] In other words, the socialist revolution rather than international law should guide GDR politics of law.

Steiniger, once again a participant at the meeting, argued for a historical perspective to guide legal interpretations. He supported Peck's focus on international law. But he also criticized Peck's focus on Allied war aims as the determining factor in the question of German sovereignty. The legal nature of occupation, he held, had to be exploited in more detail to support the notion of the existence of two separate German states. Steiniger thus turned to the same problem that the West German constitutional court had to navigate at the time. If the transition from the Reich through occupation was of consequence for domestic and international sovereignty, East German experts had to tackle the legal relationship of state succession and the new political beginning after 1945. Steiniger thus suggested that the 'uniqueness of the historical situation' had to be used to justify the legitimacy of a socialist new beginning in a sovereign state that had produced new kinds of rights.[99]

Faced with these dissenting voices, the party leadership concluded that legal scholars could not move beyond their philosophical differences on their own. In response, the SED leadership enforced a consensus in 1958. Party leaders determined that history rather than any legal theory should shape international law propaganda against the FRG. This was a turn away from legal arguments, in line with Ulbricht's agenda of a primacy of ideology and party control over socialist legal norms. Termed the effectiveness principle, a party-sanctioned historical narrative of the transition from the Third Reich to the divided Germany now centred on a legal dismemberment of Germany. By this, the party stipulated that the German Reich had been divided in 1945 and the GDR represented one of its successor states. After years of competing with the Bonn government over the representation of the German Reich's sovereignty under international law, the GDR government had decided to disavow all legal ties to the German Reich on Ulbricht's command.[100]

This was a momentous decision, with major legal ramifications, as the following chapters illustrate. Yet it did not mean that GDR legal scholars stopped paying attention to West German legal developments; on the contrary. The German Institute for Legal Science in Babelsberg monitored the development of West German legal codes as closely as possible. Yet where the institute had previously denounced West German interpretations of German law and legal tradition, it now worked on a strategy to combine domestic and international developments in attacking West German politics of law. From here on, the FRG was dubbed a 'separate state' dependent entirely on the Western allies.[101] Against this image of a 'neofascist state', the GDR's socialist rights regime should shine in international rights propaganda.[102]

Towards Independent GDR Sovereignty and Socialist Law

The battle against the West German legal sphere had kept GDR scholars locked in traditional legal frameworks for too long. At an infamous meeting on 2–3 April 1958 in Babelsberg, Ulbricht declared that 'many jurists have continued to describe the functioning of our state institutions and law with bourgeois methods'.[103] This attack on leading legal scholars in 1958 marked an important shift in the SED's official interpretation of GDR legal sovereignty and citizenship rights. Following Ulbricht's demands, Bernhard Buck working at the Institute for West German State and Legal Questions changed the ideological interpretation of previous timelines of the GDR's legal development. In a memorandum for the SED leadership, he contended that the second party conference, on which the building of socialism had been declared in July 1952, represented no 'qualitative leap' in the development of socialist law. Citing Ulbricht's speech at Babelsberg, Buck now argued that socialist law originated from 'the period around the foundation of the GDR and the enactment of the first five-year plan'.[104] Buck thus backdated the emergence of socialist law to 1949. In doing so, he ignored the fact that there was still no scholarly consensus on what socialist law and legality actually meant.

Forgotten was a decade of disputing the Bonn government's right to represent the German Reich's sovereignty and rights.[105] Buck stipulated that the evolving socialist legal system had already morphed into the blueprint for a future unified Germany. Similar to the Basic Law's elevation in the Saarland case, described in Chapter 1, the SED now declared that the GDR's socialist system had to serve as the blueprint for unification.[106] Socialist law, Buck explained, had an important twofold effect: it helped to secure the socialist revolution and served as 'an instrument for the realization of reunification on democratic foundations'.[107] Democratic centralism – Buck actually meant party control here – should dominate the court system and the legal sciences in the implementation of socialist law. Socialist legality had to be aggressively propagated as part of lived legal reality. Otherwise, the implementation of a socialist legal consciousness among the population could not be achieved.[108] Ulbricht had emphasized this importance of law propaganda and legal education at home and abroad as a key feature in his Babelsberg address in April 1958.

Yet there existed overt problems. East German legal scholars still grappled with the fact that an overwhelming amount of German legal codes remained in force in lieu of new socialist codification of law beyond the constitution. Buck instituted a classification between these older bodies of law and newly developed socialist legislation after 1949. As an interim solution, older legislation should be 'employed in the interests of the working class'. Yet it could never assume the function of socialist law. New legislation 'served a function, bourgeois law cannot have as it is supposed to secure and promote the modes of exploitation: Socialist law has to mobilize the masses and organize them in the struggle against old elements in society and for the active fight for their needs'.[109] Socialist law and rights, in other words, should empower East Germans to march on in the socialist transformation of their society.

More party control over the legal sector after 1958 provided the basis for a more effective politicization of law against the FRG in the following decade. The importance of law for the party's domestic stabilization of rule became clear in the intense efforts to hijack the whole legal sphere for the party in the late 1950s. Two special sections within the SED central committee now supervised the state and legal sciences. Ulbricht demanded that the Academy for State and Legal Sciences, which also carried his name, had to become the 'leading theoretical force in the field of state and legal sciences'.[110] The academy was therefore now directly reporting to the Council of Ministers and the SED's Section for State and Legal Questions.

Karl Polak, who had ghost-written Ulbricht's Babelsberg speech, became the guardian of the party's control over the law. During the last years of his life, a Polak cult developed that culminated in the parading of his portrait at public rallies in the late 1950s.[111] This popularity was dangerous and Polak almost fell over it.[112] Many of his colleagues, who had suffered from his attacks since 1958, now retaliated. In February 1960, the Section Sciences reported to the SED central committee. Legal concepts of *Zweistaatlichkeit* (two-state theory), developed by Polak, met with fierce ideological criticism within the party apparatus.[113] The Section Sciences vetted Polak's concept for the planned conference on the theme 'The Development of the State Question in Germany since 1945' of the Section for State and Legal Sciences at the German Academy of Sciences. Polak's analysis and proposed programme, the party ideologues judged, contained 'abstract-theoretical' and ideologically unspecific aspects.[114] These shortcomings in Polak's legal approach threatened the intended outcomes of the conference. The gathering was meant to kick off the campaign for an independent GDR rights universe.

Polak's misguided analysis ran deep in the eyes of party cadres. The very basis of his analysis was wrong. His premise of equality between the two German states neglected the fundamental ideological conflict between imperialist forces and the 'interests of the nation'.[115] Polak suggested that the GDR's situation had to be interpreted in a legal framework of the two German states and the four Allied powers. 'It is not enough to analyse the current situation in Germany and then to conclude that two states exist and to analyse how this situation has developed.'[116] Explanations of German division had to be developed based on Lenin's writings on imperialism and the proletarian revolution, not legal theory. In the eyes of his critics, Polak left insufficient room for the revolutionary role of the working class in the defeat of imperialism. This turn to Lenin's work foreshadowed a concentration on the right of self-determination in the coming years. Polak had failed to give party ideology a proper place in his legal appraisal of divided Germany's legal situation. The party elite dismissed Polak's version of a socialist 'scientific' legal science that still rooted the GDR's international legal status in traditional approaches to law.[117]

The intervention of the party triggered the complete overhaul of Polak's conference plans. On 8 March 1960, he called together several of his colleagues. Polak handed down the new party guidelines. He declared that Hans Gerats was tasked with an in-depth analysis of the 'development and restoration of the imperialist state in West Germany as an instrument against the people's masses'.[118] This was in line with the Section for State and Legal Questions' main criticism of Polak's concept.[119] His revised draft for the conference agenda now introduced a new key term for the future international rights strategy. Following the party's insistence on combining the concepts of state and nation, the argument of the imperialist suppression of the self-determination of the German people guided Polak's draft. In 1960, Polak introduced only a short mention in passing towards the end of the conference programme.[120] Yet self-determination soon dominated East German legal politics in the international arena.

Polak still struggled to leave a focus on a German-German framework behind. This led to renewed open criticism by fellow legal scholars. Not all legal scholars fell in line with this party-endorsed focus on West German imperialist tendencies to explain the legal situation of the German nation-state. Steiniger made another advance in a general debate on strategy of the Section for State and Legal Sciences at the German Academy. After Polak's short report on his revised preparations, Steiniger proposed a major shift in legal rhetoric. In the presence of Minister of Justice Hilde Benjamin and her deputy minister Hans Ranke, he argued that the problem of sovereignty and rights had to be discussed in the context of decolonization. None of his colleagues, however, immediately supported this suggestion. Instead, the SED's ideological commission insisted on a firm link of the national question with a Marxist-Leninist interpretation of the bourgeois state in West Germany.[121]

The departure to a new international approach to Cold War legal politics was blocked one last time by the old guard. Polak still held greater sway with the party in 1960 than Steiniger and other experts of a younger generation.[122] Their legal interpretation demanded a Marxist-Leninist focus on West German imperialism to explain the existence of two German states in international law. For Polak, everything was a question of ideological legitimacy, even more so after he had survived the attacks on his work. Under socialism, humans organized society to their benefit. Capitalism conversely turned humans into 'living instruments' rather than free individuals. The 'humane nature' of the individual that was only guaranteed in socialist society underpinned Polak's concepts of sovereignty.[123] Polak enforced this view as consensus and the group passed on its conclusion to Kurt Hager (1912–1998). After Hager, the SED's propaganda chief, had given his approval, this focus on socialist society as the core of GDR sovereignty was added to the existing 'agitation and propaganda' work plan. Despite all internal disagreements, law morphed into a more central component in the defence of East German sovereignty alongside ideology shortly before the building of the Berlin Wall in 1961.

This new emphasis on socialism and socialist legality to justify sovereignty soon prompted the question of the need for a new socialist constitution. The Academy for State and Legal Sciences kept a watchful eye on scholarly reviews of constitutional codification in the CSSR, Hungary,

Poland, Yugoslavia, Finland, France and Italy. The academy paid special attention to the prefaces giving these constitutional laws political meaning and the role of basic rights for citizens. A new GDR constitution had to foreground waning citizen rights in the FRG in the course of Western military integration in contrast to guarantees of basic rights under socialism. Socialist legality, as deliberations among party cadres in the early 1960s showed, should secure socio-economic rights such as the right to work, the right to leisure, the right to material security in old age and in case of inability to work, and the right to education. Next to these basic social and economic rights, the equality of citizens, especially the equality of men and women, and 'democratic rights' including the right of free speech, freedom of the press, freedom to assemble, freedom of conscience and the relationship between church and state, and individual freedoms should be included in a future socialist constitution. The new evolving East German constitutional doctrine constructed and legitimized sovereignty through the rights that socialist men and women actively won by their dutiful participation in building socialism.

Domestic as well as international sovereignty should now be derived from socialist citizen rights.[124] Socialist rights, the new GDR rights strategy stipulated, would become the answer to West German legal infringement on GDR sovereignty. The hard-fought shifts in legal doctrine in the late 1950s prepared a major transformation in the politics of law between the two German states in the coming decade. Active participation of citizens in the political and economic development of socialism, enshrined in socialist legality guarded by party control, had to overcome the antagonism between the individual and society. In return, this duty to engage in socialist society secured citizen rights for the individual. Yet East German legal experts expressly refused to equate these duty-bound rights with individual freedom in a liberal tradition. The individual could not be free if the collective people was not free. The socialist citizen therefore only gained rights if they observed their duties towards society.[125] This socialist rights universe would soon become central to legitimize East German claims to self-determination, territorial integrity and international sovereignty. Yet the rising stream of people leaving the GDR in the late 1950s showed that this legal utopia was a far cry from reality.

Conclusion: The Clash of Legal Identities

The building of the Berlin Wall in 1961 cemented the division of Germany. Until this time, the judiciaries, ministerial officials and legal scholars of both German states had begun to disentangle German legal tradition and moulded their shared heritage into two distinct rights systems and ideologies.[126] West German ministries could capitalize on a Western-dominated codification of rights at the international level that validated their nationality-inspired rights policies until the end of the 1950s. As Roger Normand and Sarah Zaidi have observed, it was in no way trivial what rights were codified at the UN as they validated ideological visions of rights at home.[127] Despite open attempts by West German legislators and bureaucrats to return to Third Reich citizenship rights frameworks stripped of the antisemitic Nuremberg Laws of 1935, the FRG enjoyed the – though at times reluctant – support of the Western Allies in its legal politics. As long as UN rights politics favoured the idea of closed sovereign legal systems and the nexus of nationality and international sovereignty, the Bonn government's superior position in international law politics was secure. This vision of international law defended the sovereign right of nation-states to frame their domestic rights systems independent of international rights norms.[128] As long as the US and other Western powers defended this separation of domestic and international rights, it gave the Bonn government cover to defend the perpetuation of an expansive nationality policy in the field of citizenship administration against the GDR.

East German legal politics in turn remained fixated on domestic struggles over the correct ideological interpretation of what socialist law, legality and rights actually meant. The relegation of social and economic rights in UN politics to secondary importance and the Soviet belief, expressed by Vyshinsky when the Soviet Union abstained from the vote on the UDHR in 1948, that rights 'could not be conceived outside of the state' gave little international cover for GDR initiatives to develop socialist law at home.[129] Yet aggressive rights policies surrounding the West German citizenship law amendments in 1955 and the ban of the KPD in 1956 clearly showed that the SED's strategy of contesting West German politics of law on the basis of German legal tradition did not work. After a phase of rampant 'revolutionary justice' to stamp out internal opposition until the mid-1950s, the GDR government began to search for an alternative domestic and international framework of socialist law.[130] Yet the SED leadership around Walter Ulbricht had lost touch with current developments in the Soviet Union after years of internal infighting.[131] By 1958, Ulbricht and other party leaders pursued their own version of party-state control over the legal system independently of their Soviet teachers.[132] Embroiled in internal struggles over the nature of law, East German legal experts began to view matters of domestic and international law as more and more enmeshed in the confrontation between the two German states. Yet the internal struggles over the correct ideological line at the turn of the 1960s show that the departure to a new legal language of GDR independence and sovereignty remained embattled among legal scholars and party experts. Mollnau's call of 1961, cited in the introduction to this chapter, for a 'practice-oriented' field of scholarship showed that the impact of socialist law and GDR legal politics inside and outside of East Germany was still found wanting.

The period in which the legal battle between the two German states was fought on the basis of German legal tradition would soon come to an end. While the two German states, their judiciaries and ministerial officials remained locked in a battle over rights and sovereignty based on German legal tradition until the early 1960s, as I have shown in the first two chapters, anti-colonial movements across the globe advanced a new framework and language of the right of self-determination in their struggles for independence.[133] German politics of law would soon be sucked into these global forces of decolonization. Despite Decker's work on behalf of the Federal Ministry for All-German Affairs and Steiniger's repeated attempts to draw attention to decolonization and the importance of Chinese national division for GDR legal politics, both German governments remained oblivious to this new opening front line of global legal politics for a long time. West German ministries stuck to their legalist agenda rooted in *Staatsrecht* and Western international legal norms of sovereignty and rights. In the GDR, the party-internal struggle over the party's control of the legal sector caused a similar initial rejection of self-determination as a guiding concept in East German reconfigurations of international sovereignty and rights. Yet it was in the Third World and at the UN, as I discuss in the next chapter, that GDR leaders would finally find new alliances to overcome West German legal politics of non-recognition grounded in *Staatsrecht* and intrusions into the East German state's administration of citizenship.

Notes

1. This SED commission monitored West German legal developments and served as a think tank to develop strategies for how to engage with West German law and jurisprudence.
2. ASR/3417, 'Mollnau: Positivistische Methode und neothomisches Naturrecht'.
3. Howe, *Karl Polak*, 191–230.
4. ASR/3417, 'Mollnau: Positivistische Methode und neothomisches Naturrecht'.
5. Güpping, *Die Bedeutung der 'Babelsberger Konferenz'*, 96.
6. Ulbricht, *Die Staatslehre des Marxismus-Leninismus*, 14.
7. These legal frameworks remained deeply rooted in the discussion on citizenship since 1913. See: Sargent, 'Diasporic Citizens'.

8. Walter Ulbricht outlined the official position on the nature of the socialist state in his keynote address at the Babelsberg Conference in 1958. See: Ulbricht, *Die Staatslehre des Marxismus-Leninismus*. See also: Güpping, *Die Bedeutung der 'Babelsberger Konferenz'*, 70–85; Stolleis, *Sozialistische Gesetzlichkeit*, 138–61. For the development of a two-state framework out of the competition over the German Reich's sovereignty, see: Hacker, *Der Rechtsstatus Deutschlands*, 81–90.
9. Hacker, *Der Rechtsstatus Deutschlands*, 116–48.
10. Palmowski, *Inventing a Socialist Nation*, 23–64.
11. For first signs of this fundamental reorientation after 1953, see: Hacker, *Der Rechtsstatus Deutschlands*, 133–53.
12. Brubaker, *Citizenship and Nationhood*, 16. For a summary of the main strands in research into German citizenship law, see: Fahrmeir, 'Coming to Terms with a Misinterpreted Past?'.
13. This expansive definition allowed the return of so-called *Aussiedler* from Eastern Europe and the former Soviet Union after 1989/91. For the difficulties in defining 'German descent' in court to access German citizenship after 1989, see: Senders, '*Jus Sanguinis* or *Jus Mimesis*?'. See also: Klusmeyer and Papademetriou, *Immigration Policy in the Federal Republic of Germany*, 53–143.
14. BArch, B106/73195, letter Ministry of the Interior (Hesse), 13 December 1951.
15. BArch, B106/73195, memorandum working group Ministries of the Interior, 22–23 April 1952.
16. BArch, B106/73195, registry addendum: citizenship questions of the Soviet zone, 25 April 1952.
17. BArch, B106/73195, letter Federal Minister for All-German Affairs, 10 June 1952.
18. See: Ther, 'Expellee Policy in the Soviet-Occupied Zone'.
19. BArch, B106/73195, letter Hessian Ministry of the Interior, 18 June 1952.
20. This was a strategy used by the East German secret service: Allen, *Interrogation Nation*, 177–206.
21. BGH, 23.02.1954.
22. BArch, B106/73195, letter Hessian Ministry of the Interior, 18 June 1952.
23. BArch, B106/73195, letter Königstein Circle, 19 June 1952.
24. BArch, B106/73195, letter Kleberg, 22 August 1952.
25. See: Klusmeyer and Papademetriou, *Immigration Policy in the Federal Republic of Germany*, 53–75.
26. BArch, B106/73195, notes meeting on citizenship questions, 27 March 1953.
27. PA/AA, B82/217, letter exchange between ministries and expellee associations, 1952.
28. 'Gesetz über die Angelegenheiten der Vertriebenen und Flüchtlinge (Bundesvertriebenengesetz)'.
29. AdsD, 1/MHAC01431, letter Hacks to Kunze, 25 June 1953; AdsD, 1/MHAC01431, ASJ meeting minutes, 7 April 1951.
30. Schätzel, 'Die Staatsangehörigkeit der Volksdeutschen', 231–44.
31. For the administrative practice of naturalization in occupied Poland, see: Wolf, *Ideologie und Herrschaftsrationalität*. See also: Heinemann, *Rasse, Siedlung, deutsches Blut*.
32. See: Panagiotidis, '"The Oberkreisdirektor Decides Who Is German"', 506–14.
33. Schätzel, 'Die Staatsangehörigkeit der Volksdeutschen', 233.
34. Ibid.
35. See the chapters in: Ericsson and Simonson, *Children of World War II*.
36. For the maintenance of unequal legal standards within the UN, see: Normand and Zaidi, *Human Rights at the UN*, 212–24 and 230–35; Mazower, *Governing the World*, 191–231.
37. BVerwGE 1, 206.
38. BVerfGE 1, 322.
39. BArch, Z22/55, letter exchange von Armin, May 1949.

40. See: Makarov, 'Entscheidungen: Staatsangehörigkeit'.
41. BVerfGE 1, 322.
42. Makarov, 'Entscheidungen: Staatsangehörigkeit'.
43. Ibid.
44. 'Gesetz zur Regelung von Fragen der Staatsangehörigkeit'.
45. 'Gesetz über die Angelegenheiten der Vertriebenen und Flüchtlinge (Bundesvertriebenengesetz)', 204. For the long-term consequences of this policy, see: Senders, 'Jus Sanguinis or Jus Mimesis?'.
46. BVerfGE 4, 322.
47. Ibid.
48. 'Zweites Gesetz zur Regelung von Fragen der Staatsangehörigkeit'.
49. PA/AA, B82/217, letter exchange West German embassy Vienna, July 1960.
50. Wildenthal, *The Language of Human Rights*, 45–62.
51. Ibid., 57f.
52. Ibid., 49–50.
53. Ibid., 45–62.
54. For the interwar origins of German legal minority concepts, see: Salzborn, '"Volksgruppenrecht"'.
55. Such outsourcing of public relations work had also been used in promoting the FRG's inclusion into NATO. See: Uelzmann, 'Building Domestic Support'.
56. BArch, B241/4, press review institute opening, 1956.
57. For the rise of a language of self-determination, see: Manela, *The Wilsonian Moment*; Fisch, *The Right of Self-Determination of Peoples*; Getachew, *Worldmaking after Empire*, 71–106.
58. BArch, B241/4, press review institute opening, 1956.
59. Herbert Kraus looked back on an esteemed career. In 1923, he had been appointed to a chair at the University of Königsberg. In 1927, he taught for one summer at the Hague Academy of International Law before teaching at summer schools in Philadelphia and Chicago. In 1928, he moved to Göttingen where he founded the Institute for International Law. Under the Third Reich, Kraus was forced out of his academic post. He had been a doctoral student of Adam von Trott zu Solz, who was involved in the attempt on Hitler's life in 1944. After the end of the war, Kraus was reinstated in his academic positions. He specialized in the status of former Eastern territories in international law until his retirement.
60. BArch, B241/29, appendix letter, 13 March 1956.
61. Ibid.
62. Ibid.
63. BArch, B241/24, memoranda Decker, 16 August 1956, 18 August 1956, 15 January 1957.
64. BArch, B241/24, confidential report on 7th Congress of the Federal Unions of European Ethnic Minorities, 13 June 1957.
65. BArch, B241/15, memorandum Decker, 19 November 1956.
66. Decker also kept himself busy travelling in the ministry's service. See: BArch, B241/3, letters Decker to the UN at Geneva and New York from 12 and 21 July 1955.
67. Fisch, *The Right of Self-Determination of Peoples*, 190–217; Getachew, *Worldmaking after Empire*, 71–106.
68. BArch, B241/6, report Research Centre for the Right of Self-Determination and Nationality Politics, 15 January 1958.
69. See: Normand and Zaidi, *Human Rights at the UN*, 243–88.
70. PA/AA, B82/901, letter Schäfer, 14 October 1958; see also: PA/AA, B82/530.
71. For example, the Belgian embassy inquired in 1959. See: BArch, B106/73195, letter Dlugosch, 27 May 1959.

72. BArch, B106/73195, note on awarding of German citizenship by GDR authorities, 23 March 1960; memorandum on naturalizations by GDR authorities, 31 March 1960.
73. Ibid.
74. BArch, B106/73196, minutes of meeting on citizenship questions with state-level officials, 18 September 1959. For the treatment of Jewish applicants, see: Panagiotidis, 'The Oberkreisdirektor Decides Who Is German' and 'Germanizing Germans'.
75. BArch, B106/73195, memorandum on recognition of GDR naturalizations, 6 April 1962.
76. Ibid.
77. The Foreign Office internally questioned this strategy. If citizenship law should change in one of the German states, such administrative acts would inevitably turn into sovereign acts. BArch B106/73195, memorandum on recognition of GDR naturalizations, 10 July 1962.
78. For the controversy over the role of socialist legality for state planning in the 1950s, see: Caldwell, *Dictatorship, State Planning, and Social Theory*, 57–96.
79. BArch, DP1/6166, Statutes German Institute for Legal Sciences.
80. BArch, DP1/6166, letter Toeplitz, 11 July 1953.
81. Until 1948, the SED dismissed 12,985 judicial employees (out of 16,267). See: Feth, 'Die Volksrichter', 354. Between 1947 and 1961, 2,700 academics fled the GDR, which exacerbated the crisis in training a new legal elite. See: Krönig and Müller, *Anpassung, Widerstand, Verfolgung*, 400f.
82. This had also to do with the lack of literature and resources. Polak assumed the role of Ulbricht's leading legal advisor and set the agenda towards a Soviet-style legal system. See: Güpping, *Die Bedeutung der 'Babelsberger Konferenz'*, 101f.
83. BArch, DP1/6166, action points from IV. SED Party Convention. See also Güpping, *Die Bedeutung der 'Babelsberger Konferenz'*, 58–67.
84. BArch, DP1/6166, '"Thesen zum Thema: Das Rechtssystem der DDR" von Prof. Dr. Steiniger', 21 June 1955. Güpping discusses the reception of Vyshinsky's doctrine by GDR scholars in the 1950s. See: Güpping, *Die Bedeutung der 'Babelsberger Konferenz'*, 180f.
85. BArch, DP1/6166, '"Thesen zum Thema: Das Rechtssystem der DDR" von Prof. Dr. Steiniger', 21 June 1955.
86. See: Caldwell, *Dictatorship, State Planning, and Social Theory*, 57–96.
87. Ibid., 96.
88. BArch, DP1/6166, meeting minutes of Section State and Legal Theory, German Institute for Legal Sciences, 4 July 1955.
89. Ibid.
90. ABBAW, Klassen, No. 224, minutes first meeting Section Legal Sciences, 12 October 1955.
91. Brentzel, *Die Machtfrau*, 289f.
92. ABBAW, Klassen, No. 224, communiqué on the foundation of a Section Legal Science, German Academy of Sciences.
93. ABBAW, Klassen, No. 224, minutes first meeting Section Legal Science, 12 October 1955.
94. See: Hacker, *Der Rechtsstatus Deutschlands*, 154–279.
95. ABBAW, Klassen, No. 224, minutes meeting Section Legal Science, 15 April 1957. See also: Güpping, *Die Bedeutung der 'Babelsberger Konferenz'*, 73–77.
96. The phase of open criticism by legal scholars of the GDR legal system's shortcomings was stopped and would harm many scholars in the coming years. See: Güpping, *Die Bedeutung der 'Babelsberger Konferenz'*, 105–36; Howe, *Karl Polak*, 191–230; Caldwell, *Dictatorship, State Planning, and Social Theory*, 63–74.
97. For the framing of GDR independence in constitutional terms, see: Güpping, *Die Bedeutung der 'Babelsberger Konferenz'*, 73–98.
98. ABBAW, Klassen, No. 224, minutes meeting Section Legal Science, 15 April 1957.
99. Ibid.

100. BArch, DY30/IV2/13/459. See also: Hacker, *Der Rechtsstatus Deutschlands*, 340.
101. BArch, DY30/IV2/13/487. See also: Stolleis, *Geschichte des Öffentlichen Rechts*, Bd. 4, 189f.
102. Hacker, *Der Rechtsstatus Deutschlands*, 300–306.
103. Ulbricht, *Die Staatslehre des Marxismus-Leninismus*, 5.
104. BArch, DY30/IV2/13/459.
105. Hacker, *Der Rechtsstatus Deutschlands*, 105–15.
106. Güpping, *Die Bedeutung der 'Babelsberger Konferenz'*, 76f.
107. BArch, DY30/IV2/13/459.
108. BArch, DP1/6166, working group meeting trial law, German Institute for Legal Science, 12 November 1958.
109. Ibid.
110. Cited in: Güpping, *Die Bedeutung der 'Babelsberger Konferenz'*, 164. See also: Howe, *Karl Polak*, 210–21.
111. Howe, *Karl Polak*, 221–25.
112. Ibid., 225–30.
113. For Polak's draft, see: BArch, DY30/IV2/48.
114. Ibid.
115. Ibid.
116. Ibid.
117. Ibid.
118. ABBAW, Klassen, No. 225, protocol of meeting on 8 March 1960.
119. Ibid.
120. ABBAW, Klassen, No. 225, draft 'The Development of the State Question in Germany since 1945 (with Special Attention to the National Question)'.
121. ABBAW, Klassen, No. 225, minutes of first secretariat meeting, 8 April 1960.
122. Polak secured his dominant position by authoring an authoritative volume together with Ulbricht on the nature of the socialist state. See: Ulbricht and Polak, *Beiträge zur Staatslehre*. Polak's instructional volume on the nature of law and the function of the legal sciences was reprinted in three editions between 1959 and 1963. See: Polak, *Zur Dialektik in der Staatslehre*. The emphasis was on the state and the party in contrast to law and the legal sciences, as the titles of these volumes indicate.
123. ABBAW, Klassen, No. 225, minutes of first secretariat meeting, 8 April 1960.
124. ASR/5599.
125. For the social and legal construction of socialist citizen rights, see: Betts, 'Socialism, Social Rights, Human Rights'; Palmowski, 'Citizenship, Identity, and Community'.
126. For a parallel history of German-German legal reconstruction and the development of separate university teaching, legal doctrine and legal institutions, see: Stolleis, *Geschichte des Öffentlichen Rechts*, Bd. 4.
127. Normand and Zaidi, *Human Rights at the UN*, 200.
128. Ibid., 103.
129. Cited in: ibid., 194.
130. See: Fricke and Engelmann, *'Konzentrierte Schläge'*; Engelmann and Vollnhals, *Justiz im Dienste der Parteiherrschaft*. 'Revolutionary justice' would remain a tool for enforcing party discipline until 1989. See: Raschka, *Zwischen Überwachung und Repression*.
131. Dina Moyal's work shows the reinterpretation of socialist legality as part of de-Stalinization. See: Moyal, 'Did Law Matter?'. The Soviet Union also re-engaged with UN legal debates; see: Mazower, *Governing the World*, 244–72.
132. See: Güpping, *Die Bedeutung der 'Babelsberger Konferenz'*, 175–82.
133. Fisch, *The Right of Self-Determination of Peoples*, 190–217; Getachew, *Worldmaking after Empire*, 71–106. For the origins of these movements after World War I, see: Manela, *The Wilsonian Moment*.

Part II
INTERNATIONALIZATION

Chapter 3

The Clash of Legal Universes

On 28 February 1966, SED leader Walter Ulbricht submitted an official application for UN membership.[1] The GDR's admission as a full member remained unlikely at this point, but the SED leadership hoped to make inroads into international legal affairs. Ulbricht set out a clear goal for his initiative. He aimed at breaking the barring clause that only permitted UN members and official observer states to join UN conferences, programmes, conventions and special organizations.[2] This practice had been established under the aegis of UN Secretary-General Dag Hammarskjöld (1905–1961) in the 1950s to slow down access to UN politics before the wave of decolonization fully unleashed in the 1960s.[3] The FRG had secured UN observer status in 1952 at the height of the Korean War, when Western countries still comfortably dominated UN affairs after the Soviet Union's temporary retreat from the organization.[4] In the late 1940s, the Soviets protested the relegation of social and economic human rights to secondary importance within UN politics and the seating of the ROC to represent China in the UN Security Council instead of the PRC.[5] Short of full membership, Ulbricht hoped to attain at least the same official observer status that the Bonn government enjoyed. He imagined that such equal treatment of both German states by the UN could then be propagated as international recognition of the GDR's independent sovereign statehood.

In the historiography on German-German relations, the period from the late 1960s into the 1970s is commonly analysed through the lens of West German Ostpolitik, in which Willy Brandt's social liberal government moved to politics of détente with the GDR, Poland and the Soviet Union. Brandt hoped to normalize relations with the GDR to allow for increased family contacts across the Iron Curtain or, in the words of his

---

Notes for this chapter begin on page 136.

chief advisor Egon Bahr (1922–2015), to trigger 'change through rapprochement' in German-German Cold War politics.[6] Scholarship on East German foreign policy in turn has centred on the question of whether the GDR was more an 'object' between Bonn and Moscow rather than having independent agency in foreign affairs. If we look beyond the diplomatic history of Ostpolitik, the Cold War legal battle between the two legal universes of Western rule of law and socialist legality reveals the GDR's attack on established international law standards. In its legal foreign policy, the SED displayed much more independence from Moscow than diplomatic histories have often assumed.[7]

For East German legal experts, as the previous chapters have illustrated, the attack on West German frameworks of German sovereignty and citizenship was part of the struggle between two legal universes. After years of internal struggles over the primacy of the party-state over law, the SED commanded its legal experts to depart from German legal tradition and develop a socialist legal universe at home and in international law in the late 1950s.[8] In the year before his early death at the age of fifty-eight in 1963, the doyen of GDR law Karl Polak had acknowledged that the 'Third World's struggle for liberation has returned international law to a place of prime importance'. In contrast to Third World rights campaigns, however, Polak firmly rooted the birth of 'international law of our epoch' in the October Revolution and Lenin's writings on self-determination.[9] In his view, the Bolshevik revolution had decisively transformed the legal issue of the equality of nations and their political representation.[10] Crucially, Polak still endorsed the traditional view that domestic legality did not directly relate to international law.[11] For him, the turn to self-determination in a Leninist tradition may have been an internationalist project, but it was one that was propelled by sovereign socialist states.

The East Berlin leadership had constantly hit roadblocks in its quest for international recognition as long as it had worked solely within the restrictive framework of the four Allied occupation powers and two German governments. By the mid-1960s, East German diplomats realized that the growing number of governments of decolonized states might be supportive of a renewed bid for GDR recognition by the international community.[12] The GDR and newly independent governments in Africa and Asia had much in common. They all questioned the unequal legal logics that had dominated the UN since its foundation and, as Antony Anghie has argued, rested on a 'sovereignty doctrine' which colonial powers had built to exclude colonized peoples from international law affairs.[13] Adom Getachew has explored how anti-colonial leaders set up new frameworks for international governance, in which they tried to overcome the ideological separation of collective and individual human rights and rejected the UN's internal hierarchy. Referencing Lenin's endorsement of a right of self-determination to secure national independence, Third World leaders proposed a new framework that reconciled the desire for independence from colonial rule through sovereignty, the guarantee of human rights through citizenship rights and the impact of international legal norms on nation-states.[14] This vision of realizing the promise of universal legal rules for all after the end of empire was not without problems, but it matched the GDR's desire to have its independence recognized.

Even though the GDR and many African and Asian states had ideological differences, the new East German legal universe centred on the same core principle that Third World liberation movements advanced in their quest for independence: the right of self-determination.[15] By the mid-1960s, in its new international law venture, GDR international law propaganda thus constructed a direct link to rights campaigns in the Third World. Ulbricht sensed that he also had a powerful ally within the UN administration. His demands for UN recognition of GDR sovereignty matched UN Secretary-General Thant's (1909–1974) political agenda. Since his election in 1961, Thant had advocated that the UN had to fulfil its charter's promise of universal membership of all sovereign states.[16] While he primarily advocated equal rights for decolonized states, Thant could not overlook the connected issue of divided countries. It was this new emphasis on legal universality of the UN's own rules of membership and the Third World's pressure to make the General Assembly an equality-based decision-making body to break the Security Council's veto powers that gave Ulbricht confidence to launch an international law campaign in the corridors of the UN. The hope was that if the GDR rallied support for Third World countries' causes such as anti-apartheid, they would support the demand for UN recognition of GDR state sovereignty.[17] This strategy, however, had important consequences for the UN as a whole.

The East German departure towards a vision of sovereignty that put rights guaranteed under socialism at the core of claims to self-determination was significant because it questioned the mid-century international law consensus of the intrinsic link of nationality and international sovereignty. This chapter explores how the SED's international law campaign to have the GDR's territorial integrity and sovereignty recognized by the UN not only undermined traditional German concepts of statehood, rights and sovereignty, but also questioned the UN's core doctrine of membership. After 1945, the UN system was designed to ensure that one seat in the General Assembly represented one nationality. From the early 1950s onwards, the Bonn government had used this convention to represent 'Germany' as an official observer state within the UN and its associated organizations and keep the GDR out of UN affairs. The GDR now proposed that the sovereignty of 'divided nations' such as Germany, China, Korea and Vietnam could legitimately be divided, putting socialism at the core to legitimize an East German right of self-determination.

This new international campaign had important consequences at home. If socialism and the rights it bestowed on GDR citizens formed the core of the SED's bid for an East German right of self-determination, nationality could no longer play a central role in legal definitions of sovereignty and citizenship. This turn to new ideological foundations of the East German state, as Jan Palmowski has shown, forced the SED to invent a socialist nation for its citizens at home.[18] It also required that the GDR create a new image of a socialist sovereign state abroad. The international law politics surrounding divided nations catapulted the two German states to the heart of UN clashes over international sovereignty and the lawful representation of statehood in the late 1960s and early 1970s.[19] In these clashes, the strict separation of the GDR's domestic legal sphere and international legal norms, which Polak had still insisted on in 1962, loosened.

Catching Up

The GDR government had long underestimated the importance of the UN. In the early 1950s, the SED leadership had missed the opportunity to engage with UN affairs. On 28 June 1950, the first UN Secretary-General Trygve Lie (1896–1968) offered a personal meeting with GDR president Wilhelm Pieck (1876–1960) at the UN headquarters in Geneva. Lie suggested that the UN might be able to broker and monitor an all-German referendum on unification. Despite the fact that this offer tied directly into the GDR's legal politics supporting communists before West German high courts at the time, the SED leadership openly rejected such international involvement in German affairs. Pieck's explanation then was reminiscent of old European reflexes of superiority. In a letter to federal president Theodor Heuss (1884–1963), Pieck defamed UN oversight over German affairs as the degradation of Germany to a 'colonial people'.[20] In 1950, Pieck saw the UN in the tradition of the League of Nations' mandate system, which he felt did not apply to the German postwar situation.[21]

When the Allied powers released the two German states from occupation in 1954–55, the SED leadership painfully realized the consequences of ignoring international legal politics and sought ways to quickly deal with this lacuna.[22] International law became the second main focus of the German Academy of Science's Section for Legal Science, the same section that had debated the nature of the domestic socialist legal system discussed in the last chapter. Two of the legal scholars in the group, Heinrich Brandweiner (1910–1997) and Elfried Härle (1908–1978), were tasked with international law and UN affairs. Brandweiner had begun his career in Austria and emigrated to the GDR after he had visited Korea in 1952 and accused the US of bacterial warfare. Härle became professor of law in Jena and would leave the GDR for West Germany in 1959 after the purge following the Babelsberg Conference. After the Section for Legal Science was constituted in 1955, its first demand was for a swift and accurate translation of new international laws and conventions into German. Having accessible texts was important because GDR scholars lacked basic information to establish a legal position towards the UN at the time. Brandweiner and Härle demanded that translated UN materials should be circulated as part of the training of legal personnel, which the GDR was still lacking in great numbers.

Many within the party did not share this enthusiasm for international law as they sensed its 'subversive' potential. Herbert Kröger, now the new director of the German Academy for State and Legal Sciences, savvily cautioned against immediately circulating international legal texts within the GDR. He argued that the dissemination of UN conventions should always be accompanied by an appropriate commentary and in coordination with the Ministry for Foreign Affairs. Having been involved in the KPD trial in West Germany, Kröger had plenty of experience with the ways in which law could be politicized. The group therefore agreed that Soviet counter-resolutions had to be published alongside all UN conventions. Legal trainees and students had to be led to see UN developments in the appropriate ideological context of Soviet opposition to Western domination of the organization at the time. Otherwise, they would not develop the 'correct' political position towards international legal norms.[23]

Internal discussions over the correct approach to socialist law, traced in the previous chapter, replicated in early debates on a UN legal campaign. At the section's next meeting, members discussed the GDR's new international strategy and Baumgarten opened with a paper on 'The World Peace Movement and Its Historical Importance for International Law, Democracy and Socialism'.[24] For Baumgarten, it was clear that the US and 'capitalist governments under the US's spell' had taken over the UN. And he supported the Soviet Union's search for an alternative global institutional network to oppose the UN as a 'Western organization'. The people of the world, first and foremost those under colonial rule, had to find new avenues to secure peace and self-determination by putting pressure on the UN from outside of the institution.[25] Baumgarten proposed that a deeper understanding of the world peace movement therefore had to be the first priority in advancing scholarship in international law.

Steiniger, who had repeatedly advocated a turn to international law and self-determination, was of a different opinion during the discussion that followed. He went straight to the main problem of the GDR in international legal politics: the SED leadership, he argued, lacked alternative legal categories to confront West German legal concepts. Steiniger was an authority on this subject. He had experienced the West German exclusion of GDR rights groups in the UN context first-hand. Since 1954, Steiniger had served as the president of the East German League for the United Nations.[26] This new East German NGO should build contacts with Third World delegations and rally support for GDR membership in UN-associated organizations. When Steiniger had witnessed how these attempts first failed, he argued that one had to attack the very definition of international sovereignty on which the UN was built. If the SED planned to promote the legal existence of two German states, possible distinctions between 'the state' and 'the nation' under law needed more exploration. For Steiniger, the solution was to contest the convention that only 'nations' represented subjects of international law.[27]

East German legal scholars should also pay more attention to comparative perspectives on the situation of divided countries in Asia and Europe. Communist China, Steiniger proposed, was as much a sovereign state and a legitimate UN member state as the GDR. It had only been US dominance over UN affairs that had prevented the implementation of this fact in 1949, with the result that the ROC on Taiwan now represented China in the UN although the Chinese Communist Party (CCP) governed the whole of the Chinese mainland. For disadvantaged states such as the GDR and the PRC to overcome this situation, the UN's focus on nationality in legal definitions of sovereignty had to be countered by socialist legal frameworks. The new question among party cadres and legal scholars was how socialist definitions of people's sovereignty might become the legal core of their state's international legitimacy. In the years that followed, the Institute for International Law at Babelsberg and the German Law Institute spearheaded the formulation of such new legal concepts along these political guidelines.[28]

The international outrage over an epidemic of swastika paintings and antisemitic attacks in the winter of 1959 made the FRG the subject of UN debates on racial discrimination. The fear of a return of Nazism sparked unexpected consensus within the UN Sub-commission on Prevention of Discrimination and Protection of Minorities, that was in session when reports on antisemitic attacks emanated from West Germany, on the need for a new convention on racial discrimination.[29] Suddenly, the SED leadership realized that its own anti-fascist language was compatible with Third World demands if it was connected through anti-racism rhetoric.

The international outcry over neo-Nazi attacks accelerated the shift in GDR legal debates on a new framework of international sovereignty. In the years following 1959, the SED doubled its efforts to appeal to Third World liberation groups and emerging African and Asian states. The party's mouthpieces *Neues Deutschland*, *Neue Zeit* and *Berliner Zeitung*, ran articles on racial discrimination and apartheid in increased frequency to propagate the GDR's solidarity with the Third World to domestic and international audiences. These papers denounced the 'Regime of Inhumanity' and called for 'Sanctions against South Africa'.[30] The SED had found its first rallying cry that allowed a connection to newly decolonized states through a law campaign.[31]

If the SED wanted to engage with UN debates directly, however, the focus on self-determination needed a more solid legal basis.[32] Pressure quickly mounted on international law experts because the GDR government was itself under intense international pressure after the Berlin Wall had cemented German division. By autumn 1962, the Ministry for Foreign Affairs grew impatient. Amidst the second Berlin crisis since 1958, which culminated in the building of the Berlin Wall in 1961, legal scholars were still focused too much on refuting West German positivist and bourgeois-imperialist approaches to law.[33] Just as they had not come up with a genuinely socialist rights framework for GDR law in their domestic legal sphere, they also had still not developed any socialist approaches to international law that could be used as foreign policy tools. East German diplomats urgently needed legal concepts that had the potential to challenge Western dominance in the field of international law.[34] Steiniger's repeated calls for an inclusion of decolonization and self-determination in the deliberations on sovereignty now finally caught the ministry's attention and silenced the older guard of scholars' legal orthodoxy that had demanded a focus on divided Germany.

Hopping on the Third World Bandwagon

In February 1964, the SED officially launched its UN publicity campaign. It began with Deputy Foreign Minister Georg Stibi's (1901–1982) telegram to the delegates of the XX. Conference of the Human Rights Commission that had convened in New York and debated global issues of racial discrimination.[35] Addressing African delegates in particular, Stibi associated the FRG with the South African apartheid regime. He opened his telegram by making the connection between the experience of fascism and apartheid. Stibi declared: 'The government of the German Democratic Republic sees it as its duty towards the nation and the global public to speak up in this important matter as racial discrimination and racial persecution have caused millions of deaths across Europe under the rule of German fascism'.[36] The FRG, he wrote, was an accomplice in 'the withholding of human rights from millions of Africans, that rests on the direct application of Hitler-fascist racial laws'.[37] The GDR, in contrast, supported Third World liberation. Stibi linked this East German advocacy of anti-racial discrimination legislation to the GDR's international recognition. He bemoaned the fact that the SED could not more effectively support anti-racial discrimination policies because East Germany was barred from UN affairs and was unable to sign UN conventions.[38] Stibi promised East German support for Third World rights campaigns if decolonized states facilitated the GDR's accession to the UN through their votes in support of East German membership.

The GDR sought to make use of the ongoing shift in the UN's balance of power. In 1961, the Burmese UN Secretary-General Thant had become the first UN leader from the Global South. Under his leadership, the UN turned its focus to decolonization, Third World economic development, human rights and universal UN membership. It was thus no coincidence that Thant was the first secretary-general to visit a meeting of the UN's International Law Committee on 16 July 1964. The committee's meeting incidentally marked the departure of its long-standing head Yuen-li Liang (b. 1903). Liang and Thant shared many concerns in common. A former professor of international law at Shanghai's Soochow University, Liang had worked on questions of international law since the interwar period. Liang knew the obstacles in advancing international law full well. He had been instrumental in including a commission for international law in the drafting of the UN Charter in 1945. The establishment of this commission had enabled the UN to become an active institution in the drafting and codification of international law after 1945. Liang, who was appointed on behalf of the ROC, perpetuated the Chinese demand for the continuous development and codification of international law, now enshrined in Article 13 of the UN Charter against Western reservations. Maybe even more importantly, the ROC's involvement in the drafting of the charter ensured that trusteeship of colonies, as codified in Article 76, should lead progressively to self-governance or independence.[39] This laid the groundwork for Thant's agenda of promoting the right of self-determination and universal UN membership within his own institution.

Throughout the 1960s, owing in great part to Thant's activist interpretation of his office, the UN matured into an active arbiter and producer of international law, a fact that would greatly aid the GDR's cause. Thant wanted to turn the UN into an agenda-setting institution rather than a mere venue of international diplomacy. And the International Law Committee was one of the prime venues to achieve this goal, especially given its mission, which Liang's successor Robert Ago (1907–1995) outlined as follows: 'Thanks to the vision and action of a group of enlightened men, some of whom are in this very room, the idea of the progressive development of international law and its codification was embodied in the Charter as a matter for the General Assembly to initiate studies and make recommendations'. With Thant's support, Ago suggested, 'the time has come for it [the commission] to devote itself to the revision, clarification and codification of the main topics of international law'.[40] The commission was prepared to take on new drafts concerning special missions and relations between states and international organizations. This went to the heart of legal conflicts surrounding decolonization and divided states. 'Evolution must be provoked', Ago urged Thant; 'for this reason the Commission boldly put on its agenda the principal chapters of contemporary international law, like the law of treaties, State succession and State responsibility'.[41] GDR legal experts and diplomats would utilize all these themes in the coming years in their quest for UN recognition.

As part of his new agenda to institute universal international rules, Thant elevated the legal conundrum of divided countries within the UN. This provided the GDR with a new opportunity to make inroads into UN politics. To begin with, Thant ended Hammarskjöld's hard line against the GDR. Hammarskjöld had only communicated with the GDR government via mid-level administrative staff. In contrast, within a few months of his appointment, Thant met with the GDR Deputy Foreign Minister informally during a dinner hosted by the Polish UN league in Warsaw.[42] To acknowledge GDR support for Thant's ambitious agenda to make the UN a universal global organization by enabling the accession of decolonized states to the UN, East German international law propaganda soon after moved to a strong focus on anti-imperialism that replaced anti-fascism as the East German core foreign policy concept of the late 1940s and 1950s.

The Ministry for Foreign Affairs revamped its international rhetoric accordingly in the mid-1960s. With this shift, SED cadres had finally found a rights language that connected them directly to the demands of African, Arab and Asian states. The adoption of UN conventions on Granting Independence for Colonial Countries and Peoples in 1960 and the Elimination of All Forms of Racial Discrimination in 1965 kickstarted the transformation of UN legal politics by decolonized states. The GDR's campaign against anti-racial discrimination and 'neo-colonial' Western exploitation of former colonies was designed to speak to this Third World coalition.[43] Socialist bloc rights activism soon extended to attacks on the US for war crimes committed in Vietnam and Israel's treatment of Palestinians. At the same time, Third World countries with the help of socialist states hoped to transform the continued prosecution of Nazi crimes after the Second World War into a wider anti-racial discrimination framework that could be mobilized against Western countries and South Africa.[44] GDR propaganda now painted the FRG as a 'neo-colonial' and 'neo-fascist' state that helped reassert Western dominance over Africa through economic exploitation. Until the late 1960s, 'neo-fascism' became an umbrella term in GDR propaganda that included such diverse phenomena as the alleged West German governmental support for fascist groups within the FRG and GDR, 'race terror in the US' and the apartheid regime in South Africa.[45] In other words, the GDR government painted a picture of international politics in which East Germans and peoples suffering under colonial rule faced the same foe: a 'neo-colonial' and 'neo-fascist' Western bloc. The SED government hoped that African states in turn would actively support its campaign to be recognized as a sovereign state.[46]

Linking Self-Determination and Socialist Human Rights

The SED's turn to self-determination compelled it to engage with human rights norms. The East German Committee for the Protection of Human Rights was founded in 1959, and in March 1963 its members for the first time visited a meeting of the UN Human Rights Committee in Geneva as an unofficial delegation without an official invitation.[47] Preparing for its new international rights campaign, the SED leadership realized that the internal struggles of the 1950s had sidelined and largely silenced scholars who had the crucial expertise in human rights norms. One prominent example was Hermann Klenner, who had been denounced by Ulbricht at the Babelsberg Conference in 1958. In 1964, Klenner, having returned from his political exile serving as mayor of a small town, put forward a socialist interpretation of human rights as part of the SED's turn to Third World legal politics. According to him, human rights could only be secured through political and economic participation in 'real existing socialism'.[48] This was to be the basic premise for future work and it was the foundation for linking the legality of socialist society to international sovereignty through human rights language in the coming decade. Klenner's conceptual shift, moreover, also prepared the ground for an independent definition of socialist citizenship and the beginning of a public campaign for East German national independence.

It did not take long for East German legal experts to realize that they needed a more comprehensive language to set themselves apart from renewed human rights campaigns of West German expellee organizations. In 1965, Klenner used the commemorations of the end of the Second World

War to demarcate the distinction between West German basic rights and socialist human rights. Rage fuelled Klenner's intervention in front of GDR human rights activists. West German expellee organizations, labelled 'revanchist organizations' in East Germany as they called for a return of lost Eastern territories, had announced a year of human rights in the FRG for 1965. These organizations wanted to use the publicity surrounding this campaign to renew their demand for a human right to homeland grounded in West German notions of self-determination described in the previous chapters.[49] To Klenner, the right to homeland, which West German expellee groups rooted in natural law and Christian ethics, was nothing other than revanchist legal politics. 'Bonn's annexation policies', Klenner warned the members of the East German human rights league, were disguised as a human right to appeal to international audiences. The GDR's state-sponsored human rights activists urgently needed to contest such interpretations of human rights in international rights debates.[50]

Klenner tied the development of human rights in Germany since 1945 to the UN Charter and tried to intervene in the still ongoing controversies over the two UN human rights covenants on civil and political as well as social and economic human rights. In contrast to older rhetoric that had emphasized the importance of the Soviet Union for German liberation, he explicitly rooted his ideas in the 'liberation of the German people through the forces of the United Nations'.[51] While the US Bill of Rights from 1776 and the French Declaration of the Rights of Man and of the Citizen from 1789 had highlighted the four human rights to life, liberty, property and the pursuit of happiness, Klenner demanded the abolition of any form of exploitation. This fifth basic human right was aimed at ongoing UN conflicts over the two human rights conventions.[52] In 1965, negotiations over the precise wording of the human rights covenants neared their end after Cold War conflicts over law had split the original plans for one comprehensive UN human rights convention into two separate covenants. Klenner highlighted the importance of social and economic human rights for the ongoing international human rights norms codification.[53]

A closer look at Klenner's rebuttal of West German advances illustrates how human rights rhetoric paved the way for a convergence of East German human rights language and concepts of self-determination. In Klenner's view, the GDR needed to exploit the fact that the US, the UK and France had prevented the implementation of a right to national self-determination in the UDHR in 1948. Klenner emphasized the absence of the right to work and education, which the socialist basic rights catalogue guaranteed. He concluded that the 'universal and timeless aura' that Western legal thought had attempted to instil in human rights was nothing but a smokescreen.[54] Against such mere rhetoric, the 'historical greatness' of socialist basic rights was grounded in their actual application and lived reality. Klenner reminded the members of the GDR's German League for the United Nations that socialists had to realize that not the declaration, but the implementation of rights was at the centre of the ideological battle over human rights. In this demand, he met with Third World critiques of UN rights politics. He reminded his fellow human rights activists that, 'in Germany, for a long time, there has existed an exceptional mismatch between the talking about human rights and acting for human rights, between the formulation of and the implementation of human rights. This discrepancy has become unbearable in recent years'.[55]

GDR legal scholars had to act fast to rebuff West German activities in the international arena. The West German BdV's year of human rights in 1965 included a petition to Thant to intervene on their behalf and advocate for their legal right to have their homelands reinstated.[56] For Steiniger, then still acting as president of the GDR's League for the United Nations, this was a personal matter. He lashed out against this West German legal 'aggression', accusing leading West German international law scholars of preparing to recapture lost German territory. Steiniger was the son of a Bohemian Jewish father whose mother had converted to Judaism. Moreover, he knew leading proponents of a human right to homeland well because he had worked towards his doctorate under the guidance of Carl Schmitt in 1928 and then pursued a career in law before losing his German citizenship in 1935. Now he decried 'those in Bonn who feel themselves legally identical with the aggressors [the Third Reich] and who are, at least some of them, actually identical in person with them'.[57]

Archival evidence suggests that by the mid-1960s East German legal scholars had moved to an integrated approach to law that connected international law and domestic socialist legality.[58] Socialist legality was now pitched against the concept of a *formierte Gesellschaft* (uniform society), promoted by West German conservative politicians, intellectuals and academics at the time. The liberating quality of socialist law was contrasted with the pressure to conform in such West German concepts of society.[59] In this process of unifying domestic and international perspectives on law, SED cadres streamlined legal language. Human rights, basic rights, citizens' rights and individual rights taken together described the principal legal status of socialist citizens and their relationship to one another and the state. As Willi Büchner-Uhder (1928–2003) declared in 1966, with the transformation of East German society from an 'antifascist-democratic to a socialist social order', basic rights had also evolved.[60] Through his work for the publishing house Urania, Büchner-Uhder, professor for *Staatsrecht* and member of the draft commission for the new GDR constitution that would be first proclaimed in 1968, became one of the influential legal scholars to explain citizenship rights and duties to a wider East German readership.[61]

This was the moment when the GDR's Third World strategy centred on the right of self-determination merged with socialist human rights concepts. In 1966, East German legal scholars established causality between the right of self-determination and human rights. Only when the international community universally respected the right of self-determination, they argued, could human rights be secured.[62] This exactly matched anti-colonial rights frameworks that saw the validation of self-determination as a human right as the guarantee of independence from colonial domination and thus sovereignty as the only way to guarantee human rights protected in sovereign citizenship rights.[63] In an interview with the *Deutschlandsender* in December 1966, the radio reporter invited Klenner to comment 'on human rights in the GDR and the emergency surrounding human rights in the Federal Republic'.[64] Following Ulbricht's official application for UN membership in February 1966, Klenner summarized the five central norms in the GDR's UN campaign. These were 'unambiguous international legal norms', Klenner declared on the radio, including 'the ban on aggression, the right of self-determination of people including state sovereignty, the right to peace, and [the protection against] racial discrimination'. Those rights had universal legal validity, Klenner claimed, whether they had been implemented by states as part of domestic legislation or not.[65] He thus argued that certain international rights penetrated the sovereignty of national legal systems.

Renewed clashes between East Berlin and Bonn over law in 1966 illustrated why GDR legal cadres now saw a need for a causal link between domestic legality and international sovereignty. On 29 July 1966, the West German parliament passed the Law on the Temporary Exemption from German Jurisdiction. This law temporarily exempted leading SED cadres, against whom warrants had been issued in the FRG, from legal prosecution. In preparation for talks between SED leaders and SPD members that were to take place in West Germany, the GDR government had demanded full diplomatic protection of SED delegates during their stay in the West. In response, the Bonn parliament passed its Law on Temporary Exemption, granting 'Germans living outside the territory governed by the Basic Law' one-week exemptions from being subject to West German law enforcement agencies. The SED leadership reacted with outrage to this new legislation. While the exemption was what they wanted, the phrasing of the law in practice assumed legal authority over high-ranking SED cadres who visited West Germany. In response, the GDR government enacted the Law for the Protection of Citizenship and Human Rights of Citizens of the German Democratic Republic. This law, in turn, threatened that anyone who supported either the West German claim to exclusive representation of German sovereignty, the enlargement of West German jurisdiction to the territory of the GDR or the prosecution of East German citizens would be sentenced to a maximum of five years' imprisonment if caught.[66]

SED leaders had had enough of West German infringements on GDR law. International recognition for the territorial integrity and sovereignty of the GDR had to be won somehow. After 1966, the GDR intensified its efforts to conform to international law standards and UN regulations. The East German League for People's Friendship, the League for Human Rights, the Association for International Law and especially the German League for the United Nations pushed for the GDR's international recognition in many different international venues. In 1966, the State Council officially endorsed the new legal doctrine of GDR sovereignty built on the right of self-determination.[67] In order to challenge the FRG's 'revanchist policies' of claiming to be the only legitimate successor state of the German Reich, the East German government stipulated that the 'people of the GDR' had chosen to be a sovereign people.[68] The East German state machinery now doubled its efforts to finally break free from international isolation.

Members Only?

The year 1966 foretold fundamental shifts in the international Cold War architecture. Within the UN, the power balance within the General Assembly began to shift as a result of thirty-eight new member states gaining admission after 1960, the opening of the human rights covenants for signature and the announcement of an official Year of Human Rights in 1968.[69] In the US and across Western countries, these changes in the UN's internal architecture spurred public mistrust. Conflicts over the representation of divided countries meanwhile came down to questions of rules and regulations. Membership applications were one of the most divisive topics since the acceleration of decolonization. Legal experts disagreed over the question of whether the Security Council should be able to block membership before an application could even reach the floor of the General Assembly. While African states demanded an end to the Security Council's unequal dominance of UN politics, Western observers such as Arthur Larson, the former head of the United States Information Agency under the Eisenhower administration, realized that there existed gaps in UN regulations that decided whether the veto of Security Council members applied to requests for admission.[70] For the time being, the US insisted on the primacy of the Security Council over the General Assembly. In spring 1966, the Soviet delegation bitterly complained in a private note to Thant about the US. The Americans prevented the immediate circulation of the GDR's UN application outside of the Security Council through their veto.[71] Such a suppression of the GDR's voice, the Soviet representative claimed, was nothing other than 'a discriminatory, unwarranted and hostile policy towards the German Democratic Republic'.[72]

Non-recognized countries such as the PRC and GDR now planned to attack unequal UN regulations to make their voices heard.[73] Reactions within the UN bureaucracy showed that not everyone agreed with the GDR's exclusion from UN politics. In March 1966, the UN Political and Security Council Affairs Department endorsed East German claims in response to the veto against the circulation of the GDR's application within the General Assembly. The department compiled a memorandum for Thant that explicitly concentrated on supporting East German arguments for UN membership. The advisors began by quoting Thant's recent public statements in support of universal membership. If full membership for sovereign states could not be achieved due to Cold War restraints, Thant favoured official observer status for all states as the bare minimum to realize the UN Charter's goals. If the UN still had to recognize the Western argument that UN membership of the GDR would cement division and prevent German unification, the department predicted that this position would change in the near future by a shift in West German foreign policy. UN officials kept an eye on emerging Ostpolitik negotiations given its potential ramifications for the rules of international recognition of statehood. The department argued that the Western camp might quickly drop its current legal positions on German sovereignty. After all, both the US and Soviet Union increasingly saw German division as an annoyance, not least because their negotiations over détente in Europe had in recent years been constantly torpedoed by German clashes over sovereignty.[74]

The battle for access to UN politics was now underway in the corridors of the UN in New York and Geneva. Against the advice of his legal counsellor Konstantinos A. Stavropoulos and other high-ranking UN officials, Thant began to elevate the GDR's visibility at the UN.[75] He had to tread carefully though as he was running for a second term in office in 1966. When Thant met with the GDR Foreign Minister Otto Winzer (1902–1975) in Moscow in July 1966, he was thus at first reluctant to put his full public support behind the GDR's application.[76] His own institution, moreover, was also still divided over the issue of divided countries. In opposition to the UN Political and Security Council Affairs Department that advocated for the GDR, the UN legal division still blocked any official accreditation of a GDR observer in Geneva or New York. The UN legal experts also supported the Security Council's veto to circulate the GDR's membership application within the General Assembly. Desperate to make progress, the GDR Foreign Office even briefly contemplated simply announcing the current Allgemeiner Deutscher Nachrichtendienst (ADN, General German News Service) correspondent in New York as an official UN observer.[77] Without open support from the UN departments, however, these plans too were quickly abandoned.[78] Third World demands to realize universality and equality nonetheless were moving things in the GDR's favour. So much so that the West German magazine *Der Spiegel* saw 'communist miners' at work, who were whispering ideas of universal membership in Thant's ear during his visit to Moscow.[79]

By late 1966, the GDR's strategy of courting Third World states showed its first effects.[80] On 2 December 1966, Thant was reappointed UN Secretary-General for a second term, and on 16 December, the UN Covenants on Civil and Political Rights as well as Economic, Social and Cultural Rights were opened for signature and scheduled to take effect by December 1976. This changed climate brought the GDR its first international diplomatic success. Both the German League for the United Nations and its West German counterpart were admitted as equal members to the World Federation of United Nations Associations (WFUNA).[81] The GDR's new anti-imperialist rhetoric had appealed to newly decolonized Third World states. This admission to an NGO with close ties to the UN encouraged the GDR to target a major UN special organization such as the World Health Organization (WHO) next. The goal was to trigger a chain reaction that would finally catapult East Germany into the midst of the international community.

For this strategy to work, it was crucial to frame the idea of human rights in a distinct socialist language.[82] By the late 1960s, the East German government was confident that it could convince Thant to take the GDR's side publicly. With the GDR's direct access to the UN still blocked, Deputy Foreign Minister Stibi asked the Soviet embassy in East Berlin how he could meet Thant personally. Western media had reported that Thant planned a trip to Moscow in 1967, and the GDR government hoped to influence the UN Secretary-General in favour of granting the GDR observer status. In Moscow, the advantage of exclusive access was for once on the side of the East Germans as the Soviet government could grant them privileged access to Thant. Yet it was important that if Thant was going to move to support the GDR, he did not move too fast. GDR diplomats hoped that the Soviet Union would discourage Thant's plan for an immediate vote on UN membership in the General Assembly. More new member states from Asia and Africa had to be admitted first, so that the voting balance within the General Assembly was certain to tip in favour of the GDR.[83]

With the human rights covenants opened for signature in 1966, the GDR Ministry for Foreign Affairs noted once more that the socialist bloc needed to be prepared for the battle over human rights language in the coming years. GDR diplomats now hoped that it was only a matter of time until their quest to break the FRG's legal and diplomatic isolation strategy within the UN was successful. East German unofficial UN observers targeted the WHO, the International Atomic Energy Agency (IAEA), the World Metrological Organization (WMO), the International Telecommunication Union (ITU), UNESCO and the Inter-Governmental Maritime Consultative Organization (IMCO), trying to get admitted to as many of these UN special organizations as possible. Although admission backed by socialist and Third World votes would not immediately equal the establishment of formal diplomatic ties with states that supported GDR membership in these organizations, it would still advance East German bilateral diplomatic relations with states in Asia, the Middle East, Africa and Latin America.[84] It was one backdoor to international recognition of GDR statehood and sovereignty.

The Socialist Assault on UN Procedural Rules

Procedural rules offered another backdoor to recognition. After the failed circulation of the GDR membership application in February 1966, the Eastern bloc exploited procedural rules to allow for the circulation of GDR policy statements within the UN. Socialist member states simply provided their delegation cover page and attached East German policy papers for circulation in the Security Council and General Assembly. Every new GDR document submitted to the General Assembly or the Security Council stirred institutional conflicts over appropriate ways of circulation. The socialist states demanded the open distribution of GDR policy statements to all UN delegations. By 1967, the high volume of East German interventions proved increasingly disruptive. Western UN member states opposed this attempt to treat the GDR as a sovereign state. They argued for a ban of all GDR documents. In response, Stavropoulos called for a new 'stable modus vivendi' and tried to peddle the middle ground. He insisted on a qualified circulation of GDR memoranda. UN member states would be able to send GDR statements as part of a 'note verbale' or as direct quotations in their own UN circulars.[85] The GDR had found a way to circulate its demands officially within the UN sanctioned by the UN's legal counsel.

What may have seemed mere haggling over procedural issues formed part and parcel of proving international sovereignty for all parties involved. Documents from the West German official observer delegation suggest that Bonn's emissaries at the UN only woke up to this new threat to their non-recognition policy of the GDR in 1968. On 10 April, the West

German representative at the UN in Geneva, Rupprecht von Keller (1910–2003), sent a cable to Bonn to request that the head of the Foreign Office's Political Unit I should be sent as reinforcement of his delegation. Keller was worried about an upcoming WHO meeting scheduled for 6 May. On the meeting agenda was a discussion of the admission of new members, and the GDR was among the states that had applied for membership. Keller anticipated an attack of socialist bloc countries aided by non-aligned states on the West German claim of representing 'Germany' within the WHO. He predicted that the West German delegation needed to be able to move quickly within negotiations and decide on potential changes in strategy on the spot. Worried that such decisions were beyond the remit of his post, Keller was asking for a leading diplomat to join him.[86]

The matter reached beyond simply increasing the size of the West German delegation. The GDR's WHO application, as documents of the West German chancellery show, caused internal conflict within the Bonn government. Studies on the history of Ostpolitik have paid ample attention to the conflicts within West German party politics over politics of détente.[87] Yet how these conflicts unfolded in the context of UN politics has attracted less attention.[88] By 1968, the SPD ministers Willy Brandt and Herbert Wehner (1906–1990) advocated for the admission of the GDR to the WHO. Both argued that the FRG could not be seen in opposition to humanitarian action within Germany. Moreover, they hoped to use the promise of WHO membership in ongoing German-German negotiations over West German access to West Berlin, which Brandt, as Foreign Minister, and Wehner, heading the Ministry for All-German Affairs, oversaw. Exchanges between doctors from both German states seemed, to both, good publicity for the Bonn government. In opposition to this SPD position, however, the chancellery under CDU chancellor Kurt Georg Kiesinger (1904–1988) feared a chain reaction once the GDR government managed to get its foot into the WHO door.[89] The chancellery ultimately kept the upper hand. No concessions were to be made. When it came to the vote on East German WHO membership in 1968, the West German delegation was able to unite the Western camp one last time behind its position and the GDR application was voted down.[90]

Yet broader shifts in global Cold War politics threatened West German legal positions by the late 1960s. US support for the legal position of a sole representation of 'divided nations' by only one state was rapidly declining. In private conversations with US journalists, US ambassador to the UN Arthur Goldberg (1908–1990) argued that there should be an East and West German presence in the UN. The US administration hoped to apply the same principle to South and North Vietnam to bolster the South

Vietnamese government's position in the ongoing war in Vietnam. When the West German and Taiwanese delegations inquired about the relevance of Goldberg's statements for US foreign policy, as both delegations feared their non-recognition policy of their socialist counterpart was at stake, the US delegation merely pointed to their private character. The circumvention of a clear denunciation of Goldberg's remarks by the State Department shocked the West German UN delegation.[91]

Reports from the West German UN observer delegation back to Bonn became ever more alarming. At the end of his tenure, the West German UN ambassador Sigismund von Braun (1911–1998) pointed to the erosion of West German influence during his last six years in office. By January 1968, only the delegates of the Philippines, Luxembourg, Belgium, Argentina, France, Turkey, Austria, Togo, Gabon, Ruanda, Madagascar and Cyprus spoke on behalf of the Bonn government's cause when the issue of divided Germany was discussed in the General Assembly. These twelve statements, a decline from twenty-three statements in 1967, had been sympathetic, but vague in their support for the privileged West German position within the UN. Thant's renewed call for the introduction of universal membership in the UN's Year of Human Rights in 1968 flew in the face of the West German delegation's efforts to keep the Vienna Formula alive, which stipulated that only members of UN sub-committees would be eligible for application to full membership.[92] Under the aegis of Hammarskjöld, this rule was introduced to UN institutional practice to slow down accession of decolonized states in the 1950s.[93]

Braun warned that fending off East German advances into UN affairs put the FRG on the wrong side of many political issues. West German observer status and official membership in some UN special organizations forced the delegation to vote on an increasing number of controversial issues. The West German South Africa policy in support of the apartheid regime, in particular, was a problem. Braun had to explain West German support for South Africa at the UN's human rights conference in Tehran in 1968 and at a conference on treaty law in Vienna later in the same year. Predictably, this support upset African countries to the extent that they had abstained in protest when the GDR's application for WHO membership came to a vote. Only the threat of recalling development aid had compelled them not to vote for GDR admission.[94]

Braun doubted that such neutrality could be bought for much longer. He stated:

> It is regrettable from our point of view that Secretary General U Thant has again called, as last year, for the admission of observers from 'all countries' to the UN in his annual report to the General Assembly. The language used indicates that U Thant also thinks about the dispatch of an observer from the SBZ.[95]

Support for West German claims to represent Germany was ever-more quickly eroding within the UN departments. The current leading UN legal adviser still opposed Thant's attempt to fast-track universal membership and insisted on adherence to the Vienna Formula. A new legal adviser could very well reverse this legal viewpoint and support the Soviet Union's view of an 'All States Formula'. The Afro-Asian bloc supported such a shift in membership policies as well. In short, the ban of the GDR from UN membership was increasingly difficult to maintain. Braun cautioned that one single East German success would not represent a 'gradual nuance' but a 'full breakthrough'.[96] It was prescient advice: in a later vote of the Sixth Committee of the UN General Assembly on the membership formula in November 1969, the margin in favour of the Vienna Formula would decrease to a mere seven votes.[97]

At the same time, the question of the 'two Chinas' and the tensions between the Soviet Union and PRC impacted the observer delegation's work to keep the GDR barred from UN affairs.[98] West Germany had to lobby smaller countries intensely now. Poor financial support and limited communication with their governments made UN delegations from small decolonized countries easy targets. Their voting behaviour would, Braun stated, 'more often than not rest not so much on guidelines received from their capitals, but which UN representatives they lent their ear'.[99] Yet the FRG was ill-prepared for these challenges: the Foreign Office still had no special section exclusively tasked with UN-related issues. Braun felt that his superiors in Bonn paid too much attention to the Allied framework of German division and were in danger of being blindsided. In anticipation of a future GDR entry into the UN, he argued that: 'Not just in the political, but also in the administrative field should we prepare ourselves rigorously to enter as an equal partner into "world domestic politics"'.[100]

The GDR meanwhile strategically used the UN's Year of Human Rights in 1968 to link human rights to the issue of universal membership more broadly.[101] On 20 September 1968, the Council of State declared the GDR government's readiness to accede to the International Covenant on Economic, Social, and Cultural Rights and the International Covenant on Civil and Political Rights. The legal challenge to the FRG's international dominance necessitated that the East German government pledged to join a wide range of human rights and international law treaties in exchange for UN admission. Since 1966, the East Berlin government had supported the conventions on the elimination of all forms of racial discrimination, the prevention and punishment of the crime of genocide, the rights of women, against discrimination in education, the abolition of slave labour, against discrimination in respect to employment and occupation, equal remuneration of men and women for work of equal value, freedom of association and the abolition of slavery. All these promises had made the GDR government a credible supporter of Third World issues.[102]

The new GDR constitution draft of spring 1968 promised to turn UN human rights norms into socialist constitutional law and played an important role in making these promises credibly to international audiences. By autumn 1968, the GDR leadership demanded that the UN now do its bit. Winzer wrote to Thant and stated:

> The government of the German Democratic Republic holds the view that it would correspond with the lofty aims of the International Year for Human Rights proclaimed by the United Nations Organization and with the 'Proclamation of Teheran' of the United Nations Conference on Human Rights of 13 May 1968 if the restrictive conditions of accession to the respective United Nations conventions were amended and harmonized with the principles and objectives of the United Nations. It is inconsistent with the basic principles of the United Nations, among them in particular the principle of universality as anchored in the United Nations Charter as well as the world-wide humanitarian objectives of the conventions in the field of human rights, if the universal application is substantially hampered by unjustified restrictive conditions of accession.[103]

In other words, in not allowing GDR membership, the UN itself was preventing a universal implementation of its own conventions.

Conflicts over procedural questions between socialist states and the UN bureaucracy had in the meantime become ritual. East German diplomats besieged UN offices with constant complaints and requests. By 1969, Stavropoulos felt compelled to reiterate the UN's procedural rules to the Soviet delegation in the hope that the Soviet UN ambassador would rein in the East Germans. In a confidential memo, Stavropoulos also included an internal ten-page 'lex GDR' on documents emanating from East Berlin. He had drafted these regulations for internal use in 1968 following the repeated Soviet complaints and public attacks on the UN administration. Stavropoulos fought hard to uphold administrative regulations against what he viewed as constant subversion of institutional rules.[104]

By 1970, the days of a mere focus on the German situation in international politics of law were gone. The East Berlin government explicitly endorsed and welcomed the codification of international law. The inalienable rights to independence and the formation of independent states, GDR foreign policy experts stressed, should be enforced as an unrestricted legal principle.[105] This claim strengthened once more the link of Third World demands to the East German international legal position. Foreign Minister Winzer constantly repeated his support for the implementation of full sovereign equality of all states of the international community if African and Asian states threw their weight behind the GDR's membership application.[106]

The year 1970 saw the twenty-fifth anniversary of the UN, a cause that gave the East German government another opportunity to confirm its turn towards international legal language. In his congratulatory message, Ulbricht described the GDR as the 'anti-imperialist, socialist German nation-state, committed to humanitarianism, peace and international understanding'.[107] The 1968 GDR constitution stipulated that the international legal norms enshrined in the UN Charter were binding for all GDR citizens. The SED had thus opened up its own legal system to international norms. While the interpretation of these norms strictly followed party interpretation in domestic law, the GDR government nonetheless conceded that international rights norms had some bearing on its domestic legal system. The case for UN membership was now exclusively made through compliance with the UN charter and declarations. To appear impartial in the support for the UN's universalist vision, Ulbricht linked his reaffirmation of the GDR's application for membership in 1970 with the East Berlin government's call on Bonn to apply simultaneously for full membership.[108]

Double Standards

German and Chinese national division came to dominate UN politics simultaneously in the early 1970s. Similar to the GDR's case within the UN, the PRC's bid for a reversal in Chinese UN representation had been a long time in the making, beginning in the early 1950s following the establishment of the PRC. In 1961, the Western bloc had been forced to permit debate on the Chinese question on the floor of the General Assembly for the first time.[109] Following Article 18, Section 2 of the UN Charter, the issue of divided China was now classified as an 'important question'.[110] In a vote of sixty-one in favour against thirty-four in opposition, the question of Chinese membership had been officially made part of international negotiations. By 1965, the resolution to classify the representation of China an 'important question' had been reaffirmed and a consecutive vote on seating communist China instead of Taiwan in the UN ended in a tie of forty-seven in favour and against with twenty abstentions.[111] This outcome might have encouraged the SED leadership to submit their first application for GDR membership only months later. In 1966, legal experts in East Berlin anticipated that this conflict would end in the representation of both Chinese governments following Thant's agenda of universal membership.

While the issue of Chinese UN representation captivated audiences within and outside the UN, the GDR tried to keep the momentum of its own campaign going. By 1970, the FRG was under pressure. The GDR had successfully established diplomatic relations with ten non-aligned states since 1969. Hermann Axen (1916–1992), SED central committee secretary for international relations and foreign policy architect since 1966, now confidently remarked that GDR membership in UN committees had become ever more likely.[112] The GDR government was now confident that the breakdown of West German dominance in the field of international law was imminent.[113] At the Vienna conferences on the law of treaties in 1968 and 1969, socialist states had agreed to support the Afro-Asian bloc in efforts to implement the universality principle. The technical issue of treaty law, GDR foreign policy experts determined, represented an important diplomatic lever for the GDR. If the convention on treaty law implemented a right for all sovereign states to partake in international treaty relations, the GDR's case for recognition of sovereignty would be strengthened once more.[114]

The SED's success in raising the international profile of the GDR became visible in a shift in official UN terminology. In January 1970, the Soviet UN ambassador Yakov A. Malik (1906–1980) tried to ambush Thant with a press statement during a joint press conference in the hope of implementing a terminological shift as a fait accompli. In his statement, Malik requested the official change from referring to the GDR as 'Eastern Germany' to 'German Democratic Republic'. He also suggested that the legal counsel Stavropoulos supported such a change in terminology. Malik probably gambled on Thant supporting his statement if he thought Stavropoulos approved of this shift. Stavropoulos immediately protested in a memorandum to Thant against Malik's suggestion that he had signalled an official change in the UN secretariat's position on the German question.[115]

Malik's suggestion that Stavropoulos had changed his mind was odd. After all, Stavropoulos had been instrumental in streamlining UN terminology for over a decade, since 1958, and he had helped to create the policy that the GDR should officially be referred to as 'Eastern Germany' at the UN. Before 1958, a variety of terms had been used to address the East German government and state, ranging from 'East Germany' to 'Eastern Germany' and 'Soviet Occupation Zone'. On Stavropoulos' suggestion, Hammarskjöld had decreed to implement the UN Economic Commission (ECE)'s terminology for all UN institutions. The GDR thus became 'Eastern Germany' within UN politics. Yet, while he had protested Malik's suggestion that he supported a change in terminology when it came to the GDR, Stavropoulos could not deny that the situation had rapidly changed since the failed GDR attempts to apply for membership of the UN in 1966 and the WHO in 1968. Even the Bonn government had recently changed its official language from 'Soviet Occupied Zone' to 'GDR' as part of Ostpolitik negotiations. In light of these changes, Stavropoulos suggested implementing the requested terminological shift, but only if it was accompanied by an explicit denial of any recognition of GDR sovereignty. Yet he wanted to avoid the impression that he had bowed to Malik's pressure. To downplay the issue, Malik's aggressive demand should be met with an explicitly administrative reaction rather than a policy statement.[116]

Such incremental changes made the GDR government ever more confident in UN affairs. In February 1970, the West German UN diplomat Swidbert Schnippenköter (1915–1972) relayed back to Bonn that the East Germans seemed reluctant to advance German-German talks. The East Berlin leadership sensed that it could be successful in its quest for recognition outside the German-German framework.[117] The West German legal front crumbled even further when, in March, US environmental agencies sent a cable to Bonn stating that it was increasingly difficult to accept that GDR delegations should be excluded on diplomatic grounds from important negotiations such as battling the pollution of the Danube. The quibbles over the representation of German sovereignty within the ECE reached a new high when Schnippenköter engaged in an almost comical exchange between Bonn, US governmental agencies and the ECE executive secretary Janez Stanovnik (1922–2020) in March 1970. Schnippenköter outlined strategies in case a GDR representative were to show up at the next ECE meeting and put a self-made sign denoting himself as representative of the GDR on the conference table. He expected that an unannounced GDR delegation might turn up and demand to be seated as an official delegation. To make this point, the East Germans might bring self-fabricated table signs to blend into the ECE meeting. Schnippenköter insisted that the GDR could not be seen to ambush official ECE meetings like this. Such small symbolic East German provocations seemed serious enough in the extremely volatile diplomatic climate of 1970.[118]

Documents from the Bonn chancellery suggest that this East German pressure triggered a public relations campaign to minimize the impact on public opinion within the FRG. The West German public somehow had to be prepared for the anticipated changes in Bonn's position towards the GDR. Contrary to what legal frameworks of German sovereignty and the Hallstein Doctrine had suggested to West Germans for two decades, the international status of the GDR was no longer dependent on Bonn's position by 1970. Since 1949, the West German public had been well-acquainted with an official political and legal rhetoric of complete non-recognition of GDR statehood. Many West Germans were now ill-prepared to adjust to the rapid turnaround on central foreign and legal policies that Ostpolitik negotiations signalled by 1970.[119] The CDU opposition mobilized public opinion at home and the expellee associations suspected a betrayal of their national mission.[120] Facing intense international and domestic pressure, the Bonn government suddenly received help from unexpected places.

By June 1970, the issues of Chinese and German division converged in UN politics. Only intimate observers of UN affairs at first noticed a renewed repositioning of the UN bureaucracy. In June 1970, Stavropoulos once more clarified the UN's legal terminology when referring 'to certain of the divided nations'.[121] He now excluded the Chinese case and only focused on Germany, Korea and Vietnam. At first glance, Stavropoulos seemed to merely be indulging in an exercise of bureaucratic hair splitting. He proposed that:

> If we change from 'Eastern Germany' to 'German Democratic Republic', logic would seem *prima facie* that we also change from 'North Viet-Nam' to 'Democratic Republic of Viet-Nam' and from 'North Korea' to 'Democratic People's Republic of Korea'.[122]

Despite the fact that the UN had not recognized North Vietnam, North Korea or the GDR, Stavropoulos nonetheless maintained that the UN clearly dealt with North Vietnam 'on the basis that it is a state'.[123] The same applied to North Korea, where the UN had adopted the term Democratic People's Republic of Korea in its institutional practice regardless of the 'hostilities' the UN had found itself engaged in with the state. Thus, not even the UN's direct involvement in the Korean War was seen as an obstacle by the legal division to normalize terminology. To soften the blow and demarcate this linguistic shift as a mere terminological change, Stavropoulos suggested the following disclaimer to the next UN bulletin on terminology:

> The designations [of states] employed and the presentation of the material in this publication do not imply the expression of any opinion whatsoever on the part of the secretariat of the United Nations concerning the legal status of any country or territory or of its authorities, or concerning the delimitations of its frontiers.[124]

This statement was obviously beside the point. The recent conflicts over the acknowledgement of GDR sovereignty had amply exemplified that a terminological shift would signal the UN secretariat's support for the recognition of national sovereignty of divided countries. Stavropoulos's recommendation to Thant for an exclusion of the Chinese problem from the list of changes revealed this all too clearly.

> There is the more difficult question of the terminology used when referring to the 'People's Republic of China', the secretariat generally employing the designation 'China (mainland)'. I personally feel that it would not be possible to make a change at the present time, as the General Assembly continues, in the annual debate on the representation of China, to treat the Government of the Republic of China as the Government of all China. I do not believe that the secretariat can depart, or appear to depart, from this position until there is a change in the Assembly.[125]

The fact that the UN administration could not even afford the impression of challenging the 'one China' concept while signalling support for the recognition of all other divided countries marked the separation of China within UN politics from the treatment of the other three divided Cold War front line states.

Thant now publicly called for wider recognition of divided countries and even mentioned the possibility of according observer status to the GDR. To accommodate the West German 'two states in one nation' formula, which the Bonn government had devised to pacify the public and conservative party at home and retain certain citizenship regulations that allowed GDR citizens a claim to West German passports, the UN political advisers pointed to 'such types of membership' that were 'based on states representing different nationalities within a state'.[126] The UN membership of the Ukrainian and Belorussian socialist republics alongside the Soviet Union could serve as a model to accommodate both German states within the General Assembly. This solution seemed to please everyone involved. Thant could point to a further accomplishment in the striving for universal membership, the West German government could insist on the legal distinction between statehood and nationhood, while the GDR would achieve international recognition of its sovereignty.

Yet East German ministries had information that the FRG would continue stressing established special clauses applying to Germany based on the Allied occupation regime since 1945.[127] These regulations implied only a temporary reorganization of Germany until a final peace settlement could be reached. If they could not prevent the GDR from entering the UN, the West Germans hoped to make a case for a temporary UN membership for both German states until a peace treaty had been signed. This would perpetuate legal references to a united Germany. Against such claims, the SED propaganda chief Axen argued that the Soviet Union, as a standing member of the Security Council that had to approve applications for UN membership unanimously, could stop all West German attempts to keep ideas of a 'provisional' settlement of the German situation alive.[128] Suddenly, the East Germans were calling into question their own earlier strategy of circumventing the Security

Council veto in putting the question of GDR membership to a vote in the General Assembly.

Documents from both German foreign ministries show how the US government also hoped to capitalize on these debates. The Nixon administration advocated the UN admission of the two German states together with North and South Korea and North and South Vietnam and pushed for UN recognition of the concept of 'two Chinas'. This demand went against the UN secretariat's decision to exclude the Chinese situation from the debate over divided countries. It also met with ardent resistance from Beijing. In East Berlin, Axen urged his comrades that the GDR should not accept any special regulations that tied a potential UN membership to the status of West Berlin (as Allied governed territory) or restrictions on GDR sovereignty grounded in a 'one nation, two states' paradigm.[129] Yet the GDR government was also aware of certain limits to its bargaining position. The extremely volatile situation within the UN could change as quickly again in similar unexpected ways as it had turned in the GDR's favour in the mid-1960s.[130] First the Congo Crisis and later the Biafran War from 1967 to 1970 had shown the detrimental effects of the open question of whether the right of self-determination should grant sovereignty based on shared ethnicity and how a 'people' was defined under international law.[131]

In the meantime, Thant continued to use his administration to bolster the GDR's position. In mid-April 1971, the UN Economic Commission for Africa (ECA) in Addis Ababa withdrew its delegates from the next meeting in West Berlin. Asked for an explanation by the Bonn Foreign Office, the ECA declared that the Soviet Union saw the UN involved in yet another Berlin crisis.[132] The UN Industrial Development Organization (UNIDO) based in Vienna followed suit only days later. The UNIDO confirmed that the action had been taken following an order sent from the UN headquarters in New York. The West German press reported on the Foreign Office's inquiry into the incident.[133] The Bonn diplomats worried this step could mark the official shift of the UN's policy towards Germany. As an article in *Der Spiegel* noted, only a mid-level aide of the UN Secretary-General declared in response to an inquiry of the West German UN observer delegation that the UN was observing a policy of strict neutrality in the ongoing Berlin negotiations between the FRG and the Soviet Union.[134]

In this situation, money remained one of the last and most effective West German tools by which to maintain its diplomatic and legal position. In response to the recalling of UN officials from travels to West Berlin, hoping to force UN officials to resume attending diplomatic functions in West Germany, the Bonn government threatened to withhold funds from the UN.[135] This threat came not even a year after Foreign Minister Walter Scheel (1919–2016) had promised Thant an increase in West German payments to support the UN Development Programme (UNDP) and a contribution of one million dollars to the peace-keeping mission in Cyprus. On 16 May 1971, the GDR Foreign Ministry bitterly complained about these recent West German actions. Foreign Minister Winzer encouraged Thant to withstand West German pressure and maintain his decision to prohibit UN officials from attending official functions in West Berlin.[136]

The Western policy of preventing East German officials from physically entering UN affairs by attending meetings at the UN headquarters bought more time for the FRG one last time. During the twenty-fifth and twenty-sixth sessions of the UN General Assembly in 1970–71, the institutional restrictions that Stavropoulos had fought so hard to uphold in the 1960s crumbled. Socialist governments invited Winzer to the UN headquarters in New York. And the head of the Soviet delegation, Malik, who chaired the twenty-sixth session, encouraged his 'comrade' Winzer to discuss political questions of mutual interest. Before Winzer set out to plan his journey to New York, he contacted Thant to again request permanent observer status for the GDR. Aware of this request, Winzer feared that the US government might revert to withholding his visa to stop his visit. And this was exactly what happened.[137]

The GDR government was outraged. But it was not in Thant's power to grant Winzer access to the UN in New York. Neither the Headquarters Agreement with the US government, nor the Convention on Privileges and Immunities of the UN provided any legal means for the Secretary-General to grant travel visas for the UN. The UN administration could only plead with the US government to grant visas for UN representatives that allowed entry via New York airports to the US and transport to the UN headquarters in Manhattan. Entry to the US was a strictly bilateral issue between the US administration and the East German government.[138] In his reply to Winzer, transmitted through Vittorio Winspeare (1912–1995) who served as the director-general of the UN at Geneva, Thant also had to decline Winzer's request for an announcement of permanent GDR observer status. Stavropoulos had renewed his concerns to move beyond terminological changes without a vote in the General Assembly. Thant nonetheless reiterated his dissatisfaction with the current state of affairs in no uncertain terms. Neither the UN Charter nor the Headquarters Agreement with the United States government or the UN resolution 257 of 3 December 1948 included any provisions on the status of UN observers. The current state of affairs was purely shaped by institutional practice since 1945. In other words, the Western member states had established a policy the UN Secretary-General was yet unable to break completely, but he was working on it.[139] The US had reminded the GDR brutally of how effective politics of sovereignty were in the Cold War.

Just at the time when all signs pointed towards the adoption of some sort of legal framework to accommodate divided countries within the UN's membership framework in the near future, the change in Chinese UN membership transformed the situation once more. The Beijing government had kept a watchful eye on German debates and viewed the growing success of the GDR's two states paradigm with great suspicion.[140] On 25 October 1971, UN resolution 2758 transferred Chinese UN representation from the ROC to the PRC. For the first time, the US government suffered a major defeat in the UN as the Nixon administration was unable to protect Taiwan's simultaneous UN membership.[141] The balance of power within the UN suddenly shifted again, and the fact that a member state and Security Council member was expelled by a two-thirds majority in the General Assembly sent shockwaves around the world. Resolution 2758 marked a controversial turning point in the UN's history. Many observers saw UN regulations and international law broken with this resolution as it circumvented the Security Council altogether, in which the ROC would have had a right to veto the decision. For a moment, decolonization seemed to have broken the control of the Security Council and made the General Assembly the decision-making body of the UN. George Bush (1924–2018), at the time Permanent Representative of the US at the UN, tried to roll back the success of the passed Albanian resolution draft that denied the ROC any UN representation and disputed the political legitimacy of the Taiwanese government altogether. Yet the US could not muster enough votes to bring a revised resolution to the floor of the General Assembly that could have proposed to acknowledge the ROC's continued right to remain a UN member.[142] The vote on Chinese representation showed Western disunity when it came to Cold War politics in Asia. The United Kingdom, France, Italy, Belgium, the Netherlands and Canada had all voted for the PRC's entry and helped pass the Albanian draft.

This major shift in UN politics questioned the admission of both German states on equal terms. The change of Chinese representation within the UN also dealt a major blow to Thant's agenda for universal membership of all states based on legal concepts of sovereignty that acknowledged statehood independent of rivalling national claims. And it dealt a fatal blow to US plans for UN representation of all divided countries including South Vietnam. The Nixon administration, while instructing Bush to vote against PRC membership, had secretly embarked on rapprochement with Mao's China to weaken the Soviet Union's position in Asia. The shift in Chinese representation was thus not entirely unwelcome in Washington. Yet the terms were. On 22 December 1971, Thant appealed one last time to the General Assembly. He stated:

The participation of the People's Republic of China is a major step on the road towards universality which will no doubt increase the United Nations capability of working for the objectives of the Charter. A further step in this direction would be the admission of the divided countries which I hope will be brought about in the not too distant future.[143]

He urged all delegations to implement universal UN membership for all sovereign states. Thant had to witness a major defeat in this quest only weeks before his departure from office. The entry to the UN of the Beijing government, that had replaced the Taiwanese delegation in the Security Council on 25 October 1971, reinforced the nexus of sovereignty and nationality at the UN once more as the PRC insisted on its 'one China' paradigm as soon as it entered the UN.

The separation of the China question from other divided countries – a separation Stavropoulos had implemented in 1970 – now came to the rescue for the GDR government. As Stavropoulos had already begun to separate the China issue from the problem of 'divided countries' in 1970, his terminological adjustments now served as the basis for legal interpretations of how the Chinese situation differed from divided Germany. The international community welcomed the GDR as a fully sovereign state on 18 September 1973, when the General Assembly simultaneously approved full membership of both German states after the Ostpolitik treaties had been ratified in 1972. The PRC did not veto the representation of two German states because the UN's legal division had devised a new legal doctrine to account for a German legal exceptionalism. In contrast to Chinese national division, which the UN now classified as having arisen from the civil war after the end of the Second World War, Germany had been divided after its unconditional surrender and Allied occupation. These unique circumstances set Germany apart from both divided Korea and China as well as war-torn Vietnam. This unique historical trajectory served as the legal foundation for two German delegations within the UN and trumped Thant's vision of universal legal standards of sovereignty and UN representation for all sovereign states. Now that it had won UN membership, the East Berlin government saw a major goal in international legal politics achieved: the 'whole construction' of the West German *Alleinvertretungsanspruch* in international law had broken down.[144]

Conclusion: A German Legal Exceptionalism

The clash between the two German states in the corridors of the UN signalled a fundamental wider shift in international debates on nationhood and statehood, state sovereignty and national self-determination. The West German dominance in international law had been built on legal understandings of the nation-state that stemmed from the interwar period.[145] In the particular German *Staatsrecht* tradition, the *Staatsvolk* resembled an ethnic collective legal category for which West German legal experts had claimed international representation. At the same time, as earlier chapters demonstrated, the West German state managed to promote the idea of a direct West German state succession between the German Reich and the FRG within and beyond the Western Cold War camp in the late 1940s and 1950s.[146]

Decolonization attacked this definition of national sovereignty rooted in nationality politics of the interwar period that had been reserved for sovereign states and excluded colonial peoples from the right to have sovereign rights. Older notions of state sovereignty grounded in ethnic definitions of the nation had been severely damaged by GDR legal propaganda and law making. The GDR's new framework of socialist self-determination appealed to the anti-colonial leaders as it also attacked the unequal hierarchy within international politics that the UN had helped to maintain after 1945. By the late 1960s, the international legal position on which ideas of a 'provisional' West German state had been built in the late 1940s appeared outright revisionist. The idea of a continued existence of the German Reich in its borders of 1937 seemed particularly antiquated in the context of UN legal politics once debates on decolonization and the human rights covenants gained traction.[147] From a West German perspective, decolonization thus had started the timer on a ticking bomb that could eventually destroy the entire West German international legal framework of German division.

Ostpolitik seen from a UN perspective was thus – underscoring Mary E. Sarotte's findings on the SED's internal perspective on German-German diplomatic encounters during Ostpolitik – as much determined by the GDR government's agenda as it was a West German project.[148] Using the threat of taking the backdoor to international recognition at the UN, the East German government could extensively pressure the West German government to come to a bilateral agreement that would acknowledge GDR statehood and sovereignty. In the early 1970s, a report composed by the West German Christlich Soziale Union (CSU, Christian Social Union) retrospectively bemoaned the GDR's 'great aggression' within the UN.[149] The memorandum highlighted the GDR's successful inclusion of human rights language in its foreign policy, stating that socialist states had capitalized on new opportunities in rights diplomacy that arose from changing majorities in the UN since the acceleration of decolonization. In the eyes of Bavarian conservatives, the Western camp had left this Cold War battlefield to the socialist camp almost unchallenged in the 1960s.

In the historical moment between 1966 and 1973, new unequal legal concepts of sovereignty were implemented in UN politics. Decolonization helped to enlarge the UN at an unprecedented speed and pushed the right of self-determination to the top of the priority list of UN affairs. At the same time, decolonization questioned old Western legal logics of international sovereignty. While Thant's agenda of universal membership played into the hands of East Berlin's rights diplomacy, both Korean states remained excluded from the UN until 1991. The ROC lost international recognition in favour of PRC membership in 1971 and Vietnam was unified through war before it gained membership as a united country in 1977. The admission of the two German states remained a legal exception until 1991 when both Korean states acceded as full members to the UN General Assembly. In the years following 1973, it became clear that conflicts surrounding divided countries were not merely about diplomatic representation but formed part of reconfigurations in the fundamental legal concepts of self-determination and sovereignty under the pressures of decolonization and the Cold War.

Attempts to unify legal definitions of international sovereignty and enable universal UN membership failed in the early 1970s. The historical significance of this moment thus lay elsewhere: the confrontations over the recognition of their national self-determination and international sovereignty pushed many governments towards linking the legitimacy of their national legal systems to international legal norms (if not in effect then at least rhetorically). When self-determination was replaced by the struggle over collective and individual human rights norms as the major legal battlefield of the 1970s, legal claims to international sovereignty increasingly had to be formulated in accordance with international legal norms and language formulated within the UN. More and more states implemented international norms into national law to bolster their legitimacy at home and abroad. The legal politics surrounding the Helsinki Accords between 1973 and 1975 with their focus on territorial integrity, collective security, peaceful co-existence and human rights mirrored this willingness to legal reform within both the socialist and Western Cold War camps. In this process, as the next chapters show, the role of the citizen and legal rights of citizenship were heavily politicized and the individual moved to the forefront of Cold War legal politics.

Notes

1. UN ARMS, S-0884-0008-06, GDR application for UN membership, 28 February 1966. The application was submitted on 1 March 1966 by the Polish UN ambassador, see: Stein, *Der Konflikt um die Alleinvertretung*, 126.

2. Ibid.
3. See: Aust, *Modern Treaty Law and Practice*, 106.
4. Hüfner, 'Allgemeinpolitische Rahmenbedingungen', 17f.
5. Normand and Zaidi, *Human Rights at the UN*, 199–208.
6. For a global perspective on Ostpolitik, see: Fink and Schaefer, *Ostpolitik 1969–1974*.
7. For a historiographical overview of these controversies, see: Scholtyseck, *Die Außenpolitik der DDR*, 60–69. See also: Wentker, *Außenpolitik in engen Grenzen*, 211–318. The Soviet Union hoped to contain rights activism centred on a human right of national self-determination to anti-colonial struggles in Africa and Asia to avoid criticism of the Soviet leadership's disregard for self-determination calls of ethnic minorities within the Soviet Union. The GDR leadership's focus on self-determination in a European context was thus not welcomed unreservedly in Moscow. See: Gehrig et al., 'The Eastern Bloc'.
8. Polak defended his ideological approach to law centred on party control until his last days. In 1963, he fiercely rebutted Heinz Such's attempt to reconfigure the approach to socialist law. Polak suspected a veiled attack on party dominance and a resurgence of law as a system that theoretically functioned partly outside of party control. For the exchange between Such and Polak, see: Polak, 'Über die weitere Entwicklung der sozialistischen Rechtspflege'; Such, 'Gegen Erscheinungen des Dogmatismus und Rechtsnihilismus'; Polak, 'Zur weiteren Vervollkommnung der sozialistischen Rechtspflege'. For Polak's approach, see: Reichhelm, *Die marxistisch-leninistische Staats- und Rechtstheorie Karl Polaks*.
9. Lenin, 'The Right of Nations to Self-Determination'.
10. For the Soviet rights universe, see: Weitz, *A World Divided*, 281–319; Newton, *Law and the Making of the Soviet World*; Quigley, *Soviet Legal Innovation*.
11. Polak, *Gesellschaftliche Gesetzmäßigkeit und Völkerrechtswissenschaft*, 4–20.
12. Especially African leaders developed new visions of international governance at the time based on the principle of self-determination. See: Getachew, *Worldmaking after Empire*, 71–106.
13. Lydia Liu has pointed to Western dominance over the underpinning intellectual frameworks of the UN and the crucial influence of P.C. Chang in breaking free from Western ideas of civilization in the drafting process of the UDHR. See: Liu, 'Shadows of Universalism'. For the colonial roots of 'sovereignty doctrine' see: Anghie, *Imperialism, Sovereignty, and the Making of International Law*, 1–12; 32–195.
14. Getachew, *Worldmaking after Empire*, 71–106.
15. Gehrig, 'Reaching Out to the Third World', 576–84.
16. At the same time, Thant had to navigate the issue of secessions from newly independent states, which he opposed in his role as UN Secretary-General. Yet he stood firm on the demand that all decolonized states had to be recognized as sovereign states. The transformation of former colonies into sovereign states took precedence in this transition for the UN before the question of internal minority conflicts and the arbitrary nature of many colonial borders from the perspective of decolonizing peoples.
17. Gehrig, 'Reaching Out to the Third World', 576–84.
18. For the only partly successful campaign of instilling a party-controlled East German national identity into GDR citizens from the 1960s onwards, see: Palmowski, *Inventing a Socialist Nation*.
19. For the PRC's interference in Ostpolitik negotiations, see: Schaefer, 'Ostpolitik, "Fernostpolitik," and Sino-Soviet Rivalry'; Sarotte, *Dealing with the Devil*, 87–112.
20. Stein, *Der Konflikt um die Alleinvertretung*, 35 and 40.
21. See: Pedersen, *The Guardians*, 195–232.
22. Early initiatives to apply for admission into the World Federation of United Nations Associations (WFUNA) from 1954 onwards failed. See: Horn, 'Die Deutsche Liga für die Vereinten Nationen', 89–94.
23. ABBAW, Klassen, No. 224, minutes first meeting Section Legal Science, 12 October 1955.

24. Ibid.
25. The Soviet Union had long pursued the implementation of 'wars of aggression' into the canon of international law in response to the German attack in the Second World War. One of the leading legal minds of the Soviet Union, Aron Trainin, introduced this legal idea into the Nuremberg Trials backed by the doyen of Soviet law Andrey Vyshinsky. See: Hirsch, 'The Soviets at Nuremberg'.
26. Hüfner, 'Die deutsche Gesellschaft für die Vereinten Nationen', 47–55.
27. The turn to the invention of a socialist nation tied into these debates. See: Palmowski, *Inventing a Socialist Nation*.
28. ABBAW, Klassen, No. 224, minutes meeting Section Legal Science, 11 November 1955.
29. Normand and Zaidi, *Human Rights at the UN*, 261.
30. E.g. 'Regime der Unmenschlichkeit', *Neue Zeit* 16(74) (27 March 1960); 'Sanktionen gegen Südafrika gefordert', *Neue Zeit* 16(80) (3 April 1960). In 1960, articles on apartheid and racial discrimination surged to thirty-one in those three papers, up from none the year before. By the mid-1960s, there were routinely more than one hundred articles per year in these three newspapers on these topics.
31. For the GDR's anti-apartheid campaign, see: Gehrig, 'Reaching Out to the Third World', 576–84.
32. BArch, DY30/IV2/13/559, confidential material on German question, 9 May 1961; argumentation self-determination, no date; memorandum on the right of self-determination of both German states, no date.
33. Major, 'Innenpolitische Aspekte der zweiten Berlinkrise'.
34. ASR/3180, evaluation of Institute of International Law, 20 September 1962.
35. Published as: 'Gegen jede Rassendiskriminierung: Stibi: Menschenrechtskonvention sollte allen Staaten zur Unterzeichnung offenstehen', *Neue Zeit* 20(49) (1964), 1–2.
36. 'DDR-Telegramm an Uno-Komission: Konvention gegen Rassismus befürwortet', *Neues Deutschland* 19(58) (1964), 1.
37. Ibid.
38. Ibid.
39. Liang had been part of international law debates since he attended the League of Nations' meeting on codification of international law in 1930. Hsieh, 'The Discipline of International Law', 114f.
40. UN ARMS, S-0285-0002-18.
41. Ibid.
42. The new East German strategy of bridging the Second–Third World divide overcame initial Soviet criticism as it undermined Cold War détente in Europe. See: Stein, *Der Konflikt um die Alleinvertretung*, 109f.
43. The Congo conflict put Africa and human rights abuses at the centre of UN activities from 1960 onwards. See: O'Malley, *The Diplomacy of Decolonisation*; Betts, 'Socialism, Solidarity and Decolonization'. African revolutionary leaders developed their own alternative approach to global governance while Thant tried to reshape the UN. See: Getachew, *Worldmaking after Empire*.
44. Grosescu, 'State Socialist Endeavours', 255–57.
45. Gehrig et al., 'The Eastern Bloc', 293–303.
46. See: Gehrig, 'Reaching Out to the Third World', 576–84.
47. For GDR human rights language, see: Richardson-Little, *The Human Rights Dictatorship*, 53–137.
48. Richardson-Little, '"Erkämpft das Menschenrecht"', 120–43.
49. Wildenthal, *The Language of Human Rights*, 45–62.
50. BArch, DZ23/26, minutes of committee meeting, manuscript Klenner, 'Twenty Years of Human Rights in Germany', 26 April 1965.
51. Ibid.
52. Ibid.

53. Normand and Zaidi, *Human Rights at the UN*, 197–241.
54. BArch, DZ23/26, minutes of committee meeting, manuscript Klenner, 'Twenty Years of Human Rights in Germany', 26 April 1965.
55. Ibid.
56. The exile representative of the Free City Danzig, for example, petitioned Thant in 1964. See: UN ARMS, S-0285-002-05.
57. BArch, DZ23/26, minutes of committee meeting, discussion paper Steiniger, 26 April 1965.
58. BArch, DZ23/26, manuscript Meister, 'Emergency of Political Human Rights in West Germany', 6 December 1966.
59. For West German debates on the nature of society, see: Nolte, *Die Ordnung der deutschen Gesellschaft*, 280–390.
60. BArch, DZ23/26, manuscript Büchner-Uhder, 'Human Rights in the GDR and Their Realization', 6 December 1966.
61. Büchner-Uhder and Beil, *Staat und Recht in der Staatsbürgerkunde*; Büchner-Uhder, *Menschenrechte – eine Utopie*.
62. BArch, DZ23/26, manuscript Gräfrath, 'Human Rights and International Law', 6 December 1966.
63. See: Getachew, *Worldmaking after Empire*, 71–106.
64. BArch, DZ23/26, interview Klenner, 9 December 1966.
65. Ibid.
66. See: 'Gesetz über die befristete Freistellung von der deutschen Gerichtsbarkeit', 453f. For the official GDR reaction, see: Toeplitz, 'Ein Dokument westdeutscher Rechtsanmaßung', 419.
67. BArch, DY30/IVA2/10.02/145, brochure 'Declaration of the GDR State Council on the Legal Development of Both German States'.
68. BArch, DY30/IVA2/13/231, memorandum 'GDR – the legitimate German *Rechtsstaat*'.
69. For Third World rights activism during the human rights year, see: Jensen, *The Making of International Human Rights*, 174–208.
70. Larson, *Questions and Answers on the United Nations*, 56.
71. Hüfner, 'Allgemeinpolitische Rahmenbedingungen', 21–23.
72. UN ARMS, S-0878-0001-17.
73. ASR/3377, 'GDR – the legitimate German *Rechtsstaat*', 17 August 1966.
74. UN ARMS, S-0884-008-06, memorandum on GDR UN membership application, 31 March 1966.
75. Stein, *Der Konflikt um die Alleinvertretung*, 106fn651.
76. Ibid., 132.
77. PA/AA, MfAA A 9744.
78. See the intensifying confrontation around German NGO membership in the WFUNA. Hüfner, 'Die Deutsche Gesellschaft für die Vereinten Nationen', 75–80; and Horn, 'Die Deutsche Liga für die Vereinten Nationen', 94–101.
79. 'Vereinte Nationen: Tat bei Tisch', *Der Spiegel* 42 (1966), 34.
80. BArch, DZ23/143, Concept for Engagement with the UN, 17 July 1965.
81. BArch, DZ23/143, report on activities of German League for the UN and plans for 1968, 2 November 1967.
82. Betts, 'Socialism, Social Rights, Human Rights'.
83. PA/AA, MfAA C 1284/77, meeting minutes Stibi-Shiljakow, 27 June 1967.
84. BArch DZ23/141, strategy paper on GDR UN policy, 1 April 1969.
85. UN ARMS, S-0884-0008-06, 'Annex: Note for the record on the circulation of communication emanating from the German Democratic Republic', 15 January 1968; UN ARMS, S-0291-0008-09, 'Circulation of communication from non-members', confidential circular, 6 February 1970.
86. BArch, B136/6536, telegram no. 258, 10 April 1968.

87. For West and East German contexts as well as the global ramifications of Ostpolitik, see: Grau, *Gegen den Strom*; Sarotte, *Dealing with the Devil*; Fink and Schaefer, *Ostpolitik 1969–1974*.
88. A rare exception is Stein, *Der Konflikt um die Alleinvertretung*.
89. BArch, B136/6536, report on GDR admission to WHO, 2 May 1968.
90. Gray, *Germany's Cold War*, 205.
91. BArch, B136/6388, telegram no. 619, 19 June 1968.
92. BArch, B136/6388, report '6 Years at the UN', 17 July 1968.
93. Aust, *Modern Treaty Law and Practice*, 106.
94. See: Gray, *Germany's Cold War*; Gehrig, 'Reaching Out to the Third World'.
95. BArch, B136/6387, report of the UN Observer of the XXII. General Assembly, 25 January 1968.
96. BArch, B136/6388, report '6 Years at the UN', 17 July 1968, 8–9.
97. BArch, B136/6388, telegram on *Deutschlandpolitik*, 24 November 1969.
98. BArch, B136/6387, report of the UN Observer of the XXII. General Assembly, 25 January 1968.
99. BArch B136/6388, report '6 Years at the UN', 17 July 1968, 4.
100. Ibid.
101. The human rights conference at Tehran in honour of the UN's Year of Human Rights quickly descended into open political conflict between Third World countries and Western delegations. See: Jensen, *The Making of International Human Rights*, 174–208; Burke, *Decolonization and the Evolution of International Human Rights*, 92–111.
102. The GDR's support for Arab and African groups including the denunciation of the state of Israel further bolstered Third World support for the East Berlin government. See: Herf, *Undeclared Wars with Israel*; and Gehrig, 'Reaching Out to the Third World'.
103. UN ARMS, S-0291-0008-09, letter Winzer, 9 October 1968.
104. UN ARMS, S-0291-0008-09.
105. UN ARMS, S-0291-0008-09, letter Winzer, 3 April 1970.
106. Ibid.
107. UN ARMS, S-0291-0008-09, 'Message of the Chairman of the Council of State of the German Democratic Republic', 14 October 1970.
108. Ibid.
109. Several countries, chiefly Albania, advocated on behalf of the PRC in the General Assembly in the 1960s and demanded an annual debate on the issue of Chinese UN representation.
110. UN Charter, Article 18, Section 2: 'Decisions of the General Assembly on important questions shall be made by a two-thirds majority of the members present and voting. These questions shall include: recommendations with respect to the maintenance of international peace and security, the election of the non-permanent members of the Security Council, the election of the members of the Economic and Social Council, the election of members of the Trusteeship Council in accordance with paragraph 1 (c) of Article 86, the admission of new Members to the United Nations, the suspension of the rights and privileges of membership, the expulsion of Members, questions relating to the operation of the trusteeship system, and budgetary questions'.
111. Larson, *Questions and Answers on the United Nations*, 52f.
112. BArch, DC20-I/4/1956.
113. Stein, *Der Konflikt um die Alleinvertretung*, 133.
114. For a documentation of negotiation plans for the conference, see: BArch, DC20-I/4/1956.
115. Incident described in: UN ARMS, S-0285-0002-33, confidential memorandum, 'Question of the terminology to be used when referring to the "German Democratic Republic"', 10 February 1970.
116. Ibid.

117. BArch, B136/6388, confidential telegram, 5 February 1970.
118. BArch, B136/6388, confidential telegram, 12 March 1970.
119. BArch, B136/6388, report on public relations work within the FRG, 10 March 1970.
120. See: Grau, *Gegen den Strom*.
121. UN ARMS, S-0285-0002-33, confidential memorandum, 'Terminology Bulletin No. 263: Names of Countries and Adjectives of Nationality', 29 June 1970.
122. Ibid.
123. Ibid.
124. Ibid.
125. Ibid.
126. UN ARMS, S-0291-0008-09, 'Membership of the GDR and FRG in the United Nations', confidential report, 14 April 1970.
127. BArch, DZ23/141, memorandum on Western positions regarding GDR and FRG UN membership, 28 April 1970.
128. Ibid.
129. Ibid.
130. BArch, B136/6388, telegram no. 258, 16 March 1971.
131. Getachew, *Worldmaking after Empire*, 100–103. For a critique of the right of self-determination based on this lack of clarity in defining what a people constitutes in international law, see: Fisch, *The Right of Self-Determination of Peoples*.
132. UN ARMS, S-0878-0001-17.
133. 'Berlin: Stein des Anstoßes', *Der Spiegel* 19 (1971), 25–26.
134. Ibid.
135. UN ARMS, S-0878-0001-17.
136. Ibid.
137. UN ARMS, S-0884-008-06, letter Thant, 25 November 1971.
138. Ibid.
139. Ibid.
140. See Schaefer, 'Ostpolitik, "Fernostpolitik," and Sino-Soviet Rivalry'; Sarotte, *Dealing with the Devil*, 87–112.
141. United Nations General Assembly, Resolution 2758.
142. 'Agenda Item 96'.
143. UN ARMS, S-0291-0008-11.
144. Institut für Internationale Beziehungen, *Außenpolitik der DDR*, 263.
145. In the tradition of international law making of the mid-century from the 1920s to the 1960s, 'civilized nations' and 'citizens' held sway over colonized 'peoples'. For conflicts within the League of Nations surrounding this basic unequal divide of the international system, see: Pedersen, *The Guardians*; Manela, *The Wilsonian Moment*; Fisch, *The Right of Self-Determination of Peoples*, 126–74.
146. NARA II, RG 59, Entry 5389, LOT 70D448, Box 2, Folder 'Germany: Frontiers 1960–1963'.
147. See: Normand and Zaidi, *Human Rights at the UN*, 243–88.
148. Sarotte, *Dealing with the Devil*.
149. Cited in: Richardson-Little, '"Erkämpft das Menschenrecht"', 132.

Chapter 4

Entangled Citizenships

On 5 September 1967, Czechoslovak State Airlines (CSA) flight number 523 crashed on the climb-out from Gander Airport, Canada. The crash, en route from Prague to Havana via Shannon and Gander airports, left four crew members and thirty-three passengers dead. The Ilyuschin Il-18D, which had only been handed over to the airline in April 1967 from the Soviet manufacturer, took off at an unusually shallow angle, struck a supporting wire of a mast, continued to climb to approximately 40 metres before taking an abrupt dive, hitting the ground and coming to a complete stop at a nearby railway embankment. Among the survivors were two GDR citizens on their way to Cuba. When news of the crash reached the GDR embassy in Havana, the ambassador tasked two of his staff members to travel to Canada and assist the two East German victims. Much to their outrage, the Canadian Foreign Ministry declined their applications for entry permits. The ministry claimed that the embassy staffers had no business looking after the interests of injured German citizens in Canada. Instead, West German officials were allowed onto the scene.[1]

Beyond the corridors of national governments, international organizations and courts, the legal Cold War was ultimately about people.[2] Overshadowed by the diplomatic battle over sovereignty at the UN and Ostpolitik, the conflict over citizenship turned into a global battle in the late 1960s.[3] This chapter shifts perspective away from international legal politics at the UN to focus on how the GDR's departure to a socialist framework of sovereignty underpinned by socialist legality that Ulbricht had announced in the late 1950s affected ordinary people.[4] During the same period that saw German-German clashes over UN politics, explored in the previous chapter, ordinary Germans became the subjects of legal Cold

---

Notes for this chapter begin on page 175.

War confrontations. The GDR used citizenship law to push back against West German claims to represent Germans around the world. The SED demanded the right to fulfil consulate duties and thus represent GDR citizens even in countries with which it had no official diplomatic ties at the time. The SED leadership was no longer willing to accept that GDR citizens had to be represented by proxy by other socialist countries outside of the Eastern bloc or that West German embassies claimed diplomatic responsibility. After the plane crash, the West German Foreign Office contacted relatives in the GDR and offered them travel assistance to Canada.[5] This was another insult to the SED leadership. The fact that the GDR government had legislated an independent GDR citizenship law only months earlier in February 1967 seemed to matter little.

During the 1950s and early 1960s, the West German claim to the German Reich's sovereignty and aggressive citizenship regulation, discussed in chapter 2, had allowed the containment of the GDR government's powers to represent its citizenry to the Eastern bloc. By the 1960s, this position came under severe pressure after anti-colonial movements made a powerful bid in international rights politics to secure their sovereignty and citizenship rights for their people through the recognition of the right of self-determination as a human right.[6] Against growing sympathy of decolonized states with GDR legal diplomacy at the UN, the West German NATO delegation used the Canadian case to remind NATO member states that enforcing visa restrictions for GDR officials remained vital in 1967.[7] Apart from growing Third World support for GDR rights policies centred on the recognition of East German sovereign rights, the Bonn government had noticed a growing impatience of their Western partners with their hard line on visa restrictions for SED officials and GDR cultural delegations.[8] Many NATO members grew impatient with the Bonn government as it seemed one of the hindrances in moving to a politics of détente. The GDR's shift in legal foundations to the right of self-determination and socialist legality and its global campaign for diplomatic recognition had begun to undermine the legitimacy of the West German grip on Germans' legal representation around the world. This loss of West German influence in international legal affairs formed part of the tectonic shifts in international law politics that saw the old legal logics of empire in the politics of belonging crumble under the pressures of decolonization.[9] By the late 1960s, and despite many member states' reservations, NATO remained one of the last transnational networks that supported the Bonn government's legal policies against the GDR.

To claim East Germans as GDR citizens through law, as the GDR did in 1967 by means of proclaiming a citizenship law, meant that there now existed two separate German citizenships. The legal redefinition of East

Germans as *DDR-Bürger* (GDR citizens) in 1967 was backdated and it was declared that independent *DDR-Staatsbürgerschaft* (GDR citizenship) had emerged with the foundation of the GDR in 1949. In contrast, the FRG now exclusively represented *deutsche Staatsangehörigkeit* (German citizenship) over which both governments had competed until 1967. The immediate effect of this new GDR law was that all those Germans who had escaped the GDR since 1949 could now be threatened with forced naturalization. The SED leadership claimed that these East Germans had possessed GDR citizenship since 1949 and the East German state had never accepted their release from this citizenship. The effects of the new East German law were thus quite different to the West German expansionist politics of citizenship a decade earlier. While the West German government had opened the door to West German citizenship in the tradition of wartime legislation for people who were considered ethnically German and continued a legal tradition that had evolved in the interwar period and put ethnicity and (later in the Third Reich) race at the heart of citizenship policies, the GDR government now robbed people of their individual right to rescind and control their citizenship status.[10]

The approach the GDR now took to citizenship was not entirely new. The first ideas to separate the legal status of East Germans decisively from all West German claims dated back to the late 1950s when the SED leadership realized that they could not compete with West German dominance in the field of *Staatsrecht* and needed an alternative socialist approach to domestic and international law.[11] Making *Republikflucht* (escape from the republic) a criminal offence had not deterred droves of East Germans from escaping SED rule in the 1950s. After the Berlin Wall became the physical manifestation of separating the East German citizenry from the FRG in 1961, SED legal cadres moved to sever all legal ties between East and West German citizens. This legal reform matched the attempt of the SED leadership to fence in and control its own citizens ever more tightly.

This chapter asks how the GDR's law campaign for international recognition translated into a new citizenship regime. In keeping with the Leninist tradition of legal doctrine, SED legal cadres saw citizenship law as a 'weapon' to both pressure the Bonn government into accepting East German terms in Ostpolitik negotiations and to threaten former East Germans with the legal reach of the East German state. The SED leadership responded to the invisible legal wall in the 1960s that West German ministries and high courts had built during the 1950s to fence in the GDR's legal reach by deploying law as a threat to East Germans beyond the GDR's borders. West German ministries in response failed to preserve Bonn's citizenship regime internationally after the GDR citizenship law was proclaimed in 1967. Their attempt to fight back exposed the fact that the competition over citizenship had held back reform efforts to modernize West German legislation. The struggle over the entangled citizenships of the two German states and the East German campaign to disentangle them permanently also triggered the legal recalibration of relations between the West German judiciary, the Allied powers and the GDR that crystallized when both German states moved to détente after 1973. Similar to the local fortification of the German-German border from both sides, as Edith Sheffer has argued, both German governments drove this legal battle over citizens that complemented the physical division of the two German states and split Germans legally into two separate citizenries in the late 1960s and early 1970s.[12]

Breaking Down the Invisible Western Wall against the GDR

The GDR government's isolation after 1949 through the West German Hallstein Doctrine and legal non-recognition policy was not just a figurative restriction to the Eastern bloc, but often a literal one. With the foundation of the two German states in 1949, the Western Allies together with the FRG had begun to use visa restrictions to bar East German diplomats, politicians and cultural ambassadors from participating in international affairs. This visa regime was built on the West German claim that the FRG exclusively represented German sovereignty and citizenship. As long as the GDR competed for the representation of an undivided German sovereignty, the Western alliance resorted to a policy of non-recognition. In this, they followed West German demands to dispute the right of the East German state to represent its citizens.[13]

This visa policy severely impeded East German diplomacy and international cultural and economic relations. East Germans could only travel in Western countries if they held so-called Temporary Travel Documents (TTDs) issued by the Allied Travel Office (ATO) in West Berlin.[14] First run by the three Western Allies, the ATO was administered after 1949 by the British authorities.[15] This arrangement ensured Western unity and control over the official movements of GDR cadres in Western countries. With the waning credibility of Bonn's claim to the German Reich's sovereignty in its 1937 borders within the UN and elsewhere, the West German government was keen to ensure that NATO retained the Allied travel regime as an organization-wide policy. Once it had become NATO policy in 1955, the visa regime could not easily be undermined by individual member states and boxed in SED cadres to the Eastern bloc. The NATO Council ensured that governments of individual NATO member states were 'not the controlling factor' in barring East Germans from entrance to Western countries.[16]

One example of this restrictive visa policy, discussed in the previous chapter, was the prevention of SED cadres from travelling to the main sites of UN politics. Yet this policy extended much further. The ATO frequently classified GDR state officials as 'presumed German' or even stateless if they applied for exit visas to travel to NATO countries.[17] By not acknowledging the GDR's power to represent German citizens living in East Germany or elsewhere, NATO thus gave crucial support to the West German legal claim to represent Germans internationally. As a result, East German attempts to send representatives abroad could already be stopped at the East German border. This NATO-wide policy enforced discipline within the Western bloc. It also ensured the GDR's diplomatic isolation even after the early 1960s when the phase of intense anti-communist mobilization across West European states had ended.

The criminalization of emigration from the GDR was the first step to an independent East German citizenship framework. On 29 January 1958, Heinrich Toeplitz, at the time state secretary in the Ministry of Justice, addressed the members of the People's Chamber's delegate cabinet. Explaining recent changes to criminal law, he also touched on the fact that new legislation on passport regulations had been passed on 13 December 1957 and that 'many questions have been asked by the people'.[18] Toeplitz alluded to the fact here that East Germans were shocked by the criminalization of leaving the country. Fleeing the republic, Toeplitz indeed cautioned the delegates, was now a criminal offence. Even worse, Toeplitz stressed that the SED viewed leaving the GDR unauthorized as ideological betrayal. He told People's Chamber delegates: 'We should express in all seriousness in answer to the manifold questions, which we are being asked, that fleeing the republic is treason against the German people'.[19] Toeplitz insisted it was the right of every sovereign state to protect its borders through such legislation. Yet he added that some citizens might insist on their freedom of movement as guaranteed in the GDR constitution and instructed his audience that these people had to be told that the GDR government could only guarantee freedom of movement within the GDR.[20] Such an approach to freedom of movement was also prevalent in the FRG at the time when it came to national security. In 1957, the constitutional court ruled that the withholding of a passport from the former conservative mayor of Mönchengladbach Wilhelm Elfes (1884–1969) had been lawful as his advocacy for German unification and against rearmament had threatened the national security of the state.[21]

To separate East German citizenship from the FRG meant delineating a terminology for socialist citizenship based on class. By 1960, the Foreign Ministry saw an 'absolute necessity' to propagate the class character of the citizenships of the two German states through targeted propaganda. The difference between East and West Germans was not just their different legal treatment by the two German states, but the fundamentally different class-consciousness of East Germans. To express this more clearly to domestic and international audiences, systematic unification of terminology in legislation, official forms and documents, and questionnaires was needed to set GDR citizenship apart from West German legislation. In short, GDR ministerial officials decided that the 'process of the constitution of the citizenship of the GDR had to be systematically prepared'.[22] So far, the socialist notion of citizenship had found a variety of expressions in East German constitutional language, ranging from *Staatsangehörige* to *Staatsbürger* and *Bürger*. All these terms indicated identical legal validity, but to build a viable international propaganda campaign they needed streamlining. The traditional legal term *Staatsangehöriger*, also used in the FRG, suggested passive belonging of individuals to the state. It was clearly a remnant of the legal culture of the German Empire and Prussian bureaucracy, GDR officials determined, which had instituted this term in the citizenship law of 1913.[23] The new central socialist term should signal active citizenship rights rooted in socialist society.

Documents of the GDR Ministry of the Interior show that East German legal experts wanted to blame the FRG for the division of German citizenship. Two secret drafts on the 'Question of the Citizenship of the German Democratic Republic' from 1960 proposed that it had been the FRG that had formed a 'separate imperial citizenship of the West German state' by 'tearing out West Germany from the German national union'.[24] Preparations for an official announcement of the end of the 'fiction' of a unified citizenship were first dominated by such strategic political rather than legal questions.[25] The origins of GDR legal reform of citizenship were thus much more shaped by the German-German ideological confrontation than by domestic East German agendas.

Law should serve as an additional deterrence against even more people leaving the GDR. From the outset, citizenship reform had a crucial punitive element to discourage people from leaving the GDR and threaten those who had already fled to the West. With the 1960 internal decision to backdate the existence of GDR citizenship to the foundation of the state in 1949, the GDR government embarked on a gradual tightening of legal guidelines from 1961 onwards. In 1964, a decree stipulated that the state only granted exemption from prosecution to those former East Germans who had left the country before 13 August 1961. Anyone who had fled the GDR after the building of the Berlin Wall was to be subject to legal prosecution for violation of citizenship duties.[26] Any East Germans wishing to leave now had to apply for permission to change their citizenship and leave the country. Legal regulations mirrored the physical barrier along the German-German border.

These changes did not go unnoticed in Bonn. A dossier compiled by the UfJ, the West German lawyer's association that monitored the legal situation in the GDR, for the Ministry of the Interior suggests that authorities in Bonn began to wonder in 1964 about shifts in citizenship terminology that were now openly promoted by leading GDR scholars. One example drew particular attention: Gerhard Riege (1930–1992), professor of *Staatsrecht* at the University of Jena at the time, had published an article in the academic journal *Staat und Recht* (State and Law) advocating for the introduction of the legal term *Staatsbürgerschaft*. In a socialist society, Riege wrote, citizenship went beyond mere membership implied by the term *Staatsangehörigkeit*. Based on his Habilitation titled 'The Citizenship of the GDR', Riege's article was preparing a wider scholarly audience for the shift in legislation that followed in 1967.[27] Yet few people were paying proper attention. At the time, the UfJ lawyers spitefully noted that the East German 'two state theory' and Riege's notion of citizenship were still grossly underdeveloped.[28] Yet they soon realized the magnitude of this theoretical shift. In 1966, preceding the promulgation of its new citizenship law by several months, the GDR propaganda department began distributing pamphlets about GDR citizenship. These materials were distributed in East and, as far as possible, West Germany, underscoring the claim that GDR citizenship was a topic relevant to all Germans.[29]

Only months later, these propaganda efforts were followed by legislation. On 20 February 1967, the GDR officially proclaimed its own citizenship law. *DDR-Staatsbürgerschaft* now denoted a separate, intrinsically socialist citizenship. In the eyes of the SED, GDR citizens no longer had a claim to German citizenship. They had become *DDR-Bürger* (GDR citizens). Rights of East Germans were now no longer conceived outside of the state and rooted in concepts of ethnicity. Instead, the new socialist citizenship came with a set of rights and restrictive duties that were guaranteed through the existence of the socialist state. Violations of the new law were treated as criminal offences. This was reminiscent of Soviet citizenship regulations that had developed since the interwar period.[30] The government commissioned new encyclopaedia entries, published in dictionaries of the leading publisher Dietz, which warned readers that an escape from the GDR would not end prosecution by GDR authorities. These entries clearly stated that if GDR citizens left the country without having undergone the proper procedure and being released from citizenship by the state, GDR authorities would continue treating them as GDR citizens. East Germans were now physically but also legally trapped in their state.[31]

At the same time, the law reinforced the split from German legal unity by treating West German applicants for GDR citizenship as applications by foreigners. Henceforth, no special privileges were to be granted to such applicants.[32]

Despite the sizeable propaganda effort underway since the early 1960s to promote the official language of East German independence and the right of self-determination, ordinary East Germans were deeply irritated by these legal reforms. In town hall meetings, organized to discuss the drafting and implementation of a new socialist constitution promised for 1968, citizens gave voice to their confusion and concerns. These comments were then captured in internal reports. Local residents were especially confused about what they felt to be a rather sudden policy shift that declared Germany non-existent.[33] Over time, the party had to adjust to a new cultural project of a socialist nation to pacify people around the country and offer regional cultural identities to replace the outlawed German national identity.[34]

Trying to Hold the Line

West German media immediately rallied against this 'legal aggression'. The *Frankfurter Allgemeine Zeitung* (FAZ) reprinted the whole text of the new law on the front page two days after its proclamation. The editorial office had chosen to simply comment with subheadings on the law's specific stipulations in order to explain their effects. Headlines read: 'Children of Refugees Too Are "GDR Citizens" – Even If Only One Parent Came from the Zone' and 'A Hold on Humans'.[35] That same day, the Ministry for All-German Affairs circulated an internal memo to other ministries detailing the flaws in the legal logics of the new GDR law.[36] The ministry's legal experts focused on the inconsistencies they detected in relation to prior GDR rules that had still referenced the 1913 citizenship law as a basis for GDR regulations. Regardless of all inconsistencies, however, they could not avoid concluding that German legal unity had been ended unilaterally by the GDR.

The citizenship battle was no longer focused on the question of which state rightfully represented German citizenship, even if West German officials wanted to cling to this idea. West German ministries spent the next weeks working to deny the legality and legitimacy of the GDR's legislative move. Yet information about the new law remained scarce. Foreign Office experts complained that eight days after the law had been proclaimed by the People's Chamber, West German legal experts were still working from the text that the FAZ had published on 22 February.[37] For the time being, West German experts could do no more than compare the new law to legal precedent. Working on sketchy information, the Section Law of the Foreign Office did what it did best: legal experts attempted to update legal arguments to dispute the legitimacy of socialist law and citizenship based on the claim that only the FRG lawfully represented the German Reich's sovereignty.[38] The section highlighted the distinctions drawn by Third Reich citizenship legislation, which had first introduced the legal term *Staatsbürgerschaft*. The Third Reich's racial categorization of its citizenry had granted its Jewish citizens mere *Staatsangehörigkeit* but denied them full *Staatsbürgerschaft*. Yet it seemed problematic to highlight such historical precedents. In light of West German attempts to return to Third Reich regulations in the 1950s, discussed in Chapter 2, the Foreign Office thought such comparisons would invite another round of GDR propaganda efforts pointing to the complicated legal legacies within the FRG.

Efforts to discredit the new East German legalization ironically highlighted problems with West German legal positions. In trying to make their case, West German legal experts accidentally implied that their own government circumvented international legal norms.[39] When they pointed to the GDR's international campaign for national self-determination, Bonn's officials assumed that the primary purpose of the GDR citizenship law was to prove the existence of an independent *DDR-Staatsvolk* (GDR people). To disprove this argument, West German experts sought to provide arguments for the claim that the GDR violated international law. The preface of the GDR's citizenship law explicitly mentioned its compliance with international law. Based on provisions of the Hague Convention enacted on 12 April 1930, the GDR stipulated that individuals acquired citizenship of the state in which they resided or citizenship of the state to which the individual 'appeared to have the closest ties'. Assuming that this was 'Germany' in the case of GDR citizens, West German experts argued, the East German government violated the Hague Convention. The new law forced GDR citizenship onto individuals who saw themselves as 'Germans', not as 'citizens of the GDR'.[40]

The FRG's institutions, however, made similar assumptions. The West German government had assumed citizenship representation over 'all Germans' who had held German citizenship in the Third Reich in its borders of 1937. Therefore, the FRG's official claim to represent 'all Germans' including GDR citizens could also be seen as a violation of international law. The decisive distinction between GDR legislation and West German citizenship law of course remained the right of the individual to renounce West German citizenship and apply for foreign citizenship without asking for governmental approval first, a right that East German citizens did not have. The fact remained, however, that both governments employed similar arguments in conflicts over citizenship, which could be challenged with international law provisions. West German legal diplomacy was suddenly trapped by its own arguments.

The deliberations of West German ministries show that governmental experts were concerned about the ramifications of the new law for their domestic legal sphere. Ministries in Bonn wanted to continue to assume the unity of German citizenship, a unity administered by two separate bureaucracies. Yet if they did so, some people might start to claim GDR rights in the FRG. For example, the new GDR law formally enabled its citizens to claim voting rights at age eighteen. In 1967, the West German voting age remained twenty-one. Ministerial officials worried that former East Germans might claim the same lower voting age in the FRG. 'It is possible that a refugee could try to use the citizenship of the GDR in the Federal Republic to their advantage.'[41] Legal experts were also anxious that former East Germans who now lived in the FRG might refuse certain civic duties by pointing to their 'still existing GDR citizenship'.[42] The number of legal uncertainties, with which the West German public was presented overnight, triggered a flood of inquiries by concerned citizens. Due to their high number, the Ministry for All-German Affairs swiftly issued a standardized letter and an information sheet to answer all queries efficiently.[43] Former East Germans in general followed all these developments with heightened interest and insecurity.[44]

The situation was serious, and the Foreign Office quickly warned other government ministries against downplaying or even ignoring the potential effects of the law. Governments that had recognized the GDR as a sovereign state were going to incorporate the new law into their legal apparatuses. This might shift the administration of German citizenship abroad and undercut the NATO travel regime. Former GDR citizens and their children, as the FAZ had rightly warned, also faced a new legal threat when travelling behind the Iron Curtain. Eastern bloc governments could now grant the GDR legal aid in extraditing former GDR citizens to the GDR despite their West German passports.[45]

Given these legal uncertainties, the GDR citizenship law became a governmental priority. On 1 March 1967, Hubert Schnekenburger (1894–1979), Special Deputy to the Chancellor for Berlin, summarized what West German offices knew about the law. His conclusion was bleak. The FRG's options to respond to GDR legislation remained extremely limited. It had yet to be determined if the new GDR law was to be accompanied by further restrictions in passport and visa regulations for West Germans intending to travel to the GDR. Schnekenburger saw continued family contacts across the Iron Curtain, one of the main priorities of the Bonn government in dealing with the SED leadership, in serious jeopardy.[46] Schnekenburger's report, moreover, also showed that the Bonn government was entirely dependent on the Western Allies as their extraterritorial powers over Berlin determined the effectiveness of a West German response to a potential introduction of new passport and visa regulation on the German-German and Berlin borders. Even worse, he sensed internal division in Bonn. The only effective response was economic sanctions and the restriction of exports of goods to the GDR.[47] The Federal Ministry of Economy and the Ministry for All-German Affairs, however, strongly resisted any such suggestions. The majority of West German ministries agreed that economic sanctions would only increase the danger that the SED would cut off German-German family contacts even more severely than was already the case in 1967.[48]

Most branches of government initially agreed that the new GDR law was about underscoring East German international sovereignty. While the proclamation of the law seemed to have had no immediate effects, it was still early days. Schnekenburger cited a public statement of the East German Minister of the Interior Friedrich Dickel (1913–1993), who had declared in early March 1967 that the GDR government intended to exercise its authority over GDR citizens independent of their current place of residence. Ministerial officials took this statement to mean that the SED leadership considered all Germans who had fled the GDR after 7 October 1949 to be GDR citizens. One immediate effect of the law could thus be a deepening of German division in everyday life. Former East Germans were effectively being deterred from visiting their relatives in the GDR for fear of being arrested for violation of the new law as almost all of them had left the country without applying for release from GDR citizenship.[49]

At first, these were theoretical concerns in the absence of hard evidence. In March 1967, West German security services remained confident that there existed no increased danger to persons who had not been previously threatened by GDR prosecution.[50] While there had been some worrying incidents in the past, when former East German citizens were temporarily held in the GDR after returning for family visits, the security services insisted that the GDR State Council decree from 21 August 1964 would still guide East German practice.[51] This decree only threatened legal action against former East Germans who had fled after the building of the Berlin Wall. Such persons had to expect 'difficulties' if they returned to the GDR. Persons wanted for alleged acts of espionage or economic crimes would have to be as cautious as before, so for them nothing much had changed.

Despite these assurances, West German security services strongly reiterated their warning that the FRG had no means to protect former East Germans if they were pressed into their 'duties as GDR citizens' on travels to the GDR. They concluded that due to the 'unpredictability of the authorities in *Mitteldeutschland* [Middle-Germany]', absolute security on travels through Eastern Europe could no longer be guaranteed.[52] The security services assumed that the East German change in legislation had the backing of the Soviet Union and that the East German government had first sought approval from Moscow before implementing the law.[53] West German officials were tempted to treat the law as a mere tool of psychological warfare designed to intimidate former East Germans now living in the FRG. The East Berlin government was clearly trying to undercut the core of West German Ostpolitik strategies. In 1966, 1.5 million West Germans had visited the GDR and 1.2 million had travelled within Eastern Europe.[54] Legal threats were to discourage Germans from crossing the border into the GDR.

Catching Up with East German Legal Reform

Bonn did not have many options at this point in time. Recent changes in West German foreign policies that chancellor Kurt-Georg Kiesinger (1904–1988) had announced in 1966 did not allow a return to stricter anti-communist arguments that legal experts in Bonn had peddled in the 1950s. After the Cuban Missile Crisis, the superpowers moved to a politics of détente that the West German government had to account for to maintain good diplomatic relations with the US. Kiesinger had shifted tactics by no longer directly demanding unification based on West German legal frameworks discussed in the first two chapters. Engaging with the GDR's rhetoric of self-determination, he had instead demanded free elections in the GDR. In case East Germans voted for GDR independence, Kiesinger announced, the Bonn government would acknowledge and respect such an expression of self-determination.[55] In making allowances for such a legal route to GDR sovereignty, Kiesinger had made himself vulnerable to socialist bloc and Third World criticism in the international arena that showed in UN politics in the late 1960s, as discussed in the previous chapter. The West German practice of projecting automatic citizenship upon all persons and their descendants who had lived in the Third Reich could easily be denounced as a form of imperial citizenship.[56] The denial of the GDR's power to legislate citizenship, which the Kiesinger government also continued as Bonn's official position, seemed even more anachronistic as West German courts had proceeded to acknowledge GDR legislation in the fields of civil and criminal law in the 1960s. For many international observers, it appeared illogical to accept GDR jurisdiction in some legal matters, but to refuse the East Berlin government's right to legislate a new citizenship law.[57]

The GDR government took its time to publish administrative directives of how the new law was to be implemented. In light of the continued legal uncertainty, the Minister of Justice Gustav Heinemann (1899–1976) ordered seven divisions of his ministry to evaluate the potential impact of the new GDR citizenship law. Twenty-seven deputy assistant undersecretaries and senior governmental officials were given twelve days to come up with answers. Most of the reports they produced stated that the repercussions of the GDR law were minimal. This seemed a rather tendentious conclusion in the absence of hard information. Yet some divisions of the justice ministry went to the heart of East German politics of law in their reports. Evaluating potential consequences for criminal law, Deputy Assistant Under Secretary Erich Corves declared: 'The answer to this question depends concretely on the fact whether state and constitutional lawyers recognize or deny the legal validity of the citizenship law'.[58] In other words, Corves argued that if constitutional law experts in the FRG and abroad accepted the new GDR legal framework, it would enter into legal practice. If the GDR government successfully propagated its new legal position in the international arena, the GDR citizenship law would become accepted legislation sooner or later regardless of what West German ministries thought. Corves thus acknowledged that international public opinion and legal practice would decide the issue, not West German legal non-recognition policies.

Divisions tasked with international law questions within the Federal Ministry of Justice saw these consequences more clearly than other sections. As Corves had pointed out as well, there were direct consequences in international criminal law. Deputy Assistant Under Secretary Heinrich Grützner, head of the international law section, assumed that foreign governments could deny West German legal aid for GDR citizens living abroad whom the GDR prosecuted for political reasons. They also might deny extraditions to the FRG based on East Germans' claim to a West German passport. If East Germans made it across the Iron Curtain, they could so far claim German citizenship and thus a West German passport to immigrate to the FRG. Depending on how foreign governments would implement the new GDR citizenship law in their diplomatic practice, it might cut off escape routes for East Germans to the FRG via third countries. Egypt was a case in point for Grützner where such policy changes already seemed to be visible and East Germans were no longer given an option to leave the country with a West German passport if the authorities knew them as GDR citizens.[59]

There still remained many questions for West German officials: What would happen to persons born after the enactment of the new law? How could *deutsche Staatsangehörigkeit* (German citizenship) be secured for them? Deputy Assistant Under Secretary Wilhelm Bertram concluded that the GDR might reference the West German constitutional court's 1955 decision on the citizenship status of Austrians remaining in the FRG after 1945, discussed in Chapter 2. Austrians were not permitted to decide between Austrian and German citizenship but had to accept decisions made by the West German and Austrian governments. The East Berlin government thus might not be under any legal obligation to give East Germans a choice between *deutsche Staatsangehörigkeit* and GDR citizenship. This implied that the GDR had a right to legislate citizenship. In the end, however, Bertram also declared that all depended on whether other states accepted the new citizenship law in international affairs.[60]

With uncertainty mounting, West German ministries vehemently disagreed about how to respond. The Ministry of the Interior insisted on the continuation of an absolute non-recognition policy and denial of all sovereign legal powers of the GDR government. Against this, the Foreign Office under the new minister Willy Brandt promoted pragmatic and fast solutions to react to this new situation.[61] Citizenship legislation, the Foreign Office maintained, had already significantly differed before 1967. Total opposition to any GDR legislative power would threaten a substantial number of individuals with statelessness, a result that had to be avoided for political reasons. The Foreign Office argued that attempts to prove that the new law contradicted previous GDR legislation only highlighted how far removed from reality and the actual international political situation the Ministry of the Interior's position actually was in 1967.[62] What was needed was a shift in policies, not a stubborn insistence on established legal opinions from the 1950s.[63]

The Foreign Office had an agenda: it wanted to protect nascent policies of a new approach to Ostpolitik. Playing the East German game of legal escalation only undermined West German efforts to work for better German-German relations and ultimately any chance for unification.[64] The notion of a 'common house', in which two sets of regulations to administer German citizenship existed, the Foreign Office experts concluded, would serve as the best way forward. This rhetoric, matching the later famous formula of 'two states in one nation' of Brandt's Ostpolitik as chancellor after 1969, flew in the face of all Cold War legal arguments that the West German judiciary had established since 1949.

The events of the spring of 1967 showed West German ministries how little they actually knew about GDR legal realities.[65] Officials went on fact-finding missions, working through East German legal scholarship and governmental notices, to reconstruct the GDR's legislative path to the new citizenship. It was only then that they realized that this process had already accelerated in 1961 when, one day after the construction of the

Berlin Wall started, the GDR government 'had purposefully dropped the term *"deutsche Staatsangehörige"* (German citizens) and replaced it across the board with the term *"Bürger der DDR"* (citizen of the GDR)'.[66] They also discovered that it was in 1964 that party officials had first spoken of the existence of a GDR citizenship.[67] Reconstructing these developments, the Foreign Office concluded that the proclamation of the law in 1967 should have come as 'no surprise'.[68]

It was again Gerhard Riege, the professor who had already proposed the existence of an independent GDR citizenship in 1964 when few West German experts had been willing to listen, who provided a first scholarly interpretation of the new law from an East German perspective. In the summer of 1967, he expanded on his previous publications from 1964, and explicitly declared that the law underpinned the development of legal concepts designed to protect GDR sovereignty. He contrasted the new GDR law with West German legislation since 1949 that had accepted all collective naturalizations conducted by the Third Reich before and during the war.[69] The FRG, he reminded his audience, had excluded all French, Luxembourgers and Austrians who had become German under the Third Reich, but still retained legal claims to German citizenship for persons from 'areas of the now existing people's democracies' in the east.[70] For him, the GDR government now simply reversed the tables on West German policies and reclaimed citizens who resided in Western countries while leaving the rights of Germans living in other Eastern bloc countries untouched.

Uncertainty ended on 3 August 1967. The GDR government finally enacted and published specific regulations that governed its new citizenship in everyday practice. Beyond the anticipated implications for current and former East Germans, GDR legislators had also included a provision that asked all GDR citizens to register their marriages with state authorities. Given the inclusive approach of the law and the backdating of the emergence of GDR citizenship to 1949, this provision extended also to former East Germans living in West Germany. Residency or change in citizenship was not a factor in these new legal guidelines. In essence, the law now required second- or third-generation children of former East Germans to ask permission before getting married in the FRG. If state authorities had not released them from citizenship, the GDR government now also treated descendants of former East German citizens as part of their citizenry even if they were born in the FRG. As marriage registration was mandatory under GDR law, the GDR government demanded that such persons now had to register with GDR authorities when they got married.[71] In response, the West German Ministry of the Interior began to contact close allies such as the Austrian government and asked Austrian authorities to remove all references to former GDR citizenship in marriage certificates recording the unions between Austrian and GDR citizens.[72] Yet, when couples submitted certificates to the East German authorities denoting the GDR spouse as a 'German citizen', the GDR authorities refused to recognize the validity of such documents. The immediate impact of the GDR law on everyday legal affairs clearly showed that the West German government had to find a more comprehensive response.

Putting Pressure on the Bonn Government

By September 1967, *Der Spiegel* reported that at least sixty-four West German citizens were being held prisoner in Eastern Europe as a result of the new GDR citizenship regulations.[73] That summer, West German media had begun a campaign to alert the public to the fact that those arrests were based on the recent changes in GDR citizenship legislation. Press coverage told the story of these arrests as Cold War narratives. Journalists seldom appreciated the legal dimension of these developments. There were only few commentators who paid close attention to GDR legal reform. Already in January 1967, the *Christ und Welt* journalist Peter Jochen Winters (b. 1934) had dubbed the shifts in GDR policy 'Ulbricht's own Hallstein Doctrine'.[74] Another journalist who saw what was happening was Winters' colleague, Giselher Wirsing. After a journalism career in the Third Reich and service in the Reich Main Security Office, Wirsing had become one of the influential journalists of the early FRG and was now editor-in-chief of *Christ und Welt*, a newspaper owned by the Protestant Church which he had turned into the weekly newspaper with the highest print run nationwide by the early 1960s. He was carefully following the events and concluded that the arrests of the summer of 1967 were not a political 'demonstration without consequences'.[75] Wirsing used his influence to try and draw public attention to the events' international legal dimension.

The human and emotional dimension to these developments was paramount. When in August 1967 newspapers began covering stories of West Germans facing court action in the GDR after being arrested in Eastern Europe, the case of Annemarie Derlig attracted special attention.[76] A former East German citizen and governmental official, Derlig had escaped to the FRG in 1960.[77] Shortly thereafter she had gained West German citizenship and moved to Münster in Westphalia. Now she had been arrested on her way back from her summer vacation in Hungary in 1967. During her stay, she had met her sister for a family reunion. Her brother-in-law, a high-ranking SED member, reported their meeting in the Hungarian town of Tihany at the shores of Lake Balaton to his superiors in East

Berlin. On her journey home, the Hungarian border patrol and East German secret police arrested Derlig at the border crossing Hegyeshalom on the Hungarian-Austrian border.[78] On 18 January 1968, Derlig's trial concluded and she was sentenced to three years and ten months in prison on charges of espionage in East Berlin.[79] On 1 September 1968, following several months in a GDR prison, the West German government negotiated her release and she returned to Münster via West Berlin.[80] Derlig's case lent itself well to newspaper coverage. Her party background suggested that the East German secret police had arranged her arrest as revenge for her desertion. Worried by these developments, West German politicians called on their fellow countrymen not to travel to Eastern Europe.[81] Yet this popular narrative distracted from the important legal aspects of the case.

At the end of 1967, it was clear to government ministries that the new GDR citizenship law had fundamentally transformed the legal contest between the two German states and was only one element in wider legal reform efforts. In December, with the Derlig case still in the papers, the newspaper *Die Welt* warned readers of the effects of the new GDR criminal code. They told readers that, using the new GDR criminal code and citizenship law, the GDR government now threatened prosecution of GDR citizens if they violated any GDR law while living outside of East Germany. The newspaper made sure to emphasize this new 'political part' of the criminal code, including provisions that threatened sentences of up to ten years' imprisonment if GDR citizens were hindered from fulfilling their 'constitutional duties' abroad. 'The political "special (political) part" of the criminal code provides a broad scope for interpretation for severe penalties.'[82] For the crimes of treason against the state and high treason as well as 'terror', the GDR justice system still threatened the death penalty.[83] These stipulations, while addressed to citizens, were clearly also aimed at the West German international legal blockade and visa regime that was obstructing GDR access to international legal and political bodies based on the argument of sole legal representation of Germany by West German authorities.

West German ministries could no longer pretend that the new GDR law did not warrant a revision of their own guidelines and administrative practice. In a confidential directive, the Ministry of the Interior advised state-level ministries in December 1967 how to proceed in future. The directive stated that all persons treated as GDR citizens following the GDR citizenship law remained German citizens according to West German law.[84] To avoid illegal naturalizations, however, governmental offices were told to continue to withhold passports from all those persons who qualified for GDR citizenship but who could not be declared German citizens following the ethnic logics of West German legislation. Such persons had to be treated as foreigners.[85] To avoid unnecessary public attention, the state-level ministries were urged to apply 'most generous' criteria. If GDR citizens who had applied as foreigners for GDR citizenship and had been granted a GDR passport under the new stipulations of the 1967 law, but had no claim to German citizenship under West German regulations, applied for West German citizenship after moving to the FRG, West German local authorities should grant them residence permits without much delay.[86]

In 1968, the political rifts between the government coalition partners CDU and SPD over Ostpolitik became ever more apparent in the negotiation of a West German response to the GDR's ongoing legal offensive. Heinemann, the SPD Minister of Justice, complained to the inner-German committee of parliament about the Ministry of the Interior's stubbornness and unwillingness to cooperate with other ministries. Interior ministry officials were worried that foreigners could now acquire GDR citizenship and inherit an immediate legal claim to a West German passport if they then relocated from the GDR to the FRG. Such persons should be excluded from access to West German citizenship, because they were seen as ethnic foreigners. Heinemann stressed that this position undermined the West German legal claim that all East Germans were still German citizens. He acknowledged that issues of uncontrolled immigration by way of GDR naturalization had to be considered. Yet blind adherence to the antiquated provisions of the 1913 citizenship law, Heinemann argued, was no solution to the problem. Heinemann, moreover, had serious doubts that the current treatment of male and female foreigners married to Germans conformed to gender equality as stipulated by the Basic Law. West German regulations still demanded that female foreigners give up their citizenship if they married a German as the male line determined citizenship. The FRG could no longer ignore the violation of international legal standards such as the UN convention on the rights of unmarried and married women by standing West German administrative practice.[87] The Ministry of the Interior should no longer hide behind Cold War legal concerns to block the modernization of West German law.

While West German officials concurred that the goal of retaining 'German citizenship in the territory of the German Reich' should be upheld, the above discussions between the Ministries of Justice and the Interior illustrate that they disagreed over how to do so. The SPD-led Ministry of Justice and Foreign Office supported the argument made by Herbert Wehner (SPD), in charge of the Ministry for All-German Affairs, that all GDR passport holders had to be acknowledged as German citizens if they crossed the border into the FRG. Wehner further demanded that West

German citizenship regulations needed to accommodate claims to citizenship of children from non-German fathers and acknowledge naturalizations of foreigners by GDR authorities. Yet in practice this meant adopting new GDR legal stipulations, something that seemed unacceptable to the CDU. The Ministry of the Interior, led by the conservative Paul Lücke (1914–1976), took a contrasting position to these SPD arguments, arguing that the issue of GDR citizenship had to be treated 'as part of the big picture' due to its far-reaching political consequences. By this, Lücke meant sticking to established legal positions set up in the 1950s. Lücke refused to accept the changed international situation that no longer allowed for aggressive legal policies of non-recognition that conservative governments had maintained since 1949.[88] Lücke left office shortly afterwards, on 2 April 1968, seemingly freeing the way for progress. Yet his successor Ernst Benda (1925–2009), who would later become president of the constitutional court, tried to straddle the line between Wehner, Heinemann and Brandt. His aim was to outmanoeuvre them to avoid official changes in West German legislation. He argued for an administrative rather than legislative approach and suggested that outdated provisions of the 1913 law could be silently ignored in the administration of citizenship.[89] For Wehner, however, this was bending the law. The GDR citizenship law posed a challenge that could not simply be ignored or pushed down to the level of administrative practice. In response, Wehner complained to Benda that the Ministry of the Interior was clearly dragging its feet. None of this was merely theoretical. Queries from foreign countries about how citizenship questions should be handled had remained unanswered since April 1967.[90] Yet despite Wehner's vocal complaints, Benda prevailed with his tactics until the next general election in 1969. Benda's administrative solution allowed a continuation of conservative legal rhetoric for one more year until the social-liberal coalition took over government.

The citizenship challenge to the FRG, as GDR Foreign Ministry records show, soon extended to attacks on the restrictive NATO travel policies imposed on GDR citizens. On 12 June 1969, the GDR Foreign Ministry official Ingo Oeser (1930–1998), in charge of the Western Europe section, reaffirmed the need to break travel restrictions for GDR citizens in NATO countries. NATO travel policies, enforced by the ATO, were still upholding the FRG's claim to represent German citizenship exclusively. NATO's reassurance, in response to GDR inquiries, that it had officially suspended the work of the ATO in West Berlin in 1969 was a ruse. Oeser pointed out that restrictions were being enforced through the ATO's direct intervention with Western embassies and consular offices in West Berlin whenever GDR citizens applied for travel visas to their countries. While East Germans no longer had to apply centrally at the ATO when they planned travels to NATO countries, but could apply directly to national embassies, NATO travel restrictions still remained active. NATO now circulated lists of GDR citizens who should be blocked from travelling directly to national embassies. As a targeted administrative provocation, moreover, Western authorities still entered the nationality as 'German' or 'East German' on travel documents for GDR citizens, thus not acknowledging the legal validity of GDR citizenship and the new official terminology of 'citizens of the GDR' that had replaced 'German' as the nationality category.[91]

In response, Oeser advocated in his letters to GDR embassies in October 1969 for a public relations campaign against NATO policies. GDR offices abroad should distribute details and arguments against the ATO to other socialist embassies. He also asked the head of the GDR's trade office in Brussels, Max Kleineberg, to target Western journalists and politicians already critical of NATO policies and feed them with information so they could 'agitate' against the ATO.[92] While neither ATO nor NATO had directly refused any visa applications since June 1969, the ATO now sent regular lists to Western embassies in West Berlin naming GDR officials who were to be blackballed from travelling to NATO countries. Officially, embassies then rejected visas on the basis of their national regulations. The real reasons for rejections, however, as GDR officials suspected, were driven by Cold War politics. The GDR Foreign Ministry therefore prepared brochures in several languages. These pamphlets invoked the principle of sovereign equality put forward by the UN special committee on principles of international law. This principle stood in opposition to the argument that states would be entitled to refuse the acknowledgement of the citizenship of a state with which they had no official diplomatic relations. The rejection of GDR citizenship by NATO member states therefore violated Article 15 of the UN Human Rights Convention that proclaimed the right of every individual to citizenship. Oeser argued that East German officials abroad should blame NATO for violating human rights norms.[93]

Eastern European governments bolstered the GDR's legal attack by threatening the citizenship status of double-citizenship holders on travels to their countries. Previously, former East German citizens with a West German or another foreign passport could use this foreign passport to avoid difficulties. By 1971, the West German Ministry of the Interior, acting on warnings from the Foreign Office in this matter, reinforced prior warnings to state-level authorities. In a confidential letter, the head of the constitutional law section, Eckart Schiffer, emphasized that double-citizenship holders continued to experience severe difficulties travelling behind the Iron Curtain. Persons, he wrote, 'who travelled with German documentation in their luggage in Eastern bloc countries, have to be prepared that they might be denied return to the Federal Republic or even be restricted in their personal freedom in a different manner'.[94] Schiffer was hinting here at the possibility of imprisonment.

The problem was that the FRG could not provide legal shelter for persons with double citizenship. 'Given recent incidents', Schiffer instructed state-level ministries once again to communicate to all offices in charge of processing citizenship certificates, ID cards or passports, or that supplied other travel documentation, that they had a duty to alert endangered individuals.[95] This instruction extended not only to individuals holding two passports, but also included persons who held legal rights as Germans through *Volkszugehörigkeit* based on Article 116 of the Basic Law but did not possess full German citizenship. *Volkszugehörigkeit* pertained to persons who were recognized as belonging to German minority groups abroad. Such recognition of belonging to the German people opened up an avenue to West German citizenship on application. This category of limited rights below full citizenship stemmed from imperial times when the British and French Empire or the US, for example, instituted overseas citizenships that did not grant full citizenship status.[96] Against prior guidelines from the mid-1960s, Schiffer emphasized that governmental offices should only in special cases process applications for German citizenship without official documentation detailing the applicant's release from his previous citizenship if they came from Eastern Europe. By this point, the FRG had come under legal pressure not just from the GDR, but the entire Eastern bloc.[97]

This legal struggle between the FRG and the GDR made it very difficult for some affected citizens to determine their citizenship status. In 1971, a woman inquired with the German embassy in Vienna whether she still possessed German citizenship. The woman had been born in 1939, had lived in the GDR and later married her Polish husband. Both of them now worked in Vienna and did not plan to migrate to the FRG. The woman successfully applied for release from GDR citizenship and received a certificate of release signed by the Chairman of the Council of Ministers Willy Stoph (1914–1999) dated 18 August 1970. At the point of writing, she was only in possession of a Polish alien passport. In response, the Ministry of the Interior confirmed that the woman still possessed German citizenship. Her Polish documentation indicated that she never acquired full citizenship and the release from GDR citizenship would not equal the loss of German citizenship. Austrian authorities in response inquired if they should treat her as a German citizen, which the Foreign Office agreed to on behalf of the Ministry of the Interior.[98] Such cases indicated that there needed to be new guidelines, accessible to lower administrative staff, foreign authorities and also to ordinary citizens.

During the negotiations over the Basic Treaty in 1970–71, that aimed to move German-German diplomatic relations to a new plane of mutual recognition, the controversy over citizenship became a potent bargaining chip for the East German government. On 23 April 1971, a confidential UN report emphasized that the GDR was still exerting political pressure on the FRG. East German authorities were arresting West German citizens on visits to the GDR and had increased surveillance of the German-German border.[99] The changed practices of other Eastern European governments, the report remarked, demonstrated the limits of the FRG to fulfil the self-proclaimed duty to represent and protect all German citizens. The cornerstone of Egon Bahr's (1922–2015) concept of 'change through rapprochement', which he promoted as one of Chancellor Brandt's closest political advisers and that underpinned New Ostpolitik, was therefore threatened by new GDR citizenship legislation enforced all over Eastern Europe. Bahr wanted to keep feelings of German national unity alive through everyday contacts between East and West Germans. He predicted that the political legitimacy and stability of the GDR could be undermined through sustained East-West family and everyday contacts. Yet during the ongoing German-German negotiations, the GDR was only willing to disarm its citizenship 'weapon' in return for West German recognition of GDR state sovereignty.[100] This GDR usage of citizenship reform as political leverage forced the West German government to adopt the 'two states in one nation' formula as a legal rather than just a political category.

However, it was not a full East German victory. When the two states concluded their negotiations on new bilateral relations in 1972, the confrontation over citizenship resulted in separate letters from both German governments clarifying disagreements in the interpretation of the Basic Treaty. In its letter, the GDR once again stipulated the existence of an independent GDR citizenship. The Bonn government, by contrast, continued in its position that only a single undivided German citizenship existed.[101] Yet the FRG had acknowledged GDR sovereignty, thereby ending the West German strategy of disputing GDR citizens' citizenship abroad. The Basic Treaty permitted the GDR's entry into international affairs, which culminated in the simultaneous admission of both German states as UN member states in 1973. With this success, the GDR dramatically altered its legal position in the field of citizenship once again. With the international recognition of GDR sovereignty, the East Berlin government renounced all special ties to the FRG. From 1972 onwards, the GDR government argued that no all-German connections or special inner-German regulations existed.[102] Where the GDR had previously tried to claim control over all people it could possibly denote as citizens, the Law on the Regulation of Citizenship Questions of 17 October 1972 released all former East Germans who had left the country between 7 October 1949 and 31 December 1971 from GDR citizenship. These regulations extended to the children of former GDR citizens.[103] When the Basic Treaty was signed on 21 December 1972, the threat of prosecution, which had haunted former East Germans living in the FRG since 1967, had once again disappeared.

Socialist Pressure for Modernization

The West German insistence that the 1913 Reich State and Citizenship Law remained in force stalled legal modernization in the FRG. By the late 1960s, many observers were no longer sure whether bureaucrats in Bonn purposefully used the legal confrontation with the GDR to slow down domestic legal modernization. By that time, West German domestic debates on legal reform turned to gender equality and family law. In this climate of social reform, the GDR citizenship law amplified the shortcomings of existing West German regulations. The East German guarantee of equal citizenship rights for women, which the GDR hailed as a socialist achievement, pointed to the absence of similar legal guarantees in West Germany and persisting patriarchal regulations.[104] One example that showed how West German regulations hindered modernization of immigration and gender equality rules surfaced in 1972 when the West German embassy in Amsterdam pointed to the 'modified form of jus sanguinis' now in place in the GDR since 1967. The embassy asked for clarification of an issue that diplomats in Amsterdam expected to face frequently and in more complicated fashion in the future: a female GDR citizen married to a Zairian husband, who had fled the GDR from the city of Halle, had contacted the embassy. She planned to travel via Amsterdam to the reception centre at Gießen to apply for a West German passport. The couple had a child registered in the mother's GDR passport. The embassy inquired with the Foreign Office whether the child had any claims to German citizenship now that the couple had left the GDR.[105]

The Reich citizenship law still in place in West Germany only acknowledged the lineage of the father as the determining factor of children's nationality. Following the ministerial circulars from Bonn since 1967, the embassy thus assumed that the child only possessed Zairian citizenship. But the embassy staff pre-emptively pointed to dissenting scholarly assessments when they inquired in Bonn about how to proceed. One of the leading legal scholars in citizenship questions, Alexander Makarov, had already argued in the 1950s that new GDR legislation on double citizenship allowed for children's claims to German citizenship in such cases. While the embassy still assumed that the child only possessed GDR citizenship, but did not qualify for German citizenship, cases such as this were opening up in practice the issue of whether naturalized GDR citizens only acquired GDR citizenship or both GDR and German citizenship. There were, moreover, also questions about the mother's citizenship status: did an 'alien citizen' such as the mother qualify for legal aid or would he or she be treated as a foreigner and immigration law applied? Did such persons who had escaped from the GDR require living permits to stay in the FRG? Did they possess voting rights and the duty to serve in the military? Could such persons be extradited or did citizenship rights protect them?[106] In the Amsterdam case, the woman and child were forced to apply as foreigners for citizenship. In the mid-1970s, the West German parliament finally amended legal regulations to ensure gender equality and modernized other outdated regulations of the original 1913 law to conform to international standards.[107] But, for one thing, West German legislators always made sure not to portray this publicly as also being influenced by East German legal reform, and, for another, reforms were proceeding at a very slow pace.

The government's accompanying letter to the Basic Treaty in 1972 further complicated cases such as the one raised by the diplomats in Amsterdam. The federal government had stated that the two German states had not come to an agreement on the question of citizenship. The Bonn government remained of the official opinion that there was no need for the FRG to amend citizenship law as a result of the treaty. Yet, the Amsterdam embassy staff argued, existing law created what West German jurisprudence described as unnecessary hardship. The embassy thus requested new administrative guidelines to ensure uniformity in processing such cases.[108] And they were not the first. Herbert Wehner had already warned of such complications when Bonn ministries coordinated their first response to the GDR law in 1967. Back then, Wehner had argued that the Bonn government was de-facto acknowledging that a *DDR-Staatsvolk* existed if not all GDR citizens had an automatic right to a West German passport, naturalized foreigners or not.

Diplomatic practice and West German citizenship regulations urgently needed to be amended if the Bonn government wanted to maintain the notion of a still existing unified German citizenship. The events between 1967 and 1972 made it necessary to investigate carefully how citizenship matters were actually administered, not least because the legacies of the Second World War were still exerting pressure on administrative practice. The Ministry of the Interior, now under the leadership of Hans-Dietrich Genscher (1927–2016), continued the conservative practice of using administrative directives to avoid changes to the actual citizenship law. Yet in May 1972, the case of the so-called Tyrol *Optanten* demanded another change in policy. In 1950, the ministry had decreed that only Germans who had been naturalized until 1942 and moved from South Tyrol into the territory of the German Reich would remain German citizens. This policy was adopted to avoid the loss of property of German South Tyroleans who still lived in Italy at the end of the war. Their property had otherwise been treated as enemy property. Now, in 1972, the ministry advocated for accepting all citizenship certificates of *Optanten* that had been issued by the Third Reich. Similar to the Amsterdam embassy staff, the ministry legitimized this shift in policy with the intention to ease 'social hardship'. To avoid any politicization of the issue, it decreed that this was to be enacted on a case-by-case basis and not as a uniform policy.[109] Governmental policies could show flexibility in citizenship questions whenever it came to persons who were considered ethnically German. Ministerial officials therefore continued in their practice of undercutting standing legislation with administrative acts if they wanted to avoid publicity or new conflicts with the GDR or other foreign countries.

Over time, the Bonn government remained above all interested in how foreign governments reacted to German-German clashes over citizenship. In February 1973, the chancellery requested a report for Brandt detailing citizenship terminology and practice in the treatment of West German citizenship abroad. The head of the Bureau of State Secretaries in the Foreign Office, Peter Schönfeld, investigated how foreign visa documentation classified West Germans in sections denoting nationality and citizenship. Were West Germans now classified as 'West German', 'German' or otherwise? This was a priority request, the chancellery impressed on Schönfeld, who reported that for the most part the term 'German' was used abroad as the GDR government now insisted on the denomination 'GDR citizens' in the nationality column.[110] The Bonn government still did not wish to abandon a unified German citizenship. Yet legal experts across government ministries no longer knew how this legal position could be effectively maintained and how it translated into everyday realities for ordinary Germans living outside of the FRG. At the same time, the first foreign governments were inquiring directly with the GDR government in East Berlin about the specifics of the new citizenship law, thus indicating that they accepted the international legal validity of the GDR law.[111] It was now clear that the West German government could no longer insist on the diplomatic representation of 'Germans' around the world.

Waning West German Legal Home Fronts

The international recognition of the GDR as a sovereign state prompted another round of conflicts between West German ministries, the constitutional court, the GDR government and the Western Allies. These clashes centred on claims to jurisdiction over citizens within divided Germany and Berlin in particular. The Western Allies were no longer willing to back West German revanchist legal positions. In the attempt to fend off the GDR's attack on the West German legal framework of sovereignty and citizenship, West German institutions pushed against Allied special rights to reassert dominance in legal politics. In the early 1970s, the constitutional court schemed to enlarge its jurisdiction to West Berlin in response to the GDR's diplomatic recognition. After the end of the war, the Allied powers had demanded special rights in the administration of Berlin. After 1949, they retained these extraterritorial rights. In 1957, East Berlin became part of the GDR's jurisdiction. This change in administration had angered West German ministries and high courts ever since. In the face of East German advances in international rights politics, West German high courts attempted to boost the Basic Law's authority in Berlin in the early 1970s.[112]

One prominent example in which these post-Ostpolitik conflicts between the Allied powers, the Bonn government and its own high courts crystallized was the case of Ingrid Brückmann. Her case was a German-German family tragedy. Brückmann was born in East Berlin in 1956, the year her parents got divorced. One year later, mother and child moved to West Berlin. In 1959, her father took his daughter against her will back to East Berlin. After the building of the Berlin Wall in 1961, Brückmann had to remain in the GDR. It was only in 1972 that her stepfather managed to organize her escape to West Berlin. On 4 May 1973, the GDR General Prosecutor issued a warrant demanding the release of Brückmann to the GDR. She was accused of having murdered her father near Senzig in the District of Königs-Wusterhausen in July 1972. Aged sixteen at this time, she had been sexually and physically abused by her father from an early age. After being taken into custody in West Berlin, Brückmann confessed, but stated that the assault on her father had been in self-defence, triggered by further attempted sexual abuse.[113] West German authorities initially complied with the GDR extradition request. On 10 August 1973, the General Prosecutor of the West Berlin Higher State Court ordered the release of Brückmann to the GDR on the charge of murder. In response, Brückmann's attorney appealed to the constitutional court and the European Commission of Human Rights.[114] With these appeals pending, Brückmann had to remain in custody in West Berlin until the case was settled.

In the summer of 1974, the Brückmann case developed into an international diplomatic affair. As the case had clear basic rights implications, the constitutional court at Karlsruhe requested the West Berlin case files to determine whether it could admit the case. In this process, the court communicated through backchannels with the Ministry of Justice. The judges were trying to find out whether the case had the potential to become a 'fundamental confrontation' over the court's jurisdiction in Berlin matters. For years, the court had tried to expand its direct jurisdiction to Berlin but had been repeatedly blocked by the Allied authorities. Kai Bahlmann (1927–2009), a former academic assistant at the court between 1958 and 1960 who now served as Head of Department for Public Law at the Ministry of Justice, contacted vice-president Walter Seuffert (1907–1989) on 28 February 1974. Bahlmann had made a name for himself by introducing a much more activist and independent role to his administrative post. His approach resulted in frequent clashes with the ministers Gerhard Jahn (1927–1998) and later Hans-Jochen Vogel (b. 1926) under whom he served in the ministry.[115] Bahlmann called Seuffert to pass on information off the record. He explained that the Berlin Justice Senator Horst Korber (1927–1981) had voiced uncertainty about the constitutional court's request to send case files to Karlsruhe. Korber's request for clarification had led the Foreign Office to consult the Western Allies about the case. The Allied authorities decreed that it was prohibited to release the files to the Karlsruhe court. Bahlmann had been unable to move his minister to make a public statement in the matter. The Foreign Office, too, was unwilling to explain the events publicly. He therefore wondered whether Seuffert could declare the court's request for the case files void before an official refusal by the Allied Kommandatura drew even more publicity to the case.[116]

Yet the constitutional court purposefully accelerated the controversy surrounding the case. On 7 March 1974, Bahlmann wrote a summary of the Brückmann case that he circulated within government ministries in Bonn. The Foreign Office especially needed all available information for further negotiations with the Allied representatives. Yet an additional unofficial copy also reached the court at Karlsruhe. Seuffert had asked Bahlmann to be kept informed about government-internal debates. In his report, Bahlmann reiterated that the Foreign Office had set events in motion by raising the Brückmann case in a regular meeting with representatives of the three Western Allies in Bonn on 15 February 1974. The Allies had no prior information about the constitutional court's request for the case files to begin a judicial review of the case. Bahlmann was insinuating that the Bonn government had informed the Allies purposefully to block any involvement of the constitutional court.[117]

It was clear from the Allies' response that they opposed the court's request. They ordered the Berlin authorities to refrain from releasing any files until an official decision had been reached. Bahlmann, meanwhile, convinced that the constitutional court should play a role in the case, urged the Foreign Office to intervene on behalf of the Karlsruhe court.

He stressed that no official request for judicial review in the Brückmann case had been submitted yet and the court only planned to engage in a preliminary evaluation. Trying to make the court's case, Bahlmann argued that the constitutional court had never openly questioned Allied authority over Berlin. Still, he insisted, the judges needed to have the authority to request files as part of legal aid legislation *within* the FRG 'without any necessity of an explanation or even "legitimation" on part of the constitutional court'.[118] The request for case files would not constitute an 'act of "ruling" of Berlin by the federal government'. Bahlmann closed his report by pointing out that a potential official decree by the Allied authorities banning Berlin courts from sharing files with the constitutional court would constitute a troubling precedent. He argued that the federal government, and with it the Foreign Office, had to strongly oppose any such act in defence of the legal unity of the FRG and West Berlin.[119]

The Allies' intervention to restrain the court had a longer history. In 1952, the Allies had first refused to adopt the Law on the Constitutional Court (BVerfGG) for Berlin. Since then, the court had pushed to gain official recognition of its jurisdiction over West Berlin. This question was tied to the official recognition of West Berlin as a state of the FRG, which the Allies, too, had been unwilling to grant since 1949. The international protests of the Soviet Union against treaties signed by the FRG including Berlin, after the Soviets had acknowledged East Berlin as the official capital of the GDR, hardened the position of many West German jurists over time.[120] In response, many leading high court judges had pushed for the legal inclusion of Berlin in the FRG's sovereignty since the building of the Berlin Wall in 1961.[121]

The Brückmann case deepened existing rifts between the court, governmental ministries and the Allied powers. Through Bahlmann's indiscretion, the court knew that Foreign Minister Scheel had informed the Allies about the court's initial request for the Brückmann files. This came after the Ministries of Justice and the Interior had already advised the Berlin court to send the court files to Karlsruhe. The Foreign Office thought it had been time to retaliate and diminish the court's political influence, not least as payback for the court's major interference in foreign affairs through the Basic Treaty verdict in 1973, discussed in the next chapter. The judges at Karlsruhe now debated whether they should protest this Foreign Office interference in an official letter and combine it with a public demand for support in opposing the Allies' assertion of their special rights in Berlin. Via backchannels, Seuffert continued to inform Bonn that the court was pondering a plenum resolution to protest the Foreign Office's interference in the case. After all, only Scheel's actions had alerted the Allies to the complications of the Brückmann case.

The internal struggles between the court and government ministries soon became public and quickly riled up public opinion in favour of Brückmann.[122] As the court pressed to receive the Brückmann files, the Allies eventually released an aide-mémoire that asserted their authority in Berlin and prohibited any release of court files to the constitutional court on 12 March 1974. Feeling that the diplomats had sabotaged him, the court's new president Benda sent a letter to the Foreign Office, requesting a personal meeting with the Foreign Minister. In his letter, he expressed his dissatisfaction with the Foreign Office's 'uncoordinated activity'. The court, he argued, should have been consulted and given the opportunity to explain the judges' view of their role in the current delicate legal situation.[123]

Eventually, the court found a procedural trick that enabled it to comment officially on Brückmann's case. The judges argued that they had the authority to evaluate Brückmann's case based on the underlying legal aid legislation from 1953. In 1953 and 1965, the Berlin Senate had adopted the legal aid law and its amendments that regulated how the Bonn and West Berlin governments dealt with matters that affected both West Berlin and the FRG. Following procedures that respected Allied prerogatives, federal law had thus become law in Berlin since the legal aid laws had been implemented. Given the constitutional court's responsibility to judge whether federal law accorded with constitutional norms, the judges saw it within their powers to admit Brückmann's appeal. They argued that while the court would not evaluate the court ruling against Brückmann directly, it was in the court's power to evaluate the legal norm on which the West Berlin court had based its decision.[124]

The constitutional court judges knew that they could not rule on Brückmann's case. All they wanted to do was to make a public statement on the matter. Yet when they released their ruling on the legal norm that the West Berlin court had used in the case against Brückmann on 27 March 1974, the constitutional court judges simply expanded their legal brief and also addressed the legal substance of Brückmann's case itself. The court stated that Brückmann would not receive due process and a fair sentence in the GDR. The judges therefore suggested that German citizens could only be extradited 'if it is beyond any reasonable doubt that all preconditions are met that an extradition is in accordance with the ordre public [the West German understanding of the rule of law] of the Federal Republic of Germany'.[125] This implied that the judges thought a fair trial was not guaranteed within the GDR court system. 'Doubts on the lawful use of the legal and administrative aid [between the two German states] cannot be dismissed out of hand if it cannot be safely ruled out that hidden political goals of the prosecution in the German Democratic Republic play a part [. . .]. This will not seldom be the case when so-called *Republikflücht-linge* [persons who fled the GDR] are concerned.'[126] The judges ended their criticism by pointing once more to Article 116 of the Basic Law, which ensured the protection of all Germans living under protection of the Basic Law. In the eyes of the court, this included the FRG and Berlin as well as the GDR.[127] In other words, the court saw the West Berlin court's order to proceed with Brückmann's extradition as an unconstitutional verdict. While prohibited from ruling on the case itself, the judges had thus made their opinion on the matter amply clear.

Two days after the court's decision, the president and vice-president of the court, Benda and Seuffert, finally met with the federal ministers of the interior, justice and foreign affairs. Benda and Seuffert stressed that the judges at Karlsruhe were unhappy that the court had been forced to back down from claiming direct jurisdiction in the Brückmann case under pressure from the federal government and the Allies. Both urged the ministers to press the Allied powers for a specification of their aide-mémoire, which should outline that the document only addressed the Brückmann case and would not outline a general Allied position on the relationship between the constitutional court and Berlin.[128] Yet the government disagreed with the court. The Foreign Office official Guntram von Schenck (b. 1942) pointed out that the Allies had paid close attention to the court's actions since the signing of the Four Power Agreement on Berlin on 3 September 1971. The agreement guaranteed that West Berlin would not become an integral part of the FRG and it preserved the Allied status and authority over Berlin. The Soviet Union would react particularly sensitively to any attempt at subversion by the court that indicated the inclusion of West Berlin in the legal realm of the FRG. The lifting of certain travel restrictions between both parts of the city had been contingent on the signing and honouring of the agreement. The court's recent actions, von Schenck implied, had jeopardized the government's politics of détente.[129]

But the court had provided enough publicity and public pressure on the Bonn government and West Berlin Senate not to release Brückmann to the GDR. To satisfy GDR demands for a necessary prosecution of Brückmann's father's death, Brückmann's case was tried before a West Berlin court. Brückmann then appealed to the European Commission of Human Rights, an action that even resulted in the commission's president Anthony B. McNulty (1911–1992) visiting her in prison in 1974. Following this appeal, the Bonn government used human rights norms to argue publicly that she could not be extradited to the GDR as the death penalty was still in force in East Germany. Such human rights norms could still not be directly applied in West German law, however, and in the end the legal explanation for why Brückmann was not extradited was that there was proof that she might attempt suicide if the West Berlin Senate sent her back to the GDR. It was the West German constitutional norm that the state had a responsibility to ensure that its citizens came to no harm that prevented her extradition.

The claim to the representation of German citizenship remained the last legal bond between the two German states. West German lawmakers and high court judges were not willing to relinquish it after the Bonn government had accepted GDR sovereignty with the signing of the Basic Treaty in 1972. Still, the restriction of the West German *Alleinvertretungsanspruch* (claim to exclusive representation of German statehood) from sovereignty to citizenship caused much unease among West German legal experts. With some months' distance from the events, even Walter Seuffert publicly expressed his bewilderment over the rapid and politically motivated transfer of old legal arguments on sovereignty to citizenship legislation. Seuffert wrote a reader's letter to the weekly newspaper *Die Zeit* in which he strongly refuted the argument that the Basic Law prohibited the acknowledgement of a GDR citizenship.[130] Instead, he argued, the Basic Law only prevented the FRG from denying GDR citizens their claim to German citizenship. If legal scholars, high court judges and government officials had done a better job explaining this legal situation to the public, the heated public conflict surrounding Brückmann's case could have been avoided. Seuffert signed his reader's letter 'Walter Seuffert, lawyer', thus making clear that the letter was an expression of his private opinion rather than an intervention in his official capacity as constitutional court judge. Still, it was a published reader's letter from a high court judge in a leading national newspaper and as such yet another unofficial intervention in an ongoing debate.

Seuffert was obviously taking aim at popular revanchist arguments. Public debate was still dominated in the early 1970s by narratives of a West German claim to the German Reich's sovereignty. In his reader's letter, Seuffert argued that the formula of a legal duty for reunification extrapolated from the Basic Law preface had too often been instrumentalized. The Basic Law's preface called for unity and freedom, but it put greater importance on personal freedom than national unity. In his opinion, it would be an enormous achievement if all Germans enjoyed the freedom guaranteed by the Basic Law. Whether this equalled national unification was a secondary question for him.[131] In 1974, his intervention went unheard. In public debates, the notion of a legally binding prohibition to acknowledge GDR citizenship that officials in Bonn had promoted in response to the GDR citizenship law between 1967 and 1972 still dominated public debate in the FRG for years to come. Yet Seuffert had prepared the ground for legal arguments centred on individual self-determination that eventually rose to prominence in the 1980s.

Conclusion: Forced Naturalization

As a result of the Cold War ideological confrontation between the two German governments, both statelessness and citizenship became a possible threat to individual freedom and security. In the first half of the twentieth century, threats of denaturalization and statelessness had haunted individuals. Now, the GDR aided by other Eastern European states threatened former citizens with re-naturalization. Where the major legal threat to individuals had once been the removal of rights, it was now the exercise of state power. Drawing on the Soviet model, the GDR used citizenship for 'the creation, preservation and defence' of the state. Similar to Eric Lohr's argument that he made for the case of the Soviet Union, the East German government's guiding principle in legislating citizenship was the development of the state's capacity 'to control its borders and population movements across them, making great strides towards overcoming the traditionally huge gap between policy intentions and actual practices'. In contrast to the Soviet Union, however, the GDR required a physical wall to enforce one of 'the hardest, most rigorously enforced citizenship boundaries the world has ever seen'.[132]

Ostpolitik, as this chapter has demonstrated, reframed the legal contest between the two German states. The GDR's strategy of threatening forced legal repatriation effectively countered the West German *Alleinvertretungsanspruch* of German citizens. The GDR based its quest for the international recognition of GDR sovereignty on the use of citizens as political leverage. By the early 1970s, the new West German formula of 'two states in one nation' was the only framework left that countered the GDR's firm position on state sovereignty and national self-determination in the international arena. The battles over citizenship restricted the foreign policy of future West German governments. The constitutional court's statement in the Brückmann case led to renewed calls that the West German government had a duty to protect GDR citizens abroad. In the eyes of many West German observers, such calls equalled a court-sanctioned duty to help East Germans escape from the GDR, something that was treated as *Fluchthilfe* (aid to escape) and penalized under the new GDR criminal and citizenship law. The constitutional judges had also used the Brückmann controversy to reiterate their belief that the German-German border was 'similar to borders between federal states' and emphasized the status of Berlin as a state of the FRG.[133] These court-sanctioned definitions harshly restricted the government's options in foreign affairs in the future. In combination with the Basic Treaty decision of the constitutional court on the legal validity of the treaty between the two German states, discussed in the next chapter, the court made a full legal acknowledgement of East German legal positions almost impossible.

The latent aura of a GDR legal threat to former East German citizens remained until 1989. In 1972, the GDR had merely suspended its legal citizenship weapon. From 1980 onwards, the SED leadership started another large-scale campaign for a full official acceptance of GDR citizenship by West German authorities. On 18 November 1980, the SED mouthpiece *Neues Deutschland* proclaimed that peace in Europe could only be achieved if the equality of all existing states was guaranteed. This meant the full acknowledgement of an independent GDR citizenship.[134] West German media immediately refuted such East German advances and insisted on the primacy of the West German citizenship legislation.[135] In a *Spiegel* interview, the constitutional court judge Martin Hirsch (1913–1992) returned to controversial legal arguments in his rejection of East German attempts to establish GDR citizenship in perpetuity. Hirsch stated that the Basic Law assumed that the German Reich's sovereignty would be re-instituted someday. When asked where in the constitution such an assumption was laid down, Hirsch answered that such an understanding was implied by the preface of the Basic Law. While the German Reich had indeed perished in 1945, he explained, there was a promise of resurrection of the unified nation-state.[136] In the atmosphere of renewed global Cold War tensions, the Soviet invasion of Afghanistan and tensions surrounding the deployment of new US and Soviet mid-range nuclear missiles to Europe in the early 1980s, the continuity theory thus remained the instinctive touchstone in moments of GDR attacks among West German constitutional judges.

The East German use of citizenship law as a legal 'weapon' shows that for SED cadres it was not 'the path, but the result that matters'.[137] The GDR government was above all interested in clearly delineating the GDR citizenry from West German legislation. This was not about rights so much as it was about securing West German recognition of GDR sovereignty, territorial integrity and self-determination. Yet the SED leadership adopted many international legal norms and tied the drafting of a GDR citizenship law to its international rights campaign. While the GDR used citizenship law as a repressive tool in the late 1960s and early 1970s, the next chapters show that this move to a new rights language also permanently tied the GDR government to international rights languages of human rights.

Notes

 1. PA/AA, B82/530, restricted NATO circular, 30 November 1967.
 2. For the reconfigurations in European understandings of citizenship, see: Gosewinkel, *Schutz und Freiheit?*, 413–69; Palmowski, 'Citizenship, Identity, and Community'; and Fulbrook, 'Germany for the Germans?'. There exists of course a plethora of legal scholarship on the topic, but these studies usually treat the issue of German citizenship between 1949 and 1989 in the separate logics of the East and West German legal systems instead of exploring their entangled history. See, e.g. von Münch, *Die Deutsche Staatsangehörigkeit*, 90–109.
 3. See: Fink and Schaefer, *Ostpolitik 1969–1974*.
 4. Ulbricht outlined this new framework for a socialist state and the role of law for the transformation of society in his 1958 speech at the Babelsberg Conference. See: Ulbricht, *Die Staatslehre des Marxismus-Leninismus*, 5–48.
 5. PA/AA, B82/530, restricted NATO circular, 30 November 1967.
 6. See: Getachew, *Worldmaking after Empire*, 71–106.
 7. PA/AA, B82/530, restricted NATO circular, 30 November 1967.
 8. Thomas, '"Aggression in Felt Slippers"', 37–41.
 9. For the European context, see: Gosewinkel, *Schutz und Freiheit?*, 284–345.
10. For the shift to an ethnicity-based framework in the Weimar era and after, see: Fahrmeir, 'Coming to Terms with a Misinterpreted Past?'. This shift blurred the borders between 'inner' and 'outer' citizenship that Dieter Gosewinkel put forward as a framework for the history of citizenship. See: Gosewinkel, *Schutz und Freiheit?*, 12–30.
11. BArch, DO1/7772, letter Kaudelka, 29 June 1960.
12. Sheffer, *Burned Bridge*, 167–212.
13. These restrictions allowed for a speedy implementation of the Hallstein Doctrine. See: Kilian, *Die Hallstein-Doktrin*.
14. Thomas, '"Aggression in Felt Slippers"', 37–41.
15. For the organization of the Allied Travel Office through the British Foreign Office and NATO, see: FCO33/228–301; 316–321; 1722–1723; FO1071/134, 142, 171.
16. NATO Archives, AC 52-R(62)05.
17. For this administrative policy, see: FCO33/228–301; 316–321; 1722–1723; FO1071/134, 142, 171.
18. BArch, DP1/6767, manuscript talk Toeplitz, 29 January 1958. In the following years, the GDR government began to enforce citizenship on West Germans who had left the country after 1949. See: Gehrig, 'Cold War Identities', 796–97.
19. DArch, DP1/6767, manuscript talk Toeplitz, 29 January 1958.
20. Ibid.
21. The court internally acknowledged that West Germans should have a guaranteed right to leave and enter their country, but upheld the withholding of a passport in Elfes' case. Such infringements on freedom of movement were also used against West German communists in the 1950s. See: Rojahn, 'Elfes'.
22. BArch, DO1/7772, letter Kaudelka, appendix 2, 29 June 1960.
23. BArch, DO1/7772, letter Kaudelka, appendix 1, 29 June 1960.
24. Ibid.
25. Confidential plans to announce a GDR citizenship commenced at a time when the inclusive nature of the 1913 citizenship law was no longer needed. In 1959, the Minister of the Interior Karl Maron (1903–1975) had ended the Action Family Reunion (*Aktion Familienzusammenführung*). This programme had organized the repatriation of Germans from Poland to the GDR based on their ethnicity. See: BArch, DO1/19072, report of visit to People's Republic of Poland from 20–26 June 1961.

26. 'Erlass des Staatsrates der Deutschen Demokratischen Republik über die Aufnahme von Bürgern der Deutschen Demokratischen Republik, die ihren Wohnsitz ausserhalb der Deutschen Demokratischen Republik haben'.
27. ASR/3625, invitation to public lecture 'The GDR Citizenship', 20 June 1964.
28. BArch, B106/73196, dossier 'The Legal Development of the Soviet Zone during February 1964'.
29. BArch, DP2/249, letter Herrmann, 30 January 1967.
30. Lohr, *Russian Citizenship*, 132–76.
31. BArch, DO1/7670, letter on the dictionary entry 'citizenship' to be published by Dietz Publishing House, 11 January 1967.
32. BArch, DY30/IV2/3/1325, minutes SED Central Committee Meeting, 23 August 1967.
33. BArch, DY30/IVA2/13/47, report secretariat for State and Legal Questions, 2 February 1968.
34. See: Palmowski, *Inventing a Socialist Nation*.
35. 'Auch Kinder von Flüchtlingen sind "DDR-Bürger"', *FAZ* (22 February 1967).
36. BArch, B136/6536, report on GDR citizenship law, 22 February 1967.
37. PA/AA, B82/913, memorandum on GDR citizenship law, 28 February 1967.
38. BArch, B136/6536, report on GDR citizenship law, 22 February 1967.
39. Ibid.
40. Ibid.
41. Ibid.
42. Ibid.
43. BArch, B136/6536, standardized letter on GDR citizenship.
44. See articles 'Das "DDR"-Staatsbürgerschaftsgesetz – Unruhe unter Flüchtlingen' and 'Wer ist gefährdet?' in: *Leipzig Neuste Nachrichten* 5 (March 1967).
45. PA/AA, B82/913, memorandum GDR citizenship law, 28 February 1967.
46. BArch, B136/6536, report on countermeasures to GDR citizenship law, 28 February 1967.
47. Mary E. Sarotte has pointed to the central importance of economic relations for the GDR government in Ostpolitik negations. See: Sarotte, *Dealing with the Devil*.
48. BArch, B136/6536, report on countermeasures to GDR citizenship law, 28 February 1967.
49. BArch, B136/6536, report on GDR citizenship law, 15 March 1967.
50. BArch, B136/6536, excerpt from 'Internal Security – Information on Questions of State Security'.
51. Ibid.
52. Ibid.
53. BArch, B136/6536, report on GDR citizenship law, 21 March 1967.
54. Ibid.
55. Gray, *Germany's Cold War*, 198.
56. See: Gosewinkel, *Schutz und Freiheit?*, 284–345.
57. BArch, B136/6536, report on GDR citizenship law, 21 March 1967.
58. BArch, B141/59339, memorandum on GDR citizenship law, 31 March 1967.
59. BArch, B141/59339, memorandum on GDR citizenship law, 22 March 1967.
60. BArch, B141/59339, memorandum on GDR citizenship law, 29 March 1967.
61. PA/AA, B82/913, meeting on GDR citizenship regulations, 12 April 1967.
62. For the transformation of debates on citizenship from the 1940s to the 1960s, see: Gosewinkel, *Schutz und Freiheit?*, 413–68.
63. PA/AA, B82/913, position paper on Interior Ministry policy regarding GDR citizenship.
64. PA/AA, B82/530, internal memorandum Treviranus, 21 April 1967.
65. PA/AA, B82/913, confidential report Treviranus.
66. Ibid.
67. Ibid.
68. PA/AA, B82/530, letter on GDR citizenship in Austrian marriage certificates, 24 April 1967.

69. Riege, 'Das Staatsbürgerschaftsgesetz der DDR', 701–13; Riege, *Zwei Staaten*.
70. Riege, 'Das Staatsbürgerschaftsgesetz der DDR', 710.
71. 'Durchführungsbestimmungen zum Gesetz über die Staatsbürgerschaft der Deutschen Demokratischen Republik vom 3. August 1967'.
72. PA/AA, B82/530, letter on GDR citizenship in Austrian marriage certificates, 24 April 1967.
73. 'DDR: Republikflucht: Teure Genossen', *Der Spiegel* (4 September 1967).
74. Winters, 'Absage an Deutschland', 1.
75. Wirsing, 'Riskante Reise', 1.
76. 'Bonn: Ostblock-Reisen: "Gewisse Sorge"', *Der Spiegel* (28 August 1967); 'Deutsche Touristin in Ungarn festgenommen', *FAZ* (4 August 1967).
77. 'Annemarie Derlig in Zone verurteilt', *FAZ* (30 January 1968); 'Annemarie Derlig', *FAZ* (2 September 1968).
78. 'Bonn: Ostblock-Reisen: "Gewisse Sorge"', *Der Spiegel* (28 August 1967), 19f.; 'Deutsche Touristin in Ungarn festgenommen', *FAZ* (4 August 1967), 1.
79. 'Annemarie Derlig in Zone verurteilt', *FAZ* (30 January 1968), 7.
80. 'Annemarie Derlig', *FAZ* (2 September 1968), 7.
81. 'Bonn spricht von persönlichem Risiko bei Ost-Reisen', *FAZ* (19 August 1967); 'Festnahmegefahr schreckt Touristen ab', *FAZ* (16 August 1967); 'Marx vermutet Aktionen östlicher Geheimdienste', *FAZ* (14 August 1967); 'Mahnung', *FAZ* (19 August 1967); 'Bonn: Ostblock-Reisen: "Gewisse Sorge"', *Der Spiegel* (28 August 1967).
82. 'Mitteldeutschland: Strafrecht mit Stoßrichtung gegen die Bundesrepublik', *Die Welt* (12 December 1967).
83. Ibid.
84. BArch, B136/6536, directive on citizenship questions concerning foreigners, 4 December 1967.
85. For the drafting of the 1913 citizenship law, see: Sargent, 'Diasporic Citizens', 25–30.
86. BArch, B136/6536, directive on citizenship questions concerning foreigners, 4 December 1967.
87. BArch, B136/6536, letter Heinemann, 6 February 1968.
88. BArch, B136/6536, minutes section meeting, 1 April 1968.
89. BArch, B136/6536, letter Benda, 25 April 1968.
90. BArch, B136/6536, letter Wehner, 15 May 1968.
91. PA/AA, MfAA C 277/73, letter Oeser, 12 June 1969.
92. PA/AA, MfAA C 277/73, letter Oeser, 31 October 1969.
93. PA/AA, MfAA C 277/73, letter Haupt, 22 November 1969.
94. PA/AA, B82/974, letter Schiffer, 26 July 1971.
95. Ibid.
96. Gosewinkel, *Schutz und Freiheit?*, 284–345.
97. Ibid.
98. PA/AA, B82/994, letter Ministry of the Interior, 10 December 1971.
99. UN ARMS, S-0884-0008-05.
100. BArch, DY30/11331, report on Basic Treaty negotiations, 11 October 1972.
101. 'Erklärungen zum Grundlagenvertrag zwischen der Bundesrepublik Deutschland und der Deutschen Demokratischen Republik'.
102. BArch, DY30/JIV2/3J/1544, position paper on citizenship, 18 October 1972.
103. AdsD, 1/GJAA000349, Nachlaß Gerhard Jahn, report 'SPD-Bundestagsfraktion, AK I: Staatsangehörigkeit der DDR-Bürger', 18 October 1972.
104. For a discussion of the problems of this state-mandated gender equality, see: Gerhard, 'Die staatlich institutionalisierte "Lösung" der Frauenfrage'.
105. PA/AA, B82/994, letter FRG embassy Amsterdam, 17 November 1972.
106. Ibid.

107. 'Gesetz vom 8. September 1969'; 'Kostenermächtigungs-Änderungsgesetz vom 23. Juni 1970'; 'Gesetz vom 20. Dezember 1974'; 'Zuständigkeitslockerungsgesetz vom 10. März 1975'; 'Adoptionsgesetz vom 2. Juli 1976'; 'Gesetz zur Verminderung der Staatenlosigkeit vom 29. Juni 1977'.
108. PA/AA, B82/994, letter FRG embassy Amsterdam, 17 November 1972.
109. BArch, B122/12778, letter Ministry of the Interior, May 1972.
110. PA/AA, B82/972, letter Chancellery, 2 February 1973.
111. BArch, DO1/14241, draft for consultation meeting with Austrian authorities, 22 October 1973.
112. The constitutional court's verdict on the Basic Treaty only one year earlier heralded a conservative revolution in constitutional jurisprudence. See: Grigoleit, *Bundesverfassungsgericht und deutsche Frage*, 271–85.
113. 'Prozesse: Auf der Kippe', *Der Spiegel* 51 (1974), 47–48.
114. The case fell into the transformation period of the ECHR. See: Bates, *The Evolution of the European Convention on Human Rights*, 277–318.
115. Görtemaker and Safferling, *Die Akte Rosenburg*, 356.
116. AdsD, 1/WSAE000196, Nachlass Seuffert, minutes Brückmann case, 28 February 1974.
117. AdsD, 1/WSAE000196, Nachlass Seuffert, letter Bahlmann, 7 March 1974.
118. Ibid.
119. Ibid.
120. BArch, B141/59040, circular Foreign Office, 16 April 1962.
121. The Third Criminal Senate of the BGH had already included Berlin in the sovereign territory of the FRG in a decision from 1960 (3 StR 34/60). See B141/74089, letter BGH president Bruno Heusinger, 24 November 1961.
122. 'Drübiges Rechtsgebiet', *Der Spiegel* 26 (1973), 68–69; 'Auf der Kippe', *Der Spiegel* 51 (1974), 47–48; 'Ein Stück Schicksal der Nation. Der Fall Ingrid Brückmann: Menschlichkeit aus den Mühlen der Justiz', *Die Zeit* (12 April 1974); 'Lex Brückmann', *Die Zeit* (1 November 1974).
123. AdsD, 1/WSAE000196, Nachlass Seuffert, letter Benda, 19 March 1974.
124. See: BVerfGE 37, 57.
125. Ibid.
126. Ibid.
127. Ibid.
128. AdsD, 1/WSAE000196, Nachlass Seuffert, minutes of Foreign Office meeting regarding the Brückmann case, 29 March 1974.
129. Ibid.
130. AdsD, 1/WSAE000144, Nachlass Seuffert, reader's letter Seuffert, 3 December 1974.
131. Ibid.
132. Lohr, *Russian Citizenship*, 133.
133. 'Grundvertrag: Dogmatischer Hauch', *Der Spiegel* 35 (1973), 23–25.
134. 'DDR-Staatsbürgerschaft anerkennen: Frieden in Europa kann nur auf Gleichheit aller Nationen basieren', *Neues Deutschland* (18 November 1980).
135. 'Ost-Berlin will Änderung des Grundgesetzes: Die Agitation für die Anerkennung der DDR-Staatsbürgerschaft', *FAZ* (14 November 1980); 'Stoph fordert die Respektierung einer Staatsbürgerschaft der DDR', *FAZ* (18 December 1980); Otto-Jörg Weis, 'Nur Bremsinstrument für die Entspannungspolitik', *Stuttgarter Zeitung* (24 October 1980); 'Sozialistische Staatsangehörigkeit', *Bayernkurier* (3 May 1980); Jens Feddersen, 'Deutsch bleibt deutsch: Zu Honeckers Staatsbürgerschaft', *Neue Ruhr-Zeitung* (18 October 1980); 'Staatsbürgerschaft als Abgrenzungsvehikel', *Der Tagesspiegel* (7 December 1980); Alfons Heutgen, 'Der doppelte Staatsbürger', *Deutsches Allgemeines Sonntagsblatt* (11 January 1981).

136. 'Erstens pharisäerhaft, zweitens falsch: Bundesverfassungsrichter Martin Hirsch über den Anspruch der DDR auf eine eigene Staatsbürgerschaft', *Der Spiegel* 5 (1981), 34–37, 34.
137. BArch, DY30/22276, letter Sorgenicht, 13 November 1984. By 1984, even members of the CDU-FDP coalition publicly speculated about recognizing GDR citizenship. See: 'Auch Bonn denkt jetzt über eine DDR-Staatsbürgerschaft nach', *FAZ* (24 September 1984).

Part III
UNIVERSALISMS

Chapter 5

International Networking

Gifts were part of the German-German legal battle. On 22 May 1975, the GDR Deputy Foreign Minister Peter Florin (1921–2014) wrote to Ismat T. Kittani (1929–2001), the Executive Assistant of the UN Secretary-General Kurt Waldheim (1918–2007), to inform him that the GDR government wished to present the UN with a gift: a sculpture by the artist Fritz Cremer (1906–1993) titled *Der Aufsteigende* (The Rising Man). The gift, Florin explained, symbolized 'the rise of man towards an awareness of his historic role and the unfolding of his strength'. The sculpture, he added, 'must also be seen as a historic symbol of the German Democratic Republic's twenty-five years of development'.[1] The Art Committee of the UN swiftly approved the acceptance of the GDR's gift and the sculpture was erected in the UN Northern Gardens in autumn 1975 at the beginning of the forthcoming UN General Assembly session to shine light on the GDR's international rights activism (Figure 5.1).[2] Three years later, the Bonn government followed with its own gift to the UN Security Council. On 15 March 1978, the designers Paolo Nestler (1920–2010) and Günter Fruhtrunk (1923–1982) unveiled the interior design for a Quiet Room in the presence of Waldheim that serves as a common room for the Security Council (Figure 5.2).[3]

In many ways, these two gifts symbolized the attitude of the two German states and their judiciaries to international rights politics in the 1970s. The SED leadership used its newfound international access through UN membership to branch out into transnational legal networks. GDR legal experts also reached out within their own bloc to learn about legal practice in other socialist states. The intrinsic link between human rights, socialist legality and a new form of constitutionalism guided the SED's law pro-

---

Notes for this chapter begin on page 215.

Figure 5.1. The Rising Man, sculpture, Northern Gardens, UN Headquarters, New York City, 1975. Artwork: © DACS, used with permission. Photo: © UN Photo Library, Photo # 142342, used with permission.

Figure 5.2. The Quiet Room, Security Council, UN Headquarters, New York City, 1978. Photo: © UN Photo Library, Photo # 70453, used with permission.

paganda at home and abroad that accompanied these endeavours. While East German legal experts confidently ventured into the wider world of legal politics, West German high court judges and legal scholars conversely tried to salvage whatever they could of the remains of the FRG's Cold War legal framework. While the old West German framework of sovereignty, rooted in imperial legal traditions, had lost much of its international appeal after decolonization, the constitutional court judges tried to reinforce their international legal influence by setting up new transnational high court networks in Europe. This legal diplomacy happened in the secluded atmosphere of conference centres and courthouses far away from the public. While many GDR legal experts saw their legal universe on the rise, like the sculpture their government gifted to the UN, the mood among their West German counterparts was often subdued after the West German Cold War framework of the 1950s had crumbled under the changes in international politics accompanying decolonization.

From the 1960s into the 1970s, adherence to international law standards, and not just signing up to UN conventions without implementation of international rights norms at home, became particularly essential for states such as the FRG and GDR that directly competed for legitimacy of their legal systems to make moral claims to ideological superiority. Ideological conflicts over law during the 1970s seemed to render any walled-off domestic judicial system untenable. With the 1975 Helsinki Accords, a shared legal framework across Cold War borders in Europe came into being.[4] In an age of economic and political integration that reshaped fundamental principles of thinking about the state, sovereignty and rights, international legal norms had to become an accepted part of national jurisprudence east and west of the Iron Curtain.[5] This forced both German states to forge international expert networks as the confrontation over what legal ideology should dominate international law and human rights frameworks continued with undiminished intensity. Yet the premise of international rights conflicts was changing. Pressure from Third World leaders to secure sovereignty and transform the international political and economic system at the same time forced Western and Eastern bloc politicians, lawyers and legal experts to contemplate how international and domestic legal spheres were linked.[6]

During the second half of national division, the international battle over German law turned into a German-German confrontation over international law and rights. Historiography has begun to integrate human rights scholarship into the development of new international legal networks on both sides of the Iron Curtain.[7] While clashes over human rights and new intensified grassroots human rights activism captured the headlines, the increasing number of international legal, economic and political frameworks that developed in Europe and beyond alongside each other in the 1960s and 1970s made the evolution of transnational legal networks inevitable.[8] There was no sudden 'shock of the global' to domestic legal frameworks. Pressure to adopt new legal languages and norms gradually increased.[9] Attempts to frame questions of social peace and justice, human rights of the individual and international security in new ways – most famously advocated by supporters of a New International Economic Order (NIEO) – transformed debates in East and West and forced legal scholars and practitioners to look to international legal spheres.[10] In this international climate, the judiciaries of the two German states had to justify their legal standards and rights provisions no longer solely in relation to each other, but they also had to explain how their legal norms related to international rights standards in the face of ever-growing grassroots rights activism.[11] In a variety of new venues, from constitutional court networks to socialist scholarly and ministerial networks as well as the UN, legal experts from both German states grappled with the challenges of the internationalization of their legal worlds.

The Last Attempt to Hold the Line

The 8 o'clock weather map had shaped West German public perceptions of Germany since 1960 (Figures 1.3 and 1.4). The arrival of colour television was more than mere technological modernization; it transformed the West German imaginary of what Germany was. When the leading evening news show *Tagesschau* broadcast in colour for the first time on 29 March 1970, three years after the start of colour TV had been celebrated in the FRG, the weather forecast was projected on a geographical map of Europe that drew instant criticism. The map no longer included national borders. Recall that since 1960, the TV weather map had been the political map of the German Reich in its borders of 1937. During early Ostpolitik negotiations, this public depiction of a still existing German Reich in its borders of 1937 caused friction with the Polish government in particular and attracted much ridicule in political magazines such as *STERN* and *Der Spiegel*. One cartoon summarized this conundrum for the government by depicting chancellor Willy Brandt, sitting in the chancellor bungalow's living room watching the news (Figure 5.3). When the weather report is shown at the end of the news broadcast, he turns to his Foreign Minister Walter Scheel and tells him: 'You can call the gentlemen of the Polish delegation back in – the weather report is almost over'. The TV image shows a map of Germany in the 1937 borders at the same time. In response to the change to the new weather map, Herbert Schwarzer, the general secretary of the national expellee organization BdV, stated that 'we will certainly protest this change. ... The weather map has to remain the way it is'.[12] Such public criticism in response to this shift in representing Germany on TV showed that many West Germans still clung to the idea of a still existing German Reich under international law.

Familiar constructs of Germany were also under attack in the legal sphere, as the case against the Basic Treaty demonstrates. Once negotiations over détente between the two German governments had been concluded in 1972, this case radicalized West German legal rhetoric in response to Ostpolitik in 1973. It also marked the beginning of a fundamental reorientation of West German frameworks of sovereignty and rights. Klaus Joachim Grigoleit has described the domestic political upheaval caused by personal attacks and frequent insults surrounding the Basic Treaty case, which culminated in the recusal of judge Joachim Rottmann (1925–2014).[13] The case marked the peak of the constitutional court's engagement with the continuity theory which argued that the German Reich's sovereignty existed unabated after 1945. At the same time, it also heralded much-needed reform in West German legal frameworks of sovereignty.

Aus „Stern"

„Sie können die Herren von der polnischen Delegation wieder hereinrufen — der Wetterbericht ist gleich zu Ende"

Figure 5.3. Cartoon, 'TV-Wetterkarte: Lästige Gemüter', *Der Spiegel* 7 (1970), 39. Artwork: © Markus.

In May 1973, the Bavarian state government played the conservatives' last card in preventing the outcomes of Ostpolitik. The Bavarian legal brief to support a case against the government's treaty with the GDR deployed the politics of sovereignty. The Bavarian state's lawyers criticized the fact that the German Reich was not even mentioned as a legal basis in the Basic Treaty. This, they argued, equalled the acceptance of the East German theory of an end of the German Reich's existence and the foundation of two new states in 1949, a direct violation of the Basic Law's legal sentiment and therefore unconstitutional.[14] Conservatives felt deeply frustrated when the West German government retreated from the right to represent the whole of prewar Germany.[15] The Bonn government's claim that the Basic Treaty would not affect any third-party agreements and treaties, the Bavarian government argued, could no longer sufficiently defend vital West German legal positions. In the eyes of the Bavarian government, the letter accompanying the Basic Treaty, discussed in the previous chapter, diminished former exclusive claims to German sovereignty and citizenship beyond anything that was acceptable to them.

For many conservatives, the Basic Treaty seemed to be a complete capitulation to the East German 'two-state theory' in *Staatsrecht* and international law.[16] To make their case, the Bavarian legal team deployed international law in making its case at the constitutional court. If the letter that had accompanied the treaty, in which the government stated its continued disagreement with East Berlin over the issue of German citizenship, constituted a legal document with binding quality – following the UN treaty convention's Article 31 – the government should have also outlined that the FRG insisted on legal rights in the field of national unity and self-determination. This was a complicated reading of the UN treaty convention. The Bavarian lawyers omitted to mention the UN treaty convention's insistence on state sovereignty as the basis for the conclusion of treaties between states. This already indicated a legitimate GDR claim to statehood.[17]

The Brandt government tried to free West German jurisprudence from the German Reich as the anchor of West German legal foundations. Yet many leading members of the judiciary did not want to be liberated. For them, the acknowledgement of GDR sovereignty as an equal in legal quality to the FRG's international status rendered toothless previous policies of containing the legal reach of the SED leadership. The disagreement over citizenship with the GDR, which the government had registered in the letter accompanying the treaty, was irrelevant in the international arena. Even worse, in the eyes of many conservatives, the treaty transformed 'the demarcation line, which the Allied powers had forced on the German Reich' into an international border.[18] Against this perceived capitulation of the FRG, the Bavarian Minister President Alfons Goppel (1905–1991), who had signed the appeal to the constitutional court on behalf of the Bavarian government, called the preface of the Basic Law 'an immovable constitutional cornerstone' of binding legal quality.[19] Goppel saw in the preface the bulwark against any retreat from claims that the united prewar nation-state still existed. The Basic Law's preface, in his interpretation, clearly demanded from the Bonn government that it pursue national unification in the existing framework of the German Reich in its borders of 1937. For Goppel, the court had an obligation to protect the Basic Law. It should therefore have no choice but to strike down the treaty between the two German states.[20]

One day after the submission of the legal brief, the Bavarian government added a further part to the argument that 'unfortunately', as the Bavarian government wrote, had been forgotten a day earlier.[21] The first version had not spoken in great detail about the right provided by the Basic Law for the parts of Germany not belonging to the FRG to join its territory.[22] Based on the court's verdict in the Saar Statute case, discussed in Chapter 1, the Bavarian government now argued that the acceptance of GDR sovereignty made it harder to achieve unification. Recall that the Saar verdict had prohibited any action that 'hampered or made it more difficult' for another part of Germany to join the FRG. The Bavarian legal team opined that the Basic Treaty did just that: it had made unification exceedingly harder to achieve. The treaty, as they wrote, 'added additional legal difficulties' to already existing political realities of national division.[23] The Bavarians had made a substantial case of some magnitude and it forced the vice-president of the court, Seuffert, who also played a key role in the Brückmann case discussed in the previous chapter, to ask the government to hold off the exchange of ratification documents with the GDR government. Seuffert wrote to the Minister of Justice Gerhard Jahn (1927–1998) directly, but Jahn emphatically rejected the very premise of the case and refused to hold off the ratification.[24]

With the case officially submitted, the time had come again for the legal scholars to make arguments to support political agendas. Wilhelm Wengler (1907–1995), professor at the Free University in West Berlin and a leading scholar of international law and international private law, drafted the expert opinion for the Bavarian government.[25] Ardently attacking the acceptance of GDR sovereignty and the GDR's territorial integrity, Wengler claimed that the treaty undermined the possibility of any future attacks on a legitimate East German claim to self-determination 'in the spirit of the UN Charter'. Wengler suggested that the UN's concept of self-determination 'as some have argued' would only apply to colonial peoples.[26] Anti-colonial leaders had indeed insisted that a human right of self-determination first and foremost applied to colonized peoples. Yet decolonization had questioned old Western imperial legal traditions to such an extent by the late 1960s that the West German scholarly frameworks of state sovereignty and their neglect of popular sovereignty in the construction of state continuity between the Reich and the FRG had lost international appeal. Against the GDR's rights rhetoric of self-determination rooted in socialism, Wengler called for a return to the strict focus on *Staatsrecht* that West German scholars had established in the 1940s and 1950s. His opinion also reflected the deep-seated suspicions of international legal norms that many within an older generation of West German legal scholars harboured. It was too far removed from their *Staatsrecht* universe.

The human rights situation in the GDR formed another central argument of Wengler's rejection of the treaty. He argued that the acceptance of GDR self-determination and protection of internal affairs would prevent future West German governments from criticizing the GDR government's authoritarian character. Wengler opined that the 'Basic Law, however, demands to react more intensively to human rights violations of Germans by another German government, even if it were a recognized state in international law, than to human rights violation of Jewish or non-Jewish citizens of the Soviet Union by their regime'.²⁷ Wengler's comparison of the human rights of Germans and Jews was most unfortunate and it showcased the emotional tensions surrounding the case that affected the arguments of all parties involved. Stressing the importance of *Staatsrecht*, Wengler disregarded potential new avenues for UN inquiries into the human rights situation in member countries that would become possible with the ratification of the UN human rights covenants by enough UN member states.

The case was as much about history as it was about law. Against the conservative assertion of standing legal orthodoxy, Martin Kriele (b. 1931), professor of law at the University of Cologne and lead representative for the government, historicized the drafting of the Basic Law in his closing arguments on behalf of the government. The political situation, he explained, had changed greatly in the last twenty years.²⁸ Kriele accused the Bavarian government of misinterpreting the content, goals and results of the Basic Treaty.²⁹ He argued that in light of the GDR's international law campaigns during the 1960s, the 'legal opinions expressed by the plaintiff are not only understood in the East, but also the West – or misunderstood which is the same in its political consequences – as keeping the option open to reverse the territorial status by non-peaceful means'.³⁰ Kriele here referred to the insistence of conservative legal scholars on the German Reich's continued legal existence 'in its borders of 1937', which seemed anachronistic to international audiences in East and West by 1973, and also possibly belligerent. The Basic Treaty, Kriele continued, included no mention of a full international recognition of GDR sovereignty and excluded the issue of citizenship. In short, the treaty was in accordance with the Basic Law's goal to secure peace and supported the ideal of humanitarian governance. The treaty improved people's living situations, observed the notion of a continued existence of Germany as a whole in the formula 'two states in one nation', improved the situation not only of the FRG but the whole nation, and kept the question of unification open. *Staatsrecht*, so Kriele argued, was increasingly unfit for capturing the legal status of German sovereignty in a world of developing international law. The 'relationship between the Federal Republic and Germany [is] primarily not a *Staatsrecht* question but an international law question'.³¹

Armed with the archive of the West German government, Kriele mounted a general attack on the established politics of law and sovereignty. He exposed how politicized the legal doctrine of state continuity actually was that West German legal experts had built in the 1950s. In his opinion, there had been three options in 1945 to determine legal sovereignty: the concept of state succession, the idea that the sovereignty of the German Reich and the FRG were identical, or the representation of the legal duties of the German Reich through the FRG. The majority of legal scholars had supported the last option in the immediate postwar period. Kriele exposed largely unknown agreements that the Adenauer government had made with the Allied powers shielded from the West German public in the 1950s. Already at the foreign ministers' conference in New York on 19 May 1950, he explained, Adenauer accepted that speaking for Germans did not equal state identity with the German Reich. This declaration was only declassified in 1971 and Kriele now drew the attention of the general public to this fact.[32] Kriele thus showed how the Adenauer government had actually agreed to the Western Allies' demands not to promote legal claims of state identity between the FRG and the German Reich. West German government ministries had only been able to promote the continuity theory with all its problematic territorial claims, which the Bavarian brief now claimed was a historical fact, once the West German legal sphere had been free of direct Allied control. Kriele thus dismantled the normative Bavarian argument by exposing its historical origins and inconsistencies.

Kriele's presentation was a sharp exposition of West German legal experts' semantic dance on a knife-edge in the late 1940s and early 1950s that had resulted in the blurring of legal distinctions between the goal of claiming state identity of the Reich and the FRG and ensuring the foundation of a new democratic state at the same time. Kriele stressed that the American and British foreign ministers had emphasized in 1955 that 'following international law Germany continues to exist. . . . The Federal Republic and the so-called GDR however do not represent – either separate or together – an all-German government which would be allowed to act for Germany within international law'.[33] This meant that the two German states had to deal with the legal obligations that the German Reich had signed up to, but had no claim to represent Germany as a whole any longer.

The trial drew intense media attention.[34] Kriele's contribution to the courtroom proceedings exposed to the West German public how sovereignty had been politicized in the immediate postwar years. He skilfully narrated the story of how West German high court judges, legal scholars and government officials had elevated their legal doctrine of a still existing German Reich in its borders of 1937 in court verdicts, rules and regulations and scholarly work against the Allies' position.[35] Bernhard Leverenz (1909–1987), former Minister of Justice of Schleswig-Holstein and legal expert for the government, then wrapped up the government's case with a discussion of relevant aspects of international law.[36] Leverenz emphasized the politics of all legal theories that had tried to capture Germany's postwar status of sovereignty. Germany as a legal concept continued to exist. Yet, he stated, 'it would neglect all rules of logic if a part would be identical with the whole. ... Thus, all Germany theories are theorems, which try to explain political developments and systematize them in legal categories of thought'.[37] All these theories, then, had to be understood in their specific historical contexts and none of them had ever managed to create a consensus. More importantly, Leverenz argued that 'none of these "Germany-theories" has any legal validity or even constitutional quality. It therefore comes as no surprise that no ruling of the constitutional court exists that treats these theorems as legal or constitutional questions'.[38] Leverenz thus implicitly warned the court not to make the mistake of adopting one theory over another in the coming verdict and infuse it with some sort of legal quality. It was precisely the political nature of all these theories that had allowed the court to react flexibly to shifting Cold War politics in the previous decades.[39]

One Last Radicalization

However, the court did just that. The majority of the judges voted for the elevation of the theory that the German Reich and the FRG's sovereignty were identical. As the internal documents of the court show, the judges had to decide whether they wanted to label the GDR a 'foreign state' as a first step to reach a verdict. As vice-president of the second senate that was hearing the case, Seuffert compiled material on this question for his colleagues.[40] Unsurprisingly, the expert literature overwhelmingly made a case against the idea that the GDR was a foreign state. But there existed grey areas. Seuffert cited the work of Theodor Maunz (1901–1993) who had written the authoritative teaching manual on *Staatsrecht* in 1951.[41] Maunz had defined foreign countries as 'any state that is neither the Federal Republic nor one of the *Gliedstaaten* (member states) of the Federal Republic'. Yet Maunz as one of the leading *Staatsrecht* scholars also stated that 'the GDR is no foreign state in relation to the FRG'.[42] This ambiguity opened up the room for interpretation that Seuffert needed. He pushed against the recognition of the GDR's full legal sovereignty: 'It seems for many reasons important to avoid the impression as if we take part in deciding this question [of whether the GDR is a fully-sovereign state], and in fact [that we answer this question] in a positive sense (GDR is a foreign state)'.[43] For him, the duty to work for unification, which the court's own interpretation of the legal quality of the Basic Law's preface had established in the 1950s, came closest to a guiding authority in this case. His preferred solution was adding a very brief mention of the fact that the

GDR constituted no foreign state 'if the conceptualization of the verdict allows for it'.[44] This followed Leverenz's suggestion in his closing remarks for the government to avoid lengthy discussions of the competing legal theories that tried to capture German postwar sovereignty.

The other judges saw the matter differently. It is well documented how the trial developed hereafter: under the pressure of the public controversy surrounding Ostpolitik, the court moved to radicalize its rhetoric on German sovereignty.[45] Despite Seuffert's cautioning against a lengthy engagement with this issue, the verdict explicitly addressed the question of sovereignty. The court chose the most radical rhetoric possible and deemed the FRG's sovereignty to be 'identical' with the German Reich's sovereignty. This was legal posturing to satisfy the many West Germans who had great difficulties accepting the outcome of Ostpolitik. Under the cover of this radical legal language, the judges hid the actual reasoning for their rejection of the Bavarian case. The verdict discussed the idea of an identical sovereignty of the Reich and FRG at length, but the judges then made a sharp turn and argued that this issue was not the actual legal substance of the Bavarian case. The court actually had to decide if the judges had the authority to dictate foreign policy. The judges acknowledged that the court had ultimately no business in intervening in international treaty negotiations. Foreign policy was the executive's prerogative. On this basis, the case was dismissed, but the radicalized legal rhetoric that served as cover would dominate public debate for years to come.

The judges restricted the political room for manoeuvre for future negotiations between the two German governments.[46] Earlier generations of judges had carefully constructed strategic interpretations of sovereignty in the 1950s, but the court now declared the direct continuity between the German Reich's sovereignty and the FRG a legal fact.[47] It was a contradictory verdict. On the one hand, it radicalized domestic legal rhetoric. On the other hand, it climbed down from previous claims of a West German legal right to enforce the German Reich's sovereignty internationally. The judges accepted that their interpretation could only claim legal authority in the FRG, as the treaties did not 'establish a special legal order' within international law.[48] Yet the court suggested that this status could still be challenged by West German lawmakers and treated as a special relationship when laws were concerned that affected both German states.[49]

Enough political damage was nonetheless done. Right-wing conservative activists quickly read this verdict to their advantage, brushing aside the fact that the case had been rejected because of a 'technicality', and focusing instead on the parts of the verdict that claimed that the FRG and the German Reich were identical. When a new wave of right-wing militancy erupted in the late 1970s and early 1980s, right-wingers pointed out that the court, the country's authoritative legal voice, had clearly legitimized their territorial claims towards Poland. The new generation of activist conservative judges who dominated the court in the early 1970s had shown little concern for such political fallout when they supported the sentiment of the Bavarian government's case in the radicalized legal rhetoric of the verdict.

Another often-overlooked side-effect of the verdict was the court's postulate of the Basic Law's order as the future constitutional basis of a united Germany. The verdict stated that the FRG would only represent a 'complete state' once 'the other parts of Germany belong to her'.[50] State institutions, the verdict argued, were prohibited from amending or abolishing the Basic Law's democratic order. Once 'other German territories' declared their will to join the political order of the Basic Law, the FRG's political institutions had to set the rules for this process without any foreign interference.[51] The incorporation of German territories, for example the GDR, had to be possible at any point in time. Yet the court declared that such a territorial change would only be lawful if and when, in this process, the Basic Law's political order was fully preserved. The verdict therefore closed with the predictable conclusion that unification of the two German states under a communist political order was unconstitutional.[52] Without knowing it, the judges had outlined the legal unification process that was set in motion in 1990.

High Court Networks

If West German high court judges wanted to reassert their authority in German-German legal politics, the judges realized in the course of Ostpolitik negotiations, they had to engage with legal publics outside of the FRG. Ostpolitik put the necessary pressure on West German jurists to leave their domestic focus behind. But détente also opened up new possibilities for legal dialogue across the Iron Curtain. The waning influence of West German frameworks of sovereignty prompted high court judges, in particular, to reflect on the increasing pressure on traditional *Staatsrecht* positions through international law and rights politics. The GDR's success in UN rights politics, the ongoing drafting and revision process of a new constitution and legal codes in the GDR, and the fundamental shifts in Cold War politics in an era of détente forced West German jurists into the international arena. After decades of devising and advancing legal arguments in a German-German framework taking the rights of the Allied powers into account, West German legal experts realized that they needed to gain a better understanding of the changing legal worlds around them.

This included in particular the reach of high courts and constitutional courts and their powers to influence bilateral and international politics in an era of legal internationalization.

At first, however, West German high court judges saw this nascent international cooperation as another vehicle to persuade their international colleagues of their hard line taken in the Basic Treaty verdict. On the initiative of the West German, Italian and Yugoslavian constitutional courts, a first conference of European constitutional courts took place in Dubrovnik from 17 to 20 October 1972. Due to Yugoslavia's unique position in Europe and its leading role in the non-alignment movement, this new high court network also allowed West German judges contact with socialist law experts. Preparations for this meeting had already begun in 1969 when Yugoslavian judges had first visited the FRG and invited their hosts for a visit to the Yugoslavian constitutional court in 1971.[53] It would be another year until the three constitutive courts had put together plans for the first official conference that took place in 1972 at a time when the West German government concluded Ostpolitik negotiations.

To find common ground between the delegations, UN norms governed the preparations for this new network. The final communiqué of the conference at Dubrovnik in 1972 explicitly referenced the 1965 UN resolution that had stipulated that 'any improvement of the relations between European states with different socio-political systems ... has a positive impact on international relations in general'.[54] The new network was thus put in the context of the ongoing negotiations over détente surrounding Ostpolitik. The conference attendees set aside the officially still prevailing ideological non-recognition of each other's national legal cultures and discussed two fundamental questions: the juridical powers of constitutional courts and their jurisdiction, and the legal impact of decisions made by such courts and institutions tasked with the protection of constitutional legal standards. 'In a friendly and sincere spirit', the high court judges discovered 'shared values and interests ... despite all the contradictions and differences that surfaced concerning the development of the world and the European realm'.[55] The final statement highlighted the importance of such conferences in the future to enhance international legal cooperation. European meetings of constitutional judges and experts should transcend existing bilateral cooperation and develop into a multinational forum.[56] This was an important first step to acknowledge the authority of courts operating in ideologically opposed political systems, something West German courts and governmental officials had long denied East German courts in particular.

The West German constitutional court was keen to bring the second conference to Karlsruhe in 1973. Just two months after the end of the inaugural conference in 1972, the constitutional court's president Benda met with his deputy Seuffert and the judges Theodor Ritterspach (1904–1999), Hans Brox (1920–2009) and Hans Georg Rupp (1907–1989) to discuss plans for a second meeting. Ritterspach and Rupp were tasked with heading a working group, drafting a preliminary programme and suggesting themes for the conference.[57] When the Minister of Justice Jahn visited the court in February 1973, he pledged his support. As the conference seemed to be in line with his government's politics of détente, Jahn's ministry would supply financial support, send interpreters and could organize some leisure activities or a visit to Bonn if necessary.[58] In March 1973, the working group agreed that the meeting's themes would be: international treaty evaluation by constitutional jurisprudence, a pressing topic given the ongoing controversy surrounding the Basic Treaty, and the interpretation of laws according to the constitution.[59]

When the rifts within the court and between the court and the Bonn government became evermore apparent, the Karlsruhe court hoped to enlarge the number of delegations to have a wider international audience for their agenda of building support for the idea that constitutional courts should be able to evaluate international treaties between states before those treaties were signed.[60] Yet the preparations for the conference took too long. Benda, Walter Antoniolli (1907–2006), Blazo Jovanovic (1907–1976) and Francesco Paolo Bonifacio (1923–1989) only agreed on coming together in Karlsruhe in autumn 1973 to discuss further details. At this point, the Basic Treaty verdict had already been handed down. Now, the West German mission turned into bolstering support for their contentious verdict. Although the presidents agreed to enlarge the planned conference at Karlsruhe beyond the founding members, Bonifacio voiced doubts about the choice of conference themes. He agreed that the second theme, the interpretation and evolution of laws according to the constitution, represented a shared task of all participating courts. The first theme, however, seemed highly dependent on national regulations. Many constitutional courts had no judicial powers to evaluate international treaties at all.[61] Benda on behalf of the Karlsruhe court, however, insisted on retaining the treaty theme. The Basic Treaty case had centred precisely on this issue and the court hoped to rally international support among constitutional courts. If their foreign colleagues endorsed the idea that courts should have a greater voice in international treaty questions, this would have been a welcome counterweight to the intense domestic criticism of the court from many West German legal scholars and the government.[62]

By the time the second conference took place at Karlsruhe and Baden-Baden from 14 to 16 October 1974, open conflict had broken out between the federal government and the West German court.[63] Since the verdict on the Basic Treaty in the summer of 1973, the relationship between the social-liberal coalition and the court had been extremely difficult. When Benda asked again for assistance in the organization of the conference, the Ministry of Justice reacted without much enthusiasm. The government had little appetite for foreign constitutional judges adding to their troubles with their own constitutional court. The conference themes by now reflected the recent clashes over the Basic Treaty. Delegates discussed three topics: the constitutional interpretation of legislation, the pathways to a judicial evaluation of current legislation, and the evaluation of international treaties by constitutional courts.[64] In essence, the conference asked what role courts should play in governing states in domestic and international affairs.

The conference was well attended given this direct reflection of Cold War legal politics in the proceedings and the larger issue of the role of courts for national governance. Next to the West German, Italian and Yugoslavian delegations, judges and legal experts from Austria, France, Romania, Switzerland, Luxembourg, Turkey, Greece, Ireland and the European Court of Justice at Luxembourg joined as delegates. Observers from Denmark, the Netherlands, Norway, the Vatican and the United Kingdom also attended the sessions in Baden-Baden. The West German delegates had reserved the right to provide the introductory lecture on the theme of international treaties.[65] The judges anticipated further cases in relation to the treaties with the Soviet Union and Poland and wanted to get their message out to an international audience to strengthen their hand against the Bonn government.[66]

The West German judges tried to turn the meeting into an endorsement of their own politics of law, and the West German government tried as best it could to counter this move. When Federal President Walter Scheel welcomed the delegations to Karlsruhe on 14 October 1974, he looked to give the conference a different emphasis. Courts from Eastern and Western Europe, he explained, should meet and think about shared problems, pointing specifically to shifts in state–citizen relations and the ability and legal pathways for citizens to appeal to constitutional courts that were tasked with guaranteeing the legal security of Europeans. Scheel thus focused on the role of courts in strengthening citizens' rights, a demand that had underpinned many social protests since the 1960s across Europe and the world. He said no word about the theme of treaty evaluation. This was no surprise. Scheel had, after all, already been at loggerheads with the constitutional judges only a few months earlier during the Basic Treaty trial when he was still foreign minister. The wounds were too fresh.[67]

The judges, however, were determined to make their views heard. When they opened proceedings, the West German judges Helmut Simon (1922–2013) and Hans-Justus Rinck (1918–1995) pushed back at Scheel's diversion from the conference agenda in their speeches and explicitly focused on the treaty issue.[68] In a following set of remarks, Judge Hans Georg Rupp (1907–1989) then went to the heart of controversies surrounding the constitutional court. First, he pointed out that ideas of sovereignty, which traditionally had separated national from international law, had declined. While Anglo-Saxon jurisprudence had allowed for some impact of international law on 'the law of the land' since the eighteenth century, he explained that German jurisprudence had only begun to discuss this issue in the interwar period.[69] Rupp argued that the participants lived in revolutionary times. The mid-century's 'overemphasis of national sovereignty has today given way to a tendency in domestic legal orders that is generally *völkerrechtsfreundlich* (sympathetic towards international law) and aimed at the further integration of the community of states'.[70] Rupp thus acknowledged the impact of international rights norms on national legal systems, a link that anti-colonial leaders had promoted against Western resistance since the end of the Second World War.

National jurisprudence, Rupp maintained, had to account for international law's ever-growing influence in domestic legal affairs. The same applied to international treaties. Given the increased weight of international law, Rupp rhetorically asked participants how clashes between constitutional law and treaty conventions could be avoided.[71] He had of course already arrived at a conclusion: only constitutional courts were fit to resolve legal conflicts arising from international treaties for domestic legal systems. In view of recent events, legal conflicts between national law and international treaties, he insisted, could only be effectively avoided if the courts were given the opportunity for judicial scrutiny before the ratification of treaties. His government in recent months had denied exactly such a process. Achieving such a change in procedure was vital for the authority of courts. This issue had become even more important since the UN convention on treaty law from 1969 had stipulated that states could not retreat from treaties after ratification even if they later were deemed in violation of domestic law. All this allowed Rupp to come to the central question of whether courts would have the legal authority to test treaties against the constitution. The West Germans were looking for reaffirmation from their colleagues. The Austrian constitution, in Article 140a, granted the constitutional court the right to evaluate treaties. Karlsruhe had only established such a view through its institutional practice, beginning with the verdicts on Western integration in the 1950s.[72] In the verdict on the General Treaty, signed on 26 May 1952 to organize the return of sovereignty to West Germans and the relation between the three Western Allies and the Bonn government, the court had first assumed such jurisdiction in disputes over international treaties.[73]

Following Rupp's speech, Benda continued with the heavy focus on current West German legal politics. He tried to reinforce the political function of constitutional courts. To strengthen this self-image of constitutional jurisprudence, he suggested a debate on the very purpose of constitutions as the guiding theme for the next meeting. And Benda, the West German constitutional court's controversial president, certainly did not shy away from an open discussion of politics of law, choosing instead to address recent accusations against constitutional judges candidly. West German media and members of the government had criticized the fact that the increased importance of law for policy making would enable high court judges to build *Richterstaaten* (judges' states). Rather than trying to prove that this was not the case, Benda encouraged his colleagues to explore the political potential of constitutional jurisprudence 'to the fullest' in an open provocation to the present federal president.[74] Legal scholars and judges should claim their key role in connecting domestic legal norms and international law and embrace their political role. This was a call that the European Court of Justice (ECJ) judges would take up in the coming years when they developed powerful new doctrines with the help of national courts and turned their court into an influential supranational actor.[75]

While Benda continued the political skirmishes with the government over the court's constitutional powers, the critical responses of many of their peers showed the limits of the West German constitutional judges' campaign to justify their aggressive rhetoric in the Basic Treaty verdict.[76] Commentators within the FRG attacked the many inconsistencies in the court's discussion of German sovereignty and severely criticized what many observers viewed as an untimely return to outdated modes of legal thinking.[77] *Der Spiegel* provocatively asked Benda in an interview: 'Mr. Benda, does the constitutional court plan to take power in Bonn?'[78] After Benda's open provocation of the government at the conference of European courts in 1974, some of Benda's colleagues saw him overstepping the lines of judicial restraint in highly politicized cases such as German-German legal relations. In dissenting votes, *Der Spiegel* argued, Benda was accused of '*Amtsammaßung* (unlawful assumption of public authority)' by some of his peers.[79] When such public pressure mounted on Benda to change course, the court finally had to acknowledge that the international debate on state sovereignty and self-determination had moved on. Those judges at Karlsruhe who had been instrumental in the Basic Treaty case had to realize that they could not reset the parameters of German-German legal conflicts on their own any longer. They had to accept the breakdown of expansive frameworks of German sovereignty in their jurisprudence. Time was of the essence as the Helsinki Accords negotiations demanded the recognition of the territorial integrity of European states, something current West German high court jurisprudence did not yet adhere to.

The opportunity for the judges to change course and rein in their own controversial rhetoric in the Basic Treaty verdict came in the summer of 1975. When a group of claimants filed cases concerning citizenship and property rights related to their expulsion from former Eastern territories in 1945, the court dismissed all of their claims on 7 July 1975.[80] With the imminent signature of the Helsinki Accords on 1 August 1975, the court could no longer be seen to question the territorial integrity of sovereign states and UN members. This would have openly contradicted the very basis of the new security architecture for Europe. The judges therefore acknowledged that the Allies had agreed in 1945 that former German Eastern territories should become parts of Poland and the Soviet Union. While they stressed the option that borders might be redrawn one day in peace treaty negotiations, the aggressive doctrinal rhetoric of state identity between the German Reich and FRG completely vanished in favour of a historical description of the immediate postwar agreements between the Allies.[81] The territorial realities created with these agreements might change again in the future, the court maintained, but they could only be altered if all people living in these territories were to opt for a shift in borders based on their right of self-determination.[82]

Unfortunately, the court's retreat from the much more controversial rhetoric of the Basic Treaty verdict of 1973 went almost unnoticed in public debates. The 1975 verdict focused on people and their rights. The omission of a discussion of German sovereignty in the 1975 ruling thus resulted in right-wing conservatives constantly referencing the 1973 verdict. They now mobilized for a return of the sovereignty framework of the German Reich in its borders of 1937, deploying selective references to the constitutional court ruling to bolster the legitimacy of their claims. The court's decision to play politics openly in the early 1970s radicalized legal debates for decades to come and is still used by so-called *Reichsbürger* ('citizens of the Reich') who claim that the Reich still legally exists today.[83]

East German Fact-Finding Missions

While West German high court judges, legal scholars and the general public were embroiled in conflicts over West German legal frameworks of sovereignty and the institutional reach of high courts, East German legal scholars and ministerial officials used the new opportunities for international recognition to decisively sever all ties to German legal tradition and move to socialist law. They joined the wave of constitutional reform that resulted in the proclamation of new socialist constitutions across the Eastern bloc, including a new GDR constitution that developed between 1968 and 1974, and peaked with the new Soviet constitution of 1977. The conflicts over the drafting of the human rights covenants and their implementation, the ideological clashes over a new international economic order based on human rights claims, and the growing international integration of markets forced socialist legal experts to engage in more intense legal exchanges to cope with these new challenges. Yet this endeavour lacked sufficient institutional underpinnings. While decolonization dominated UN politics into the 1970s, the socialist bloc had still not managed to build counter-networks to develop socialist international law work against the international legal venues set up by Western powers until 1945 and after.

East German legal experts realized that they lacked basic knowledge about the work of their colleagues across the socialist bloc. For too long, socialist states had failed to develop their own legal networks and international bodies beyond shared international rights propaganda. Getting inspiration from abroad was crucial for several reasons. GDR scholars had only begun to move into transnational socialist legal debates by the mid-1960s. It was only then that the GDR legal sector had developed sufficient new academic structures and expertise in international law.[84] East German scholars now sporadically attended international conferences of Eastern bloc states. By that point, their Hungarian colleagues were already a step further. In December 1964, the Law Faculty of the University of Szeged had invited representatives from all socialist bloc states for a first international scholarly conference. The meeting heralded the new role of law as the guiding source for transnational governance across the socialist world. At the meeting, Imre Szabó, an expert in constitutional law and leading socialist mind on human rights, lectured on the theme 'The Position of the Socialist Constitution within the Legal System'.[85] Hungarian legal scholars were already thinking about the role of law under socialism in a much more complex way than their East German colleagues, and the GDR delegation was impressed by these attempts to use 'international socialist legal science' to capture the social development towards a socialist people's state and its consequences for constitutional law and international cooperation.[86]

Of particular note to the GDR delegation were debates at this conference that returned to the question of how law could become an active transformative force under socialism. The discussions during the conference panel on constitutionalism highlighted the importance of including the public in the drafting of new laws. Public endorsement for the codification of new constitutional law would bolster the power of ruling parties. Yet it was not at all clear how public support could be won. The Soviet Union had practised rights talk as a way to include the population in codification drives since the 1930s.[87] The PRC had pushed the boundaries of disseminating law even further in the 1950s with mass campaigns for popular legal education.[88] Yet dissident activism using constitutional law had alerted the Soviet authorities to the dangers of law propaganda at home since the early 1960s.[89] It was therefore important to instil the 'correct' legal consciousness into citizens. Economic integration was the second big theme at the conference. The question of economic organization, formerly a domain of ministries of the economy, was now seen as part of debates on constitutional law. The Soviet delegates insisted that socialist legal scholars could no longer dispute the existence of economic law as a separate branch of law making. All this pointed to the complex issue of incorporating the state's role in commanding the economy and society into constitutional law.[90] These two themes would structure the GDR's work to frame a new kind of socialist constitutionalism in the rhetoric of the 'unity of social and economic policy' once Erich Honecker (1912–1994) took over the reins from Walter Ulbricht in 1971.

These early meetings with socialist peers did not yield many concrete results as long as the GDR legal sphere remained embroiled in intense conflicts with the FRG over Ostpolitik. One notable exception was the constitution draft debate that the SED staged in spring 1968.[91] In 1969, exasperated with what it felt to be too much academic discussion and too little practical action, the Ministry of Justice finally took away the coordination of international legal exchanges from academic institutions. The drive towards internationalization in the legal sphere, the ministry argued, called for immediate cooperation with the Ministry for Foreign Affairs. Relations with foreign states, socialist or not, had to be organized through a uniform ministerial legal policy. Legal scholars had mainly focused on learning about international legal developments in the 1960s. The Ministry of Justice now reversed course and demanded proactive popularization of the GDR's achievements in building socialist legality. Simply adapting abstract legal norms and policies developed in other Eastern bloc states without sufficient information about the context in which these norms had been developed seemed an insufficient basis for the internationalization of the GDR's legal field. To cope with the new pressures of implementing international law norms at home, the Ministry of Justice now decided that regular annual work should include exchanges with study groups from socialist brethren states.[92] The ministerial legal experts wanted everyone to focus on popularizing and propagating the socialist legal system's potential to prevent crime and eventually overcome criminality altogether and organize socialist social and economic life more efficiently.[93] Law thus assumed an evermore important role in proving the ideological superiority of socialism against the FRG, not just in the field of law and criminality, but also for the economy and the individual citizen.

Socialist legal reform efforts translated into transnational legal networks in the 1970s. International law conferences provided welcome spaces and opportunities for socialist delegations to plan their future cooperation. Conversations between GDR legal experts and their peers from other Eastern bloc states at the Fourth UN Congress on Crime Prevention in Kyoto in 1970 resulted in the planning of a European regional conference of socialist experts. Party leaderships realized that socialist countries needed to do more than contribute to international legal debates at the UN and elsewhere. The new goal was to build an alternative international legal universe underpinned by independent socialist expert networks. The Hungarian government again paved the way forward. The Ministry of Justice suggested a first meeting in Budapest to devise uniform legal strategies to be deployed at the UN and in the international arena.[94] For long enough, the socialist bloc had ignored the full potential of socialist legality as a counter-model to Western ideas of international law.

This new trans-socialist project made it necessary to build new institutional nodes. In autumn 1971, the head of the revision commission of the College of Lawyers, Gerhard Häusler (1928–2012), asked permission from the Ministry of Justice to engage in discussions about a new transnational socialist lawyers' association. The Bulgarian and Soviet delegations had introduced this idea at the previous meeting of the College of Lawyers in Sofia. The proposed new international organization should help to centralize and unify legal policies and practice across the socialist bloc. The main purpose was the creation of a 'political counterweight against the already existing union of lawyers of capitalist states'.[95] The Bulgarians suggested building an International House to give the new organization a home and suggested Crimea as a suitable location. This new headquarters for socialist lawyers should ease the future exchange of new national rules and regulations.[96]

After the establishment of scholarly and lawyers' association networks, socialist ministries of justice took over the leadership in developing trans-socialist networks. The promise of active involvement of citizens in socialist legal systems had to be translated into legal realities.[97] This was government work. When the ministers of justice of socialist bloc countries met in Moscow in November 1973, the conference focused on measures to implement legal education of citizens to observe socialist law, which put the question of effective law propaganda at the heart of exchanges.[98] In

1975, socialist ministers of justice directed their propaganda departments to meet again in Budapest. Legal experts now explored different modes of legal education to put theory into practice. These meetings and ministerial exchanges marked the beginning of transnational socialist ministerial cooperation, which ensured regular meetings in an increasingly institutionalized setting.[99]

Once socialist ministries of justice were meeting regularly to discuss concrete policy measures, it did not take long for high courts to also exchange knowledge and build networks. In May 1973, the president of the GDR High Court Heinrich Toeplitz, his deputy Walter Ziegler (1912–1977), the SED liaison officer for the court at the SED central committee Erich Hänsel, and the judges Werner Strasberg and Ursula Böhm visited Moscow on a fact-finding mission. East German high court judges wanted to make sure that they remained close to the Soviet model in organizing their court system at home, despite going their own way in UN politics of law. To explore Soviet high court practice, the East Germans' list of topics to discuss with the president of the Soviet High Court Leo Smirnov (1912–1986), the Minister of Justice Vladimir Terebilov (1916–2004) and other colleagues included central questions such as the position of courts in the legal system, the active role of citizens in criminal and civil law cases, the efficiency of courts and their cooperation with local governmental office, and the potential of so-called comradeship courts.[100] Toeplitz seized the opportunity to suggest a regular exchange between the two high courts at the end of the trip.[101] After the GDR had lost its privileged position in foreign policy making with the Soviet Union after the conclusion of Ostpolitik, Toeplitz hoped to build a new special relationship in the legal field.[102]

Trying to move beyond the intense focus on German-German legal politics of the last decade, GDR legal scholars joined more and more international exchanges after 1973.[103] Conferences at the Academy for International Law in The Hague became a prime venue for the acquisition of relevant scholarly material and exchanges with foreign colleagues. In 1975, Karl Döblitz, a party member of the Babelsberg Academy for State and Legal Sciences, met with the Soviet keynote speaker Grigory Tunkin (1906–1993) at the 46th Session of the Hague Academy for International Law and took the opportunity to ask him burning questions about the relevance of international law for socialist legality at home. Tunkin had been a leading legal scholar of the Soviet Union for decades. He had headed the international law section of the Moscow Law Institute between 1946 and 1965 and the legal department of the Soviet Foreign Ministry from 1957 to 1966. Tunkin also was a long-standing member of the UN's International

Law Commission over which he had presided in 1961. Since 1970, he had argued for a new quality in the linkage of national and international law and contended that all states that had voted in favour of the declaration on principles of international law in 1970 were now bound by international legal norms.

The GDR had pledged support for many UN conventions and rights norms in its quest for international recognition. Yet if and how these norms should be translated into legal affairs at home remained a problematic issue. Tunkin could not say for certain how this should happen when Döblitz pressed him for definitive answers. East German scholars such as Döblitz still erred on the side of caution and followed the standard scholarly literature that favoured the traditional opinion of a clear separation of domestic and international legal spheres. In contrast, Tunkin supported a progressive position on the reach and legal quality of international law.[104] Döblitz took this potential shift in international affairs very seriously. Tunkin suggested that a turn towards a link between international law and domestic legal spheres would soon transform UN legal norms into binding law for national judiciaries. He saw the human rights covenants as prime examples of this development. The director of the UN's Human Rights Division at Geneva, Marc Schreiber (b. 1915), called on the Hague conference delegates to remember that the signature of human rights conventions broke down all former safeguards of sovereignty for states joining these treaties, at least in theory.[105]

On his return to the GDR from The Hague and his meeting with Tunkin in 1975, Döblitz reported to his superiors that the international law landscape might be on the brink of a momentous transformation. Tunkin had suggested that there were no longer any internal affairs of states when it came to human rights since the ratification of the Helsinki Accords. The UN wanted to implement a direct linkage of international and national legal norms when the human rights covenants' ratification period ended in 1976. Despite making a forceful argument, Döblitz nonetheless conceded in the report to his party superiors that only time could tell how states would implement these new norms. Individual national routes to the implementation of UN rights norms seemed the most likely scenario.[106] GDR legal experts and their superiors could live with such an approach as it allowed them to interpret human rights norms based on their understanding of socialist legality in the wider developing cosmos of socialist transnational legal work. Yet they also realized that they could not go back easily on their pledges to adopt international rights norms. Winning the global fight over the definition and interpretation of rights for the socialist bloc had become even more important.

The More Legitimate State

The GDR's future law propaganda activities, as a 1970 SED party directive had already outlined, were to become global. It was an ambitious goal that went beyond the Third World rights campaigns of the last decade, traced in Chapter 3. East German legal work moved on from a focus on legitimizing East German statehood to the promotion of a fully-fledged alternative rights universe. To make this case to international audiences, the GDR remained focused on UN rights work. Propagating a socialist path to realize international human rights norms in a socialist legal system became the new priority after the GDR's UN accession in 1973. The SED leadership sensed that their law propaganda work still gave them an advantage over their West German competitors who were still stuck in controversies over the relationship between *Staatsrecht* and international law.

In order to sustain recent successes in attracting international audiences to East German legal arguments, the Ministry of Justice and the Ministry for Foreign Affairs had to cooperate better. If they did not, there was a danger of mixed messages between diplomats and their ministry, something the Ministry of Justice wanted to avoid. It was a disguised claim to more political influence. If the Ministry for Foreign Affairs had set the agenda for the Third World and UN law campaigns since the mid-1960s, the Ministry of Justice now demanded control over legal politics at home and abroad. Responsibility for organizing international legal aid and expert relations shifted to Department 2 of the Ministry of Justice. Between 1968 and 1974, the pressure to implement new socialist legal codes and constitutional norms resulted in more political influence of the Ministry of Justice.[107] To showcase the new socialist legal system to the world, East German ministerial experts reasoned, the annual UN Yearbook and the UN Yearbook for Human Rights should be the main targets of GDR legal experts. These central UN publications represented the prime vehicle to reach an international and West German audience at the same time.

The West German government, meanwhile, was ill-prepared to respond to the GDR's public relations battle centring on the UN. There was little governmental funding to propagate the UN's mission within the FRG, and next to none for international activities. This led the head of the German Association for the United Nations, Annemarie Renger (1919–2008), to complain in a letter to Chancellor Brandt in June 1970. The budget for 1971, Renger declared, would make it difficult for the association to keep supporting the government's 'active foreign policy'.[108] Renger had experience with the GDR's UN tactics and growing success. As president of the West German UN association, she tried to fend off East German attempts to gain recognition for GDR sovereignty within the WFUNA in 1967.[109] In response, Foreign Minister Scheel assured Renger that the Foreign Office fully supported her association and its goals. Scheel seconded Renger's demand for a funding increase, yet the new budget, which rose from 156,000 DM in 1970 to 200,000 DM in 1971, was still utterly insufficient to cover the growing range of activities that the UN association was supposed to organize in the coming decade. Current funding, Scheel told Brandt on behalf of Renger, merely allowed the association to exist, but prevented any meaningful public engagement to support the government's agenda of increased participation in international organizations in the coming years.[110]

Funding, moreover, was not the only problem. The long-term cause of the association – to keep their East German counterpart out of WFUNA – had worn out its members. Internally, the West German UN association was deeply divided. Instead of closing ranks against the GDR, association members were arguing over what their main purpose and agenda should be during the high tide of Ostpolitik. After the GDR's human rights league had gained entrance to WFUNA in 1967, many within the West German association advocated for a new focus for their group.[111] This internal rift over the association's purpose cost Renger her leadership position and Karl-Hans Kern (1932–2014) replaced her in December 1971.[112] Renger feared that the new leadership would neglect any other functions of the association apart from development aid work. She worried that the competition between the two German UN leagues within the UN would suffer under such a reorientation of the association.

Kern, however, did not neglect German-German legal politics after he took office. He understood that the tensions surrounding Ostpolitik and the UN's withdrawal from Berlin signalled difficulties for his organization and he called on Brandt to support the expansion of German-speaking staff at the UN Information Office in Geneva. Such new personnel could then be used to influence West German public opinion as well. UN publications in German supporting West German legal positions were needed to showcase compliance with international legal norms at home. The East Berlin government had focused on the production of English-language information materials to reach international audiences since the mid-1960s. By 1971, there was therefore still a relative dearth of German-language information materials on the UN, its sub-organizations and its general mission circulating in both German publics. The West German association thought they had discovered an aspect of UN rights work that the GDR paid less attention to. The existing East German advantage within English-speaking publics, Kern suggested, should not be allowed in a German language context.[113] While the GDR government mainly targeted foreign audiences, the West German work should address German-speaking audiences and potentially undermine the SED leadership at home.

Just as Kern was making preparations to engage with SED human rights activism within German publics, the GDR Committee for Human Rights returned to the issue of West German anti-communism and neo-Nazism. The renewed East German campaign was driven by the upsurge of neo-Nazism, embodied in the Nationaldemokratische Partei Deutschlands (NPD, National Democratic Party of Germany)'s state-level electoral successes in the late 1960s. Citing UN resolutions 2545 (XXIV) and 2583 (XXIV), which condemned Nazism and racial intolerance, the GDR committee returned to old arguments. It had been their state that had provided a home for all anti-fascist fighters of the wartime resistance and had subsequently endorsed a socialist order that guaranteed self-determination. The FRG, conversely, was accused of ignoring the prosecution of Nazi criminals. There had been an outcry within and beyond the FRG after it had transpired that parliament had passed a law in 1968 that declared the prosecution period for the majority of crimes committed during the Third Reich as past.[114] The Bonn government, the East German activists now argued, failed to implement international legal norms that mandated fighting any crimes against humanity. The GDR human rights league stated that 'to grant democratic rights and liberties to old and new Nazis as is happening in the FRG is incompatible with the agreements of the anti-Hitler coalition and with the Universal Declaration of Human Rights and the UN resolutions against Nazism'.[115] To fight neo-Nazism effectively, the GDR committee thus called for the implementation of international legal norms into West German criminal law, something the GDR government had done in the new Criminal Code of 1968: international conventions were to be implemented directly into national law making as 'Nazism, neo-Nazism and racial intolerance are not an intra-state affair'.[116]

This attack on West German legality tied into the GDR league's preparations for the UN's International Year against Racism and Racial Discrimination in 1972. The year's theme gave GDR human rights activists the opportunity to reiterate their commitment to anti-apartheid policies and solidarity with Angela Davis, the famous African-American activist with ties to the US communist party and the Black Panther movement. Davis in turn endorsed the GDR government. The East Berlin government, she advocated, dealt more effectively with the issue of racism than the FRG. Hoping to forge more new alliances of this kind during this year, the GDR human rights league initiated a joint publication project that brought together Heinrich Toeplitz, the president of the GDR High Court, Claude Lightfoot, politburo member of the Communist Party of the United States, a delegate of the ANC from South Africa and students from Third World countries in Asia and Africa, Bernhard Graefrath in his function as presidium member of the GDR human rights league and the lawyer Friedrich Wolff.[117] Together, they prepared a new propaganda campaign in three languages – English, French and German – titled 'Free From Racism – How the GDR Realized Human Rights and Outlawed Discrimination'. This campaign based its central arguments on constitutional law and legal reform currently ongoing in East Germany. After East German UN membership had been won in 1973, the diplomatic ascendency of the GDR to the international arena, as Deputy Foreign Minister Oskar Fischer (1923–2020) put it, meant 'the reaching of a strategic goal of the socialist state community for which it had struggled for 24 years'.[118] With this success, Fischer explained, all GDR ministries should remember that they had a duty to contribute information and ideas to a new international rights strategy. Rather than meeting 'imperialist aggression', the goal now was to develop an 'aggressive foreign policy initiative' to implement their own socialist positions in international legal affairs.

Such projects allowed the GDR to confidently enter negotiations on the Helsinki framework, which were underway from 1973 onwards.[119] Fischer declared that one of the next strategic goals of GDR foreign policy would be to establish a system of collective security in Europe and Asia that was framed in the rhetoric of international law. He saw a continuation of the GDR's Third World strategy as the most promising avenue to rally support for important UN resolutions that concerned the GDR directly. In this process, the fast training of qualified GDR cadres to fill positions at the UN would have the highest priority. Adequate language training and diplomatic expertise were still lagging behind the efforts of other socialist and non-socialist states. Only through a fast learning curve, Fischer urged his colleagues, could the GDR live up to the challenges of entering international bodies in all fields of policy. As a first step towards streamlined coordination, Fischer instituted a higher frequency of meetings of all deputy ministers. So far, only one annual meeting had brought deputy ministers together to plan international legal work.[120]

After a decade of GDR international rights propaganda, East German ministries now had to show concretely that the GDR was the more legitimate state and that it would act on its promises. Once it had joined the UN, the Ministry for Foreign Affairs urgently needed to decide which UN conventions, treaties and multilateral agreements the GDR actually ought to join. And in order to comply with UN regulations, domestic legislation needed to be altered quickly where necessary. Deputy Foreign Minister Ewald Moldt (1927–2019) called for a comprehensive engagement and regular ministerial and central committee reports on the development of GDR–UN relations. The SED leadership wanted to put forward for service within the UN administration as soon as possible East German diplomats who could propagate this legal implementation of international law.

Yet internal rivalries over strategy and agenda setting persisted, similar to earlier clashes traced in Chapters 1 and 2. While the Ministry for Foreign Affairs had taken the lead in the rights campaign for GDR sovereignty, the Ministry of Justice claimed greater expertise now that UN membership had been won. Hans Ranke, State Secretary in the Ministry of Justice, lamented problems in the division of labour between ministries in 1973. His ministry had prepared the last UN report on the human rights covenant on civil and political rights. With UN membership, Ranke anticipated that he would be called on to compile a report on the GDR's compliance with the human rights covenant on social and economic rights as well. Yet this part of the human rights conventions fell to other ministries. Ranke demanded the centralization of UN work.[121] To avoid being pressed for time in reporting to the Foreign Minister or indeed the UN Secretary-General on legal compliance of the GDR government with international law, the ministry had to build its own material depository and reorganize work between departments to keep up with international developments.[122]

The long and exhausting uphill battle for UN membership had taught the SED foreign policy experts how important the control of administrative committees within the UN was. Influencing the UN bureaucracy from within became even more important with the US-led counter-offensive in the human rights field in the late 1970s.[123] After the civil rights legislation had passed the US Senate and House of Representatives in 1965, the US administration was free to advance human rights norms internationally without constant pushback on racial segregation at home. In 1974, Moldt singled out this new US rights activism as 'adverse to détente'. In other words, he sensed that the US administration had found a potent new cause to regain the offensive in the Cold War propaganda battle after years of being on the defensive over racial segregation and the Vietnam War.[124] State-sponsored socialist visions of human rights needed to be protected against this new threat of US advances into the socialist bloc. The West German UN representatives had already indicated that they were going to drop their long-held reservations to put human rights violations in the GDR before the UN. Before 1973, West German diplomats thought such a move too risky as it might have accidently elevated the GDR's international standing. Now that East German sovereignty had been recognized by the Bonn government, West German diplomats were free to adopt a more aggressive human rights rhetoric and strategy to attack the GDR's international law propaganda.

With the Helsinki negotiations moving towards the establishment of a treaty framework, Moldt saw the possible dangers of a 'Helsinki effect' on the internal stability of SED rule early on. Daniel C. Thomas has argued that the Helsinki Accords provided a common platform between East and West around which opposition forces could form and mobilize across Eastern Europe.[125] In the GDR, as Moldt's reaction shows, the government wanted to pre-empt such an effect by continuing to occupy the human rights discourse through a state-mandated interpretation of human rights. In addition, the self-absorbed nature of West German legal debates on sovereignty after the West German constitutional court's Basic Treaty verdict still bought the SED time. On 16 January 1974, in a meeting of all GDR ministries and mass organizations, Moldt encouraged his fellow deputy ministers to maintain a strong focus and engagement with international politics of law. Foreign Minister Winzer, intending to use the international stage provided by UN membership to the full, made sure to call on the Minister of Justice Hans-Joachim Heusinger (1925–2019) to send his deputy to this meeting in an effort to coordinate ever-closer cooperation between GDR diplomats and legal experts and to end the turf war between their ministries.[126]

After the signature of the Helsinki Accords in 1975, the pressure on national governments to address their compliance with international legal norms increased. In 1977, Peter Alfons Steiniger, who had been a long-term advocate of international law within GDR legal scholarship, emphasized that the 'politico-moral weight' of UN debates and conventions had increased once more.[127] As president of the German League for the United Nations, he had witnessed first-hand the effect of moral rights claims. While the UN was no 'world law maker' and states still decided in full sovereignty over their adherence to conventions, the moral pressure to subscribe to human rights norms in particular stemmed, as he argued, from 'the strength of state and social forces' supporting such legal norms.[128] Where Steiniger's initial work in the 1960s had focused on apartheid and socialist human rights campaigns, he now moved on to focus on disarmament.[129] In this he followed the Soviet lead. In 1977, Soviet Foreign Minister Andrej Gromyko (1909–1989) called disarmament a moral duty. The conflicts over mid-range nuclear missiles in Europe also gained speed as a rights issue at this time. The legal value of UN conventions, Steiniger argued in this context, was encapsulated in the guiding nature of UN declarations for bilateral treaties between sovereign states. The adherence to such UN pledges determined the legality of bilateral treaties in the eyes of the international community.

This shift, Steiniger suggested, meant that not only did UN norms reflect on domestic legal systems, but they now also shaped international treaties between states in crucial ways. In essence, Steiniger argued that states could no longer ignore international law when it conflicted with their national interests because the UN's 'basic principles had the character of binding law'.[130] Steiniger tied this development back to the conventions on treaties, which had figured prominently in the GDR's striving for sovereignty in the 1960s. Since the proclamation of this convention in 1969, Article 53 of the convention rendered treaties that conflicted with valid national or international law illegal. In conjunction with Article 103 of the UN Charter, which stipulated the primacy of the convention over other forms of international law, international legality and politics between states had been fundamentally reshaped. Steiniger's views on the UN Charter might have seemed theoretical at first, but they actually marked a reversal of socialist perspectives on the UN. In the 1950s and 1960s, the GDR government had seen itself embroiled in an uphill battle to secure self-determination and sovereignty together with decolonized states. In this process, the socialist bloc had often attacked the UN Charter and procedural rules governing UN affairs as serving 'Western imperialism'. Now, with the heightened influence of socialist states in the UN, Steiniger conversely hailed the proclamation of the charter as a 'fundamental and seismic shift in the international legal order of the contemporary world'.[131]

With the implementation of the Helsinki framework, GDR rights activism moved on from human rights to a focus on territorial integrity. At a time when the new US president Jimmy Carter (b. 1924) spearheaded an initiative to institute the office of a UN Human Rights High Commissioner, human rights increasingly began to disappear from socialist narratives of international law.[132] Leading East German international law scholars, such as Steiniger, now built new chronologies that explained the UN's importance within this revised understanding of the international legal world with territorial integrity at their heart. Not entirely surprising, this new official narrative now began in the late 1960s at the time when the GDR had actively joined UN debates. From the convention on treaties, Steiniger drew a line to the Declaration on Principles of International Law concerning Friendly Relations and Co-operation among States in accordance with the Charter of the United Nations adopted on 24 October 1970. It was this declaration, Steiniger posited, that turned the tables within the UN because it reflected the changed balance of power within the institution after decolonization. Declaring the convention on friendly relations 'unalienable law', Steiniger ended his revised narrative of international law's development with the implementation of a legal definition of aggression in 1974 'after half a century of Soviet advocacy'.[133] This socialist narrative, streamlined as it may have been, however, had a hollow ring to many East Germans in light of the Soviet interventions in East Germany in 1953, Hungary in 1956 and Czechoslovakia in 1968.

Steiniger's new chronology of international law reflected the appreciation of socialist governments for international law in the 1970s when it served their efforts to solidify and protect their rule. For Steiniger, the recent decision to further non-violent measures of international diplomacy was particularly important. GDR legal scholars had endorsed the unfolding of a functioning international legal system since the so-called 'principle declaration' – the convention of friendly relations – in 1970. All these legal advances aided a more effective management of international conflicts. The renewed Cold War tensions over nuclear armament now fully took over the GDR's international law politics. While the Stockholm Peace Appeal of 1950 had not had enough moral legitimacy to prevent the nuclear arms race, Steiniger argued, it was the success of the socialist bloc's advocacy for peace that had prevented the use of atomic weapons since Hiroshima and Nagasaki. He thus claimed moral supremacy for socialist states in preserving 'world peace'. This was a victory for the politics of international law driven by socialist legal experts, one made possible, he claimed, by their advocacy for friendly relations between states and the outlawing of aggression.[134] By the late 1970s, as Steiniger's intervention showed, adherence to international law and human rights norms had become essential for states to make moral claims to ideological supremacy.

Conclusion: Separated Legal Identities and the Impact of International Law

If the conclusion of Ostpolitik and the accession of both German states to full UN membership in 1973 had ended the postwar battle over a shared German legal heritage, the Helsinki Accords of 1975 destroyed West German legal foundations rooted in mid-century ideas of sovereignty. European legal politics were now anchored in the acceptance of the territorial integrity of all existing states.[135] This was in some ways an acceptance of the universality principle Thant had fought so hard to implement during his tenure as UN Secretary-General, discussed in Chapter 3. With their battle over the correct ideological interpretation and usage of German legal heritage ended, East and West German legal scholars, high court judges, policy makers, NGOs and ministerial officials turned to emerging European and international legal networks. In both East and West Germany, legal experts and state-sponsored activists felt they had to legitimize their state's domestic rights universe by proving compliance to international law norms and the human rights covenants. Across both Cold War blocs, legal experts thus accepted that international rights norms had to have an impact on domestic legal universes and treaty law between states in the 1970s.

While many West German jurists grappled with the diminished legitimacy of legal frameworks rooted in the German Reich's sovereignty set up in the 1950s, East German legal experts confidently engaged in the transnational socialist project of building an international counter-universe of law. These new socialist legal networks enabled knowledge exchange and the coordination of the development of socialist legality beyond national borders. The 1970s saw socialist legal scholars, lawyers, judges and government officials move beyond their national focus and debate the potential avenues to promote a socialist version of international law that could rival the established modes of the international legal system.

These internationalization drives of Eastern and Western bloc networks accelerated the separation of domestic legal cultures in the two German states. By the mid-1970s, West German constitutional judges had to accept that their own legal frameworks had to change. European economic integration within the European Economic Community (EEC), the growing importance of the European Court of Human Rights and the need to respond to GDR rights initiatives in the international arena forced West German judges and legal scholars out of their comfort zone. The de-facto separation of the two German legal spheres, which the constitutional court eventually had to acknowledge in 1975, posed new questions and demanded answers. These answers were formulated within revised legal mental maps of two German states that, as the next chapter shows, were now seen much more as part of their respective ideological alliances rather than tied to each other through the heritage of German law.

Notes

1. UN ARMS, S-0904-0067-23. Wolf Biermann made a mockery of the Rising Man one year later on his concert tour to the FRG. This ended in his forced emigration from the GDR as he was denied re-entry at the end of his tour, showing the popularity and political significance of Cremer's statue within the GDR.
2. UN ARMS, S-0904-0067-23.
3. UN ARMS, S-0904-0015-02.
4. Bange and Neidhardt, *Helsinki 1975 and the Transformation of Europe*; Morgan, *The Final Act*.
5. The political, cultural and economic transformation of the 1960s began to show in legal confrontations of the 1970s as well. See: Ferguson et al., *The Shock of the Global*; Brown, *West Germany and the Global Sixties*; Connery, 'The World Sixties'; Gorsuch and Koenker, *The Socialist Sixties*; Pula, *Globalisation Under and After Socialism*.
6. For the linkage of national sovereignty and international law, see: Getachew, *Worldmaking after Empire*, 71–107.

7. Recent interventions have highlighted the competition between different human rights universalisms rather than an evolutionary development leading to a 'breakthrough' in the postwar era. See: Burke, Duranti and Moses, 'Introduction: Human Rights, Empire, and After'; Betts, 'Socialism, Solidarity and Decolonization'. See also note 90 in the Introduction to this volume.
8. Next to the inter-American and European frameworks of human rights conventions and courts, African states also moved to a regional convention by the late 1970s. While Western-centric narratives of 'globalization' from the 1970s onwards are well established, the Eastern bloc and non-aligned states also continued to engage with global markets, which made more legal international regulatory work necessary. See: Getachew, *Worldmaking after Empire*, 142–75; Bockman, 'Socialist Globalization against Capitalist Neocolonialism'; Pula, *Globalisation Under and After Socialism*. See also: Sanchez-Sibony, *Red Globalization*.
9. For the fundamental social, cultural, political and economic transitions of the 1970s, see: Ferguson et al., *The Shock of the Global*. For the German context: Jarausch, *Das Ende der Zuversicht*; Raphael and Doering-Manteuffel, *Nach dem Boom*. For the transformation of state–society relations, see: Pekelder, 'Towards Another Concept of the State'.
10. For the NIEO, see: Getachew, *Worldmaking after Empire*, 142–75; Burke, 'Competing for the Last Utopia?'; Normand and Zaidi, *Human Rights at the UN*, 289–315. International rights debates at the UN and elsewhere turned to the global economic order and development as a human right in this period alongside the US turn to civil and political human rights of the individual. See: Normand and Zaidi, *Human Rights at the UN*, 289–315; Slaughter, 'Hijacking Human Rights'. For transnational socialist legal networks, see: Altehenger, 'Unlikely Heirs'; Berend, *An Economic History of Twentieth-Century Europe*, 159. During the Cold War, however, this socialist legal unification drive and its implications for sovereignty and the economy attracted intense scholarly interest. For an annotated bibliography of legal analysis from the late 1960s into the 1970s and 1980s, see: Brine, *Comecon*, 23–33.
11. For human rights grassroots activism in the German context, see: Richardson-Little, *The Human Rights Dictatorship*; Wildenthal, *The Language of Human Rights*.
12. For this public controversy, see: 'TV-Wetterkarte: Lästige Gemüter', *Der Spiegel* 7 (1970), 39.
13. Grigoleit, *Bundesverfassungsgericht und deutsche Frage*, 271–89. See also: BArch, B237/99088, dissenting votes Seuffert, Hirsch, Rupp, 1973.
14. BArch, B237/99088, legal brief Bavarian government, 28 May 1973.
15. For the CDU/CSU's fight against Ostpolitik, see: Grau, *Gegen den Strom*.
16. For a scholarly attempt to push back against the GDR and the social-liberal government, see: Hacker, *Der Rechtsstatus Deutschlands*.
17. BArch, B237/99088, legal brief Bavarian government, 28 May 1973.
18. Ibid.
19. Ibid.
20. Ibid.
21. BArch, B237/99088, annex legal brief Bavarian government, 29 May 1973.
22. Ibid.
23. Ibid.
24. BArch, B237/99088, letter exchange Seuffert-Bahlmann.
25. Stolleis, *Geschichte des Öffentlichen Rechts in Deutschland, Bd. 4*, 207. Wengler was arrested by the Gestapo in 1944 when he worked at the international law institute of the Kaiser-Wilhelm-Society and had close ties to conservative resistance circles. See: Kier, 'Die "Affäre Wengler"'.
26. BArch, B237/99088, expert opinion Wengler, 1973.
27. Ibid.
28. BArch, B237/99088, plea draft Kriele, 19 June 1973.

29. Ibid.
30. Ibid.
31. Ibid.
32. Ibid.
33. Ibid.
34. Grigoleit, *Bundesverfassungsgericht und deutsche Frage*, 271–89.
35. BArch, B237/99088, plea draft Kriele, 19 June 1973.
36. BArch, B237/99088, plea draft Leverenz, 19 June 1973.
37. Ibid.
38. Ibid.
39. Ibid.
40. AdsD, 1/WSAE000197, Nachlass Seuffert, memorandum on GDR as foreign country.
41. Theodor Maunz remained a secret supporter of neo-Nazi groups for his entire life. See: Stolleis, *Law under the Swastika*, 185–92.
42. AdsD, 1/WSAE000197, Nachlass Seuffert, memorandum on GDR as foreign country.
43. Ibid.
44. Ibid.
45. For a detailed account, see: Grigoleit, *Bundesverfassungsgericht und deutsche Frage*, 277–85. See also the text of the verdict: BVerfGE 36, 1.
46. 'Grundlagenvertrag: Dogmatischer Hauch', *Der Spiegel* 35 (1973), 23–25. For the politicization of the court after 1971, see: Collings, *Democracy's Guardians*, 126–64.
47. BVerfGE 36, 1.
48. Ibid.
49. Ibid.
50. Ibid., (74).
51. Ibid.
52. Ibid.
53. BArch, B141/96904, report on First Conference of European Constitutional Courts, 15 December 1972.
54. Ibid.
55. BArch, B136/4438, letter Ministry of Justice, 15 December 1972.
56. Ibid.
57. BArch, B141/96904, 'Ergebnisprotokoll über die Sitzung der Protokollkommission beim Bundesverfassungsgericht vom 20. Dezember 1972'.
58. BArch, B141/96904, minutes, 27 February 1973.
59. BArch, B141/96904, minutes draft programme, 16 March 1973.
60. For the domestic context of the clashes surrounding the Basic Treaty case, see: Grigoleit, *Bundesverfassungsgericht und deutsche Frage*, 271–77.
61. See letter exchange in BArch, B141/96904.
62. Grigoleit, *Bundesverfassungsgericht und deutsche Frage*, 277–85.
63. Collings, *Democracy's Guardians*, 109–82.
64. BArch, B141/96905, information conference programme, 20 November 1973.
65. Ibid.
66. For the East Treaties verdict, see: Grigoleit, *Bundesverfassungsgericht und deutsche Frage*, 285–90.
67. BArch, B141/96906, draft speech Scheel, 27 September 1974.
68. See summaries of their presentations in: AdSD 1/WSAA000028, final communiqué Second Conference of European Constitutional Court, 16 October 1974.
69. BArch, B141/96906, lecture Rupp.
70. Ibid.
71. Ibid.
72. Ibid.

73. See: BVerfGE 1, 396.
74. BArch, B141/96906, closing speech Benda, 16 October 1974.
75. See: Garrett, Kelemen and Schulz, 'The European Court of Justice', 149f.
76. 'Karlsruhe: Ein verkappter Gesetzgeber?', *Der Spiegel* 10 (1975), 68–74.
77. Grigoleit, *Bundesverfassungsgericht und deutsche Frage*, 277–85.
78. 'Karlsruhe: Ein verkappter Gesetzgeber?', *Der Spiegel* 10 (1975), 68–74.
79. Ibid.
80. Grigoleit, *Bundesverfassungsgericht und deutsche Frage*, 285–90.
81. BVerfGE 40, 141 (157).
82. See: Grigoleit, *Bundesverfassungsgericht und deutsche Frage*, 285–90.
83. Wilkins, *'Reichsbürger' – Ein Handbuch*.
84. For the internal struggles over the foundation of and control over a Working Group for International Law since 1962, see: ABBAW, AG, No. 46, letter Peck, 8 August 1962; letter Peck, 17 March 1963; work report Office for State and Legal Questions of Socialist States, 24 January 1964; working plan Office for International Law, 4 February 1965. See also ABBAW, AG, No. 45, memorandum on future work of Office for State and Legal Questions of Socialist States, 22 January 1964; concept for Office for State and Legal Questions of Socialist States, 15 June 1964; note on discussion about Office for State and Legal Questions of Socialist States, 27 June 1964; research plan state and legal sciences 1966–70, 7 December 1965.
85. See: Kopeček, 'The Socialist Conception of Human Rights'.
86. ABBAW, AG, No. 45, report on international conference of socialist legal scholars, 1 February 1965.
87. Nathans, 'Soviet Rights-Talk in the Post-Stalin Era'.
88. Altehenger, *Legal Lessons*.
89. Nathans, 'The Dictatorship of Reason'.
90. ABBAW, AG, No. 45, report on international conference of socialist legal scholars, 1 February 1965.
91. Richardson-Little, 'Erkämpft das Menschenrecht'.
92. BArch, DP1/1811, first draft working plan, 22 July 1970.
93. BArch, DP1/1811, draft working plan Section 2, 22 July 1970. This push was also meant to counter the persistence of petty crime. See: Millington, 'State Power and "Everyday Criminality"', 440–60.
94. BArch, DP1/1773, memorandum on preparations for a regional European conference following IV. UN Congress, 11 December 1970.
95. BArch, DY64/108.
96. Ibid.
97. In the GDR context, this also resulted in the formation of dispute commissions and conflict commissions in local community contexts as a new form of mediating social conflict. See: Betts, 'Property, Peace, and Honour'.
98. Altehenger, *Legal Lessons*.
99. Altehenger, 'Unlikely Heirs'.
100. For Soviet legal policies, see: Moyal, 'Did Law Matter?'.
101. BArch, DP2/1987, report on visit of GDR High Court to Soviet Union, 7 May 1973.
102. For this shift in Soviet foreign policy making away from the GDR, see: Wentker, *Außenpolitik in engen Grenzen*, 225–32.
103. Crime prevention and legal education drives drove much of these early exchanges. See: Altehenger, 'Unlikely Heirs'.
104. ASR/13385, travel report, 25 August 1975.
105. Ibid.
106. Ibid.
107. BArch, DP1/1811, first draft working plan, 22 July 1970.

108. BArch, B136/6388, letter Renger, 5 June 1970.
109. See the GDR report on Renger's attempts to deny the GDR League for the United Nations entry to WFUNA: BArch, DZ23/124, confidential report on German League for the United Nation's political activities, April 1968. See also: Hüfner, 'Die Deutsche Gesellschaft für die Vereinten Nationen', 77–82.
110. BArch, B136/6388, letter Scheel, 10 August 1970.
111. Hüfner, 'Die Deutsche Gesellschaft für die Vereinten Nationen', 82–85.
112. BArch, B136/6388.
113. BArch, B136/6388, letter Kern, 13 June 1972.
114. For the confrontation over Nazi wartime criminals in this period, see: Weinke, *Die Verfolgung von NS-Tätern im geteilten Deutschland*, 180–332.
115. BArch, DZ7/73, 'Statement of the GDR Committee for Human Rights to the 25th Session of the General Assembly', 17 November 1970.
116. Ibid.
117. Graefrath had published on UN affairs since the 1950s. See: Graefrath, *Die Vereinten Nationen und die Menschenrechte*. The SED published English-language pamphlets such as *Peace, Friendship, Solidarity*. See also: Lorenz, '"Heldin des anderen Amerika"' and Hagen, '"Free Angela Davis" Campaign'. For GDR cultural diplomacy in Asia, see: Gehrig, 'Informal Envoys'.
118. BArch, DP1/21505, note, 1 November 1973.
119. See: Bange and Neidhardt, *Helsinki 1975 and the Transformation of Europe*; Morgan, *The Final Act*.
120. BArch, DP1/21505, note, 1 November 1973.
121. Gehrig et al., 'The Eastern Bloc'.
122. BArch, DP1/21505, organization UN work, 5 November 1973.
123. Keys, *Reclaiming American Virtue*; Bradley, *The World Reimagined*; Moyn, *The Last Utopia*; Slaughter, 'Hijacking Human Rights'.
124. BArch, DP1/21505, summary report, 16 January 1974.
125. See: Thomas, *The Helsinki Effect*, 89–156.
126. BArch, DP1/21505, letter Winzer, 28 December 1973.
127. BArch, DZ23/74, paper Steiniger 'The Contribution to the Development of International Law', 1977.
128. Ibid.
129. For the shift from human rights to the European security architecture of the German League for Human Rights, see also: Horn, 'Die Deutsche Liga für die Vereinten Nationen', 102–3.
130. BArch, DZ23/74, paper Steiniger 'The Contribution to the Development of International Law', 1977.
131. Ibid.
132. For the anti-communist mobilization of human rights language in the US, see: Keys, *Reclaiming American Virtue*, 103–27.
133. BArch, DZ23/74, paper Steiniger 'The Contribution to the Development of International Law', 1977. For the origins of this legal concept, see: Hirsch, 'The Soviets at Nuremberg'.
134. BArch, DZ23/74, paper Steiniger 'The Contribution to the Development of International Law', 1977.
135. Bange and Neidhardt, *Helsinki 1975 and the Transformation of Europe*; Morgan, *The Final Act*; Snyder, *Human Rights Activism and the End of the Cold War*.

Chapter 6

Separated by Law

On 28 September 1974, SED leader Erich Honecker hailed the amendments made to the new GDR constitution that had first been proclaimed in 1968. Honecker stressed in particular that there had been a need to revise the preamble of the constitution to ensure that the GDR was now defined as 'a state of workers and peasants' in which the individual 'human being was the focus of all endeavours of the socialist society and state'. 'Our people', Honecker confidently proclaimed, 'has realized its basic rights to socio-economic, sovereign and national self-determination'.[1] In the words of the party leader, the revised GDR constitution reaffirmed 'in constitutional law the important developments, which we have achieved as part of the socialist family of peoples through economic integration, the steady protection of socialism and peace, and we endorse the glorious prospects that the cooperation between states of the liberated socialist world will yield'.[2] Socialist constitutionalism, legality and international legal cooperation, Honecker proudly proclaimed, shaped the legal culture and identity of the GDR. Yet this core of statehood would soon come to haunt the SED leadership.

The SED's vision of constitutionalism and socialist human rights turned into a state-mandated discourse of social control through an emphasis on citizens' duties towards the state when the economic crisis of the Eastern bloc deepened and social unrest worsened. Honecker's ambitious legal utopia for the development of socialism on the path to communism turned against the party-state. This was partly of the party's own making. Similar to other socialist states, socialist legality and the popularization of laws, seen as necessary to maintain party-state rule, actually subverted the party's rule in the 1980s and provided dissidents with rights language that

---

Notes for this chapter begin on page 252.

could be deployed against the party-state.³ In response, the party-state redirected attention away from the idealistic human rights rhetoric of the 1960s and emphasized a legalist agenda of social control, a civic duty to comply with socialist legality, state-mandated legal knowledge and the importance of law for international economic relations.⁴ By the late 1980s, Honecker's vision of socialist constitutionalism had proven to be a hollow promise.

In the FRG, a new West German legal identity developed as well. On 23 May 1979, the political scientist Dolf Sternberger (1907–1989) marked the thirtieth anniversary of the Basic Law with an article in the FAZ that would become famous. Under the heading 'Constitutional Patriotism', the Heidelberg professor asked if the basic rights catalogue of the West German constitution could become the new cornerstone of a West German national identity.⁵ But he was also aware that many West Germans still had difficulties in coming to terms with national division and he did not wish to brush these sentiments aside. Instead, Sternberger stated that West Germans lived in a 'wounded nation, but a whole constitution'.⁶ The memory of the lost German nation-state had to be preserved and respected. Yet it was just that: a memory. His vision for the FRG's identity firmly centred on the well-functioning constitutional order that, he explained, had provided security, prosperity and rule of law.⁷ The domestic legal culture that had developed since 1949, Sternberger concluded, was much better suited to underpin West Germans' self-understanding as *Bundesbürger* (citizens of the Federal Republic) than abstract reference to a lost national past.⁸

Law now separated the two Germanys. At the same time, the rights of the individual guaranteed in law became core components in how governmental elites in West and East Germany legitimized their political systems. While the UN membership of both German states since 1973 confirmed the existence of two sovereign states, it took the next two decades for both German societies to acknowledge that national division had resulted in independent and ideologically competing domestic legal cultures. If the focus on a shared legal heritage and battle over the representation of German sovereignty and citizenship had prevented a full public acknowledgement of this fact until the early 1970s, the subsequent years until the fall of the Berlin Wall in 1989 were marked by the embrace of distinctly East and West German legal cultures. This process unfolded in parallel in a climate of accelerating transnational links between national legal systems within each bloc. This internationalization drive in turn reinforced the acknowledgement of new domestic legal identities in both states. Even in conflicts over international law and human rights, the judiciaries and governments of both German states now treated their confrontations as disputes between sovereign states and followed international protocols in engaging with each other. What used to be a struggle over the 'correct' ideology of German law now evolved into separate domestic universes of law, legality and rights.

Socialist Constitutionalism

The SED had opened the race for new separated constitutional spheres in 1968.[9] The proclamation of the GDR Criminal Code officially began the socialist legal revolution. Recall that after the introduction of a separate GDR citizenship law a year earlier, the drafting of new East German legal codes to replace the previously only amended original German legal codes, which had originated around the turn of the century, set these new socialist legal codes distinctly apart from the FRG.[10] This transition was long in the making and it now had to be propagated forcefully. In a report of the Section for State and Legal Questions, the section's head Klaus Sorgenicht (1923–1999) called for the 'intense usage of state and legal sciences in the daily political struggle'.[11] Joachim Herrmann (1928–1992), editor-in-chief of the party's mouthpiece *Neues Deutschland* and SED central committee member, also lobbied for a 'general attack on the West German constitution'.[12]

During the constitution debate that followed in February 1968, the SED returned to public rights talk campaigns intended to instil constitutionalism and legal consciousness into GDR citizens.[13] The new constitution stated in its preface that the 'people of the German Democratic Republic have given themselves this socialist constitution'.[14] The party thus deemed it necessary to have the new constitution debated in town hall meetings across the country. To disseminate the constitution in this way was to prove that it reflected 'the will of the people'. Countering West German accusations that GDR legal reform was 'top secret', spearheaded by secretive party committees, GDR legal experts went to great lengths to prove that GDR citizens had a chance to discuss the new constitution. The Ministry of Justice claimed to have received more than eight thousand suggestions for amendments after thirty-five thousand draft copies had been in circulation across the country.[15] When Ulbricht signed the revised constitution on 8 April 1968, the implementation of the transition phase to socialist legality had been made official.

West German diplomats, hardened by the legal battles with the GDR in preceding decades, realized the significance of the East German shift in constitutional identities. They even admitted some admiration for Ulbricht's move. The Foreign Office, for example, concluded that the 'political value of the new constitution for the SBZ should not be underestimated'.[16]

Circumventing free elections, but endorsing a public debate of the constitution across the country, Ulbricht had orchestrated a fundamental change in constitutional identity. Arguing that there was no alternative to 'his socialist constitution', the Foreign Office summarized, Ulbricht had secured 'the approval of the population in *Mitteldeutschland* [Middle Germany] for the division of Germany and for all his other political convictions'. In short, 'one should not underestimate this political stroke of genius by Ulbricht'.[17]

Yet the transformation of East German law went much deeper. The SED leadership codified new law that conceived of rights as generated and secured by the state's existence. In the tradition of Soviet law, people could only hold and secure rights within a political community. The SED dismissed the idea that individuals held basic rights through their existence as for example outlined in the West German Basic Law. East Germans could thus only claim rights if they in turn actively participated in society and aided the building of socialism. The transition to such an understanding of law and rights had been a long time in the making but was now formalized in the abolition of old German legal codes and the new socialist constitution.

East German legal reform continued at a fast pace. In the days and weeks following the release of the GDR draft constitution, the East German Ministry of Justice carefully monitored international responses. The ministerial officials registered positive responses to the code's modern criminological approach. Conservative West German media and politicians, meanwhile, repeated their accusations that the GDR government had destroyed Germany's legal unity. Yet simple recourse to arguments of legal continuity now met with fierce domestic criticism in the FRG. A Norddeutscher Rundfunk (NDR, North German Broadcasting Service) commentary questioned the democratic nature of the old German criminal code still used in West German courts. No one 'should shed a tear' for the abolition of a nineteenth-century legal code, even if it was for a new socialist criminal code in the GDR. Legislation emanating from the German Reich was no guarantee for 'German unity any longer and promised no hopes for a better future for the German people'.[18] In their criticism of outdated West German law, GDR legal reform seemed modern in part to some West German political commentators.

Six years later, in 1974, Honecker declared the first phase of legal transformation complete. The proclamation of amendments to the GDR constitution in September 1974, Honecker argued, marked the realization of a socialist constitutional system that should guide the way to develop socialism further towards communism.[19] It was now time to turn to Honecker's other great project. Once the SED had announced the unity of economic and social policy in 1971, socialist legality had become the centre of attention.[20] Socialist constitutionalism was to be the glue to organize the economic, social and political transformations of the future.[21] Previously dominated by economists, historians and sociologists, legal scholars now claimed a central role in paving the road to this new 'developed socialist society' in the years between 1968 and 1974. Within the German Academy, legal debates shifted towards the study of 'objective social laws' for this new socialist legal world.[22] Heinz Such (1910–1976), professor of law at the University of Leipzig, argued that the implementation of a socialist constitution now allowed debates on the 'objective tendencies and principles in the development of socialist law'.[23] Putting people's actual conditions of living at the heart of his doctrine of law, Such demanded that law should help to improve the economic and administrative efficiency of socialist society and thus the lives of GDR citizens. Inefficiencies in the legal system could lead to 'economic slumps or downturns, to political and social loss of speed' in the development of socialist society.[24]

To put the individual human being at the core of the GDR's new constitutional framework, the party had to instil the 'correct' understanding of law and rights into socialist citizens. If 'misunderstood' by GDR citizens, the very idea of socialist legality was inherently dangerous for the GDR government. The logics of active socialist citizenship, which guided the ethos of East German sovereignty enshrined in the 1974 constitution, necessitated the propagation of legal knowledge. If citizens only gained rights through doing their duty in socialist society, the party had to fulfil its role in giving voice to citizens' needs. Following this logic, the party only expressed the will of the people and led the way in implementing it. For the legal field, this meant explaining the rights guaranteed by the state to the people in return for their active participation in developing socialism.[25]

To do so, the politburo decreed the preparation of popular law propaganda materials centred on a series called *Recht in unserer Zeit* (Law in Our Time). East German legal experts believed that the party could only effectively direct society if the legal system was properly explained to the population. In August 1974, a high-profile group of SED cadres met to coordinate future legal education work. The range of themes in the series Law in Our Time reflected the broad focus of legal education. The series started with books by Mollnau, Karl-Heinz Schöneburg (1928–2013) and Wolfgang Weichelt (1929–1993) on law and political power, followed by volumes on tasks of the courts in labour law, the transformative power of law, risk and law, civil law, legal questions surrounding housing, and a booklet on the rights of the citizen as consumer. The Urania publishing house was tasked with the preparation and marketing of these popular readings, which also included encyclopaedias on the new socialist legal codes.[26] For the socialist state, it was important to control the 'rules consciousness' of East Germans in the framework provided by socialist legality.[27]

The media offensive to educate GDR citizens in socialist legality also included TV shows such as *Polizeiruf 110* (Emergency Police Call 110), crime book series such as the *Blaulicht-Reihe* (Police Lights Series) and practical guides like the *Verkehrskompaß* (Traffic Compass) explaining traffic rules or fire prevention guides for the workplace and home.[28] The transmission of legal knowledge to the general population and the redesign of the university curriculum became major foci in the work of the Ministry of Justice from 1975 onwards. By 1977, the portfolio of the series Law in Our Time extended to topics such as young people and marriage, inheritance law and legal questions of social equality. How-to guides explained in answers to one hundred questions the themes of shopping and buying, insurance law, rights of parents and pupils in the school system, the legal framework of military service, the citizen and the court system, the legal nature of the socialist state and the question of peace and disarmament.[29] The state thus provided a comprehensive portfolio of popular readings on how citizens should understand their socialist rights in everyday life.

During the 1970s, the goal of the East German legal science and the state's legal sector was to 'perfect socialist legality'.[30] The amendment of the new criminal code (1974) and code of criminal procedure law (1977), the new civil code and code of civil procedural law (1975) and the law on the tasks and institutional role of the state prosecution (1977), the prison and social reintegration law (1977) as well as the new labour code (1977) were to pave the way to incorporating ever more international legal norms into GDR legal codes.[31] When the UN human rights covenants took effect in 1976, the legal bureaucracy made sure that the GDR complied with the language of UN rights norms.

Yet legal realities remained a different matter.[32] At the peak of legal codification in 1977, internal reports captured the frustration of officials tasked with turning the party's many legal pledges of the last two decades into reality. 'We have time and again found in connection with the human rights convention that basic rights, once they had been adopted, were hyped by the propaganda to such a degree that the limitations [to these rights] built into other passages of the same document have been pushed into the background entirely.'[33] Internal opposition formed especially within parts of the government tasked with internal security and crime prevention. Not only did everyday criminality not abate as ideology dictated under 'developed socialism', but political dissent was also on the rise.[34] Governmental officials began to push back against the Foreign

Ministry and international law scholars who had promoted adherence to UN rights norms as part of the GDR's international campaign to have its sovereignty recognized.[35]

By the early 1980s, the SED leadership was forced to rein in the party's own emancipatory legal rhetoric.[36] The persistent economic crisis and a rise in unrest and political dissent across the socialist world exerted pressure from the internationalization of legal norms on the GDR legal field. If legal experts had so far justified the development of the socialist legal system with the realization of human rights under socialism, they now focused on the importance of further economic integration of the Eastern bloc. Similar to developments within the European Economic Community (EEC) at the time, solutions to the pressing problem of the international economic integration of the Warsaw Pact states were unthinkable without the development of transnational rules and regulations.[37] Law's role in solving the economic downturn now overtook ambitious human rights rhetoric.

With renewed civil unrest across the Eastern bloc and the rise of the *Solidarność* movement in Poland in the early 1980s, the SED leadership put more and more emphasis on duty-bound citizen rights and social control through law. Leading criminologists such as John Lekschas (1925–1999) provided the academic framework for these policy adjustments around 1980 when he elaborated on civic duties to provide the party with recipes to counter domestic dissent. Lekschas based his suggestions for more party control on an analysis of human behaviour in socialist society. For him, the core of socialist law – in contrast to bourgeois legal traditions – was the arrangement of relationships of duty. Writing for his academic peers and the party leadership, he explained: 'the duty of the human being in society is rooted in the social conditions and represents a crucial aspect of these social conditions. This sense of duty is a principle aimed at creating social activity, which in itself contains the expectation, demand and right to certain actions and behaviour of the individuals who are part of society'.[38] Only socialism produced such 'truly free and self-governed citizens', choosing their duty to society and state freely. 'Bourgeois rights ideologues', Lekschas contended, equated the idea of duty with *einstehen müssen* [obligation], which equalled the subjugation under 'the ruling classes'.[39] The socio-economic conditions in the GDR, based on shared ownership of the means of production, created a qualitatively different, historically bound sense of duty and camaraderie. The active participation of citizens in the organization of state and society, ensured by the new constitution, secured the leading role of the working class in society. The party in turn had the duty to direct society.[40] In short, everyone had to do their duty to secure the party's rule and East Germans would choose to do so voluntarily. Citizens had clearly defined *Handlungsrechte* (rights of action) and *Verhaltenspflichten* (duties of behaviour). Only within these confines, citizens had the right to act autonomously.

In the eyes of the party, this system of mutual responsibilities and duties towards society and the state strengthened and protected the existing social order. With civic unrest looming large in neighbouring countries, criminologists such as Lekschas in tandem with other party experts promoted the crucial importance of law in crime prevention and public security.[41] In this context, debates across the socialist bloc on legal exchanges and a socialist counter-model to Western international law, described in the previous chapter, linked to the development of socialist constitutionalism at home.[42] GDR legal scholars made sure to point out in their published work that such internationalization drives in no way affected the full sovereignty of socialist states. The attempt to reach a uniform economic legal regime across the Eastern bloc and the defence of sovereignty represented 'two different, yet interconnected tendencies of development'.[43] Gone were the days when socialist legal scholars actively advocated the linkage between international and domestic law.

Exchanges with the Soviet Union remained the highest priority for leading legal practitioners in defending the party's grip on society. In May 1981, Toeplitz and a delegation of the high court visited the Soviet High Court in Moscow. In line with the focus on crime prevention, which meant squashing political dissent at the time, a visit to the juvenile rectification colony outside Irkutsk formed the major part of the trip. In their final meeting with the deputy of the Presidium of the Supreme Soviet W.W. Kusnezov, Toeplitz described rectification camps as a manifestation of the 'humanist education within the Soviet penal system'. In his reply, Kusnezov emphasized that socialist states had not reached their full potential in crime prevention. The education of the 'new man' and 'new woman' through legal education would help achieve this goal. Made over cocktails sponsored by the GDR embassy, these statements leisurely and grossly mischaracterized the brutal realities of Soviet prison camps.[44]

Toeplitz toured the socialist bloc in the following years to find out how his high court could help defend the party's power at home. His next trip brought him to Poland. Wlodzimierz Berutowicz (1914–2004), the president of the Polish High Court, welcomed him in May 1983. Here, Toeplitz inquired about the role of the Polish courts in suppressing the protests of 1981. In particular, he wanted to know more about why almost one third of local judges had supported *Solidarność* in recent public demonstrations and strikes, a fact that had raised alarm bells among GDR high court judges.[45] The lessons that Toeplitz learnt in the Soviet Union and Poland mirrored the SED's suppression of opposition in the late 1980s.[46] This was something Toeplitz was determined to avoid in the GDR. In the span of a decade, the GDR legal sphere had moved from a triumphant language of constitutionalism and human rights to crime prevention and social control, suspecting a threat from within society that undermined party rule.

Dealing with the Domestic Realities of Human Rights

At the time when GDR officials moved away from the emancipatory human rights rhetoric of the 1960s, the West German parliament engaged in a new form of UN-led human rights politics. The GDR legal sphere came under pressure from West German rights inquiries in the late 1970s. Conservatives revived the tradition of collecting information about rights violations in so-called White Books that had shaped much of the legal anti-communist mobilization in the early FRG. In 1977, the CDU/CSU released a report on the human rights situation in Germany and Eastern Europe.[47] The Bonn parliament now finally took up the work that the UfJ and Königstein Circle, the West German lawyers associations that monitored legal developments in the GDR, had previously conducted on behalf of the West German government. After years of socialist advances in human rights language, West German politicians and legal practitioners returned forcefully into arenas of international politics of law.

This turn to human rights reaffirmed the distinctiveness of the FRG and GDR's legal system for domestic audiences. In contrast to earlier decades, the human rights clashes between the two German governments of the late 1970s and 1980s unfolded on the basis that two separate legal systems existed. Socialist leaders suddenly found themselves on the defensive after a decade of successful attacks on Western 'imperialist' and 'neo-fascist' politics of law. They were scrambling for answers to this new challenge. The states that had signed the Helsinki Accords were scheduled to meet for their first follow-up meeting in October 1977. In March, Horst Teltschik (b. 1940), office head of the CDU/CSU leader in parliament, received a report from the US government informing him that the US administration planned a public condemnation of human rights abuses in Eastern Europe and the Soviet Union during the Conference of Security and Cooperation in Europe meeting in Belgrade later that year.[48] This was a well-timed attack as human and minority rights shaped the agenda for the conference.[49] After the conclusion of the Belgrade meeting in March 1978, the CDU put the question of the human rights situation in the GDR to the government. The CDU party apparatus called for a comprehensive West German position on the issue.[50]

Human rights inquiries now followed established UN protocols and acknowledged the judicial independence of the other German state. In 1979, the CDU opposition again demanded that the Bonn government produce a report on the human rights situation in Germany in the tense atmosphere of Cold War conflicts over missile armament in Europe, the Soviet invasion of Afghanistan and growing unrest across Eastern Europe. In response to the CDU's request, the Bonn government speakers in parliament highlighted the difference in approach to international legal norms between the FRG and the GDR. For the Bonn government, the extrapolation of human rights from an ideological notion of socialist society represented no *verstaatlichtes Recht* (stated-based law), but a political ideology. To put pressure on the GDR government, the government demanded a human right of leaving East Germany.[51] This West German demand exerted additional pressure on GDR legal experts from outside to retreat from human rights language and revert to older legal language centred on basic rights that began to crystallize in GDR exchanges with Soviet and Polish colleagues at the same time.

Conservatives challenged the Bonn government to report on the East Berlin government's compliance with economic, social and cultural human rights in accordance with UN conventions and the obstacles for East Germans to exercise their right of self-determination secured through the UN convention on civil and political human rights.[52] This mirrored the US emphasis on the individual in global human rights politics at the time. In September 1979, the government responded with a lengthy report.[53] The continued violations of citizens' rights in the GDR, the report emphasized, represented a central obstacle for better German-German relations. The Basic Treaty of 1972 had expressly included the pledge of both German states to adhere to human rights standards. Yet the diverse views of human rights across the Third World, the socialist bloc and Western countries hampered both Cold War alliances in projecting a hegemonic notion of human rights in world politics. The report thus implied that the Western camp had to strengthen its influence in the Global South to roll back socialist international rights concepts before the Bonn government could use human rights language more effectively against the GDR.[54]

In response to the report, the conservatives held that an official complaint about the GDR's approach to human rights should be lodged with the UN human rights commission. After all, the UN human rights conventions made governments accountable for their actions. Yet, as the government's report pointed out, the problem was once more in the fine print. The convention on civil and political rights included three control mechanisms: first, Article 28 empowered the human rights commission to evaluate the actions of member states; second, the member states had to submit reports on the state of human rights; and third, member states could submit complaints against other states over violations of human rights. The problem was that neither the FRG nor the GDR had ratified the protocol, which guaranteed the right to make a complaint against other states. West German legal experts feared problems of legal overlap between the UN conventions and the ECHR and on their urging the Bonn government had abstained from signing. This refusal now rendered the UN human rights conventions a somewhat toothless tool to discredit the GDR government. Yet both states had to submit reports to the commission on their effort to implement human rights.[55] This might offer a chance to discredit GDR legal realities.

The government's response showed that the power of the human rights conventions in divided Germany remained restricted to their moral and political claims. Governments could be and were held accountable by the international public for rights violations such as the GDR's militarized border regime. As the human rights conventions represented a treaty regime under international law, the Bonn government argued, accusations of human rights violations could not be brushed aside legally that easily. If member states of the conventions respected the legal principle of proportionality in their accusations against other states, such governments could not simply revert back to their sovereign right to govern their own internal affairs if criticized for their human rights record. The Bonn government's strategy now became to project the demand for more legal safeguards for East German citizens via the UN's human rights commission.[56]

The GDR government began to feel the pressure of the global turn of human rights debates to individual rights.[57] Fearing West German human rights inquiries at the UN, East German diplomats had to arm themselves with sufficient amounts of material to fend off anticipated Western attacks.[58] In 1981, GDR Foreign Minister Oskar Fischer (1923–2020) asked the high court president Toeplitz for more support of the GDR's activities within the UN. Fischer argued that 'the international work in the field of human rights demands concrete arguments in individual areas of human rights norms'.[59] GDR courts had to find ways to prove that human rights norms were applied as part of socialist legal culture. To compile effective legal propaganda materials, Fischer explained to Toeplitz, the supply of recent high court cases that had involved human rights norms would be most helpful.[60]

Toeplitz and his fellow high court judges were particularly proud of the recent reinforcement of due process procedures in high court trials.[61] In well-rehearsed socialist rhetoric, his report for Fischer argued that the GDR court system even exceeded the demands of UN human rights norms due to the transformative quality of socialist legality and its direct impact on citizens' lives. The GDR High Court now reverted back to a language of basic rights to set its socialist understanding of rights apart from the growing dominance of Western human rights languages centred on the individual in UN politics.[62] Decades of debates on basic rights and attempts to move to a unique socialist human rights language now ironically resulted in a return to similar rhetoric that shaped the legal identity that formed around the West German Basic Law's basic rights catalogue at the time.[63] The revival of basic rights in GDR jurisprudence mapped onto the language Sternberger had singled out as a basis for a West German legal identity in 1979.

This was the moment at which rights language became an acute danger for the GDR government. In the mid-1980s, dissident groups appropriated the legal rhetoric of peace and disarmament.[64] In response, the high court picked out all elements of the Helsinki Accords that bolstered the GDR's territorial integrity. Arguments that the state had made itself in the 1970s, when Steiniger and other legal scholars revised the official socialist narrative of how international law and human rights had developed, now threatened the stability of the GDR. If the GDR High Court and legal experts had a decade earlier supported a direct impact of international legal norms on national legislation, they now reconsidered this. 'The implementation of human rights has to be carried out through internal national measures', the GDR High Court proclaimed in 1983.[65] In other words, the GDR High Court wanted to re-erect a walled-off sovereign national legal system in which the state determined how international law norms should have a bearing on socialist legality.

It was the existence of two opposing ideologies of international law in the socialist and capitalist bloc, the court argued, that called for this return to national frameworks. Going against all GDR international politics of law of the 1960s and early 1970s, the high court emphasized that the UN Charter had no bearing, and more importantly, contained no legal mechanisms that impacted directly on rights of citizens of a sovereign state. This shift demanded another redrafting of the official party chronology of the development of human rights norms after 1945. The third incarnation of a socialist narrative of human rights now spanned from the 'bourgeois-dominated' declaration of human rights of 1948 to the successes of socialist international law activism. In this explanation, the Soviet bloc had implemented the right of self-determination against the Western powers, ensured that private property would not represent a human right, and shaped the human rights covenants against imperialist and colonial interests. This was a last-ditch attempt to build a socialist genealogy of international law and human rights against Western narratives. From now on,

East German legal scholars, high court judges and government officials were in retreat.

To defend socialist legality, East German legal experts returned to a firm focus on their domestic legal life. At the thirty-fifth anniversary of the GDR in 1984, socialist constitutionalism had become a cornerstone of the SED's legitimacy. The country's leading research institutes, including the Academy of State and Legal Sciences, the Institute for the Theory of the State and Law at the Academy of Sciences, and the Section State and Legal Questions at the SED Central Committee prepared the celebration of socialist legality as part of the planned festivities in 1984 with a public conference that, they explained, was of 'high propaganda value'. Legal scholars hoped to bolster their own legitimacy through this celebration of socialist legality as a major benchmark and achievement of East German socialism.[66] In the summer of 1984, a total of 154 conference participants debated the advances made since 1974. *Neues Deutschland*, TV programmes and regional press covered the conference discussions, and the keynote presentations found a prominent place as a special edition published by the state publishing house.[67] Such activities illustrated that GDR citizens were still indeed learning much more about law than West Germans in their everyday lives, yet this also taught them that legal rhetoric and reality were increasingly diverging.[68]

The SED leadership hoped to use the anniversary celebrations to refocus East Germans' attention to the party's achievements in preserving peace in Europe. A party congress followed this large-scale academic meeting, and it gave the SED leadership an opportunity to try and reclaim party control over international law and human rights language for domestic purposes. In front of more than five hundred party delegates, Egon Krenz (b. 1937), the soon to be rising star of the politburo, opened proceedings with a speech on 'State and Law in the Further Development of the Advantages and Forces of Development of Socialist Society'.[69] Ten working groups then summarized the achievements of East German legal sciences, comfortably skipping over the hostile party line against many legal scholars in the late 1950s, and also outlined avenues into the future. Rearmament and the prevention of militarizing space, Krenz highlighted in his opening address, would be the key questions for legal science in the coming years.[70] This was a jib against US president Ronald Reagan's new Strategic Defense Initiative Organization, often nicknamed 'Star Wars program'. But more importantly, this legalist party-sanctioned rhetoric of peace targeted the growing dissent of church groups advocating peace and disarmament.[71]

This attempt to regain control over domestic rights discourses culminated in a short-lived discussion of a 'Socialist Declaration of Human

Rights' in 1985.⁷² East German diplomats and legal experts inside the Ministry for Foreign Affairs had already launched plans for such a declaration in 1981. At this time, GDR legal cadres saw such a convention that rested exclusively on human rights norms developed out of frameworks of socialist legality as a promising tool to delineate a regional trans-socialist human rights regime from the existing Western European framework based on the ECHR. By 1985, the year in which Mikhail Gorbachev (b. 1931) embarked on his reform policies of glasnost and perestroika in the Soviet Union, delegations from across the socialist bloc met in Bucharest to discuss the venture in more detail. The SED's chief ideologue Kurt Hager (1912–1998) proposed matching other regional human rights regimes such as the European, American and the recently endorsed African human rights charter with a socialist counter-charter. His initiative triggered the formation of an academic think tank at the Academy for Social Science of the Central Committee.[73]

If this drafting of a socialist convention of human rights had seemed promising to SED leaders at first, it soon met with resistance from within the party. The inner circle around Honecker was intensely critical of Gorbachev's reform agenda. Conflicts between reformers and orthodox communists within party elites across the Eastern bloc following Gorbachev's announcement of perestroika and glasnost brought the project to a hold. For SED leaders, especially of an older generation, such a human rights declaration seemed too destabilizing in the current domestic situation. When a twenty-page draft had been completed for discussion in June 1987, orthodox voices among the delegates dominated once again. At a follow-up meeting in East Berlin, the East German legal scholar Eberhard Poppe (b. 1931), who had already participated in formulating the Ministry for Foreign Affairs' internal draft in 1981, reverted back to an orthodox interpretation of socialist human rights. The rising tide of open dissent to socialist governments across Eastern Europe in the late 1980s had swallowed this final attempt to come out of the defensive on human rights politics.[74]

From Rights towards Economic Regulations

In the late 1980s, with party leaderships in retreat from their own international human rights propaganda, socialist rights politics decisively turned back to the court system in defence of the socialist order.[75] By the end of the decade, the GDR High Court president Toeplitz had created a network of bilateral exchanges. Toeplitz's health, however, prevented him from witnessing the pinnacle of his efforts. In 1988, the GDR High Court hosted the first conference of all socialist high courts under the theme of

'Jurisprudence – Democracy – Human Rights in Socialism' in East Berlin. In many regards, socialist legal rhetoric came full circle shortly before the unexpected downfall of communism in Europe. The East German high court judges linked human rights directly to peace. Declaring that 'peace is the highest human right', socialist legal language returned to the very roots of communist Cold War propaganda encapsulated in the rhetoric of world peace that had been globally propagated with the Stockholm Appeal of 1950.[76]

Underneath this rhetoric of peace, the economic crisis of socialist countries that plagued the Eastern bloc in the late 1980s dominated discussions.[77] In their opening remarks to their socialist brethren, the East German judges stressed the central contribution of the legal sector to social and economic unity, the compliance of the GDR constitution and legal codes with international legal norms, the ability of socialist legality to transgress and enhance UN human rights standards beyond their 'imperialist' Western competitors, and the unity of social and cultural rights.[78] These were the topics that attending high court judges from across the socialist world were invited to discuss in order to identify the achievements of socialist legality with particular attention to the court system. In his opening address, the new president of the GDR High Court Günter Sarge (1930–2019) praised the VIII. SED Party Congress of 1971 and the new SED party programme of 1976 as landmarks in building a socialist legal system as the party had then singled out law as the connection between society and the economy and the key to organizing an efficient advanced socialist society. Legal experts, Sarge demanded, now had to turn their full attention to the new legal 'main battlefield' of the economy.[79]

The front lines between reform-minded delegations in the spirit of Gorbachev's perestroika and glasnost and more orthodox judges quickly showed.[80] When the question came of whether this new platform for socialist high courts should remain an exclusively socialist affair, the Polish delegation leader Lopatka advocated closed meetings for Warsaw Pact states and a separate conference that also included other socialist delegations from Romania and beyond Eastern Europe. Lopatka did not think socialist legal experts were ready to open up their networks to the West. The Hungarian representative Szislberesky, conversely, emphasized his country's exchanges with Western states, mentioning the FRG, Austria and France in particular. The Soviet representative Terebilov, in the spirit of perestroika and glasnost, called on his colleagues 'not to repeat old mistakes' and supported the enlargement of the circle of delegations from the Warsaw Pact states to 'everyone who wants to participate' for the scheduled second meeting in Bulgaria.[81] Yet delegates from countries in which party leaderships felt they faced heightened popular pressure, such as in

Poland, viewed such an opening up to the West very critically. Sarge tried to smooth over these conflicts in his closing remarks at the conference by pointing out: 'It was not the search for a model of [legal] work that brought us together, but the desire to exchange experience, foster cooperation and mutual solidarity'.[82]

Beyond disagreement over organization, the debates between high court judges showed that they realized the importance of having a say in the development of legal frameworks for global trade and economic relations. The conference reflected an important moment in socialist legal cooperation beyond the field of court organization. Legal experts from across the socialist world thought they had established functioning domestic systems of socialist legality until the late 1980s. It was now time that they transformed their transnational exchanges, which they had engaged in through trans-socialist scholarly, lawyer, court and ministerial networks built since the late 1960s, into a socialist counter-framework of international legal relations.

When the GDR entered the last year of its existence, legal scholars claimed that their discipline was just entering its prime. In January 1989, Weichelt, the director of the Institute for the Theory of the State and Law at the Academy of Sciences in East Berlin, announced at a conference on constitutional law that the development of socialist constitutionalism in the last two decades had produced a 'fully renewed legal system'.[83] The legal sciences had defined and implemented a theory of constitutionalism that drew on Marx's theory of development. The work in the coming years, GDR legal experts anticipated, had to centre on international law to master the unfolding transformations of international economic relations. What Weichelt called the 'primacy of international law' should guide relations with capitalist countries as well as the socialist bloc. The socialist constitution was, according to East German legal scholars, the 'basic law for the advancement of developed socialist society'.[84] With a domestic legal identity of socialist constitutionalism firmly established, Weichelt felt that the socialist bloc was ready to embark on a new transnational project to brave economic globalization.

Only two months later, the Berlin Wall crumbled. The downfall of European communism prevented socialist legal networks from creating another, now socialist, transnational moment of law and legality at the end of the 1980s.[85] Ironically, therefore, socialist legality in the GDR and across Eastern Europe broke down under popular pressure at the very moment that legal scholars, judges and lawyers and government experts had established transnational networks from academia to high courts and governmental ministries that were meant to produce an alternative legal framework of rules and regulations for international trade and economic relations based on established domestic legal cultures of socialist law.[86] Yet such an alternative transnational socialist legal universe never came into being.

Professionalizing *Rechtspolitik*

If the conclusion of Ostpolitik prompted East German jurisprudence to venture first into the international arena before retreating to a focus on domestic control in the 1980s, it led West German jurists, scholars and politicians to turn inwards. Public scrutiny of the nature of constitutional jurisprudence and the attitude of high court judges towards their work intensified debates within scholarly circles, party politics and eventually the general public about the political nature of law. Protest movements and especially the rights activism of the women's movement and Amnesty International questioned the egalitarian character of West German law and connected their activism to international rights campaigns.[87] West Germans now questioned the normative quality of law and debated law's function in actively shaping a domestic political and legal culture.

There had been early attempts to professionalize legal party politics. The SPD had emphasized the field of legal politics from the 1950s onwards when the party tried to use the constitutional court to oppose Adenauer's policies of Western integration and rearmament.[88] In 1954, the party founded the Arbeitsgemeinschaft Sozialdemokratischer Juristinnen und Juristen (ASJ, Working Group of Social Democratic Jurists).[89] The CDU took until 1963 to form a similar organization, the Bundesarbeitskreis Christlich Demokratischer Juristen (BACDJ, Federal Association of Christian Democratic Lawyers).[90] These party-based associations first remained largely shielded from the public eye, preferring to debate legal reform and judicial organization in closed parliamentary settings rather than taking their work into the media or the general public.

This slowly changed in the late 1960s. In 1967, the Deutsche Juristentag (German Lawyers Conference) established the *Zeitschrift für Rechtspolitik* (Journal for Legal Politics).[91] In the tense atmosphere of student protests and the shift in government to the social-liberal coalition, more and more groups within the general public called for legal reform. Legal experts advising party leaderships came under pressure to open up their closed circles of debate.[92] The new journal of the German Lawyers Conference, endorsed in its first issue by a preface of Minister of Justice Heinemann, should 'make it its task to judge the behaviour of judges, state prosecutors and lawyers in the appropriate language of an academic journal'.[93] The left-wing journal *Kritische Justiz* soon went further than the Journal for Legal Politics in not just criticizing judicial decision making but questioning the legal system as a whole.[94] A first public academic space was created to reflect critically on ongoing legislation and jurisprudence, to suggest reform policies to the government and review draft legislation. Legal controversies were at least supposed to play out in a wider public of legal practitioners.[95]

When the social-liberal coalition took office in Bonn in 1969, the new government under Chancellor Brandt announced an ambitious domestic legal reform agenda.[96] In 1969, the ASJ president Otto Kunze (1904–1982) called his fellow members to a congress in Mainz to discuss how law could serve the democratization of society and reshape everyday political culture. Kunze now actively promoted the SPD's *Rechtspolitische Kongresse* (Legal Politics Congresses) to a wider general public to bolster support for the party's agenda.[97] Horst Ehmke, who served as Federal Minister of Justice in 1969, opened the conference by outlining the government's programme for social change through law in his speech titled 'Legal Politics in Service of Democracy'. This ASJ congress brought together an impressive list of participants to debate the freedom of the press and information as part of Willy Brandt's call to 'dare more democracy' that had spearheaded his first address to parliament as chancellor. Under the watchful eyes of the honorary ASJ member Adolf Arndt, the current elite of social democratic lawyers and some conservative guests debated how law could help in the creation of a critical public sphere.[98]

By the early 1970s, the struggle over the political foundations of West German legal culture was in full swing. The SPD's vision of a transformative social function of the legal system triggered conservative calls for the reinvigoration of a state-centred ideal of the legal sector. Peter C. Caldwell has shown how West German legal scholars early on acknowledged the need for legal norms to guarantee the Basic Law's mission to build a social welfare state, but remained fiercely divided over the institutional legal frameworks and the scope of welfare rights needed to guarantee social and economic rights.[99] In the 1970s, this controversy resurfaced with full force. The SPD's call to see law as an active vehicle to transform society reinvigorated conservative state-centred views of law when the members of the BACDJ met in May 1971 to inaugurate their second legislature period. After conservatives had lost governmental power in 1969 for the first time, many within the CDU/CSU had to realize that they had taken their ability to shape legal politics for granted as the conservatives had continuously governed the republic since 1949. Now that they had lost direct political control over legal policies, conservatives assembled at the BACDJ conference felt that they urgently needed to find effective counterarguments to prevent social democratic dominance in the field of legal policy. The SPD had raised the idea that judges could shape legal politics actively in recent debates on a reform in the selection and appointment of judges. Conservative lawyers and judges instead demanded a return to traditional role models, opposing any attempt to use law as a means of changing society. Judges should not be 'social doctors' or 'social engineers', but rather mere executioners of existing legal codes. The 'open and hidden social democratization of law' had to be stopped at all costs.[100]

The example of the appointment of Ernst Benda as president of the constitutional court on 8 December 1971 clearly demonstrated the political polarization of the West German legal sphere. Benda was a stern conservative and had served as Federal Minister of the Interior in 1968–69, when he presided over the drafting of the new Emergency Laws amidst severe parliamentary and public conflicts. His early life had been shaped by anti-communist activism. In 1948, SED cadres pushed Benda out of the Humboldt University Berlin. After some months at the University of Wisconsin-Madison, he returned to the Free University Berlin and helped to build the KgU. Backed by CIA and Counterintelligence Corps (CIC) funding, the group organized resistance against the GDR government. In the heated early years of the Cold War, Benda helped track persons whom the GDR security service had kidnapped in West Berlin and brought to East Berlin.[101] At first, the group had been officially backed by the Ministry for All-German Affairs but support stopped after a series of show trials against KgU and UfJ members in which the GDR High Court delivered its first death sentence.[102]

Benda's appointment was therefore not greeted with much enthusiasm outside the conservative party, as talks at the official ceremony for the newly appointed and retired judges at the courthouse in Karlsruhe made clear. At this event in December 1971, Federal President Heinemann even told Benda that he would not enter his new office with 'much acclaim'. Still, in his public speech Heinemann lauded Benda's support for the continued legal accountability of Nazi perpetrators that Benda had expressed in a famous speech in parliament against the majority of his own party in 1965. But the six new appointments to the court in 1971 following the usual proportional system to represent political parties in parliament, Heinemann emphasized, had been influenced by too much party politics. He reminded the incoming judges that particularly contentious issues such as Ostpolitik and abortion rights ultimately belonged in the political rather than the legal realm. The president hoped to make this point forcefully in the current climate of political division.[103]

In his address that followed Heinemann's speech, Benda directly addressed the conflicts surrounding his election. Wilhelm Hennis (1923–2012), professor of political science at the University of Freiburg, and others had questioned Benda's ability to judge cases impartially given his political career. Now, Benda took the opportunity of his inaugural address to talk about political bias.[104] He had no intention of disguising his politics in public. Benda was not the only new appointee to the highest court in the land who intended to take the politics of high court jurisprudence to the general public. Martin Hirsch (1913–1992), a new judge with close ties to the SPD, openly addressed pressing political issues of the time in the media as well. The new crop of constitutional judges chose an activist approach in their dealings with the public. In a speech to the Federation of German Newspaper Publishers in 1972, Benda argued that judges not only had a right to involve themselves in public debate, but they had a duty to do so.[105]

For this reason, the chancellery kept a watchful eye on Benda's public statements. They also did so because Benda often cited the conservative intellectuals Helmut Schelsky (1912–1984), Richard Löwenthal (1908–1991) and Karl Steinbuch (1917–2005) who argued that the stability of the state was under threat by domestic student militancy, terrorism and Cold War tensions.[106] Referencing the US doctrine of emergency executive measures in cases of 'clear and present danger', Benda endorsed the authority of the state to protect the political order. This was a particularly contentious argument after the introduction of Emergency Laws in 1968 had fuelled student militancy and public mistrust in state institutions. Hitler and the Nazi Party had used the emergency laws of the Weimar Republic to seize power in 1933. Benda now argued in 1972 that it was not enough only to trust that the institutional order – the executive, parliament and the constitutional court – would defend the republic. He, like other conservatives, saw the state simultaneously under threat from domestic left-wing radicalism and East German pressure on formerly hegemonic West German legal positions on German sovereignty. And Benda planned to use his tenure as court president to counter these threats.[107]

For conservatives, the battle for the heart of their national politics of law soon ended in a trauma. Recall that the confrontations over the Basic Treaty questioned the very existence of Germany as a nation beyond the FRG, discussed in Chapter 5. Ostpolitik's fundamental attack on older concepts of German sovereignty questioned the stability of the state in the eyes of conservative lawyers. Before the Basic Treaty trial ended in 1973, many already felt that their hold on legal politics was slipping away. To facilitate conservative debates on law in a wider circle of practitioners, Otto Theisen (1924–2005), the Minister of Justice of Rhineland-Palatine, had instituted the so-called *Bitburger Gespräche* (Bitburg Talks) as a first annual public meeting of legal experts to counteract the SPD's Legal Politics Congresses. The first meeting commenced under the theme 'Freedom and

Responsibility' in 1972. The BACDJ, meanwhile, tried to recruit young academics and practitioners interested in conservative legal reform policies. For a congress on legal policies scheduled to take place in Trier in 1974, the CDU attracted leading intellectuals to match the SPD's close ties to academic and arts elites that chancellor Willy Brandt celebrated publicly. Because he felt that conservative legal expert debates needed a fresh start on a deeper intellectual level to match the social-liberal reform rhetoric, Winfried Tilmann lobbied Theisen to attract Nikolas Luhmann as keynote speaker. To Tilmann and many others, the politics of law was a battle for the soul of the West German state, in which conservatives had lost crucial ground since the late 1960s. Luhmann, Tilmann claimed, could become the 'Schelsky of the CDU' in legal politics. The sociologist Schelsky had been a leading public intellectual in the 1950s and 1960s and shaped longstanding hegemonic sociological diagnoses of West German society.[108] Tilmann urged Theisen to treat Luhmann as a guest speaker with the appropriate care as the BACDJ urgently needed a guiding intellectual authority.[109] By the early 1970s, both major political parties thus treated legal politics as an independent sub-field of party politics.

The open political clashes surrounding the constitutional court and its judges, the establishment of lawyers' associations with close ties to the two major political parties and their regular public meetings and congresses eventually translated into a wider public interest in legal politics. The mid-1970s saw the final breakthrough of public interest in legal politics on a wider social plain. In 1976, the Ministry of Justice reported that more and more citizens requested information about the development of the West German legal system. The government was now confronted with public demand for popular readings on law that the GDR government mandated as state-sponsored legal education at the same time.[110] This upsurge in West German public interest in law coincided with the human rights offensive of Western states in the international arena. The US administration had led this rights language charge against the socialist countries since Jimmy Carter had taken office.[111] In this climate, the West German public began to debate rights no longer exclusively in a German context, but the context of international law and human rights came into view for the general public as well.[112]

Rechtsstaat in Crisis

The new federal conservative lawyers' organizations entered public debate at a time of great uncertainty. Left-wing terrorism was challenging the West German state to behave democratically in the face of political violence.[113] Preserving the rule of law and strengthening legal core concepts such as the free and democratic basic political order to defend the republic against terrorism became a top priority for conservatives. It also provided an opportunity to criticize the SPD's activist approach to law. In December 1975, the CDU congress on politics of law, which the CDU of Baden Württemberg hosted at Karlsruhe, debated the theme 'Law Secures Freedom'. In the aftermath of the kidnapping of the West Berlin CDU frontrunner Peter Lorenz (1922–1987) three days before the state elections in West Berlin on 27 February 1975 and the subsequent release of terrorists from prison in exchange for Lorenz, the stability of the state and legal order seemed under extreme threat.[114] The State Minister of Justice Traugott Bender (1927–1979) opened the meeting. The CDU, he claimed, stood for a value-driven approach to law aimed at preserving the *Rechtsstaat*. Bender oversaw the preparations of the trial against leading terrorists of the Rote Armee Fraktion (RAF, Red Army Faction) at Stuttgart-Stammheim and had been frequently under pressure from radical left-wing protesters who suspected that the state mistreated terrorists at Stammheim. During the congress, conservative lawyers then debated what they called alternatives to 'class struggle and politics of mistrust and hatred'.[115] The threat of left-wing terrorism that had dominated West German domestic politics since 1972 turned the politics of law into a central part of the conservatives' campaign preparations for the next general election in 1976.

Other conference delegates aimed their fire directly at the SPD government. The Bavarian CSU member Alfred Seidl (1911–1993) outlined central issues in the confrontation with the SPD's approach to law in the coming election campaign. For him, a particular point of contention was the active use of law for social and political modernization by the government. Seidl accused Federal President Gustav Heinemann (SPD) of using his office to promote a transformative role of law in society. For Seidl, such initiatives had no place in the institutional office of the Federal President. Since his days as Federal Minister of Justice under the grand coalition in the late 1960s, Heinemann had indeed fought for an active role of the legal sector in society. In October 1973, Heinemann had called together leading members of the ASJ, BACDJ and the FDP's party expert group on legal matters.[116] The president wanted to discuss reforms of the immigration law and rights of foreigners, the role of judges in society and new sociological approaches in the training of judges and state prosecutors.[117] At this high-profile meeting, social democrats argued that high court jurisprudence had acquired the status of active law making. Recall that the conservative president of the constitutional court Benda had to defend himself against accusations of judicial overreach in his interpretation of his role as high court judge.[118] For social democrats, such behaviour by a leading conservative jurist proved the transformative role of law and emphasized the importance of new approaches in the training of leading legal practitioners.[119] Yet the list of suggested topics for future debates showed the gulf between the political camps. While the social democrats suggested the themes of the prison system, legal training and the rights of foreigners, conservatives wanted to discuss political radicals in the civil service, the ongoing judicial reform and legal aid and expulsion of immigrants.[120] These themes reflected the planned election campaign themes that Seidl alluded to at the conservative lawyers' congress in 1975.

During the BACDJ congress at Karlsruhe, internal security became the buzzword that allowed Seidl to channel conservative demands. Seidl singled out the SPD's claim that law was a force of social transformation as the main target for conservative criticism. 'Legal norms', Seidl declared, 'must not become instruments to further one-sided ideologies, socialist utopias, or force a form of life of a minority onto the majority of citizens'.[121] Such statements tied government policy to radical left-wing grassroots activism and GDR legal reform. Conservatives hoped such rhetoric would energize their base in the fight for a return to a conservative-dominated interpretation of the Basic Law's legal order. Legal security and the protection of citizens from harm should mark out the conservatives as a law and order party in the face of radical left-wing attacks.[122]

Calls for the protection of social peace in many ways echoed a language of crime prevention debated in the GDR under state auspices, as internal security and the legal system's contribution to social stability turned into a common theme discussed in both German states, albeit with very different political impetuses. Following Seidl, the member of the CSU steering committee Karl Hillermeier (1922–2011) outlined his ideas for legal reform. Next to 'tough on crime' measures, Hillermeier singled out the reform of legal aid for citizens from low-income backgrounds as a way to attract votes that might otherwise go to the SPD. In 1975, the Bavarian state had begun test runs at twelve district courts. Bavarian conservatives admitted to the state's responsibility to provide all citizens with access to a certain degree of legal aid to protect their rights. This programme, however, was still a far cry from social democratic agendas of including and guaranteeing access for citizens to the legal system.[123]

Legal politics and their central role in the conservatives' general election campaign made this congress a major affair in 1975. This was no longer a small, secluded meeting, and it was no surprise that in the climate of an acute terrorist threat the party leaders Helmut Kohl (1930–2017) and Franz-Josef Strauß (1915–1988) raced to Karlsruhe to attract public attention to the conservatives' legal policies of defending state institutions and the law. They were joined by Ernst Benda who spoke about '*Rechtsstaat* and Social Change', Roman Herzog (1934–2017) who at the time served as state secretary in Kohl's state government in Rhineland-Palatine and would later become president of the constitutional court and Federal President, and many other leading conservative legal scholars, state prosecutors, lawyers and ministerial legal experts.[124] Benda began his keynote lecture at the end of the first congress day with a catchy slogan. 'Social change is not a synonym for social progress', he declared, and proceeded to denounce social-liberal reform rhetoric. Citing leading conservative intellectuals of the period such as Friedrich Tenbruck (1919–1994) and Ernst Forsthoff (1902–1974), he developed his contrasting perspective on state–society relations.[125] He pitched the personal freedom of West Germans against the 'other part of Germany', in which citizens enjoyed no such independence from state control. If individual liberties caused an isolation of citizens from the state, then Benda was willing to pay this price. He endorsed a conservative view of law against left-wing policies of state planning and politically engineered social change. But he nonetheless also endorsed an interpretation of the Basic Law as a 'material constitution' with the power to frame the political process through high court action. Benda explicitly rejected criticism from the political left of the Basic Treaty and abortion rights verdicts over which he had presided.[126] The court, he maintained, had to safeguard certain 'leitmotifs' of society outlined in the Basic Law. In closing, Benda cited a passage from the 1956 KPD verdict spelling out that policies of 'social transformation' – the judges had meant state socialism in the GDR in the KPD verdict – should be curtailed in the framework of the free and democratic basic political order.[127] In other words, he implicitly compared the GDR's political and legal system with the SPD's legal politics agenda.

Infuriated by such open attacks of the constitutional court's president on behalf of the CDU, the SPD countered these conservative politico-legal manoeuvres with a comprehensive agenda. In September 1977, the party released a new memorandum titled 'Social Democratic Legal Politics: Guidelines, Potential, Perspectives' that declared law and legal politics as part and parcel of its social policy.[128] Social democrats aimed at reducing privileges and inequality in society, and the transformative power of legal reform formed an integral part of this endeavour. Chancellor Helmut Schmidt (1918–2015) demanded in his opening address to parliament in 1976 that the social and welfare promises made in the Basic Law had to be finally realized for all.[129] This rhetoric, conservative critics alleged, was reminiscent of East German promises of social and economic rights. Yet there existed a crucial difference. The SPD insisted that all social policy had to be bound up in the Basic Law's basic rights catalogue and was subject to independent judicial scrutiny.[130]

Conservatives and social democrats thus fundamentally disagreed over the very purpose of legal policy by the late 1970s. Should it be first and foremost a tool for social transformation or a harbinger of political stability? In their advocacy of social change, the battle against political extremism haunted social democratic lawyers and judges. Worried by the political and constitutional crisis sparked by terrorist attacks during the German Autumn of 1977, Willy Brandt called on Martin Hirsch, the SPD's activist voice at the constitutional court and member of the SPD's commission for legal politics, to evaluate the current party policy on the legal position of courts and public security.[131] In 1978, after the terrorist crisis had been overcome, Hirsch highlighted that the unconstitutional political screening of applicants to the civil service had to end. This had been one of the first counter-terrorism measures introduced in the early 1970s that had radicalized many left-leaning students and activists in the following years. Hirsch implicitly criticized Brandt himself as Brandt as chancellor had reluctantly endorsed such personal evaluations in 1972 after the first wave of terrorist attacks had rocked the republic.[132] Hirsch closed the report for Brandt with a reference to the changed composition of the constitutional court. The SPD had allowed the CDU/CSU to extend their influence within the court in recent years. With the retirement of Walter Seuffert and Hans Georg Rupp as judges with close ties to the SPD as well as the long-standing conservative voice of Willi Geiger (1904–1994), the appointment of the SPD candidate Wolfgang Zeidler (1924–1987) and the conservative appointees Helmut Steinberger (1931–2014) and Ernst Träger (1926–2015), the court's 1975 decision in the matter of the political screening of civil servants had maintained crucial parts of the policy.[133] High court appointments remained one crucial way to change standing legal policies in vital areas of governance and security frameworks, and the conservatives in the last round of appointments had successfully ambushed the SPD.[134]

Conservatives soon used legal politics to return to the issue of sovereignty. The pain still ran deep. In 1978, the second BACDJ congress of conservative lawyers resurrected the issue of the German Reich's sovereignty. Despite six years having passed since the ratification of the Ostpolitik treaties, the insistence on state continuity between the German Reich and the FRG was still on conservative lawyers' minds. Dieter Blumenwitz (1939–2005), professor of international law and *Staatsrecht* at the Julius-Maximilians-University Würzburg, addressed conservative lawyers and judges when the BACDJ met again at Karlsruhe city hall. Blumenwitz had written the expert opinion for the Bavarian case against the Basic Treaty in 1973. He debated Germany's legal position in international law and *Staatsrecht* after the conclusion of Ostpolitik treaties and asked how they reflected on West German national identity. Blumenwitz implored his audience not to abandon the idea of state continuity: 'As long as a *staatliches Gemeinwesen* (state and society) can credibly continue in their own idea of continuity and identity, new political conditions are not able to consolidate themselves in international law'.[135] In other words, as long as West Germans insisted on state continuity from the German Reich to the FRG, the idea of two separate German states could still be challenged in international legal affairs.

Despite this desperate claim to ignore legal realities, cultural memory politics superseded legal norms in Blumenwitz's argument. Compared to earlier conservative legal concepts, Blumenwitz's rhetoric had changed in crucial details. The phrase 'Germany in its borders of 1937' had vanished from his talking points distributed to congress attendees. Rather than emphasizing legal claims based on the Reich's sovereignty, Blumenwitz honed in on the state as an idea that could continue to exist – in the spirit of Jellinek's doctrine of the state's temporal existence – beyond historical caesuras such as wars and constitutional changes. Blumenwitz then connected this ethos of state continuity to the foundation of a nation-state in 1867 that had been enlarged to the German Empire in 1871. While advocating for a continued relevance of the lost nation-state, Blumenwitz silently acknowledged that the old revisionist territorial interpretation of the identity theory had lost international credibility. He only mentioned the ideas of state continuity and 'partial state identity' developed in the late 1940s and early 1950s in passing. Instead, he aimed at a new language of sovereignty, all the while emphasizing that German sovereignty, *Deutschland als Rechtsbegriff* (Germany as a legal term), had survived Ostpolitik and the treaties signed with Poland, the Soviet Union and the GDR. Against rightwing voices who interpreted the constitutional court's 1973 verdict as a reinforced territorial claim on the Reich 'in its borders of 1937' and conveniently ignored the 1975 ruling on the Eastern Treaties, Blumenwitz highlighted a new rising concept in international debates in the context of law: national identity. In doing so, he stripped older arguments of their aura of legal objectivity and admitted to the political nature of conservative positions on questions of German sovereignty. Conservatives, he believed, should now focus on pressuring the federal government not to abandon an understanding of national identity that emphasized a conscious sense of a shared German national history from the late nineteenth century into the era of national division.[136] In many ways, Blumenwitz prepared the memory politics that the Kohl government instituted after the conservatives took office again in 1982.[137]

Following Blumenwitz's speech, Jens Hacker, professor of political science at the University of Regensburg, pointed more directly to the central importance of the constitutional court's verdicts on Ostpolitik treaties. Author of a leading study on GDR frameworks of sovereignty, Hacker hailed the court's 1973 verdict as a major achievement.[138] The judges, he stated, had returned 'contours' to the concept of 'Germany', which had become increasingly 'fuzzy' prior to 1973.[139] A confrontation over the interpretation of German sovereignty was impending, Hacker contended, and it would be fought over the question of whether the original meaning of the Basic Law or the treaty framework of Ostpolitik should prevail as West Germany's guiding star in legal politics. Like Blumenwitz, however, Hacker also ignored older conservative positions that saw a territorial dimension inbuilt in the identity theory. For him, the legal persona of Germany in international law meant that the FRG was identical to the German Reich's sovereignty. Yet Hacker no longer argued that this legal construct implied any territorial claims to prewar German territories. Instead, he advocated that the two German states constituted the only 'parts of *Gesamtdeutschland* [the whole of Germany]'.[140] Hacker only disputed the GDR's legitimacy as a second German state. This convenient reinterpretation of the original meaning of the identity theory de-escalated older conservative legal positions.

These contributions illustrate how conservatives such as Hacker for the first time interpreted the legal status of the two German states in an international legal framework. Instead of following traditional views of state continuity that had been based on German *Staatsrecht*, Hacker now saw the UN's human rights covenants and the Helsinki treaty framework as the legal basis for determining the right of self-determination of the German people. He worried that the Basic Treaty only included references to self-determination as defined in Article 2 of the UN Charter, but had not linked this fundamental right to the German people or the continued legal existence of a united Germany. Pushing for civil rights and free political expression for East Germans, which Hacker saw included in the Helsinki Accords and based in UN human rights language, now guided new conservative legal arguments against the GDR government. In Hacker's view, the concept of a still united German citizenship acquired renewed central importance. He argued that:

> the political and psychological aspects should not be overlooked: most GDR citizens still see themselves as Germans and members of an undivided German nation and not as part of a separate socialist nation of the GDR as mandated by the SED leadership.[141]

GDR citizens' right to German citizenship under West German law thus had to be maintained at all costs due to these still exiting emotional ties that transgressed the German-German border.[142] Despite his earlier denunciation of Ostpolitik in his speech, Hacker outlined in essence the SPD position in Ostpolitik negotiations a decade earlier. Only through a continued sense of a united German national identity among the citizenries of both states could German unity be won again in the future. This marked the final departure from legal claims to unification.

Despite two large public legal congresses, many conservatives viewed the party's approach to law and legality as underdeveloped.[143] In August 1979, Tilmann cautioned the current BACDJ president Hermann Hill, counselling against elevating the CDU's scattered legal positions to a 'programme' for the coming general elections in 1980. Conservative lawyers and legal experts led by the BACDJ, he argued, had not yet arrived at a coherent vision for West German domestic legality. Instead, debates crystallized around 'singular, more or less important points, which do not amount to a programme'.[144] The rhetoric of individual freedom, the focus on internal security protecting citizens from left-wing terrorism, and conflicts surrounding the legal fallout of Ostpolitik could not compare with the social democrats' comprehensive reform agenda for the entire legal system that the SPD had put forward almost a decade earlier. Tilmann thus thought it best to refrain from making law a major topic in the coming election cycle.[145]

Tilmann was right to urge caution as the SPD lawyers' association had already moved to much more ambitious themes in the late 1970s. Since 1965, the ASJ had put the citizen front and centre at its first major congress under the motto 'The Citizen and His Law'. When the association met in Saarbrücken for its fifth congress in 1980, social democratic legal experts considered ways to move from the 'Bourgeois to a Social Legal Order'.[146] The congress, led by the head of the SPD's commission on legal politics Diether Posser (1922–2010), opened with an ambitious talk by ASJ president Rudolf Wassermann (1925–2008) on 'Law as a Means for the Powerless Against the Powerful'. In contrast to the conservatives' sketchy programme, the SPD lawyers had developed comprehensive legal policies in government. The themes of equal rights for women and basic rights to work and education were followed by a debate on the right to health led by Dieter Suhr (1939–1990) and Renate Jaeger (b. 1940), who would go on to become a constitutional court and ECHR judge. Martin Hirsch, the SPD's public voice on constitutional jurisprudence and still a sitting constitutional court judge at the time, led discussions on citizen action groups, a theme that would dominate the constitutional court's work in the coming decade in the context of anti-nuclear power protests. Linked to this problem, SPD congress delegates argued over the most effective organization of the judicial system and legal aid to enable citizens to claim their rights in courts.[147]

Social rights, however, caused most controversy at the ASJ congress. Under the guidance of Ernst-Wolfgang Böckenförde and Wolfgang Zeidler, both future judges at the constitutional court, delegates tested the limits of the Basic Law in realizing social rights within the legal system. This included the right to work, a central trope of SED legal rhetoric in the context of building socialist legality. Zeidler remained sceptical as he saw political freedom diminished by state-led initiatives to implement social and economic rights. While SPD party members pushed for the inclusion of social rights in the party's programme, Böckenförde and Zeidler as legal scholars and experts cautioned against the idea that 'social basic rights' represented 'subjective legal rights'. They saw social rights as political tools rather than legal categories. In the ideological confrontation with state socialism, social rights as political concepts bolstered the state's legitimacy to intervene and organize welfare provision.[148] Yet even progressive West German legal scholars refused to treat them as legal norms. These discussions nonetheless showed how West German left-leaning legal experts, lawyers and judges were contemplating similar topics to their East German counterparts in an era marked by international conflicts over economic and social rights at the UN.[149]

Constitutional Patriotism

Protest movements of the 1960s and 1970s, the developing Helsinki treaty architecture and controversies over the curtailing of civil rights in the fight against terrorism pushed West German debates further towards a focus on the individual citizen. This domestic focus was mirrored in international clashes over which ideological legal universe was able to provide rights of citizens more effectively. In 1978, constitutional court judges from across Europe met in Vienna for their fourth international conference. Hosted once more by the West German, Italian, Yugoslavian and Austrian constitutional courts, this conference was directly influenced by recent international clashes over human rights politics at the Helsinki Accords follow-up meeting at Belgrade in 1977–78.[150] Discussions at Vienna thus centred on 'classic liberal basic rights' and 'social basic rights'.[151] The ideological division that had divided human rights in the minds of the global public in 'Western' civil and political and 'socialist' social and economic human rights structured high court debate. In his final report on the importance of basic rights, Karl Korinek (1940–2017), member of the Austrian constitutional court, emphasized a clear connection between perceptions of basic rights and the idea of the state.[152] Cold War politics of law, he maintained, had moved basic rights and human rights language to the core of state legitimacy expressed through legal language. And the social, cultural and economic change since the 1960s had put the citizen at the core of these debates across Europe. Korinek's remarks thus reflected the shifts to citizen rights-centred frameworks of statehood both east and west of the Iron Curtain.

Guaranteeing rights of citizens now also dominated West German concepts of legitimizing statehood. Constitutional court judge Konrad Hesse (1919–2005) presented a domestic West German perspective that was devoid of all wider German-German frameworks. Hesse pointed to the shifts in the understanding of basic rights in past decades in West German debates. Rights had transformed the relationship between the state and its citizens, from a situation in which basic rights merely protected the individual against state infringements on individual rights to a more comprehensive approach in which basic rights had to play a role in ensuring the social well-being of citizens. Here, Hesse's rhetoric inched closer to elements of state-socialist rhetoric. The 'planning, guiding and forming state', he explained, had a duty to secure its citizens' livelihoods and social security. This duty extended to the negotiation of the freedom of citizens in an 'ever closer and increasingly complex world' and applied in particular to economic rights and education.[153] In this new situation, individual freedom and liberty as constitutional rights could no longer be purely defined as a 'state-free sphere'. The state had to play an active role in negotiating and realizing basic rights for its citizens. 'The state', Hesse contended, 'no longer appears as a potential enemy of freedom, but has to become an aide and protector of it'.[154] Yet he also qualified this rhetoric in view of recent advances of socialist legality in the international arena, explaining that this active role of the state could by no means be unrestricted and without legal safeguards for the individual citizen.[155] Basic rights, he concluded, had come to structure not only the legal sphere of the state, but encompassed 'the entire legal life of the Federal Republic', acquiring a 'hitherto unknown importance' in German constitutional history.[156]

Basic rights, in Hesse's opinion, thus possessed a guiding function for social values and politics. His report outlined in a nutshell what would soon be described by the term constitutional patriotism: basic rights should encapsulate the basic political values that guaranteed social cohesion and consensus within West German society.[157] They legitimized the existence of the state and guaranteed an open and free political process as a cornerstone of democratic governance. Hesse was well aware that his comments about a guarantee of basic rights would be read in the context of recent domestic clashes over the curtailing of basic rights guarantees for terrorists during the German Autumn of 1977.[158] While he fully opposed such attacks on basic rights, he also believed that legal safeguards protecting basic rights had not resulted in a 'weak state'. On the contrary, the state was instrumental in guaranteeing basic rights in modern society also in times of political crisis. Yet Hesse's vision of state power was now bound up in the 'voluntary support of citizens for shared political values', by which he meant that citizens had to actively defend their own basic freedoms. Hesse advised West Germans that the guarantees of the Basic Law's basic rights catalogue had to be continuously won in open democratic debate.[159]

Basic rights provisions guaranteed by the Basic Law, and the West German constitution as a whole, morphed into the potential core for a new rights-driven national identity.[160] But this emphasis on the centrality of basic rights still had a way to go until it reached the heart of public discourse. When Sternberger praised the Basic Law as the keystone of West German identity in May 1979, his opinion was not representative of a majority of West German elites.[161] Only when conservative memory politics pushed the question of the German Reich's sovereignty decisively into the background, after Helmut Kohl had become chancellor in 1982, did the debate on the FRG's legal identity come to focus firmly on the West German political and legal system in all major political parties.[162] Access to citizenship rights and the challenges of migration now had a much greater influence on West German legal identity politics in the 1980s than all-German frameworks.[163]

In 1984, the social democrat Hans Apel (1932–2011) declared that German division and the existence of two German states had answered the German question. Only a couple of years earlier, such a statement would have provoked aggressive conservative reactions. Now, the conservative Alois Rummel (1922–2013) merely called Apel's rhetoric 'insensitive', and remarked laconically there had been a time when Apel would have been accused of 'high treason' for such a remark.[164] For Rummel, the German question had to be decided by East Germans in free elections. Whether they voted for German unity or against it was to be entirely their decision. The right to self-determination in elections therefore determined conservative reactions to Apel's remark rather than legal claims to a unified Germany. At the same time, support for a reinstitution of the German Reich in the 1937 borders decreased to five percent in West German opinion polls. West Germans were hoping first and foremost for the political and economic stability of their own state. After almost four decades of separation, moreover, the taboo that prevented the acknowledgement of the loss of Eastern territories deteriorated in conservative milieus.[165] With the fervent intellectual clashes during the *Historikerstreit* (historian's quarrel) in 1986 and Jürgen Habermas's (b. 1929) intervention in which he reframed Sternberger's concept into a 'post-national' form of national identity, the term constitutional patriotism made its final breakthrough in West German public debate.[166]

With this turn inwards and debate on the nature of the FRG's legal culture, West German international politics of law focused almost entirely on revealing and admonishing the ways in which the GDR state was wilfully withholding rights from its citizens. Western European debates on the right to leave a country supported this agenda. At a three-day meeting at the International Institute of Human Rights at Strasbourg in November 1986, delegates formulated the fifteen articles of the Strasbourg Declaration on the Right to Free Exit and Return.[167] Citing the Universal Declaration of Human Rights, the human rights covenant on civil and political rights, the convention against racial discrimination and regional human rights declarations, the declaration was primarily aimed at developing countries. Gerhard Jahn (1927–1998), at the time judge at the West German constitutional court and a delegate at the meeting, followed these European rights debates with an eye to the GDR's border regime. But the German question and Cold War division were now a secondary issue in the Strasbourg discussions about the declaration. The hierarchy of legal issues as they were listed in the Strasbourg Declaration in fact acknowledged the rights situation of developing countries before endorsing the right to exit and return to a country, a part of the declaration that clearly took aim at Eastern bloc states. Mass emigration, the core theme of the Strasbourg debates, was seen as a major threat to developing countries and affected Europe in this context of South–North migration. Border and migration controls against uncontrolled immigration from the Global South in the interest of Western countries had come to rival and overtake criticism of socialist border regimes.[168] Even before the Cold War ended, these migration pressures put 'fortress Europe' on the agenda of legal politics where it has remained until today. The Strasbourg debate showed that most Western Europeans had accepted the division of Europe.

Conclusion: A Divided Country

By the end of the 1980s, both German states had integrated their politics of law into the legal cultures of their respective ideological alliances. Decades of legal exchanges with partners in other countries from within and beyond their ideological alliances introduced many international legal norms into an originally self-centred German legal discourse. While West German lawyers, legal experts and judges looked to Western role models, the GDR government adopted socialist legality on Soviet terms. In this process, legal politics became a core component of governance and national identity in both states. Law now formed an integral part of describing and debating two separated political cultures within the two German states in the midst of legal internationalization drives east and west of the Iron Curtain. How 'the state' provided and secured rights formed the core of these legal politics in domestic, German-German and international settings in the 1970s and 1980s.

The ideological competition between socialist legality and the West German *Rechtsstaat* caused the separation of the two German legal spheres and shaped two separate legal cultures until 1989. After 1973, politicians, ministerial officials and high court judges in both states worked to disentangle their legislation and moved to independent legal identities. In the 1970s and 1980s, the two German governments and their legal experts engaged with each other on the basis of a mutually acknowledged sovereign statehood. This shift away from all-German legal and rights frameworks to bilateral legal conflicts shifted the mindset of Germans in East and West. Four decades of national division thus resulted in separated legal systems that had established their own traditions and patterns of cultural meaning by the 1980s.[169] The separation of the once unified German legal sphere was complete.

Notes

1. 'Rede Erich Honeckers vor der Volkskammer', *Neues Deutschland* (28 September 1974).
2. Ibid.
3. For this subversive effect of socialist law propaganda and the function of legal education under socialism, see: Altehenger, *Legal Lessons*, 247–61. See also: Richardson-Little, *The Human Rights Dictatorship*, 180–221.
4. Heuer and Lieberam, 'Rechtsverständnis in der DDR', 72–74.
5. Dolf Sternberger, 'Verfassungspatriotismus', *FAZ* (23 May 1979). For Sternberger's citizen-centred social ethos, see: Kinkela, *Die Rehabilitierung des Bürgerlichen im Werk Dolf Sternbergers*.
6. Dolf Sternberger, 'Verfassungspatriotismus', *FAZ* (23 May 1979).
7. For Sternberger's concept and the intellectual environment in which it developed, see: Müller, *Verfassungspatriotismus*; Hacke, *Die Bundesrepublik als Idee*.
8. Dolf Sternberger, 'Verfassungspatriotismus', *FAZ* (23 May 1979).
9. For the clashes over how to merge state planning and socialist constitutional law in the 1950s that very much still happened in direct competition with the West German legal sphere, see: Caldwell, *Dictatorship, State Planning, and Social Theory*, 63–74 and Chapters 1 and 2 of this book.
10. For the origins of German legal codes in the late nineteenth century, see: Crosby, *The Making of a German Constitution*.

11. BArch, DY30/IVA2/13/1, media review on reporting on the state and law.
12. BArch, DP2/249, letter Herrmann, 22 September 1967.
13. For Soviet approaches to rights talk, see: Nathans, 'Soviet Rights-Talk in the Post-Stalin Era'. For Communist Chinese approaches, see: Altehenger, *Legal Lessons*.
14. The transition from all-German rhetoric to a focus on GDR sovereignty becomes most obvious through a comparison of the first preface to the new GDR constitution from 1968 and the final version of 1974. The 1968 version reads: 'Bearing the responsibility for showing the entire German nation the way toward a future of peace and socialism, in light of the historical fact that imperialism under the leadership of the USA in agreement with circles of West German monopoly capital has divided Germany in order to build up West Germany as a base for imperialism and the struggle against socialism, which contradicts the vital interests of the nation, the people of the German Democratic Republic, resting firmly on the accomplishments of the antifascist-democratic and socialist transformation of the social order, its working classes and strata united in continuing the work of the Constitution of 7 October 1949 in spirit, and suffused with the will to continue unswervingly and voluntarily along the path of peace, social justice, democracy, socialism, and international understanding, has given itself this socialist Constitution'. The 1974 version reads: 'Continuing the revolutionary tradition of the German working class and supported by the liberation from fascism, the people of the German Democratic Republic, in accordance with the processes of historical development of our epoch, have realized their right to socio-economic, governmental, and national self-determination, and have created a developed socialist society. Imbued by the will to determine their own fate freely, to continue resolutely along the path of socialism and Communism, peace, democracy, and peace among nations, the people of the German Democratic Republic have given themselves this socialist constitution'.
15. BArch, DP2/2963, report on West German and foreign reaction to GDR Criminal Code, 9 February 1968.
16. PA/AA, B82/913, foreign and German-German policy aspects of the GDR constitution, 5 February 1968.
17. Ibid.
18. BArch, DP2/2963, report on West German and foreign reaction to GDR Criminal Code, 9 February 1968.
19. 'Rede Erich Honeckers vor der Volkskammer', *Neues Deutschland* (28 September 1974).
20. For the role of consumption in political stability and the problems of a new integrated social and economic policy, see: Boyer and Skyba, 'Sozial- und Konsumpolitik als Stabilisierungsstrategie'; Hübner and Hübner, *Sozialismus als soziale Frage*, 387–424.
21. ABBAW, AKL (1969–1991), No. 1096, manuscript Such.
22. ABBAW, AKL (1969–1991), No. 1096, invitation letter and manuscripts Poppe and Such.
23. Ibid.
24. ABBAW, AKL (1969–1991), No. 1096, manuscript Such.
25. Altehenger, 'Unlikely Heirs' and *Legal Lessons*.
26. Siegfried Heger (head of the Section State and Legal Questions at the Central Committee of the SED), Hantsche (deputy head of the Section Labour Law at the *Freie Deutsche Gewerkschaftsbund* (FDGB, Free German Trade Union Federation), Stiller, Müller, Bley (Academy for State and Legal Science), Hämmerlein, Negler (Office of the GDR State Prosecutor), Strasberg, Mauer (GDR High Court), Seyfert (head of the Information of Press Office) as well as members of the FdJ, the Ministry of the Interior and the National Front attended this meeting. BArch, DP2/720, report on next steps in legal education work, 4 September 1974.
27. For a discussion of 'rules consciousness' in contrast to 'rights consciousness' in the particular cultural traditions of China, see: Perry, 'Chinese Conceptions of "Rights"'.

28. For the GDR government's use of the media to portray legality, see: Marxen and Weinke, *Inszenierungen des Rechts*; Hilgert, *Unterhaltung, aber sicher*. For the role of legal education and law propaganda in socialist states, see: Altehenger, *Legal Lessons*.
29. BArch, DP2/720, evaluation of benefits and problems of law propaganda work with focus on 'Law in Our Time' series, 5 January 1977.
30. BArch, DP1/5089, draft decree, 1977.
31. Ibid.
32. Knabe, *Zur Praxis des politischen Strafrechts in der Honecker-Zeit*.
33. BArch, DP1/21451, appendix letter Kern, 23 December 1977, 2.
34. For everyday criminality and the state's effort to combat it with law propaganda and popular legal education see: Millington, 'State Power and "Everyday Criminality"', 440–60.
35. For this campaign, see: Gehrig, 'Reaching Out to the Third World'.
36. BArch, DY30/22276, circular regarding Riege article on legal duties of GDR citizens, 24 April 1984.
37. Berend, *An Economic History of Twentieth-Century Europe*, 157–60.
38. ABBAW, AKL (1969–1991), No. 1096, manuscript Lekschas.
39. Ibid.
40. Ibid.
41. Ibid.
42. Berend, *An Economic History of Twentieth-Century Europe*, 157–60.
43. Ibid.
44. BArch, DP2/1989, report on GDR High Court visit to Soviet Union, 1981.
45. BArch, DP2/1989, report on GDR High Court visit to Poland, 1983.
46. See: Knabe, *Zur Praxis des politischen Strafrechts in der Honecker-Zeit*.
47. BArch, B136/17597, CDU/CSU report on human rights, 1976–1977.
48. ACDP, I-294/063-3, note for Teltschik, 17 March 1977.
49. Snyder, *Human Rights Activism and the End of the Cold War*, 81–114.
50. ACDP, I-294/063-3, note for Teltschik, 17 March 1977.
51. BArch, B137/10767, parliamentary inquiry into governmental human rights policy, 1979.
52. See documentation in BArch, B137/10767.
53. ACDP, I-294/063-3, reply to parliamentary inquiry into governmental human rights policy, 20 September 1979.
54. Ibid.
55. Ibid.
56. Ibid.
57. For competing arguments describing the same US turn to individual human rights, see: Moyn, *The Last Utopia*; Keys, *Reclaiming American Virtue*; Slaughter, 'Hijacking Human Rights'.
58. BArch, DP1/21394, letter Fischer, 7 April 1981.
59. Ibid.
60. BArch, DP2/2452, information on basic rights protection in GDR jurisprudence, 1981.
61. Ibid.
62. Slaughter, 'Hijacking Human Rights'.
63. BArch, DP2/2452, letter Toeplitz, 3 July 1981.
64. Silomon, *'Schwerter zu Pflugscharen' und die DDR*, 35–55; Neubert, *Geschichte der Opposition in der DDR*, 398–405.
65. BArch, DP2/2452, letter Toeplitz, 3 July 1981.
66. ABBAW, FOB Gewi, No. 243, draft programme conference 'The GDR Constitution – History and Present', May 1984.
67. Ibid.

68. Heuer and Lieberam, 'Rechtsverständnis in der DDR', 72–74; Betts, 'Property, Peace and Honour'.
69. ABBAW, FOB Gewi, No. 243, 'Konzeption zur Durchführung der Konferenz "Verfassung der DDR – Geschichte und Gegenwart"', May 1984.
70. Ibid.
71. Silomon, *'Schwerter zu Pflugscharen' und die DDR*, 35–55; Neubert, *Geschichte der Opposition in der DDR*, 398–405.
72. Richardson-Little, 'The Failure of the Socialist Declaration of Human Rights'.
73. Ibid.
74. Ibid.
75. In some ways, GDR debates came full circle by returning to the controversies over the primacy of the party, socialist legality and its role in state planning. For the origins of this debate, see: Caldwell, *Dictatorship, State Planning, and Social Theory*, 57–96.
76. BArch, DP2/2266, conference working group, 30 October 1987. For the Stockholm Appeal's global reach, see: Harrison, 'Popular Responses to the Atomic Bomb in China'.
77. BArch, DP2/2266, conference working group, 30 October 1987.
78. Ibid.
79. BArch, DP2/2266, 'Manifesto of GDR High Court President Sarge', 17 May 1988.
80. For the full protocol of conference discussions, see: BArch, DP2/594.
81. Ibid.
82. BArch, DP2/2266, closing remarks Sarge, 18 May 1988.
83. BArch, DP2/594.
84. Ibid.
85. Altehenger, 'Unlikely Heirs'.
86. Oscar Sanchez-Sibony has pointed to the Soviet Union's attempt to spearhead a socialist transformation of world trade when the Soviet leadership engaged with world trade in the interwar and early postwar period. See: Sanchez-Sibony, *Red Globalization*.
87. For women's human rights activism and activists' global rights campaigns, see: Wildenthal, *The Language of Human Rights*, 101–66; Eckel, *Die Ambivalenz des Guten*, 347–435.
88. For the SPD's extensive legal agenda to block Adenauer's policies, see: Gosewinkel, *Adolf Arndt*.
89. AdsD 1/MHAC01278, Nachlass Hirsch, draft statutes, 27 April 1954; minutes ASJ members meeting, 19 March 1954.
90. For the evolution of the BACDJ into a conservative legal think tank, see: ACDP 07-001-4004, letter Dufhues, 2 June 1966; letter Lücke, 16 May 1966; note for Heck, 3 October 1966; minutes of first BACDJ meeting, 9 May 1968.
91. The jurist and journalist Rudolf Gerhardt, writing for the FAZ at the time, initiated discussions in March 1967. He approached the Deutsche Juristentag and the publisher C.H. Beck to test the waters for such an endeavour. He proposed a journal that reacted to the changes in the perception of law as an academic discipline and in its social, cultural and political dimensions. Gerhardt proposed including not just lawyers, judges and legal scholars as potential authors, but explicitly called for the inclusion of political scientists and sociologists. See: BArch, B411/489, note on Journal for Legal Politics, 3 March 1967.
92. Stolleis, *Geschichte des Öffentlichen Rechts in Deutschland, Bd. 4*, 305–548.
93. BArch, B411/489, exposé Journal for Legal Politics.
94. For the developing landscape of legal journals see: Löhnig, 'Alternative Legal Publicism'.
95. The leadership of the Juristentag feared that a younger left-wing generation of judges would take over the new journal. See: BArch, B411/489, letter Redeker, 25 June 1968.
96. For the impact of these reforms on the legal field, see: Requate, *Der Kampf um die Demokratisierung*, 168–315.

97. Wassermann, 'Jurist im Porträt'.
98. Participants included: Martin Hirsch, Helmut Simon, Konrad Duden, Ernst-Joachim Mestmäcker, Klaus Arndt, Peter Glotz, Arnold Gehlen, Martin Ihrle, Wolfgang Zeidler, Ernst Friesenhahn, Roman Herzog, Harry Pross and Rudolf Wassermann. See: AdsD, Nachlass Zeidler, programme and other materials SPD Legal Politics Congress, 21–23 February 1969.
99. Caldwell, *Democracy, Capitalism, and the Welfare State*, 46–70.
100. AdsD, Nachlass Zeidler, programme and other materials SPD Legal Politics Congress, 21–23 February 1969.
101. See: Smith, *Kidnap City*; Heitzer, *Die Kampfgruppe gegen Unmenschlichkeit (KgU)*.
102. Wagner, *Hilde Benjamin und die Stalinisierung der DDR-Justiz*, 142.
103. BArch, B122/7550, speech Heinemann, 8 December 1971.
104. ACDP, 07-001-4105, speech Benda, 8 December 1971.
105. BArch, B136/4438, speech Benda, 26 April 1972.
106. See: Wehrs, *Protest der Professoren*; Schildt, '"Die Kräfte der Gegenreform sind auf breiter Front angetreten"'.
107. BArch, B136/4438, speech Benda, 26 April 1972.
108. Kersting, 'Helmut Schelskys "Skeptische Generation" von 1957'; Nolte, *Die Ordnung der deutschen Gesellschaft*, 230–31.
109. ACDP, 07-001-4402, letter Tilmann, 10 January 1974.
110. BArch, B136/15298, report on growing public interest in law, 29 January 1976.
111. Keys, *Reclaiming American Virtue*; Snyder, *Human Rights Activism and the End of the Cold War*. For Western human rights rhetoric as a foreign policy device, see: Eckel, *Die Ambivalenz des Guten*, 435–582.
112. See: Wildenthal, *The Language of Human Rights*, 101–66.
113. Aust, *Der Baader Meinhof Komplex*; Peters, *Tödlicher Irrtum*; Hanshew, *Terror and Democracy in West Germany*.
114. Hanshew, *Terror and Democracy in West Germany*, 138–41.
115. ACDP, 07-001-4402, Pressedienst, CDU Baden-Württemberg, 3 December 1975.
116. BArch, B122/7265, minutes of meeting with legal policy party experts, 25 October 1973.
117. Ibid.
118. See: 'Karlsruhe: Ein verkappter Gesetzgeber?', *Der Spiegel* 10 (1975), 68–74.
119. BArch, B122/7265, minutes of meeting with legal policy party experts, 25 October 1973.
120. Ibid.
121. ACDP, 07-001-4402, Pressedienst, CDU Baden-Württemberg, 3 December 1975.
122. Ibid.
123. See: ACDP, 07-001-4402.
124. ACDP, 07-001-4401, congress programme and official invitation.
125. Forsthoff had intervened in the debate on the welfare state early on in a major controversy with Abendroth in the 1950s. See: Caldwell, *Democracy, Capitalism, and the Welfare State*, 46–70.
126. For media attacks on Benda in the context of these cases, see: 'Karlsruhe: Ein verkappter Gesetzgeber?', *Der Spiegel* 10 (1975), 68–74.
127. ACDP, 07-001-4405, speech Benda.
128. AdsD, 1/GJAA000625, Nachlass Jahn, intern-documents no. 5: social-democratic legal policies, September 1977.
129. Ibid.
130. Ibid.
131. AdsD, 1/MHAC000434, Nachlass Hirsch, letter Hirsch, 10 July 1978.
132. For the history of the *Radikalenerlaß*, see: Braunthal, *Political Loyalty and Public Service*; Jaeger, *Auf der Suche nach 'Verfassungsfeinden'*.

133. AdsD, 1/MHAC000434, Nachlass Hirsch, letter, 10 July 1978. Further expert opinions were submitted to Brandt by Bernhard Schlink (b. 1944) and Ernst-Wolfgang Böckenförde (1930–2019). See: AdsD, 1/MHAC000434, Nachlass Hirsch, memoranda Schlink/Böckenförde, 28 August 1978.
134. 'Dat ham wir uns so nich vorjestellt: Der Streit um das Bundesverfassungsgericht (III): Parteienproporz bei der Richterwahl', *Der Spiegel* 46 (1978), 84–98.
135. ACDP, 07-001-4408, speech Blumenwitz, 18 May 1978.
136. Ibid.
137. For this conservative reorientation, see: Geyer, 'War over Words'; Hoeres, 'Von der "Tendenzwende" zur "geistig-moralischen Wende"'; Steber, *Die Hüter der Begriffe*.
138. See: Hacker, *Der Rechtsstatus Deutschlands*.
139. ACDP, 07-001-4408, speech Hacker, 18 May 1978.
140. Ibid.
141. Ibid.
142. Ibid.
143. For transcripts of BACDJ congress speeches, see: ACDP, 07-001-4408.
144. ACDP, 07-001-4252, letter Tilmann, 21 August 1979.
145. Ibid.
146. BArch, B136/13974, documentation 5th SPD Legal Politics Congress, 29 February–2 March 1980.
147. Ibid.
148. Ibid.
149. The legal quality of social and economic human rights continues to captivate legal debates in the post-Cold War world. See: Normand and Zaidi, *Human Rights at the UN*, 316–41.
150. See: Bilandzic, Dahlmann and Kosanovic, *From Helsinki to Belgrade*; Badalassi and Snyder, *The CSCE and the End of the Cold War*.
151. BArch, B141/96907, report Fourth Conference of European Constitutional Courts, 1978.
152. Ibid.
153. BArch, B141/96907, country report FRG, 16 September 1978.
154. Ibid.
155. Ibid.
156. Ibid.
157. Müller, *Verfassungspatriotismus*.
158. Balz, *Von Terroristen, Sympathisanten und dem starken Staat*, 278–86.
159. BArch, B141/96907, country report FRG, 16 September 1978.
160. Müller, *Verfassungspatriotismus*; Hacke, *Die Bundesrepublik als Idee*.
161. Dolf Sternberger, 'Verfassungspatriotismus', *FAZ* (23 May 1979).
162. Hoeres, 'Von der "Tendenzwende" zur "geistig-moralischen Wende"'. For debates on the modernization of political key terms within the CDU, see: Steber, *Die Hüter der Begriffe*, 164–354.
163. See: Gehrig, 'Deutsche Staatsangehörigkeit und "Deutschenfähigkeit"'.
164. Rummel, 'Ohne Kompass'.
165. Wahl, 'Deutsch-polnischer Klartext'.
166. See: Müller, *Verfassungspatriotismus*; Hacke, *Die Bundesrepublik als Idee*. For the *Historikerstreit*, see: Roth, *Die Idee der Nation im politischen Diskurs*, 254–317. See also: Conze, *Die Suche nach Sicherheit*, 654–64; Wirsching, *Abschied vom Provisorium*, 485–91; Wolfrum, *Geschichtspolitik in der Bundesrepublik Deutschland*, 303–25. For British and US perspectives, see: Evans, *In Hitler's Shadow*; Maier, *The Unmasterable Past*. For recent scholarship, see: Kailitz, *Die Gegenwart der Vergangenheit*; Kronenberg, *Zeitgeschichte, Wissenschaft und Politik*; 'Holocaust Scholarship and Politics in the Public Sphere: Reexamining

the Causes, Consequences, and Controversy of the Historikerstreit and the Goldhagen Debate: A Forum with Gerrit Dworok, Richard J. Evans, Mary Fulbrook, Wendy Lower, A. Dirk Moses, Jeffrey K. Olick, and Timothy D. Snyder', *Central European History* 50(3) (2017), 375–403.
167. AdsD, 1/GJAA000541, Nachlass Jahn, expert advice on law to leave and return to one's own country, November 1986.
168. AdsD, 1/GJAA0000541, Nachlass Jahn, Strasbourg Declaration on the Right to Leave and Return, 26 November 1986.
169. For the FRG, see: Müller, *Verfassungspatriotismus*; Hacke, *Die Bundesrepublik als Idee*; Roth, *Die Idee der Nation im politischen Diskurs*. For the GDR, see: Palmowksi, *Inventing a Socialist Nation* and 'Citizenship, Identity, and Community'; Betts, 'Property, Peace and Honour' and 'Socialism, Social Rights, Human Rights'.

Conclusion

License to Legislate

The legal battle between the two German states was about who could legitimately legislate on behalf of Germans and thus define what Germany was as well as who was German. This was not merely a legal question. After the downfall of the Third Reich in 1945, speaking lawfully and rightfully on behalf of Germans was a question of moral legitimacy. In the aftermath of the crimes of Nazi warfare and the Holocaust, this moral legitimacy was not easily obtained.[1] The moral crisis of the postwar moment made the language of law one of the few political modes Germans could use to engage with international audiences and try to claim some level of legitimacy.[2] Law, as this book has argued, thus at first became a resource for Germans to regain political agency and a language to push back against Allied policies. Thereafter, the politics of law divided Germany legally and reframed the rights of ordinary Germans along ideological lines until 1989.

German frameworks of legal sovereignty operated in a complex web of domestic and international entanglements of law. Third Reich legal legacies and the Cold War division, as Part I of this book illustrated, motivated the strategic use of sovereignty and rights frameworks in both German states. Between 1945 and 1989, lawmakers in both German states moved emphasis between the three core concepts of *Staat*, *Staatsgebiet* and *Staatsvolk* that made up statehood since Georg Jellinek had first defined it in 1895. Moving either of these three core components to the heart of legal doctrine of statehood at different moments in time allowed for flexibility and reconfigurations in East and West German legal doctrine in the attempt to dispute the legitimacy of the other state. The strict separation between international law as the law governing the relations between sov-

---

Notes for this chapter begin on page 272.

ereign states and domestic law, a doctrine that only weakened in the 1960s and 1970s, gave additional leeway in devising a variety of legal arguments against the ideological opponent in German-German and international politics.

The escalation of the Cold War battle on German soil after 1945 from the Berlin Blockade in 1948 to the East German Uprising in 1953 allowed West German jurists to reassert their own doctrinal *Staatsrecht* heritage in international affairs and undermine the initial Allied powers' programme of a fundamental reformation of the legal field.[3] Until the late 1950s, West German legal experts and politicians entrenched both German governments in a legal battle over the sovereign rights of the 'German Reich in its borders of 1937' by claiming direct continuity in state sovereignty between the Reich and the FRG. This projection of sovereignty beyond West German borders forced the GDR to remain focused on German judicial traditions in trying to refute the Bonn government's claims to the representation of the whole of Germany for much longer than the SED leadership had intended in the transition to socialism.

The parameters of established German legal doctrine thus shaped the legal new beginnings in both states, yet they often clashed with the new ideological foundations of the East and West German states. West German efforts to implement a new democratic ethos based on the Basic Law were as much tainted by continuities in bureaucratic and judicial practice from the Third Reich as were the SED leadership's attempts to mould the legal sciences to serve the party-state.[4] Underneath separate domestic constitutional frameworks, the intellectual traditions of the interwar period reigned strongly in legal debates within both states and in their struggle with each other over law until the 1960s.[5] The history of law in divided Germany therefore to some extent defied narratives of Westernization and Sovietization in this period despite the fact that both governments fell in line with their superpower's propaganda war for the hearts and minds of Germans.

If the Allied occupation framework and German *Staatsrecht* doctrine promoted by West German legal experts shaped the period until the 1960s, global conflicts over the definition of sovereignty, self-determination and the international representation of states structured the internationalization of the German legal confrontations provoked by East German legal scholars and party experts from the 1960s into the 1970s. The second part of this book showed how international pressures of decolonization and the global Cold War over international law doctrine, human rights concepts and legal frameworks of sovereignty and citizenship transformed the contest between the two German states. Promoting the GDR-*Staatsvolk*'s claim to self-determination against the West German focus on continuity in the existence of the unified German *Staat* beyond 1945 and 1949, the GDR government introduced international law languages of self-determination and human rights to the German-German contest over legality when both German governments fought over the terms of détente.[6]

This shift made the GDR a case for international law experts at the UN. East German governmental legal experts and scholars developed their understanding of sovereignty from a concept rooted in nationality into a legal framework based on socialist ideology, a shift that threatened to question established modes of international representation and diplomacy at the UN. Eventually, the UN decoupled German division from the legal issue of the representation of all sovereign states within the UN and the legal battles of other 'divided nations'. The SED leadership forced a German legal exceptionalism in UN politics by defining the GDR-*Staatsvolk* no longer primarily in ethnic terms but putting the rights of citizens guaranteed under socialism at the core of its state's legal sovereignty. In doing so, however, the GDR government also threatened former East German citizens with forced naturalization to pressure the Bonn government into accepting independent GDR statehood. The separation of the shared German legal heritage that the SED leadership forced in the 1960s and 1970s enshrined the GDR's physical restrictions of freedom of movement into a new framework of socialist legality. Law was thus instrumentalized to whittle down constitutionally guaranteed rights of East Germans and complemented the militarized border regime that the SED had established since the building of the Berlin Wall.

To acknowledge the existence of two German states with their accession to full UN membership in 1973 meant embracing two rivalling legal cultures. Part III of this book traced how two distinctly different German legal systems gave rise to separated legal cultures and contributed to distinct East and West German national identities. If the origins of the legal battle between the two German states over sovereignty and citizenship rights lay in the question of who would legitimately represent German law, legality and people, this battle turned into a confrontation of two rivalling universalisms of law that was increasingly fought in the language of human rights in the 1970s and 1980s. During the first half of the Cold War, politicians, ministerial officials, high court judges and state-sponsored activists had fought the other Germany over the 'correct' legal interpretation of German postwar sovereignty from which claims to the representation of rights of Germans flowed. It was only when the Bonn and East Berlin governments mutually acknowledged their separate statehood and territorial integrity under domestic and international law in Ostpolitik negotiations and the ratification of the Helsinki Accords that two distinct legal cultures could be fully and officially embraced. German-

German legal conflicts now centred on the ability of both states to provide their citizens with individual rights in the battle for a higher plane of ideological legitimacy. This inward turn in both German states was put in even sharper relief by the simultaneous ever-closer transnational integration of legal networks east and west of the Iron Curtain. The internationalization of legal spheres within both blocs remade law into an integral part of separated political cultures within the FRG and the GDR. Two separate forms of constitutionalism saw the East German party-state trying to infuse society with socialist legal consciousness while West Germans argued over constitutional patriotism as a new national identity.[7]

Historiography has traditionally assumed that 'the Federal Republic could exist without any problems without the GDR'.[8] Such narratives gave West German developments and political agency precedent over the history of the GDR. A focus on the German legal entanglements between 1949 and 1989 in domestic, German-German and international contexts complicates such narratives. The GDR's existence and SED rights policies shaped West German politics of sovereignty and citizenship in fundamental ways. West German legal frameworks thus cannot be studied without also paying attention to the history of GDR law making as well, and vice versa.[9] These conflicts never took place in complete isolation of the two German legal spheres from the rest of the world. German legal division unfolded against the backdrop of a multipolar world shaped by Cold War conflicts, decolonization and Third World liberation, and the rise of international organizations and rights languages. German-German clashes over legitimacy through law and rights thus can only be fully understood in these wider international contexts.

The disentanglement of German legal tradition into two separate legal systems until 1989 mirrored and formed part of broader shifts in international law and rights debates. The breakdown of imperial logics of an unequal international system of sovereign states and dependent peoples propelled the East German international rights campaign to have the GDR recognized as a sovereign state. The pressures of decolonization and Third World utopias of an equal international system allowed East German policy makers to frame their quest for independence from all-German legal frameworks of the postwar era in a Third World-inspired legal language of self-determination. This campaign forced West German legal experts and politicians to let go of turn-of-the-century concepts of state sovereignty and continuity in the state's existence. This opening up to international law and global rights languages led to an increasing influence of international legal norms on formerly closed legal systems in both German states from the 1960s onwards.

The battle for ideological legitimacy at the same time prompted both German states, their judiciaries and societies at large to negotiate how individual rights were acquired and guaranteed to justify the sovereign right to legitimate statehood. This shift, which also manifested in new forms of human rights activism, made the realization of the rights of the individual – beyond the ideological clashes over civil and political as well as social and economic rights – an equally important aspect of state authority and legitimacy at home and in international affairs than claiming sovereignty in international affairs. While the GDR government saw rights inevitably tied to the building of socialism and only secured within the context of the socialist party-state and its citizenship, West German basic rights frameworks evolved reflecting the conflicts between concepts of rights guaranteed through citizenship and universal principles of rights inherent in the human existence. These clashes over the very nature of law and rights forced both German states to open up their closed legal systems to international rights norms and made basic and human rights guarantees of the state to the individual citizen a new cornerstone in claiming legitimacy for the international and domestic representation of sovereignty and citizenship.

No Gentle Civilizer of National Self-Interest

George Kennan's assertion, made in 1950, that law could be the 'gentle civilizer of national self-interest' became its antithesis in Germany's legal Cold War.[10] The military stalemate in Europe rendered law a prime vehicle to attack, intrude into and contest political legitimacy. This focus on legal frameworks as a site of ideological conflict was further enhanced by the rise of human rights language after 1945.[11] Political legitimacy now increasingly hinged upon the adherence to international legal standards. Yet, even if East and West German jurists and legal scholars at different times and in different ways portrayed international norms as universal in their reach and validity, these norms remained ardently contested between democratic and socialist legal interpretations. The legal battle in divided Germany was thus not so much about the divide between political and civil rights and social and economic rights, but about the conflict over how the state legitimized power over people and how individuals gained rights in the first place. Against Western traditions of natural law and legal positivism, socialist law refused to accept the existence of rights outside of the existence of the state. Understanding this ideological competition over law and rights, of which the two German states formed part, is crucial for our understanding of the establishment of post-Cold War discourses of human rights and international law.[12]

This book has explored legal sovereignty as a social and political construct that – even during the times when West German high court judges, ministerial officials, scholars and politicians portrayed them publicly as impenetrable and unalterable – consisted of many strategic legal interpretations. In other words, the realities of sovereignty were always much more complicated and imperfect than legal languages of sovereignty suggested. The history of the politics of sovereignty during the Cold War puts the work of many Western political scientists, international relations scholars and legal scholars who conceptualized sovereignty in the postwar era into sharp relief. In an era in which scholars such as Hans J. Morgenthau (1904–1980) and Leo Gross (1903–1990) claimed the indivisible nature of international sovereignty as an undisputed fact and shaped hegemonic concepts for the new academic discipline of international relations based on the equality of nation-states, the history of divided nations such as Germany reveals the politics surrounding the 'Westphalian myth' that underpinned much of the scholarly work on sovereignty in the Cold War era.[13]

German conflicts over law and rights constitute an important puzzle piece in the history of global reconfigurations of sovereignty, statehood and citizenship in the postwar era. In the reconfigurations of these fundamental legal concepts, divided countries time and again became central battlegrounds. Against the backdrop of the atrocities of the Second World War, international law experts at the UN criticized ethnic concepts of self-determination and nationality policies for ignoring ethnic or religious minorities.[14] In divided Germany, a counter-framework rooted in concepts of class and property rights overtly challenged the formerly ethnically defined question of national self-determination.[15] This conflict revolved around the question of which model could formulate 'more legitimate' foundations of government.[16] Who could legitimately assert national self-determination in cases where two competing governments referred to the same ethnic tradition and citizenship as a basis for their claims? This fundamental question opened up two options in international debates on law. The first option was to establish a credible legal claim to the former nation-state's sovereignty. The second option was to formulate an accepted political claim to the representation of a new statehood based on the ideological nature of government. While the Bonn government chose the first option, the GDR opted for the second. Ultimately, the West German approach proved to be more persuasive, coupled with a decisive turn to the protection of basic rights of the individual that provided not only protection for the individual but had a bearing on the entire West German legal culture in everyday life over time.

Based on these fundamental decisions over sources of legitimacy for claims to legitimate government, Cold War legal conflicts in divided Germany created two rivalling concepts of citizenship that also had an impact on wider notions of rights. It remained of crucial importance that the state defined who was a citizen because only then could both German governments attempt to infringe on the other German state's authority. The clash of West German legal definitions of *Staatsangehörigkeit* and socialist visions of *Staatsbürgerschaft* revolved around this basic conflict over the representation of people in domestic and international settings. In blurring the boundaries of the 'inner' and 'outer' dimensions of citizenship, both German governments used citizenship legislation as a Cold War weapon.[17] Both governments instrumentalized law to restrict people's citizenship rights and freedom of movement or to force citizenship onto people as part of claiming political legitimacy.

Conflicts over citizenship over time emphasized the rights of individuals and their role in making societies.[18] Underneath the battle over the legal representation of Germans, ideological conflicts over citizenship reconfigured people's expectations towards rights guaranteed by the state. These ideological conflicts over rights of the individual propelled wider global transformations in state–society relations that challenged collective frameworks of community.[19] The socialist idea of a *Staatsbürger*, enshrined in the GDR citizenship law of 1967, appeared modern and enlightened at a time when West German law insisted on a passive concept of the ethnic *Staatsangehörige* to make Cold War legal claims. In the war over legal interpretations and rights, the GDR thus initially capitalized on the rise of human rights language much more efficiently than the FRG. Socialist 'active' citizenship challenged the traditional state-centred concepts of German citizenship, which reverberated around the right of states to grant and take away rights.[20] However, the promises of such an active role of the citizen in socialist society were suffocated by the state's insistence that rights had to be earned through 'correct' ideological behaviour.

The competing legal versions of the citizen's role in society shaped cultural difference over time. Conflicts over the role of the *mündige Bürger* within West German society resulted in restrictions to state power in favour of more individual freedoms and rights guarantees from the 1960s onwards. This shift came with an emphasis on individual responsibility beyond the state's welfare duties towards its citizens.[21] If we want to understand the post-unification conflicts over the cultural difference between 'Ossis' (former East Germans) and 'Wessis' (former West Germans), the rise of 'active citizenship' rights of the individual but also individual responsibility for one's own welfare in the FRG and the socio-economic promises in return for 'rules consciousness' promoted by socialist legality help to further sharpen historical perspectives on the *Mauer in den Köpfen* (wall in the heads) after 1990.[22] The battle between two ideological universalisms of law left not just lasting legal imprints, but also influenced how people expect the state to provide and guard civil and political, but also social and economic rights.

Divided Germany in the Global Conflicts over Legality

The ideological battle over law in divided Germany highlights the deep transnational historical entanglements that shaped German postwar history. The Allied occupation of Germany in 1945 triggered a reconstruction of German statehood in explicitly international contexts. Divided Germany became one of the test cases for the establishment of postwar international governance, first exercised by the Allied Control Council and Allied High Commission and later claimed by the UN on a global scale. Germany was made subject to transitional justice trials in the attempt to channel spontaneous outbursts of violence and retribution into an orderly legal process of justice in war-ridden societies in Europe and Asia. Mostly shielded from the public eye, these large-scale transitional justice trials at Nuremberg and Tokyo formed arenas in which ideas of the rule of law and socialist law clashed.[23] Yet this legalist moment of 1945 provided the basis for an accelerated global juridification in the postwar era.[24]

Ideological Cold War conflicts already shaped this allegedly universalist moment at the end of the Second World War. If we see postwar German history as unfolding in a wider perspective that looks beyond the framework of the two German states, we discover new avenues into writing the history of divided Germany not merely from a comparative but from an entangled perspective. Such a perspective should not be restricted to comparative themes with a 'relative independence from the systems of government'.[25] The history of Cold War legal politics, which were explicitly rooted in ideological difference and opposition, shows that entangled perspectives on the two German states in a wider international perspective do not downplay ideological difference. On the contrary, studying German Cold War history in its wider European and global contexts accentuates how once-united post-fascist societies began to be politically, culturally and economically divided.[26] The history of the politics of law during the Cold War thus shows that we need to study the history of divided Germany not just as a history of similarities and differences – which is how many contemporaries framed the divide – but also to understand better how two separated societies developed in their continued entanglement and focus on each other that was rooted in a shared national heritage.

Cold War legal politics always encapsulated combative agendas. As part of their ideological alliances, both German states designed their legal foundations to infringe on the other country's sovereignty.[27] They were not alone in such an approach to law. At the main front lines of the Cold War in Europe and Asia, the postwar settlement resulted in the division of several countries and created competing legal vocabularies. The language of 'division' framed Cold War conflicts in Germany, Korea, China and later Vietnam. Alongside these conflicts over 'divisions', postcolonial frameworks of 'partition' that had governed much of the League of Nations' legal work also continued into the postwar era. The partition of colonial India and Palestine are prominent examples here.[28] The redrawing of territorial borders across the globe after 1945 thus resulted in new unequal legal frameworks describing similar legal and political processes.

Unequal legal standards and universal legal language thus did not just clash in German conflicts over law. As these partitions and divisions of countries and former colonies unfolded after 1945, the UN's foundation institutionalized a universal vision of international politics and governance framed by international law. Recent histories of international law have shed light on the ideological conflicts that underpinned these processes within the UN from the beginning.[29] Building on these studies, this book has shown how these ideological confrontations also affected national legal reforms and domestic law making. Connecting the development of international legal norms and rights languages and the domestic politics of law reveals how international law began to shape domestic legal cultures and notions of rights and vice versa.[30] Within these global developments, in which courts, legal experts within national ministries and international organizations as well as legal scholars as academic advisors of governments played key roles, divided nations such as Germany represented unique cases in which fundamental legal conflicts over the origins and nature of law and rights played out with heightened intensity and visibility.

Ideological conflicts after 1945 questioned the protection of domestic legal sovereignty from direct infringements through international legal norms. Conflicts between two competing Cold War legal universalisms and decolonization laid bare the tension between the prerogative of states to administer their territories through national laws and the universal claims of emerging international law and human rights languages.[31] Over time, the ideological competition over law in international settings forced formerly closed-off national legal systems to open up to international rights debates and norms.[32] International rights campaigns originating in the Global South advocated a direct impact of international law and rights norms on domestic legal systems.[33] Whereas radical attempts by African anti-colonial leaders demanded a reframing of international governance and opening up of national sovereignty to international rights norms in the 1960s, their disillusion with the international system and military conflicts within Africa from the Congo Crisis to the Biafran War led them back to a reaffirmation of nation-state sovereignty in the 1970s.[34] Eastern bloc states' focus on territorial integrity in the Helsinki era and conflicts over a New International Economic Order (NIEO) thus ended nascent Eastern bloc–Third World alliances and East–South geographies of human rights advocacy and the development of international law.[35] As a result of these brittle global rights alliances, however, both German states, but also the international community at large, could no longer straightforwardly claim absolute sovereignty in domestic legal affairs from the 1960s onwards.[36]

In turn, German-German legal conflicts are one example of how national law making and jurisprudence curtailed international rights norms in the name of ideological competition. While human rights language was advanced by Third World coalitions, the socialist bloc and Western states underpinned by competing ideologies of law, national governments and judiciaries also maintained crucial influence over their domestic legal spheres, legal codes and jurisprudence in the implementation of new international law norms despite the ever-growing importance of international networks and rights languages until 1989.[37] The history of divided nations such as Germany highlights how the often-cited crisis of the sovereign nation-state in the last decades of the twentieth century was much more a transformation than a decline. The concept of sovereign states as the sole standard-bearers of national independence and guarantors of rights remained a pervasive narrative even in an age of increased transnational cooperation, the ascendancy of human rights languages and globalization until the end of the Cold War.

Even after the 1970s, when UN politics moved on to conflicts over the NIEO and economic inequality between states of the Global North and South that was still shaped by imperial legacies, the legal transformations triggered by the Cold War and decolonization did not remove imperial ideas of degrees of citizens' rights and the unequal legal treatment of people within states entirely. And these legal legacies even continue to inform debates on citizenship in the post-Cold War era. Imperial practices of instituting degrees of citizenship below full legal citizenship rights still exist in the face of the postwar human rights revolutions. The FRG, for instance, continues to recognize the status of deutsche *Volkszugehörigkeit* as a legal category below full citizenship that opens a route to a right to indefinite leave to remain.[38] Other examples also show these long shadows of the imperial era. British Overseas Territories Citizenship remained in use until 2002, and tax regimes within the UK and its dominions continue to diverge. The US government also still distinguishes between US citizens and US nationals living in overseas territories.[39] At the same time, many states have created avenues to double citizenship. European integration even saw the institution of a union citizenship, which grants and guarantees citizenship rights of the individual in other European Union (EU) member states. National and transnational reconfigurations of citizenship through legal reform therefore continue, and it is important to account for how they were shaped by Cold War conflicts over rights.[40]

These Cold War politics of law, of which divided Germany was only one part, left important legacies for the post-Cold War world that reach into the contemporary period. Legal arguments about national sovereignty and the historical transfer of sovereign territorial rights have underpinned the conflict over Russia's annexation of Crimea and its claims on territory in the Eastern Ukraine since 2014 as well as disputes over islands in the South China Sea between the PRC, Japan, the Philippines and Vietnam. The PRC's 'one China' policy also continues to view Taiwan as a part of China and infringes on the international representation of the ROC as a sovereign country as well as citizenship rights of ROC citizens.[41] Similar developments have shaped the dispute over citizens between North and South Korea. But the availability of archival records makes it possible to trace this story from both sides of the ideological divide in Germany in a way that is difficult in the case of other divided countries such as China or Korea. The history of German Cold War politics thus can be instructive for our understanding of conflicts elsewhere that developed alongside the German-German conflicts over law and rights and continue to this day.

Cold War Legal Legacies in Unified Germany

While the Cold War may be history, its legislative legacies have had a sizeable impact on legal realities in unified Germany since 1990. Unification itself, administered through the Basic Law's Article 23 in a similar manner to the return of the Saarland to the FRG in 1957, was shaped by the experience of West German constitutional law and *Staatsrecht* experts during the Cold War. Instead of reverting to Article 146 and the drafting of a new constitution, a pathway that many West German legal experts would have advocated in the late 1940s and 1950s had the opportunity arisen, the East Germans joined the sovereign legal order of the Basic Law in 1990. This fact has often been portrayed as a Western 'takeover' of East Germany. Yet recent studies have shown that the transition of 1989–90 was also marked by mutual influence of the legal cultures that had developed in divided Germany.[42] This book thus hopes to contribute to a better understanding of the 'co-transformation' of Germany after unification by drawing out the separate legal cultures that national division produced over time. Understanding these divisions helps to further study post-unification legal developments and trace East German influences on the unified Germany after 1990.[43]

Legacies of the German-German struggle for legitimacy through law also shaped developments in the field of migration and transitional justice. The unified German state has since 1990 allowed the immigration of families from Romania, Hungary, Poland and the Soviet Union (and Russia after 1991) on the basis of their continued expression of *deutsche Volkszugehörigkeit*. In 1990, politicians such as Oskar Lafontaine (b. 1943), then a leading SPD politician, denounced these kinds of citizenship practices as '*Deutschtümelei*' (ethnic jingoism) and '*Heim ins Reich Politik*' (Back into the Reich policy). Indeed, these waves of immigration into unified Germany clearly carried the mark of citizenship regulations that the West German state had instituted in the 1950s.[44] At the same time, while the East German state may have no longer existed, its laws lived on. West German high courts had to revert to GDR legal codes to decide appeal cases in civil and criminal cases that stretched across the watershed date of unification on 3 October 1990.[45] This happened most prominently in the *Mauerschützenprozesse* (trials against East German border guards), in which former GDR soldiers and their officers had to stand trial for the killings of East Germans who had tried to escape across the militarized German-German border.[46] Jurists and judges did so reluctantly, but had to accept that they had to apply GDR civil, criminal and family law after 1990. GDR legal norms thus have found entry into Germany's post-unification legal world.

But it is not merely the Cold War that left legacies to contend with. German unification also forced German society to face financial responsibility for wartime forced labour. After 1949, the West German state had deflected immediate legal responsibility by pointing to the still missing peace treaty with the four Allies. Only after such a treaty had been signed, the West German government argued, could such claims be recognized. Forced labourers who had suffered under the Third Reich thus had to wait until the late 1990s for the recognition of their suffering and some financial compensation.[47] The legacies of German atrocities also came to play a role in international controversies over the euro crisis after 2008. From the beginning of the currency crisis within the EU, the conflicts surrounding the financial collapse of the Greek state reignited the question of German reparation payments. These became prominent elements of public controversies between German and Greek politicians. As the federal government has long claimed to represent the German Reich's sovereignty, many Greek experts have argued that Germany still owes the Greek state enormous financial compensation payments for the atrocities inflicted on the Greek people during the Second World War.⁴⁸ The way in which the German government has dealt with these legal legacies thus is still in part shaped by arguments that German legal experts and jurists developed during the Cold War. They continue to influence legal realities, political disputes and memory politics in manifold ways.

If the crimes committed under the Third Reich still impact on international politics, the long shadow of Cold War legal frameworks also affects domestic German politics. Right-wing mobilization has revived the trope of the 'German Reich in its borders of 1937' and the continued existence of the Reich in public debates. Since the 1980s, first only in the 'old' FRG, German citizens who refer to themselves as *Reichsbürger* (citizens of the Reich) have resisted the idea that they are represented by the current German state and government. Their arguments resemble claims made by the SRP in the late 1940s and 1950s, in which supporters of National Socialism had disputed the legitimacy of the government in Bonn. In the 1980s, this new form of right-wing activism first developed during a time of several waves of attacks on foreigners. After the infamous arson attacks on asylum seeker homes in Solingen and Rostock-Lichtenhagen in the early 1990s, right-wing violence peaked in the murders of the Nationalsozialistischer Untergrund (NSU, National Socialist Underground). Between 1999 and 2007, the NSU terrorist cell conducted bomb attacks and murdered innocent immigrants in assassination attacks.⁴⁹

The German government has now acknowledged this right-wing activism and violence as a serious threat.⁵⁰ The refusal of *Reichsbürger* to accept the sovereignty of the FRG has its roots in the ahistorical and selective adoption of former Cold War legal arguments. Distorting the historical record in their favour, *Reichsbürger* ideologues only reference passages of such high court verdicts, treaties and statements made by the Allied powers and selective quotations by leading German politicians that serve their cause. In doing so, they purposely ignore the historical context of these strategic legal politics in which those statements were made as part of the Cold War over German law and sovereignty after 1945.

The legal conflicts that grew out of Germany's legal Cold War thus continue to reverberate in political life within Germany and beyond. Since 1945, rights languages have become a dominant mode of expression in addressing fundamental political conflicts and formulating legitimate arguments both in domestic and international politics. This turn towards law and rights languages to address questions of ideology and politics has transformed modes of political communication in the Cold War era and continues to shape our current debates on sovereignty, human rights, citizenship and migration in a world of multilateral organizations. Cold War rights languages came to form the origins of integral parts of how we negotiate contemporary politics. In the German-German battle for legitimacy, the global rise of law and rights as a central object and means of political conflict came into full force.

Notes

1. For scholarship on Germany's present and future between 1945 and 1949, see: Forner, *German Intellectuals and the Challenge of Democratic Renewal*; Wettengel, '"Politik mit dem Kopf unter dem Arm"'; Olick, *In the House of the Hangman*; Braun, Gerhardt and Holtmann, *Die lange Stunde Null*. For a contemporary perspective, see: Jaspers, *Die Schuldfrage*.
2. Diestelkamp, *Rechtsgeschichte als Zeitgeschichte*, 25-67.
3. For émigré scholars such as Karl Loewenstein, this Allied failure already showed in the first years after the end of the war. See: Kostal, 'The Alchemy of Occupation'.
4. For the role of legal professionals and intellectuals in these developments, see: Günther, *Denken vom Staat her*; Görtemaker and Safferling, *Die Akte Rosenburg*; Bösch and Wirsching, *Hüter der Ordnung*; Güpping, *Die Bedeutung der 'Babelsberger Konferenz'*; Dreier et al., *Rechtswissenschaft in der DDR 1949–1971*; Heuer, *Die Rechtsordnung der DDR*; Stolleis, *Geschichte des Öffentlichen Rechts in Deutschland*, Bd. 4; Diestelkamp, *Rechtsgeschichte als Zeitgeschichte*; Caldwell, *Dictatorship, State Planning, and Social Theory*, 57–96.
5. Recent historiography has highlighted the importance of intellectual tenets reaching from the 1930s into the 1960s. For legal thought, see: Günther, 'Ordnen, gestalten, bewahren'. For this argument in the study of more general trajectories of twentieth-century history, see: Doering-Manteuffel, 'Die deutsche Geschichte in den Zeitbögen des 20. Jahrhunderts'; Herbert, *Geschichte Deutschlands im 20. Jahrhundert*, 15–22.
6. Fink and Schaefer, *Ostpolitik 1969–1974*; Stein, *Der Konflikt um die Alleinvertretung*.
7. For a concise history of the concept of constitutional patriotism, see: Müller, *Verfassungspatriotismus*.
8. Kleßmann, 'Der schwierige gesamtdeutsche Umgang mit der DDR Geschichte', 4.
9. Anja Schröter has recently pointed to the mutual influence of East and West German legal cultures in divorce law and court practice from the divided into the unified Germany. See: Schröter, *Ostdeutsche Ehen vor Gericht*.
10. Kennan used this analogy in his 1950 Chicago lectures on American diplomacy to denote his vision for US relations to 'the orient'. See: Kennan, *American Diplomacy*, 57 and 109.
11. For a political history of human rights shaped by Cold War conflicts and decolonization, see: Normand and Zaidi, *Human Rights at the UN*.
12. Socialist concepts of rights still remain at the margins of overarching narratives of human rights. See: Hoffmann, 'Viewpoint: Human Rights and History'; Burke, Duranti and Moses, 'Introduction: Human Rights, Empire, and After'. For an account of writing socialist rights history into postwar history, see: Betts, 'Socialism, Solidarity and Decolonization'.
13. See: Morgenthau, 'The Problem of Sovereignty Reconsidered'; Gross, 'The Peace of Westphalia, 1648–1948'. For the subsequent myth of Westphalia in international relations, see: Osiander, 'Sovereignty, International Relations, and the Westphalian Myth'; Teschke, *The Myth of 1648*.

14. For UN debates on minority rights, see: Normand and Zaidi, *Human Rights at the UN*, 247–88.
15. For the Soviet roots of an alternative rights universe, see: Newton, *Law and the Making of the Soviet World*.
16. For the transformation of the German enlightenment concept of self-determination into twentieth-century collective forms of self-determination, see: Weitz, 'Self-determination'.
17. For the framework of an 'inner' and 'outer' dimension of citizenship, see: Gosewinkel, *Schutz und Freiheit?*, 12–30.
18. In West German scholarly debates, the conflicts between the Schmitt and Smend schools of thought exemplify this intellectual shift within legal scholarship. See: Günther, *Denken vom Staat her*. Simultaneously, the concept of society (*Gesellschaft*) rose to prominence in West German debates, but also in a socialist variant in the GDR. For the West German contexts, see: Nolte, *Die Ordnung der deutschen Gesellschaft*, 208–390.
19. This shift that was rooted in the economic transformations of the 1960s and 1970s left deep imprints in cultural life and is often discussed in the context of new forms of protest and the end of the postwar boom. For a German perspective, see: Raphael and Doering-Manteuffel, *Nach dem Boom*; Bösch, *A History Shared and Divided*. For a wider international framework, see: Ferguson et al., *The Shock of the Global*.
20. Crucial advances towards a European legal citizenship only occurred after 1990. See: Gosewinkel, *Schutz und Freiheit?*, 519–629.
21. For extreme neoliberal positions of individual responsibility that developed in the sphere of economic theory alongside this shift, see: Slobodian, *Globalists*.
22. For the socio-economic paternalistic promise of 'rules consciousness' against 'rights consciousness', see: Perry, 'Chinese Conceptions of "Rights"'. Elizabeth Perry traces the particular Chinese tradition of 'rules consciousness'. For the German and European context, such historical perspectives on Cold War legal history that take the social and cultural impact of socialist legality seriously are still absent. For the post-unification irritations between East and West Germans, see: Jarausch, *After Unity*.
23. Von Lingen, 'Defining Crimes against Humanity'; Priemel, *The Betrayal*; Hirsch, 'The Soviets at Nuremberg'.
24. Mazower, *Governing the World*, 191–213; Normand and Zaidi, *Human Rights at the UN*.
25. Möller, 'Demokratie und Diktatur', 6.
26. As examples of integrated German-German perspectives, see: Biess, *Homecomings*; Herzog, *Sex after Fascism*; Kretschmann, *Zwischen Spaltung und Gemeinsamkeit*; Herf, *Divided Memory*; Sheffer, *Burned Bridge*; Bösch, *A History Shared and Divided*. For wider conceptual discussions of the transformation of post-fascist societies, see: Jarausch and Geyer, *Shattered Past*; Jarausch, *After Hitler*.
27. For the origins of the conflict, see: Diestelkamp, *Rechtsgeschichte als Zeitgeschichte*, 25–84.
28. Partition as a concept used in postcolonial contexts developed from the League of Nations mandate system that developed in the interwar period. See: Pedersen, *The Guardians*. For a comparative perspective on population transfer in the context of the Second World War in Germany, British India and Palestine, but without particular attention to the differences of 'partitions' and 'divisions', see: Moses, 'Cutting Out the Ulcer'.
29. See Mazower, *No Enchanted Palace* and *Governing the World*; Moyn, *The Last Utopia*; Hoffmann, *Human Rights in the Twentieth Century*; Liu, 'Shadows of Universalism'; Quigley, *Soviet Legal Innovation*; Eslava, Fakhri and Nesiah, *Bandung, Global History, and International Law*.
30. For a recent history of human rights tied into the history of nation-states and citizenship, see: Weitz, *A World Divided*.
31. For anti-colonial perspectives on the relationship of sovereignty and international rights norms to create an equal international community, see: Getachew, *Worldmaking after Empire*.

32. For the German case, see: Home, 'Statehood at the End of the 20th Century'.
33. E.g. Gehrig et al., 'The Eastern Bloc'; Grosescu, 'State Socialist Endeavours'.
34. Getachew, *Worldmaking after Empire*, 71–106. See also: Fisch, *The Right of Self-Determination of Peoples*, 190–233; Weitz, 'Self-determination'.
35. Betts, 'Socialism, Solidarity and Decolonization'.
36. For the politicking and ideological conflict around universal rights norms, see: Normand and Zaidi, *Human Rights at the UN*.
37. For the advance of human rights language and competing views of the origins and a period of breakthrough in the influence of human rights on global politics, see: Jensen, *The Making of International Human Rights*; Moyn, *The Last Utopia*; Slaughter, 'Hijacking Human Rights'; Hoffmann, 'Viewpoint: Human Rights and History'.
38. Klusmeyer and Papademetriou, *Immigration Policy in the Federal Republic of Germany*, 159–272.
39. For imperial citizenship frameworks, see: Gosewinkel, *Schutz und Freiheit?*, 284–345.
40. Ibid., 519–629.
41. For an anthropological study on the Chinese case of citizenship, see: Friedman, *Exceptional States*. Recent pressure from the PRC government on international airlines to remove their country destination codes for the ROC shows the similarities in strategies to the German legal conflict over the representation of the nation-state in everyday affairs. See: 'Giving in to China, US Airlines Drop Taiwan (in Name at Least)', *The New York Times* (25 July 2018). See also: Chiang, *The One-China Policy*.
42. See: Schröter, *Ostdeutsche Ehen vor Gericht*; DeNike, *German Unification and the Jurists of East Germany*; Weinke, 'Die DDR Justiz in der Wende 1989/90'; von Roenne, *Politisch untragbar?*; Rennig and Strempel, *Justiz im Umbruch*; Booß, *Im goldenen Käfig*.
43. Phillip Ther has recently argued that the transformations in Europe after 1989 were not merely a West–East transfer of political and economic frameworks, but resulted in the co-transformation of the continent. See: Ther, *Die neue Ordnung auf dem alten Kontinent*, 286–312.
44. 'Aussiedler: Schwebendes Volkstum', *Der Spiegel* 3 (1990): 77–79.
45. For a recent study on how this played out in the field of marriage and divorce, see: Schröter, *Ostdeutsche Ehen vor Gericht*.
46. Grafe, *Deutsche Gerechtigkeit*; Wesel, 'Das Urteil gegen Egon Krenz'; Hertle and Nooke, *Die Todesopfer an der Berliner Mauer*.
47. See: Borggräfe, *Zwangsarbeiterentschädigung*.
48. 'Zweiter Weltkrieg', *Der Spiegel* (online).
49. Edinger and Schatschneider, 'Terrorism Made in Germany'.
50. See: Wilkins, *'Reichsbürger' – Ein Handbuch*.

Bibliography

Archive Sources

Amherst College Archives, Massachusetts
The Karl Loewenstein Papers, Amherst College Archives and Special Collections, Amherst College Library

Archiv Akademie für Staats- und Rechtswissenschaften, Babelsberg (ASR)
ASR	3180
ASR	3377
ASR	3417
ASR	3625
ASR	3775
ASR	5599
ASR	13385
ASR	13463

Archiv Berlin-Brandenburgische Akademie der Wissenschaften (ABBAW)
ABBAW	AG, No. 45
ABBAW	AG, No. 46
ABBAW	AKL (1969–1991), No. 1096
ABBAW	FOB Gewi, No. 243
ABBAW	Klassen, No. 224
ABBAW	Klassen, No. 225

Archiv für Christlich-Demokratische Politik, Sankt Augustin (ACDP)
07-001-4105	Bundesarbeitskreis Christlich-Demokratischer Juristen (BACDJ), Abteilung Rechtspolitik Arthur Herzog und Peter Scheib
07-001-4252	Bundesarbeitskreis Christlich-Demokratischer Juristen (BACDJ), Arbeitsgruppe Rechtpolitisches Programm
07-001-4401	Bundesarbeitskreis Christlich-Demokratischer Juristen (BACDJ), Hauptabteilung II Politik, Rechtspolitik Justitiar Peter Scheib

07-001-4402   Bundesarbeitskreis Christlich-Demokratischer Juristen (BACDJ), Rundschreiben Hauptabteilung II Politik, Rechtspolitik Justitiar Peter Scheib
07-001-4004   Bundesarbeitskreis Christlich-Demokratischer Juristen (BACDJ), Hauptabteilung II Politik, Rechtspolitik Justitiar Peter Scheib und Abteilung Organisation Günter Meyer
07-001-4405   Bundesarbeitskreis Christlich-Demokratischer Juristen (BACDJ), Dokumentation Reden, Grußworte, Thesen Hauptabteilung II Politik, Rechtspolitik Justitiar Peter Scheib
07-001-4408   Bundesarbeitskreis Christlich-Demokratischer Juristen (BACDJ), Hauptabteilung II Politik, Rechtspolitik Jürgen Zander
07-001-11289 Generalsekretär Bruno Heck, Bundesverfassungsgericht
I-294/063-3   Bestand Johann Baptist Gradl

Archiv der sozialen Demokratie, Friedrich-Ebert-Stiftung, Bonn (AdsD)
1 / MHAC   Nachlass Martin Hirsch
1 / GJAA   Nachlass Gerhard Jahn
1 / WSAE   Nachlass Walter Seuffert
           Nachlass Wolfgang Zeidler

Bayrisches Hauptstaatsarchiv, Munich
BayHStA   Nachlass Josef Wintrich

Bundesarchiv Koblenz (BArch)
Z 5   Parlamentarischer Rat
Z 21   Zentral-Justizamt für die Britische Zone
Z 22   Rechtsamt der Verwaltung des Vereinigten Wirtschaftsgebietes
B 106   Bundesministerium des Inneren
B 122   Bundespräsidialamt
B 136   Bundeskanzleramt
B 137   Bundesministerium für gesamtdeutsche Fragen (1949–1969) / Bundesministerium für innerdeutsche Beziehungen (1969–1989)
B 141   Bundesministerium der Justiz
B 145   Presse- und Informationsamt der Bundesregierung (BPA)
B 237   Bundesverfassungsgericht
B 241   Forschungsstelle für Nationalitäten- und Sprachenfragen
B 411   Deutscher Juristentag e.V.
N 1292   Nachlass Wilhelm Stuckart
N 1334   Nachlass Gerhard Leibholz

Bundesarchiv Berlin-Lichterfelde (BArch)
BY 1   Kommunistische Partei Deutschlands (KPD)
DC 20   Ministerrat der DDR
DD 2   Staatssekretariat für westdeutsche Fragen
DO 1   Ministerium des Inneren
DP 1   Ministerium der Justiz

DP 2   Oberstes Gericht der DDR
DP 3   Generalstaatsanwalt der DDR
DY 64   Rat der Vorsitzenden der Kollegien der Rechtsanwälte in der DDR
DZ 7   DDR-Komitee für Menschenrechte
DZ 23   Liga für die Vereinten Nationen in der DDR

Harvard University Archives, Cambridge, Massachusetts
HUGFP 17   Papers of Carl J. Friedrich

Staatsarchiv St. Gallen, Switzerland
HSGN   Nachlass Hans Nawiasky

Stiftung Archiv der Parteien und Massenorganisationen der DDR im Bundesarchiv (SAPMO), Bundesarchiv Berlin-Lichterfelde (BArch)
DY 30   Sozialistische Einheitspartei Deutschlands (SED)
DY 30 / IV 2 / 3   Parteikonferenzen der SED, 1946–1963
DY 30 / IV 2 / 13   Abteilung Staats- und Rechtsfragen des ZK der SED, 1945–1962
DY 30 / IV A2 / 10.02   Westabteilung des ZK der SED, 1963–1971
DY 30 / IV A2 / 13   Abteilung Staats- und Rechtsfragen des ZK der SED, 1963–1971
DY 30 / J IV 2 / 3   Sekretariat des ZK der SED (Reinschriftprotokolle), 1953–1989
DY 30 / J IV 2 / 3J   Sekretariat des ZK der SED (Informationen), 1954–1979

The National Archives (TNA), Kew
Foreign and Commonwealth Office (FCO)
    FCO 33 / 228   East German Question and the United Nations
    FCO 33 / 300   Marriages: DDR Rejection of Certificates of No Impediment
    FCO 33 / 301   East German Citizenship Law
    FCO 33 / 302   Niekisch Case
    FCO 33 / 316   Policy on Temporary Travel Documents for East Germans
    FCO 33 / 317   Policy on Temporary Travel Documents for East Germans
    FCO 33 / 318   Policy on Temporary Travel Documents for East Germans
    FCO 33 / 319   Policy on Temporary Travel Documents for East Germans
    FCO 33 / 320   Policy on Temporary Travel Documents for East Germans
    FCO 33 / 321   Policy on Temporary Travel Documents for East Germans
    FCO 33 / 1722   Possible Membership of United Nations by German Democratic Republic and Federal Republic of Germany
    FCO 33 / 1723   Possible Membership of United Nations by German Democratic Republic and Federal Republic of Germany
    FCO 33 / 1842   Bonn Group Study on Entry of German Democratic Republic and Federal Republic of Germany into United Nations
Foreign Office (FO)
    FO 1071 / 134   Combined Travel Board (CTB), Policy Files
    FO 1071 / 142   Combined Travel Board (CTB), Stock forms: general
    FO 1071 / 171   Combined Travel Board (CTB), Policy Files

The National Archives at College Park, Maryland (NARA II)
RG 59, Entry 5389, LOT 70D448, Box 2, Folder 'Germany – Frontiers 1960–1963' (Assistant Legal Advisor for European Affairs (L/EUR) at the Department of State)

NATO Archives, NATO Headquarters, Brussels
AC   52-R(62)05

Politisches Archiv des Auswärtigen Amts, Berlin (PA/AA)
Auswärtiges Amt (AA)
B 30   Abteilung Vereinte Nationen
B 82   Abteilung Staats- und Verwaltungsrecht

Ministerium für Auswärtige Angelegenheiten (MfAA)
MfAA A 5799   Bestand M 1 (Zentralarchiv), 1949–1979
MfAA A 6553   Bestand M 1 (Zentralarchiv), 1949–1979
MfAA A 6580   Bestand M 1 (Zentralarchiv), 1949–1979
MfAA A 9744   Bestand M 1 (Zentralarchiv), 1949–1979
MfAA C 86 / 70   Bestand M 1 (Zentralarchiv), 1949–1979
MfAA C 277 / 73   Bestand M 1 (Zentralarchiv), 1949–1979
MfAA C 1284 / 77 Bestand M 1 (Zentralarchiv), 1949–1979
MfAA C 3780   Bestand M 1 (Zentralarchiv), 1949–1979

United Nations Archives and Records Management Section, New York (UN ARMS)
S-0285   United Nations Executive Office of the Secretary-General (EOSG), Office of the Chef de Cabinet, Legal Affairs
S-0291   United Nations Executive Office of the Secretary-General (EOSG), Office of the Chef de Cabinet, Area and Country Files
S-0303   United Nations Office for Special Political Affairs, Office of the Under-Secretary-General for Special Political Affairs (OUSGSPA), Special Political Affairs
S-0878   Records of Secretary-General U Thant (Peacekeeping / Other Countries)
S-0883   Records of Secretary-General U Thant (Secretary-General's Trips and Engagements)
S-0884   Records of Secretary-General U Thant (Political Matters - Country Files)
S-0904   Records of Secretary-General Kurt Waldheim (Political Matters - Country Files)

Newspapers

Bayernkurier
Bundesgesetzblatt

Christ und Welt
Deutsches Allgemeines Sonntagsblatt
Deutschland Magazin
Frankfurter Allgemeine Zeitung (FAZ)
Leipzig Neuste Nachrichten
Merkur
Neue Ruhr-Zeitung
Neues Deutschland
Neue Zeit
The New York Times
Ostpreußenblatt
Rheinischer Merkur – Christ und Welt
Der Spiegel
Stuttgarter Zeitung
Süddeutsche Zeitung (SZ)
Der Tagesspiegel
Die Welt
Die Zeit

Court Verdicts

Bundesverfassungsgericht (BVerfG)

BVerfGE 1, 322	Auslieferungsverbot gemäß GG Art 16 Abs 2 S 1 gilt auch für zwangseingebürgerte Deutsche
BVerfGE 1, 372	Deutsch-Französisches Wirtschaftsabkommen
BVerfGE 1, 396	Deutschlandvertrag: Unzulässigkeit einer vorbeugenden Normenkontrollklage - hier: gegen Gesetzesentwurf betreffend den Vertrag über die Europäische Verteidigungsgemeinschaft nach dessen ersten Lesung im Bundestag
BVerfGE 2, 1	SRP-Verbot
BVerfGE 4, 299	Überstellung eines deutschen Staatsangehörigen an das Saarland
BVerfGE 4, 322	Erlöschen der auf Anschluß Österreichs beruhenden deutschen Staatsangehörigkeit durch Wiedererrichtung der Republik Österreich
BVerfGE 5, 85	KPD-Verbot
BVerfGE 6, 32	Elfes-Urteil
BVerfGE 6, 309	Konkordatsurteil
BVerfGE 7, 198	Lüth-Urteil
BVerfGE 19, 377	Niekisch-Fall, Berliner Sache, Berlin-Vorbehalt II
BVerfGE 36, 1	Grundlagenvertrag-Urteil
BVerfGE 37, 57	Zulieferung an die DDR, Rechtshilfegesetz
BVerfGE 40, 141	Ostverträge-Urteil
BVerfGE 65, 1	Aussetzung der auf den 27. April 1983 festgesetzten Volkszählung

BVerfGE 69, 315 Brokdorf II: Verfassungsmäßigkeit von Demonstrationsverboten und des Sofortvollzugs eines generellen Demonstrationsverbotes
BVerfGE 77, 137 Konkretisierung des Wiedervereinigungsgebots: Erwerb der Staatsbürgerschaft der DDR bewirkt in den Grenzen des ordre public den Erwerb der deutschen Staatsangehörigkeit

Bundesgerichtshof (BGH)
BGH, 23.02.1954 Staatsangehörigkeitserwerb durch Einbürgerung in der Sowjetzone
BGH, 15.12.1960 Strafrelevanz der Aufforderung zur Aufhebung des KPD-Verbotes

Bundesverwaltungsgericht (BVerwG)
BVerwGE 1, 206 Kein Verlust der deutschen Staatsangehörigkeit der im Bundesgebiet gebliebenen Österreicher

Internet Sources

'Anarchie im Gerichtssaal – Angeklagte klaut Gerichtsakten', *Süddeutsche Zeitung (online)*, http://www.sueddeutsche.de/bayern/kaufbeuren-stoerer-verursachen-chaos-im-gerichtssaal-angeklagte-klaut-akten-1.2916759 [last access: 30 July 2016].

'Geschichtsrevisionisten: Reichsbürger sind nicht bloß harmlose Verschwörungstheoretiker', *Süddeutsche Zeitung (online)*, http://www.sueddeutsche.de/politik/geschichtsrevisionisten-reichsbuerger-sind-mehr-als-harmlose-verschwoerungstheoretiker-1.3212481 [last access: 19 October 2016].

Patalong, Frank, 'Zensus-Debakel in den Achtzigern: Und bist du nicht willig...', *Der Spiegel (online)*, http://www.spiegel.de/panorama/gesellschaft/0,1518,754320,00.html [last access: 19 October 2016].

President of the BGH (ed.). *The Federal Court of Justice*, http://www.bundesgerichtshof.de/SharedDocs/Downloads/EN/BGH/brochure.pdf?__blob=publicationFile [last access: 23 August 2020].

'Razzia in Bayern: "Reichsbürger" schießt mehrere Polizisten nieder', *Der Spiegel (online)*, http://www.spiegel.de/panorama/justiz/georgensgmuend-reichsbuerger-schiesst-mehrere-polizisten-nieder-a-1117289.html [last access: 19 October 2016].

'"Reichsbürger" bedrohen Merkel und Gauck', *Der Spiegel (online)*, http://www.spiegel.de/politik/deutschland/reichsbuerger-bedrohen-angela-merkel-und-joachim-gauck-a-1102853.html [last access: 30 July 2016].

'Schießerei in Sachsen-Anhalt: Wie gefährlich sind die Reichsbürger?', *Frankfurter Allgemeine Zeitung (online)*, http://www.faz.net/aktuell/politik/inland/schiesserei-in-sachsen-anhalt-wie-gefaehrlich-sind-die-reichsbuerger-14407236.html [last access: 27 August 2016].

United Nations, Audiovisual Library of International Law, Convention on the Suppression and Punishment of the Crime of Apartheid, New York, Section

'Audio', Twenty-eighth Session of the General Assembly, Third Committee, 2008th meeting, 26 October 1973, Statement by Mr. von Kyaw (Federal Republic of Germany): Explanation of vote, http://legal.un.org/avl/ha/cspca/cspca.html# [last access: 15 January 2017].

United Nations, Audiovisual Library of International Law, Convention on the Suppression and Punishment of the Crime of Apartheid, New York, Section 'Audio', Twenty-eighth Session of the General Assembly, 2185th Plenary Meeting, 30 November 1973, Statement by Mr. Ferguson (the United States of America): Explanation of vote, http://legal.un.org/avl/ha/cspca/cspca.html# [last access: 15 January 2017].

World Jurist Association – World Peace Through Law Center, http://worldjurist.org/2011/03/our-mission/ [last access: 15 February 2016].

'Wut auf den Staat: Wie Reichsbürger deutsche Gerichte stören', *Frankfurter Allgemeine Zeitung (online)*, http://www.faz.net/aktuell/politik/inland/wut-auf-den-staat-wie-reichsbuerger-deutsche-gerichte-stoeren-14311914.html [last access: 30 July 2016].

'Zweiter Weltkrieg: Wie Griechenland von Deutschland 269 Milliarden Euro einklagen könnte', *Der Spiegel (online)*, http://www.spiegel.de/wirtschaft/soziales/wie-griechenland-von-deutschland-269-milliarden-euro-einklagen-koennte-a-1107034.html [last access: 11 August 2016].

Printed Sources

Adenauer, Konrad. 'Regierungserklärung', in *1. Deutscher Bundestag. Stenographisches Protokoll der 5. Sitzung* (Bonn: BUB Gebr. Scheuer, 1949), 22–30.

'Adoptionsgesetz vom 2. Juli 1976', *Bundesgesetzblatt*, Part I (1976), 1749.

'Agenda Item 96: The Representation of China in the United Nations', in *Official Records of the United Nations. Twenty-Sixth Session: Annexes* (New York: UN, 1972), 96–97.

Akademie für Staats- und Rechtswissenschaft der DDR (ed.). *Staatsrecht der DDR: Lehrbuch*. Berlin: Staatsverlag der Deutschen Demokratischen Republik, 1978.

Arendt, Hannah. 'The Rights of Man: What Are They?', *Modern Review* 3 (1949), 25–37.

Benjamin, Hilde. 'Die dialektische Einheit von Gesetzlichkeit und Parteilichkeit durchsetzen', *Neue Justiz* (1958), 365–68.

———. *Zur Geschichte der Rechtspflege 1945–1949: Von einem Autorenkollektiv unter der Leitung von Hilde Benjamin*. Berlin: Staatsverlag der Deutschen Demokratischen Republik, 1976.

Beyer, Wilhelm R. 'Die Sonderstellung West-Berlins: Eine Stellungnahme zu dem Schreiben der alliierten Kommandantur vom 24. Mai 1967 über den Status von Berlin (II)', *Neue Juristische Wochenschrift* (1967), 1791–92.

Böckenförde, Ernst-Wolfgang. *Die Rechtsauffassung im kommunistischen Staat*. Munich: Kasel Verlag, 1967.

Bruhn, Hanns-Henning. *Die Rechtsanwaltschaft in der DDR: Stellung und Aufgaben*. Cologne: Verlag Wissenschaft und Politik, 1972.

von Brünneck, Alexander. *Politische Justiz gegen Kommunisten in der Bundesrepublik Deutschland 1949–1968*. Frankfurt/M.: Suhrkamp, 1978.
Büchner-Uhder, Willi. *Menschenrechte – eine Utopie*. Berlin: Staatsverlag der DDR, 1981.
Büchner-Uhder, Willi, and Herbert Beil. *Staat und Recht in der Staatsbürgerkunde*. Berlin: Staatsverlag der DDR, 1981.
Büchner-Uhder, Willi, Eberhard Poppe and Rolf Schüsseler. 'Grundrechte und Grundpflichten der Bürger in der DDR', *Staat und Recht* 15 (1966), 563–76.
Dahrendorf, Ralf. *Gesellschaft und Freiheit: Zur soziologischen Analyse der Gegenwart*. Munich: Piper, 1961.
———. *Gesellschaft und Demokratie in Deutschland*. Munich: Piper, 1965.
'Der Status des Bundesverfassungsgerichts: Eine Materialsammlung mit einer Einleitung von Gerhard Leibholz', *Jahrbuch des Öffentlichen Rechts* 6 (1957): 109–220.
'Durchführungsbestimmungen zum Gesetz über die Staatsbürgerschaft der Deutschen Demokratischen Republik vom 3. August 1967', *Gesetzblatt der Deutschen Demokratischen Republik*, Part I, No. 11 (1967), 3.
'Erklärungen zum Grundlagenvertrag zwischen der Bundesrepublik Deutschland und der Deutschen Demokratischen Republik', *Bulletin des Presse- und Informationsamtes der Bundesregierung vom 8. November 1972*, No. 155 (1972), 1842–44.
'Erlass des Staatsrates der Deutschen Demokratischen Republik über die Aufnahme von Bürgern der Deutschen Demokratischen Republik, die ihren Wohnsitz ausserhalb der Deutschen Demokratischen Republik haben', *Gesetzblatt der Deutschen Demokratischen Republik*, Part I, No. 10 (1964), 128.
Finkelnburg, Klaus. 'Die Bundeszugehörigkeit Berlins und die Rechtsprechung des Bundesverfassungsgerichts in Berliner Sachen: Zugleich ein Beitrag zur Brückmann-Entscheidung des Bundesverfassungsgerichts', *Neue Juristische Wochenschrift* (1974), 1969–73.
Friedrich, Gerd. *Die Freie Deutsche Jugend: Stoßtrupp des Kommunismus in Deutschland*. Cologne: Bundesministerium für Gesamtdeutsche Fragen, 1953.
''Gesetz über die Angelegenheiten der Vertriebenen und Flüchtlinge (Bundesvertriebenengesetz)', *Bundesgesetzblatt*, Part I, No. 22 (1953), 201–21.
'Gesetz über die befristete Freistellung von der deutschen Gerichtsbarkeit', *Bundesgesetzblatt*, Part I, No. 22 (1966), 453–54.
'Gesetz vom 8. September 1969', *Bundesgesetzblatt*, Part I (1969), 1581.
'Gesetz vom 20. Dezember 1974', *Bundesgesetzblatt*, Part I (1974), 3714.
Gesetz zur Regelung von Fragen der Staatsangehörigkeit, 22 Februar 1955', *Bundesgesetzblatt*, Part I, No. 6 (1955), 65–68.
'Gesetz zur Verminderung der Staatenlosigkeit vom 29. Juni 1977', *Bundesgesetzblatt*, Part I (1977), 1101.
Graefrath, Bernhard. *Die Vereinten Nationen und die Menschenrechte*. Berlin: VEB Deutscher Zentralverlag, 1956.
Grimm, Dieter. 'Recht und Politik', *Juristische Schulung* 9 (1969), 501–10.
Gross, Leo. 'The Peace of Westphalia, 1648–1948', *American Journal of International Law* 42(1) (1948), 20–41.

Hacker, Jens. *Der Rechtsstatus Deutschlands aus Sicht der DDR*. Cologne: Verlag Wissenschaft und Politik, 1974.
Havel, Václav. 'The Power of the Powerless', in Paul Wilson (ed.), *Open Letters: Selected Writings 1965–1990* (New York: Random House, 1992), 125–214.
Hennis, Wilhelm, Peter Graf Kielmansegg and Ulrich Matz (eds). *Regierbarkeit: Studien zu ihrer Problematisierung. Band 1*. Stuttgart: Klett-Cotta, 1977.
——— (eds). *Regierbarkeit: Studien zu ihrer Problematisierung. Band 2*. Stuttgart: Klett-Cotta, 1979.
Hinksey, F.H. *Sovereignty*. 2nd ed. Cambridge: Cambridge University Press, 1986.
Institut für Internationale Beziehungen an der Akademie für Staats- und Rechtswissenschaft der DDR (ed.). *Außenpolitik der DDR – für Sozialismus und Frieden*. Berlin: Staatsverlag der DDR, 1974.
International Commission of Jurists. *The Berlin Wall: A Defiance of Human Rights*. Geneva: International Commission of Jurists, 1962.
Investigation Committee of Free Jurists (ed.). *Catalogue of Injustice*. Berlin: Investigation Committee of Free Jurists, 1956.
Jaspers, Karl. *Die Schuldfrage: Von der politischen Haftung Deutschlands*. Munich: Piper, 1946.
Jellinek, Georg. *Allgemeine Staatslehre*. 2nd ed. Berlin: Häring, 1905.
Kanzlei des Staatsrates der Deutschen Demokratischen Republik (ed.). *Das neue Strafrecht – bedeutsamer Schritt zur Festigung unseres sozialistischen Rechtsstaates. Mit dem Wortlaut der von der Volkskammer der DDR in ihrer 6. Sitzung am 12. Januar 1968 beschlossenen Gesetze*. Berlin: Staatsverlag der DDR, 1968.
Kelsen, Hans. *Allgemeine Staatslehre*. Berlin: Springer, 1925.
Kelsen, Hans. *Das Problem der Souveränität und die Theorie des Völkerrechts: Beitrag zu einer reinen Rechtslehre*. 2nd ed. Tübingen: Mohr Siebeck, 1928.
———. 'The International Legal Status of Germany to be Established Immediately Upon Termination of the War', *The American Journal of International Law* 38(4) (1944), 689–94.
———. 'The Legal Status of Germany According to the Declaration of Berlin', *The American Journal of International Law* 39(3) (1945), 518–26.
Kennan, George. *American Diplomacy. Sixtieth-Anniversary Expanded Edition*. Chicago: Chicago University Press, 2012.
Klenner, Hermann. *Formen und Bedeutung der Gesetzlichkeit als einer Methode in der Führung des Klassenkampfes*. Berlin: Deutscher Zentralverlag, 1953.
———. *Der Marxismus-Leninismus über das Wesen des Rechts*. Berlin: Deutscher Zentralverlag, 1954.
———. *Formen und Bedeutung der Gesetzlichkeit als einer Methode in der Führung des Klassenkampfes*. Berlin: Deutscher Zentralverlag, 1958.
———. *Studien über die Grundrechte*. Berlin: Deutscher Zentralverlag, 1964.
———. *The Political Civil Rights in the German Democratic Republic*. Berlin: Committee for the Protection of Human Rights, 1967.
———. 'Human Rights: A Battle Cry for Social Change or a Challenge to Philosophy of Law?', *Archiv für Rechts- und Sozialphilosophie* 64(4) (1978), 465–77.
Kokott, Juliane. 'Der Erwerb der deutschen Staatsangehörigkeit durch Einbürgerungen in die DDR', *Neue Zeitschrift für Verwaltungsrecht* 7 (1988), 799–802.

'Kostenermächtigungs-Änderungsgesetz vom 23. Juni 1970', *Bundesgesetzblatt*, Part I (1970), 805.
Kriele, Martin. *Die Menschenrechte zwischen Ost und West*. Cologne: Verlag Wissenschaft und Politik, 1977.
Kuhrig, Herta. *Equal Rights for Women in the German Federal Republic. Publications of the GDR Committee for Human Rights*, No. 5. Berlin: GDR Committee for Human Rights, 1973.
Larson, Arthur. *Questions and Answers on the United Nations*. Durham, NC: Duke University Law School, 1966.
Lenin, Vladimir Ilyich. 'The Right of Nations to Self-Determination', in Vladimir Ilyich Lenin, *Collected Works*, Vol. 20 (Moscow: Progress Publishers, 1972), 393–454.
Makarov, Alexander. 'Entscheidungen: Staatsangehörigkeit', *Juristenzeitung* 3 (1955), 80–83.
Mampel, Siegfried. *Die Verfassung der sowjetischen Besatzungszone Deutschlands: Text und Kommentar*. Frankfurt/M.: Alfred Metzger Verlag, 1962.
Mann, Francis A. 'The Present Legal State of Germany', *Jahrbuch für Internationales und Ausländisches Öffentliches Recht* 1 (1948), 27–42.
Markovits, Inga. 'Socialist vs. Bourgeois Rights: An East-West Comparison', *The University of Chicago Law Review* 45(3) (1978), 612–36.
———. 'Law or Order: Constitutionalism and Legality in Eastern Europe', *Stanford Law Review* 34(3) (1982), 513–613.
———. 'Pursuing One's Right under Socialism', *Stanford Law Review* 38(3) (1986), 689–761.
Marshall, Thomas H. *Citizenship and Social Class and Other Essays*. Cambridge: Cambridge University Press, 1950.
Ministry of Justice of the German Democratic Republic (ed.). *Decree on the Administration of Justice – The Charter of Socialist Legal Policy*. Dresden: Verlag Zeit im Bild, 1963.
——— (ed.). *Statutory Foundations of the Administration of Justice in the GDR. Documentation*. Berlin: Ministry of Justice of the GDR, 1973.
Mollnau, Karl. A. 'Theoretische Probleme der gesellschaftsorganisatorischen Funktion des sozialistischen Rechts', *Staat und Recht* (1967), 715–29.
Morgenthau, Hans J. 'The Problem of Sovereignty Reconsidered', *Columbia Law Review* 48(3) (1948), 342–65.
Müller, Reimar, and Hermann Klenner. *Gesellschaftsvertragstheorien von der Antike bis zur Gegenwart. Sitzungsberichte der Akademie der Wissenschaften der DDR: Gesellschaftswissenschaften*. Berlin: Akademie-Verlag, 1985.
Nawiasky, Hans. *Die Grundgedanken des Grundgesetzes für die Bundesrepublik Deutschland*. Stuttgart: Kohlhammer, 1950.
Oppenheim, Lassa. *International Law: A Treatise, Vol. 1: Peace*. London: Longmans, Green and Co, 1905.
Peace, Friendship, Solidarity: Angela Davis in the GDR. Dresden: Zeit im Bild Verlag, 1972.
Peck, Joachim. *Die Völkerrechtssubjektiviät der Deutschen Demokratischen Republik*. Berlin: Akademie-Verlag, 1960.

Petzold, Siegfried. 'Das Recht in der Periode des umfassenden Aufbaus des Sozialismus in der DDR', *Staat und Recht* 12(1) (1963), 17–32.

Polak, Karl. *Zur Dialektik in der Staatslehre*. Berlin: Akademieverlag, 1959.

———. *Gesellschaftliche Gesetzmäßigkeit und Völkerrechtswissenschaft*. Berlin: Akademie-Verlag, 1962.

———. 'Über die weitere Entwicklung der sozialistischen Rechtspflege in der Deutschen Demokratischen Republik: Zum Beschluss des Staatsrates der DDR vom 30. Januar 1961', in Deutsche Akademie für Staats- und Rechtswissenschaft 'Walter Ulbricht' (ed.), *Karl Polak: Reden und Aufsätze* (Berlin: Staatsverlag der DDR, 1968), 404–58.

———, 'Zur weiteren Vervollkommnung der sozialistischen Rechtspflege: Bericht der Kommission des Staatsrates der DDR über die von ihr ausgearbeiteten Maßnahmen, gegeben auf der 27. Sitzung des Staatsrates der DDR am 4. April 1963', in Deutsche Akademie für Staats- und Rechtswissenschaft 'Walter Ulbricht' (ed.), *Karl Polak: Reden und Aufsätze* (Berlin: Staatsverlag der Deutschen Demokratischen Republik, 1968), 459–69.

Polcuch, Valentin. 'Was fehlt in Brüssel?', *Ostpreußenblatt* 9(28) (12 July 1958), 3–4.

Poppe, Eberhard, and Rolf Schüsseler. 'Sozialistische Grundrechte und Grundpflichten der Bürger', *Staat und Recht* 12 (1963), 209–14.

Regierungskanzlei der Deutschen Demokratischen Republik (ed.). *Zentralblatt der Deutschen Demokratischen Republik*. Berlin: Zentralverlag, 1954.

Riege, Gerhard. 'Das Staatsbürgerschaftsgesetz der DDR', *Staat und Recht* 5 (1967), 701–13.

———. *Zwei Staaten – zwei Staatsbürgerschaften*. Berlin: Staatsverlag der DDR, 1967.

———. *Die Staatsbürgerschaft der DDR*. Berlin: Staatsverlag der DDR, 1982.

Riege, Gerhard, and Hans-Jürgen Kulke. *Nationalität: deutsch – Staatsbürgerschaft: DDR. Recht in unserer Zeit, Band 19*. Berlin: Staatsverlag der DDR, 1980.

Riemann, Tord, Hans Heilborn and Gustav-Adolf Lübchen. *Law and Justice in a Socialist Society: The Legal System of the German Democratic Republic. First-Hand Information*. Berlin: Panorama DDR, 1976.

Roggenmann, Herwig. *Die Staatsordnung der DDR*. Berlin: Berlin Verlag, 1973.

Rosenthal, Walther. *Das neue politische Strafrecht der 'DDR'*. Frankfurt/M.: Alfred Metzger Verlag, 1968.

Rosenthal, Walther, Richard Lange and Artet Blomeyer. *Die Justiz der Sowjetischen Besatzungszone Deutschlands: Bonner Berichte aus Mitteldeutschland*. Bonn: Bundesministerium für Gesamtdeutsche Fragen, 1959.

Rummel, Alois. 'Ohne Kompass: Deutschlandpolitik weiter umstritten', *Rheinischer Merkur – Christ und Welt* 33 (1984), 1.

Schätzel, Walter. 'Die Staatsangehörigkeit der Volksdeutschen', in Max Hildebert Boehm, Fritz Valjavec and Wilhelm Weizsäcker (eds), *Ostdeutsche Wissenschaft: Jahrbuch des Ostdeutschen Kulturrates, Bd. 1* (Munich: Oldenbourg, 1954), 231–44.

———. *Das deutsche Staatsangehörigkeitsrecht: Kommentar zu dem Reichs- und Staatsangehörigkeitsgesetz vom 22. Juli 1913, den Staatsangehörigkeitsbestimmungen der Verfassungen und der Saarüberleitung und den Staatsangehörigkeitsregelungsgesetzen vom 22. Februar 1955 und 17. Mai 1956*. Berlin: de Gruyter, 1958.

Sternebeck, Klaus-Dieter, and Arno Wittmann. 'Rechtshilfe in Strafsachen zwischen Bundesrepublik und DDR: Zum Brückmann-Beschluß des Bundesverfassungsgerichts vom 27.3.1974', *Neue Juristische Wochenschrift* (1974), 1841–48.
Such, Heinz. 'Gegen Erscheinungen des Dogmatismus und Rechtsnihilismus in der Staats- und Rechtswissenschaft', *Staat und Recht* 1 (1962), 122–45.
Toeplitz, Heinrich. 'Ein Dokument westdeutscher Rechtsanmaßung: Stellungnahme des Präsidenten des Obersten Gerichts, Dr. Heinrich Toeplitz, zum sog. Gesetz über die befristete Freistellung von der deutschen Gerichtsbarkeit', *Neue Justiz* 14 (1966), 419.
Ulbricht, Walter. *Die Staatslehre des Marxismus-Leninismus und ihre Anwendung in Deutschland: Referat und Schlusswort auf der Babelsberger Konferenz am 2. und 3. April 1958*. Berlin: VEB Deutscher Zentralverlag, 1958.
Ulbricht, Walter, and Karl Polak. *Beiträge zur Staatslehre*. Berlin: Deutscher Zentralverlag, 1959.
United Nations General Assembly. Resolution 2758, Session 26: Restoration of the lawful rights of the People's Republic of China in the United Nations, A/RES/2758(XXVI).
Wahl, Jürgen. 'Deutsch-polnischer Klartext: Oder-Neiße-Illusionen schaden dem ohnehin dornenreichen Dialog zwischen Bonn und Warschau', *Rheinischer Merkur – Christ und Welt* 46 (1984), 1.
Wengler, Wilhelm. 'Juristische Luftbrücken von Karlsruhe nach West-Berlin: Bemerkungen zum Brückmann-Fall', *Juristen-Zeitung* 29(17) (1974), 528–35.
Wesel, Uwe. 'Das Urteil gegen Egon Krenz und andere ähnelt verblüffend der Rechtsprechung durch die DDR-Justiz', *Der Tagesspiegel* (10 November 1999).
Westen, Klaus, and Joachim Schleider. *Zivilrecht im Systemvergleich: das Zivilrecht der Deutschen Demokratischen Republik und der Bundesrepublik Deutschland*. Berlin: Nomos, 1984.
Winters, Peter Jochen. 'Absage an Deutschland: Ulbrichts eigene Hallstein-Doktrin', *Christ und Welt* 20(1) (1967), 1.
Wirsing, Giselher. 'Riskante Reise: Helmut Schmidts Schnellinformationen', *Christ und Welt* 20(34) (1967), 1.
Zieger, Gottfried. *Das Staatsbürgerschaftsrecht der DDR: Seine Auswirkungen auf die Rechtsordnung der Bundesrepublik*. Frankfurt/M.: Alfred Metzner Verlag, 1969.
'Zuständigkeitslockerungsgesetz vom 10. März 1975', *Bundesgesetzblatt*, Part I (1975), 685.
'Zweites Gesetz zur Regelung von Fragen der Staatsangehörigkeit', *Bundesgesetzblatt*, Part I, No. 23 (23 May 1956), 431–32.

Literature

Albrecht, Clemens. 'Die Bundesrepublik als "Gesellschaft": Letztbegriffe kollektiver Selbstdeutung', in Herfried Münkler and Jens Hacke (eds), *Wege in die neue Bundesrepublik: Politische Mythen und kollektive Selbstbilder nach 1989* (Frankfurt/M.: Campus, 2009), 83–113.

Allen, Keith. *Interrogation Nation: Refugees and Spies in Cold War Germany*. Lanham, MD: Rowman & Littlefield, 2017.
Altehenger, Jennifer. 'Social Imperialism and Mao's Three Worlds: Deng Xiaoping's Speech to the UN General Assembly, 1974', in Rachel Hammersley (ed.), *Revolutionary Moments: Reading Revolutionary Texts* (London: Bloomsbury, 2015), 175–82.
———. 'Unlikely Heirs: Communist China and the Transnational Socialist Search for Law, 1972–1989', paper presented at the international conference 'Law, (Inter-)Nationalism, and the Global Cold War', Oxford, June 2015.
———. *Legal Lessons: Popularizing Laws in the People's Republic of China, 1949–89*. Cambridge, MA: Harvard University Asia Center, 2018.
Amos, Heike. *Die Entstehung der Verfassung in der Sowjetischen Besatzungszone/ DDR 1946–1949: Darstellung und Dokumentation*. Münster: LIT-Verlag, 2006.
Anghie, Antony. *Imperialism, Sovereignty, and the Making of International Law*. Cambridge: Cambridge University Press, 2005.
Angster, Julia. *Konsenskapitalismus und Sozialdemokratie: Die Westernisierung von SPD und DGB*. Munich: Oldenbourg, 2003.
Arlt, Reiner. 'Die Rezeption der sowjetischen Rechtswissenschaft (Theorie des Rechts) und die Babelsberger Konferenz', in Jörn Eckart (ed.), *Die Babelsberger Konferenz vom 2./3. April 1958. Rechtshistorisches Kolloquium 13.-16. Februar 1992, Christian-Albrechts-Universität Kiel* (Baden-Baden: Nomos, 1993), 185–93.
Aust, Anthony. *Modern Treaty Law and Practice*. Cambridge: Cambridge University Press, 2013.
Aust, Stefan. *Der Baader Meinhof Komplex*. Hamburg: Hoffmann & Kampe, 1997.
Badalassi, Nicolas, and Sarah B. Snyder (eds). *The CSCE and the End of the Cold War: Diplomacy, Societies, and Human Rights, 1972–1990*. New York: Berghahn Books, 2019.
Balz, Hanno. *Von Terroristen, Sympathisanten und dem starken Staat: Die öffentliche Debatte über die RAF in den 70er Jahren*. Frankfurt/M.: Campus, 2008.
Bange, Oliver, and Gottfried Neidhardt (eds). *Helsinki 1975 and the Transformation of Europe*. New York: Berghahn Books, 2008.
Bartelson, Jens. 'On the Indivisibility of Sovereignty,' *Republics of Letters* 2(2) (2011).
Bates, Ed. *The Evolution of the European Convention on Human Rights: From Its Inception to the Creation of a Permanent Court of Human Rights*. Oxford: Oxford University Press, 2010.
Bauerkämper, Arnd, Konrad H. Jarausch and Marcus M. Payk (eds). *Demokratiewunder: Transatlantische Mittler und die kulturelle Öffnung Westdeutschlands 1945–1970*. Göttingen: Vandenhoeck & Ruprecht, 2005.
Bauerkämper, Arnd, Martin Sabrow and Bernd Stöver. 'Die doppelte deutsche Zeitgeschichte', in idem (eds), *Doppelte Zeitgeschichte: Deutsch-deutsche Beziehungen 1945–1990* (Bonn: Dietz, 1998), 9–16.
Bauernfeind, Wolfgang. *Menschenraub im Kalten Krieg: Täter, Opfer, Hintergründe*. Halle: Mitteldeutscher Verlag, 2016.
Bavaj, Riccardo. 'Verunsicherte Demokratisierer: "Liberal-kritische" Hochschullehrer und die Studentenrevolte von 1967/68', in Dominik Geppert and Jens Hacke (eds), *Streit um den Staat: Intellektuelle Debatten in der Bundesrepublik 1960–1980* (Göttingen: Vandenhoeck & Ruprecht, 2008), 151–68.

Becker, Maximilian. '"Keine Waffen für unsere Henker!" Ehemalige Verfolgte des NS-Regimes und die westdeutsche Wiederbewaffnung', *Vierteljahrshefte für Zeitgeschichte* 66(1) (2018), 87–116.
Bender, Peter. *Deutschlands Wiederkehr: Eine ungeteilte Nachkriegsgeschichte 1945–1990*. Bonn: bpb, 2008.
Bender, Gerd, and Ulrich Falk (eds). *Recht im Sozialismus: Analysen zur Normendurchsetzung in osteuropäischen Nachkriegsgesellschaften. Band 1: Enteignung*. Frankfurt/M.: V. Klostermann, 1999.
———. *Recht im Sozialismus: Analysen zur Normendurchsetzung in osteuropäischen Nachkriegsgesellschaften. Band 2: Justizpolitik*. Frankfurt/M.: V. Klostermann, 1999.
———. *Recht im Sozialismus: Analysen zur Normendurchsetzung in osteuropäischen Nachkriegsgesellschaften. Band 3: Sozialistische Gesetzlichkeit*. Frankfurt/M.: V. Klostermann, 1999.
Benz, Wolfgang. 'Föderalisitische Politik in der CDU/CSU: Die Verfassungsdiskussion im "Ellwanger Kreis" 1947/48', *Vierteljahrshefte für Zeitgeschichte* 25(4) (1977), 776–820.
———. 'Amerikanische Besatzungsherrschaft in Japan 1945–1947', *Vierteljahrshefte für Zeitgeschichte* 26(2) (1978), 265–346.
———. *Auftrag Demokratie: Die Gründungsjahre der Bundesrepublik und die Entstehung der DDR 1945–1949*. Bonn: bpb, 2010.
Berend, Ivan T. *An Economic History of Twentieth-Century Europe: Economic Regimes from Laissez-faire to Globalization*. Cambridge: Cambridge University Press, 2016.
Berg, Maxine. *Writing the History of the Global: Challenges for the 21st Century*. Oxford: Oxford University Press, 2013.
Bergem, Wolfgang. *Identitätsformationen in Deutschland*. Wiesbaden: Springer, 2005.
Berghahn, Volker. *America and the Intellectual Cold Wars in Europe*. Princeton, NJ: Princeton University Press, 2001.
Betts, Paul. *The Authority of Everyday Objects: A Cultural History of West German Industrial Design*. Berkeley: University of California Press, 2008.
———. 'Property, Peace and Honour: Neighbourhood Justice in Communist Berlin', *Past & Present* 201 (2008), 215–54.
———, 'Socialism, Social Rights, Human Rights: The Case of East Germany', *Humanity* 3(3) (2011), 407–26.
———, 'Religion, Science, and Cold War Anticommunism: The 1949 Cardinal Mindszenty Show Trial', in Paul Betts and Stephen A. Smith (eds), *Science, Religion and Communism in Cold War Europe* (London: Palgrave Macmillan, 2016), 275–307.
———, 'Socialism, Solidarity and Decolonization: An Alternative Geography of Human Rights', in Paul Betts and James Mark (eds), *When Socialism Went Global: Eastern Europe and the Global South, 1945–1990*. Oxford: Oxford University Press, forthcoming.
Biess, Frank. *Homecomings: Returning POWs and the Legacies of Defeat in Postwar Germany*. Princeton, NJ: Princeton University Press, 2009.
Bilandzic, Vladimir, Dittmar Dahlmann and Milan Kosanovic (eds). *From Helsinki to Belgrade: The First CSCE Follow-up Meeting and the Crisis of Détente*. Göttingen: Vandenhoeck & Ruprecht, 2012.

Bock, Siegfried, Ingrid Mut and Hermann Schwiesau (eds). *DDR-Außenpolitik im Rückspiegel: Diplomaten im Gespräch*. Berlin: Ch. Links, 2004.

—— (eds). *Alternative deutsche Außenpolitik? DDR-Außenpolitik im Rückspiegel (II)*. Berlin: LIT-Verlag, 2006.

—— (eds). *DDR-Außenpolitik: Ein Überblick. Daten, Fakten, Personen (III)*. Berlin: LIT-Verlag, 2010.

Bockman, Johanna. 'Socialist Globalization against Capitalist Neocolonialism: The Economic Ideas Behind the New International Economic Order', *Humanity* 6 (2015), 109–28.

Böke, Karin, Frank Liedtke and Martin Wengeler (eds). *Politische Leitvokabeln in der Adenauer-Ära: Mit einem Beitrag von Dorothee Dengel*. Berlin: de Gruyter, 1996.

Booß, Christian. *Im goldenen Käfig: zwischen SED, Staatssicherheit, Justizministerium und Mandat – die DDR-Anwälte im politischen Prozess*. Göttingen: Vandenhoeck & Ruprecht, 2017.

Borggräfe, Henning. *Zwangsarbeiterentschädigung: Vom Streit um 'vergessene Opfer' zur Selbstaussöhnung der Deutschen*. Göttingen: Wallstein, 2014.

Borisova, Tatiana, and William Simons (eds). *The Legal Dimension in Cold War Interactions: Some Notes from the Field*. Leiden: Martinus Nijhoff Publishers, 2012.

Bösch, Frank (ed.). *A History Shared and Divided: East and West Germany since the 1970s*. New York: Berghahn Books, 2018.

Bösch, Frank, and Andreas Wirsching (eds). *Hüter der Ordnung: Die Innenministerien in Bonn und Ost-Berlin nach dem Nationalsozialismus*. Göttingen: Wallstein, 2018.

Boyer, Christoph, and Peter Skyba. 'Sozial- und Konsumpolitik als Stabilisierungsstrategie: Zur Genese der "Einheit von Sozial- und Wirtschaftspolitik" in der DDR', *Deutschland Archiv* 32(4) (1999), 577–90.

Bradley, Mark Philip. *The World Reimagined: Americans and Human Rights in the Twentieth Century*. Cambridge: Cambridge University Press, 2016.

Braun, Hans, Uta Gerhardt and Everhard Holtmann (eds). *Die lange Stunde Null: Gelenkter sozialer Wandel in Westdeutschland nach 1945*. Baden-Baden: Nomos, 2007.

Braunthal, Gerhard. *Political Loyalty and Public Service in West Germany: The 1972 Decree against Radicals and Its Consequences*. Amherst: University of Massachusetts Press, 1990.

Brazinsky, Gregg. *Nation Building in South Korea: Koreans, Americans, and the Making of a Democracy*. Chapel Hill: University of North Carolina Press, 2007.

Brentzel, Marianne. *Die Machtfrau: Hilde Benjamin, 1902–1989*. Berlin: Ch. Links, 1997.

Brine, Jenny. *Comecon: The Rise and Fall of an International Socialist Organization*. New Brunswick, NJ: Transaction Books, 1992.

Brown, Timothy. *West Germany and the Global Sixties: The Antiauthoritarian Revolt, 1962–1978*. Cambridge: Cambridge University Press, 2013.

Brubaker, Rogers. *Citizenship and Nationhood in France and Germany*. Cambridge, MA: Harvard University Press, 1998.

Büchse, Nicolas. 'Von Staatsbürgern und Protestbürgern: Der Deutsche Herbst und die Veränderung der politischen Kultur in der Bundesrepublik', in Habbo

Knoch (ed.), *Bürgersinn mit Weltgefühl: Politische Moral und solidarischer Protest in den sechziger und siebziger Jahren* (Göttingen: Wallstein, 2007), 311–32.

Bueb, Bernhard, Ute Frevert, Hans Joas, Gerhard A. Ritter, Andreas Rödder et al. *Alte Werte – Neue Werte: Schlaglichter des Wertewandels*. Göttingen: Vandenhoeck & Ruprecht, 2008.

Burke, Roland. *Decolonization and the Evolution of International Human Rights*. Philadelphia: University of Pennsylvania Press, 2010.

———. 'Competing for the Last Utopia? The NIEO, Human Rights, and the World Conference for the International Women's Year, Mexico City, June 1975', *Humanity* 6 (2015), 47–61.

Burke, Roland, Marco Duranti and A. Dirk Moses, 'Introduction: Human Rights, Empire, and After', in idem (eds), *Decolonisation, Self-Determination, and the Rise of Global Human Rights Politics* (Cambridge: Cambridge University Press, 2020), 1–31.

Büschel, Hubertus. *Hilfe zur Selbsthilfe: Deutsche Entwicklungshilfe in Afrika 1960–1975*. Frankfurt/M.: Campus, 2014.

Caldwell, Peter C. *Dictatorship, State Planning, and Social Theory in the German Democratic Republic*. Cambridge: Cambridge University Press, 2003.

———. *Democracy, Capitalism, and the Welfare State: Debating Social Order in Postwar West Germany, 1949–1989*. Oxford: Oxford University Press, 2019.

Carter, Erica. 'Culture, History and National Identity in the Two Germanys 1945–1999', in Mary Fulbrook (ed.), *20th Century Germany: Politics, Culture and Society 1918–1990* (London: Bloomsbury, 2001), 247–69.

Chen Jian. 'China, the Third World, and the Cold War', in Robert J. McMahon (ed.), *The Cold War in the Third World* (Oxford: Oxford University Press, 2013), 85–100.

Chiang, Frank. *The One-China Policy: State, Sovereignty, and Taiwan's International Status*. Amsterdam: Elsevier, 2018.

Coleman, Peter. *The Liberal Conspiracy: The Congress for Cultural Freedom and the Struggle for the Mind of Postwar Europe*. New York: The Free Press, 1989.

Collings, Justin. 'Gerhard Leibholz und der Status des Bundesverfassungsgerichts: Karriere eines Berichts und seines Berichterstatters', in Anna-Bettina Kaiser (ed.), *Der Parteienstaat: Zum Staatsverständnis von Gerhard Leibholz* (Baden-Baden: Nomos, 2013), 227–57.

———. *Democracy's Guardians: A History of the German Federal Constitutional Court, 1951–2001*. Oxford: Oxford University Press, 2015.

Connelly, John. *Captive University: The Sovietization of East German, Czech, and Polish Higher Education, 1945–1956*. Chapel Hill: University of North Carolina Press, 2000.

Connery, Christopher Lee. 'The World Sixties', in Rob Wilson and Christopher Leigh Connery (eds), *The Worlding Project: Doing Cultural Studies in the Era of Globalisation* (Berkeley: North Atlantic Books, 2007), 77–108.

Conze, Eckhard. *Die Suche nach Sicherheit: Eine Geschichte der Bundesrepublik Deutschland von 1949 bis in die Gegenwart*. Munich: Siedler, 2009.

Cook, Alexander. 'Introduction: The Spiritual Atom Bomb and Its Global Fallout', in Alexander C. Cook (ed.), *Mao's Little Red Book: A Global History* (Cambridge: Cambridge University Press, 2014), 1–22.

Creuzberger, Stefan, and Dierk Hoffmann (eds). *'Geistige Gefahr' und 'Immunisierung der Gesellschaft': Antikommunismus und politische Kultur in der frühen Bundesrepublik*. Berlin: de Gruyter, 2014.

Crosby, Margaret Barber. *The Making of a German Constitution: A Slow Revolution*. Oxford: A&C Black, 2008.

von Dannenberg, Julia. *The Foundations of Ostpolitik: The Making of the Moscow Treaty between West Germany and the USSR*. Oxford: Oxford University Press, 2008.

Darnstädt, Thomas. *Verschlusssache Karlsruhe: Die internen Akten des Bundesverfassungsgerichts*. Munich: Piper, 2018.

Das Gupta, Amit. *Handel, Hilfe, Hallstein-Doktrin: Die deutsche Südasienpolitik unter Adenauer und Erhard 1949–1966*. Husum: Matthiesen, 2004.

DeNike, Howard J. *German Unification and the Jurists of East Germany: An Anthropology of Law, Nation and History*. Mönchengladbach: Forum-Verlag, 1997.

Detjen, Marion, Stephan Detjen and Maximilian Steinbeis. *Die Deutschen und das Grundgesetz: Geschichte und Grenzen der Verfassung*. Munich: Pantheon, 2009.

Diestelkamp, Bernhard. *Rechtsgeschichte als Zeitgeschichte: Beiträge zur Rechtsgeschichte des 20. Jahrhunderts*. Baden-Baden: Nomos, 2001.

Doering-Manteuffel, Anselm. *Wie westlich sind die Deutschen? Amerikanisierung und Westernisierung im 20. Jahrhundert*. Göttingen: Vandenhoeck & Ruprecht, 1999.

———. 'Westernisierung. Politisch-ideeller und gesellschaftlicher Wandel in der Bundesrepublik bis zum Ende der sechziger Jahre', in Axel Schildt, Detlef Siegfried and Karl Christian Lammers (eds), *Dynamische Zeiten: Die 60er Jahre in den beiden deutschen Gesellschaften* (Hamburg: Hans Christians, 2000), 311–41.

———. 'Freiheitliche demokratische Grundordnung und Gewaltdiskurs: Überlegungen zur "streitbaren Demokratie" und politischen Kultur der Bundesrepublik', in Frank Becker (ed.), *Politische Gewalt in der Moderne: Festschrift für Ulrich Thamer* (Münster: Aschendorff, 2003), 269–84.

———. 'Die deutsche Geschichte in den Zeitbögen des 20. Jahrhunderts', *Vierteljahrshefte für Zeitgeschichte* 62(3) (2014), 321–48.

Donert, Celia. 'From Communist Internationalism to Human Rights: Gender, Violence, and International Law in the Women's International Democratic Federation Mission to North Korea, 1951', *Contemporary European History* 25(2) (2016), 313–33.

Döring, Hans-Joachim. *'Es geht um unsere Existenz': Die Politik der DDR gegenüber der Dritten Welt am Beispiel von Mosambik und Äthiopien*. Berlin: Ch. Links, 1999.

Dreier, Horst. 'Das Bundesministerium der Justiz und die Verfassungsentwicklung in der frühen Bundesrepublik', in Manfred Görtemaker and Christoph Safferling (eds), *Die Rosenburg: Das Bundesministerium der Justiz und die NS-Vergangenheit. Eine Bestandsaufnahme* (Göttingen: Vandenhoeck & Rupprecht, 2013), 88–118.

Dreier, Ralf, Jörn Eckert, Karl A. Mollnau and Hubert Rottleuthner (eds). *Rechtswissenschaft in der DDR 1949–1971: Dokumente zur politischen Steuerung im Grundlagenbereich*. Baden-Baden: Nomos, 1996.

Duranti, Marco. *The Conservative Human Rights Revolution: European Identity, Transnational Politics, and the Origins of the European Union*. Oxford: Oxford University Press, 2017.

Duve, Thomas (ed.). *Entanglements in Legal History: Conceptual Approaches*. Frankfurt/M.: Max Planck Institute for European Legal History, 2014.
Echternkamp, Jörg. '"Verwirrung im Vaterländischen?" Nationalismus in der deutschen Nachkriegsgesellschaft 1945–1960', in Jörg Echternkamp and Sven Oliver Müller (eds), *Die Politik der Nation: Deutscher Nationalismus in Krieg und Krisen 1760–1960* (Munich: Oldenbourg, 2002), 219–46.
Eckart, Jörn (ed.). *Die Babelsberger Konferenz vom 2./3. April 1958. Rechtshistorisches Kolloquium 13.-16. Februar 1992, Christian-Albrechts-Universität Kiel*. Baden-Baden: Nomos, 1993.
Eckel, Jan. *Die Ambivalenz des Guten: Menschenrechte in der internationalen Politik seit den 1940er Jahren*. Göttingen: Vandenhoeck & Ruprecht, 2014.
———. 'Menschenrechte und der Wandel der Außenpolitik in den 1970er Jahren: Die Bundesrepublik im internationalen Vergleich', in Sonja Lesen and Cornelius Torp (eds), *Wo liegt die Bundesrepublik? Vergleichende Perspektiven auf die westdeutsche Geschichte* (Göttingen: Vandenhoeck & Ruprecht, 2016), 185–204.
Eckel, Jan, and Samuel Moyn (eds). *Moral für die Welt? Menschenrechtspolitik in den 1970er Jahren*. Göttingen: Vandenhoeck & Ruprecht, 2012.
Edinger, Michael, and Eugen Schatschneider. 'Terrorism Made in Germany: The Case of the NSU', in Johannes Kiess, Oliver Decker and Elmar Brähler (eds), *German Perspectives on Right-Wing Extremism: Challenges and Comparative Studies* (London: Routledge, 2016), 122–44.
Eley, Geoff. 'Some General Thoughts on Citizenship in Germany', in Geoff Eley and Jan Palmowski (eds), *Citizenship and National Identity in Twentieth-Century Germany* (Stanford, CA: Stanford University Press, 2008), 233–46.
Elzer, Herbert. *Konrad Adenauer, Jakob Kaiser und die 'kleine Wiedervereinigung': Die Bundesministerien im außenpolitischen Ringen um die Saar 1949 bis 1955*. St. Ingbert: Röhrig, 2008.
Engel, Ulf, and Hans-Georg Schleicher. *Die beiden deutschen Staaten in Afrika: Zwischen Konkurrenz und Koexistenz*. Hamburg: Institut für Afrikakunde, 1998.
Engelmann, Roger, and Ilko-Sascha Kowalczuk (eds). *Volkserhebung gegen den SED-Staat: Eine Bestandsaufnahme zum 17. Juni 1953*. Göttingen: Vandenhoeck & Ruprecht, 2011.
Engelmann, Roger, and Clemens Vollnhals (eds). *Justiz im Dienste der Parteiherrschaft: Rechtspraxis und Staatssicherheit in der DDR*. Berlin: Ch. Links, 1999.
Epp, Charles R. *The Rights Revolution: Lawyers, Activists, and Supreme Courts in Comparative Perspective*. Chicago: University of Chicago Press, 1998.
Ericsson, Kjersti, and Eva Simonson (eds). *Children of World War II: The Hidden Enemy Legacy*. New York: Berghahn Books, 2005.
Eslava, Luis, Michael Fakhri and Vasuki Nesiah (eds). *Bandung, Global History, and International Law: Critical Pasts and Pending Futures*. Cambridge: Cambridge University Press, 2017.
Etzel, Matthias. *Die Aufhebung von nationalsozialistischen Gesetzen durch den alliierten Kontrollrat (1945–1948)*. Tübingen: Mohr-Siebeck, 1992.
Evans, Richard J. *In Hitler's Shadow: West German Historians and the Attempt to Escape from the Nazi Past*. New York: Pantheon Books, 1989.

Fahrmeir, Andreas. 'Coming to Terms with a Misinterpreted Past? Rethinking the Historical Antecedents of Germany's 1999 Citizenship Reform', *German Politics & Society* 30(1) (2012), 17–38.

Felske, Karsten. *Kriminelle und terroristische Vereinigungen. §§ 129, 129a, StGB. Reformdiskussion und Gesetzgebung seit dem 19. Jahrhundert*. Baden-Baden: Nomos, 2002.

Ferguson, Niall, Charles S. Maier, Erez Manela and Daniel J. Sargent (eds). *The Shock of the Global: The 1970s in Perspective*. Cambridge, MA: Harvard University Press, 2011.

Feth, Andrea. 'Die Volksrichter', in *Steuerung der Justiz in der DDR: Einflussnahme der Politik auf Richter, Staatsanwälte und Rechtsanwälte* (Bonn: Bundesministerium der Justiz, 1993), 351–77.

Fink, Carol, and Bernd Schaefer (eds). *Ostpolitik 1969–1974: European and Global Responses*. Cambridge: Cambridge University Press, 2009.

Fisch, Jörg. *The Right of Self-Determination of Peoples: The Domestication of an Illusion*. Cambridge: Cambridge University Press, 2015.

Fischer, Wolfgang. *Heimat-Politiker? Selbstverständnis und politisches Handeln von Vertriebenen als Abgeordnete im Deutschen Bundestag 1949 bis 1974*. Düsseldorf: Droste, 2010.

Forner, Sean A. *German Intellectuals and the Challenge of Democratic Renewal: Culture and Politics after 1945*. Cambridge: Cambridge University Press, 2014.

Forster, Elisabeth. 'Threatened by Peace: The PRC's Peacefulness Rhetoric and the "China" Representation Question in the United Nations (1949–1971)', *Cold War History* (online first).

Foschepoth, Josef. 'Das Kreuz mit dem Davidstern: Christen und Juden nach dem Holocaust', in Arno Herzig, Karl Teppe and Andreas Determann (eds), *Verdrängung und Vernichtung der Juden in Westfalen* (Münster: Arday, 1994), 231–44.

———. *Überwachtes Deutschland: Post- und Telefonüberwachung in der alten Bundesrepublik*. Göttingen: Vandenhoeck & Ruprecht, 2013.

———. *Verfassungswidrig! Das KPD-Verbot im Kalten Bürgerkrieg*. Göttingen: Vandenhoeck & Ruprecht, 2017.

Franczak, Michael. 'Human Rights and Basic Needs: Jimmy Carter's North-South Dialogue, 1977–81', *Cold War History* 18(4) (2018), 447–64.

Frei, Norbert. *Karrieren im Zwielicht: Hitlers Eliten nach 1945*. Frankfurt/M.: Campus, 2001.

———. *Vergangenheitspolitik: Die Anfänge der Bundesrepublik und die NS-Vergangenheit*. Munich: Beck, 2003.

Fricke, Karl Wilhelm, and Roger Engelmann. *'Konzentrierte Schläge': Staatssicherheitsaktionen und politische Prozesse in der DDR 1953–1956*. Berlin: Ch. Links, 1998.

Friedman, Sara L. *Exceptional States: Chinese Immigrants and Taiwanese Sovereignty*. Berkeley: University of California Press, 2015.

Friedrich-Ebert-Stiftung (ed.). *Archiv für Sozialgeschichte, Band 44: Die Siebzigerjahre: Gesellschaftliche Entwicklungen in Deutschland*. Bonn: Dietz-Verlag, 2004.

Friedrich, Jörg. *Freispruch für die Nazi-Justiz: Die Urteile gegen NS-Richter seit 1948*. Reinbek: Rowohlt, 1983.

———. *Die kalte Amnestie: NS-Täter in der Bundesrepublik*. Frankfurt/M.: Fischer, 1984.
Fulbrook, Mary. 'Germany for the Germans? Citizenship and Nationality in a Divided Nation', in David Cesarini and Mary Fulbrook (eds), *Citizenship, Nationality, and Migration in Europe* (London: Routledge, 1996), 88–105.
———. *Anatomy of a Dictatorship: Inside the GDR, 1949–1989*. Oxford: Oxford University Press, 1997.
———. *German National Identity after the Holocaust*. Cambridge: Wiley, 1999.
———. '*Ossis* and *Wessis*: The Creation of Two German Societies 1945–1990', in idem (ed.), *20th Century Germany: Politics, Culture and Society 1918–1990* (London: Bloomsbury, 2001), 225–46.
——— (ed.). *Power and Society in the GDR, 1961–1979: The 'Normalisation of Rule'?* New York: Berghahn Books, 2009.
Garrett, Geoffrey, R. Daniel Kelemen and Heiner Schulz. 'The European Court of Justice, National Governments, and Legal Integration in the European Union', *International Organizations* 52(1) (1998), 149–76.
Gassert, Philipp. 'Amerikanismus, Antiamerikanismus, Amerikanisierung: Neue Literatur zur Sozial-, Wirtschafts- und Kulturgeschichte des amerikanischen Einflusses in Deutschland und Europa', *Archiv für Sozialgeschichte* 39 (1999): 531–61.
Gassert, Philipp, and Alan E. Steinweis (eds). *Coping with the Nazi Past: West German Debates on Nazism and Generational Conflict 1955–1975*. New York: Berghahn Books, 2006.
Gehrig, Sebastian. 'Cold War Identities: Citizenship, Constitutional Reform, and International Law between East and West Germany, 1967–75', *Journal of Contemporary History* 49(4) (2014), 794–814.
———. 'Recht im Kalten Krieg: Das Bundesverfassungsgericht, die deutsche Teilung und die politische Kultur der frühen Bundesrepublik', *Historische Zeitschrift* 303(1) (2016), 64–97.
———. 'Reaching Out to the Third World: East Germany's Anti-Apartheid and Socialist Human Rights Campaign', *German History* 36(4) (2018), 574–97.
———. 'Informal Envoys: German Cold War Cultural Diplomacy along the Bamboo Curtain', *Journal of Cold War Studies* (in print).
———. 'Deutsche Staatsangehörigkeit und "Deutschenfähigkeit": Das Teso-Urteil und die Debatten um Migration und bundesdeutsche Selbstbilder in den achtziger Jahren', in Martin Löhnig (ed.), *Juristische Zeitgeschichte der 1980er Jahre* (Tübingen: Mohr-Siebeck, forthcoming).
Gehrig, Sebastian, James Mark, Paul Betts, Kim Christiaens and Idesbald Goddeeris. 'The Eastern Bloc, Human Rights, and the Global Fight against Apartheid', *East Central Europe* 46(2–3) (2019), 290–317.
Geiger, Tim. *Atlantiker gegen Gaullisten: Außenpolitischer Konflikt und innerparteilicher Machtkampf in der CDU/CSU 1958–1969*. Munich: Oldenburg, 2008.
Geppert, Dominik, and Jens Hacke (eds). *Streit um den Staat: Intellektuelle Debatten in der Bundesrepublik 1960–1980*. Göttingen: Vandenhoeck & Ruprecht, 2008.
Geppert, Dominik, and Udo Hengst (eds). *Neutralität – Chance oder Chimäre? Konzepte des Dritten Weges für Deutschland und die Welt*. Munich: Oldenburg, 2005.

Gerhard, Ute. 'Die staatlich institutionalisierte "Lösung" der Frauenfrage: Zur Geschichte der Geschlechterverhältnisse in der DDR', in Hartmut Kaelble, Jürgen Kocka and Helmut Zwahr (eds), *Sozialgeschichte der DDR* (Stuttgart: Klett-Cotta, 1994), 383–403.

———. *Soziologie der Stunde Null: Zur Gesellschaftskonzeption des amerikanischen Besatzungsregimes in Deutschland 1944–1945/46.* Frankfurt/M.: Suhrkamp, 2005.

Getachew, Adom. *Worldmaking after Empire: The Rise and Fall of Self-Determination.* Princeton, NJ: Princeton University Press, 2019.

Geyer, Martin H. 'Die Gegenwart der Vergangenheit: Die Sozialstaatsdebatten der 1970er Jahre und die umstrittenen Entwürfe der Moderne', *Archiv für Sozialgeschichte* 47 (2007), 47–93.

———. 'War over Words: The Search for a Public Language in West Germany', in Willibald Steinmetz (ed.), *Political Languages in the Age of Extremes* (Oxford: Oxford University Press, 2011), 293–330.

Gißibl, Bernhard. 'Deutsch-deutsche Nachrichtenwelten: Die Mediendiplomatie von ADN und DPA im frühen Kalten Krieg', in Gregor Feindt, Bernhard Gißibl and Johannes Paulmann (eds), *Kulturelle Souveränität: Politische Deutungs- und Handlungsmacht jenseits des Staates im 20. Jahrhundert* (Göttingen: Vandenhoeck & Ruprecht, 2017), 227–56.

Glaab, Manuela. 'Geteilte Wahrnehmungswelten: Zur Präsenz des deutschen Nachbarn im Bewußtsein der Bevölkerung', in Christoph Kleßmann, Hans Misselwitz and Günter Wichert (eds), *Deutsche Vergangenheiten – eine gemeinsame Herausforderung: Der schwierige Umgang mit der doppelten Nachkriegsgeschichte* (Berlin: Ch. Links, 1999), 206–20.

Glaeßner, Gert-Joachim. *Herrschaft durch Kader: Leitung der Gesellschaft und Kaderpolitik in der DDR am Beispiel des Staatsapparates.* Berlin: Springer, 2013.

Go, Julian. 'Modelling States and Sovereignty: Postcolonial Constitutions in Asia and Africa', in Christopher J. Lee (ed.), *Making a World after Empire: The Bandung Moment and its Political Afterlives* (Athens, GA: Ohio University Press, 2010), 107–39.

Goebel, Michael. *Anti-Imperial Metropolis: Interwar Paris and the Seeds of Third World Nationalism.* Cambridge: Cambridge University Press, 2015.

Göhring, Joachim. 'Ohne pauschale Verdammnis und Nostalgie – Überlegungen zur aktuellen Beschäftigung mit dem ZBG der DDR', in Jorn Eckert and Hans Hattenhauer (eds), *Das Zivilgesetzbuch der DDR vom 19. Juni 1975* (Goldbach: Keip, 1995), 9–17.

Görtemaker, Manfred, and Christoph Safferling. *Die Akte Rosenburg: Das Bundesministerium der Justiz und die NS-Zeit.* Munich: C.H. Beck, 2016.

Gorsuch, Anne E., and Diane P. Koenker (eds). *The Socialist Sixties: Crossing Borders in the Second World.* Bloomington: Indiana University Press, 2013.

Goschler, Constantin. *Schuld und Schulden: Die Politik der Wiedergutmachung für NS-Verfolgte seit 1945.* Göttingen: Wallstein, 2013.

Gosewinkel, Dieter. *Adolf Arndt: Die Wiederbegründung des Rechtsstaats aus dem Geist der Sozialdemokratie (1945–1961).* Bonn: Dietz, 1991.

———. *Schutz und Freiheit? Staatsbürgerschaft in Europa im 20. und 21. Jahrhundert.* Berlin: Suhrkamp, 2016.

Graf Kielmansegg, Peter. *Das geteilte Land: Deutsche Geschichte 1945–1990*. Munich: Pantheon, 2007.
Grafe, Roman. *Deutsche Gerechtigkeit: Prozesse gegen DDR-Grenzschützen und ihre Befehlshaber*. Munich: Siedler, 2004.
Granieri, Ronald J. *The Ambivalent Alliance: Konrad Adenauer, the CDU/CSU, and the West 1949–1966*. New York: Berghahn Books, 2003.
Grau, Andreas. *Gegen den Strom: Die Reaktion der CDU/CSU-Opposition auf die Ost- und Deutschlandpolitik der sozialliberalen Koalition 1969–1973*. Düsseldorf: Droste, 2005.
Gray, William Glenn. *Germany's Cold War: The Global Campaign to Isolate East Germany, 1949–1969*. Chapel Hill: University of North Carolina Press, 2003.
Greenberg, Udi. *Weimar Century: German Émigrés and the Ideological Foundations of the Cold War*. Princeton, NJ: Princeton University Press, 2014.
Greven, Michael Th. *Politisches Denken in Deutschland nach 1945: Erfahrung und Umgang mit der Kontingenz in der unmittelbaren Nachkriegszeit*. Opladen: Budrich, 2007.
Grigoleit, Klaus Joachim. *Bundesverfassungsgericht und deutsche Frage: Eine dogmatische und historische Untersuchung zum judikativen Anteil an der Staatsleitung*. Tübingen: Mohr-Siebeck, 2004.
Grimm, Dieter. *Souveränität: Herkunft und Zukunft eines Schlüsselbegriffs*. Berlin: Verlagshaus Römerweg, 2009.
Grosescu, Raluca. 'State Socialist Endeavours for the Non-Applicability of Statutory Limitations to International Crimes: Historical Roots and Current Implications', *Journal of the History of International Law* 21 (2019), 239–69.
Gu Weiqun. *Conflicts of Divided Nations: The Cases of China and Korea*. Westport, CT: Praeger, 1995.
Güpping, Stefan. *Die Bedeutung der 'Babelsberger Konferenz' von 1958 für die Verfassungs- und Wissenschaftsgeschichte der DDR*. Berlin: A. Spitz, 1997.
Günther, Frieder. *Denken vom Staat her: Die bundesdeutsche Staatsrechtslehre zwischen Dezision und Integration 1949–1970*. Munich: Oldenbourg, 2004.
———. 'Wer beeinflusst hier wen? Die westdeutsche Staatsrechtslehre und das Bundesverfassungsgericht während der 1950er und 1960er Jahre', in Robert Chr. van Doyen and Martin W.H. Möllers (eds), *Das Bundesverfassungsgericht im politischen System* (Wiesbaden: Springer, 2006), 129–39.
———. 'Ordnen, gestalten, bewahren: Radikales Ordnungsdenken von deutschen Rechtsintellektuellen der Rechtswissenschaft 1920–1960', *Vierteljahrshefte für Zeitgeschichte* 59(11) (2011), 353–84.
———. 'Vom "Rising Star" zum Sündenbock: Ernst Rudolf Huber und die deutsche Staatsrechtslehre', in Ewald Grothe (ed.), *Ernst Rudolf Huber: Staat – Verfassung – Geschichte* (Baden-Baden: Nomos, 2015), 101–18.
———. 'Autonomie im Recht der DDR', in Joachim Rückert and Lutz Raphael (eds), *Autonomie des Rechts nach 1945* (Tübingen: Mohr Siebeck, 2020), 77–88.
Gusy, Christoph. 'Verfassungsumbruch und Staatsrechtswissenschaft: Die Verfassung des Politischen zwischen Konstitutionalismus und demokratischer Republik', in Willibald Steinmetz, Ingrid Gilcher-Holtey and Heinz-Gerhard

Haupt (eds), *Neue Politikgeschichte: Perspektiven einer historischen Politikforschung* (Frankfurt/M.: Campus, 2005), 166–201.

———. 'Laws as the Basis and Object of Political Communication', in Willibald Steinmetz, Ingrid Gilcher-Holtey and Heinz-Gerhard Haupt (eds), *Writing Political History Today* (Frankfurt/M.: Campus, 2013), 191–206.

Haase, Norbert, and Bert Pampe (eds). *Die Waldheimer 'Prozesse' – fünfzig Jahre danach: Dokumentation der Tagung der Sächsischen Gedenkstätten am 28. und 29. September 2000 in Waldheim*. Baden-Baden: Nomos, 2001.

Hacke, Jens. *Philosophie der Bürgerlichkeit: Die liberalkonservative Begründung der Bundesrepublik*. Göttingen: Vandenhoeck & Ruprecht, 2006.

———. 'Der Staat in Gefahr: Die Bundesrepublik der 1970er Jahre zwischen Legitimationskrise und Unregierbarkeit', in Dominik Geppert and Jens Hacke (eds), *Intellektuelle Debatten in der Bundesrepublik 1960–1980* (Göttingen: Vandenhoeck & Ruprecht, 2008), 188–206.

———. *Die Bundesrepublik als Idee: Zur Legitimationsbedürftigkeit politischer Ordnung*. Hamburg: Hamburger Edition, 2009.

Häberlen, Joachim C. *The Emotional Politics of the Alternative Left: West Germany, 1968–1984*. Cambridge: Cambridge University Press, 2018.

Hagen, Katrina. '"Free Angela Davis" Campaign', in Quinn Slobodian (ed.), *Comrades of Color: East Germany in the Cold War* (New York: Berghahn Books, 2015), 157–87.

Hailbronner, Michaela. *Traditions and Transformations: The Rise of German Constitutionalism*. Oxford: Oxford University Press, 2015.

Hanshew, Karrin. *Terror and Democracy in West Germany*. Cambridge: Cambridge University Press, 2012.

Harms, Michael, and Karla Popp (eds). *Westarbeit der FdJ, 1946 bis 1989: Eine Dokumentation*. Berlin: Metropol Verlag, 1997.

Harrison, Henrietta. 'Popular Responses to the Atomic Bomb in China, 1945–1955', *Past & Present* 218(8,1) (2013), 96–118.

Hein, Bastian. *Die Westdeutschen und die Dritte Welt: Entwicklungspolitik und Entwicklungsdienste zwischen Reform und Revolte 1959–1974*. Munich: Oldenbourg, 2005.

Heinemann, Isabel. *Rasse, Siedlung, deutsches Blut: Das Rasse- und Siedlungsamt der SS und die rassenpolitische Neuordnung Europas*. Göttingen: Wallstein, 2003.

Heitzer, Enrico. *Die Kampfgruppe gegen Unmenschlichkeit (KgU): Widerstand und Spionage im Kalten Krieg, 1948–1959*. Cologne: Böhlau, 2015.

Henne, Thomas, and Arne Riedlinger (eds). *Das Lüth-Urteil aus (rechts-)historischer Sicht: Die Konflikte um Veit Harlan und die Grundrechtsjudikatur des Bundesverfassungsgerichts*. Berlin: Berliner Wissenschaftsverlag, 2005.

———. 'Von 0 auf "Lüth" in 6 ½ Jahren: Zu den prägenden Faktoren der Grundsatzentscheidung', in Thomas Henne and Arne Riedlinger (eds), *Das Lüth-Urteil aus (rechts-)historischer Sicht: Die Konflikte um Veit Harlan und die Grundrechtsjudikatur des Bundesverfassungsgerichts* (Berlin: Berliner Wissenschaftsverlag, 2005), 197–224.

Herbert, Ulrich. 'Liberalisierung als Lernprozess: Die Bundesrepublik in der deutschen Geschichte – eine Skizze', in idem (ed.), *Wandlungsprozesse in*

Westdeutschland: Belastung – Integration – Liberalisierung (Göttingen: Wallstein, 2002), 7–49.

———. 'Drei politische Generationen im 20. Jahrhundert', in Jürgen Reulecke (ed.), *Generationalität und Lebensgeschichte im 20. Jahrhundert* (Munich: Oldenbourg, 2003), 95–114.

———. *Geschichte Deutschlands im 20. Jahrhundert.* Munich: C.H. Beck, 2014.

Herf, Jeffrey. *Divided Memory: The Nazi-Past in the Two Germanys.* Cambridge, MA: Harvard University Press, 1997.

———. *Undeclared Wars with Israel: East Germany and the West German Far Left, 1967–1989.* Cambridge: Cambridge University Press, 2015.

Hertfelder, Thomas, and Andreas Rödder (eds). *Modell Deutschland: Erfolgsgeschichte oder Illusion?* Göttingen: Vandenhoeck & Ruprecht, 2008.

Hertle, Hans-Hermann, and Maria Nooke (eds). *Die Todesopfer an der Berliner Mauer: Ein biographisches Handbuch.* Berlin: Ch. Links, 2019.

Herzog, Dagmar. *Sex after Fascism: Memory and Morality in Twentieth-Century Germany.* Princeton: Princeton University Press, 2005.

Heuer, Uwe-Jens (ed.). *Die Rechtsordnung der DDR: Anspruch und Wirklichkeit.* Baden-Baden: Nomos, 1995.

Heuer, Uwe-Jens, and Ekkehard Lieberam. 'Rechtsverständnis in der DDR', in Uwe-Jens Heuer (ed.), *Die Rechtsordnung der DDR: Anspruch und Wirklichkeit* (Baden-Baden: Nomos, 1995), 25–74.

van der Heyden, Ulrich. *GDR Development Policy in Africa: Doctrine and Strategies between Illusions and Reality, 1960–1990. The Example (South) Africa.* Münster: LIT-Verlag, 2013.

Hilgert, Nora. *Unterhaltung, aber sicher! Populäre Repräsentationen von Recht und Ordnung in den Fernsehkrimis 'Stahlnetz' und 'Blaulicht', 1958/59–1968.* Berlin: transcript, 2014.

Hirsch, Francine. 'The Soviets at Nuremberg: International Law, Propaganda, and the Making of the Postwar Order', *American Historical Review* 113(3) (2008), 701–30.

Hirsch, Martin, Dietmut Majer and Jürgen Meinck (eds). *Recht, Verwaltung und Justiz im Nationalsozialismus.* Baden-Baden: Nomos, 1997.

Hobson, John M. 'Provincializing Westphalia: The Eastern Origins of Sovereignty', *International Politics* 46(6) (2009), 671–90.

Hochgeschwender, Michael. *Freiheit in der Offensive? Der Kongress für Kulturelle Freiheit.* Munich: Oldenbourg, 1996.

Hochscherf, Tobias, Christoph Laucht and Andrew Plowman (eds). *Divided, But Not Disconnected: German Experiences of the Cold War.* New York: Berghahn Books, 2010.

Hockerts, Hans Günter (ed.). *Koordinaten deutscher Geschichte in der Epoche des Ost-West-Konflikts.* Munich: Oldenbourg, 2004.

von Hodenberg, Christina. *Konsens und Krise: Eine Geschichte der westdeutschen Medienöffentlichkeit 1945–73.* Göttingen: Wallstein, 2006.

Hoeres, Peter. 'Von der "Tendenzwende" zur "geistig-moralischen Wende": Konstruktion und Kritik konservativer Signaturen in den 1970er und 1980er Jahren', *Vierteljahrshefte für Zeitgeschichte* 61(1) (2013), 93–119.

Hoffmann, Stefan-Ludwig (ed.). *Human Rights in the Twentieth Century*. Cambridge: Cambridge University Press, 2011.
———. 'Viewpoint: Human Rights and History', *Past and Present* 232(2) (2016), 279–310.
Home, Stephan. 'Statehood at the End of the 20th Century – The Model of the "Open State": A German Perspective', *Austrian Review of International Law* 2 (1997), 127–54.
Hong, Young-sun. *Cold War Germany, the Third World, and the Global Humanitarian Regime*. Cambridge: Cambridge University Press, 2015.
Horn, Albrecht. 'Die Deutsche Liga für die Vereinten Nationen (LVN) in der WFUNA', in Klaus Hüfner (ed.), *Kalter Krieg zwischen den deutschen UN-Gesellschaften 1952–1968: Die Auseinandersetzung in der Weltföderation der UN-Gesellschaften* (Berlin: Frank & Timme, 2017), 89–104.
Horster, Maximilian. 'The Trade in Political Prisoners between the Two German States, 1962–89', *Journal of Contemporary History* 39(3) (2004), 403–24.
Howe, Marcus. *Karl Polak: Parteijurist unter Ulbricht*. Frankfurt/M.: Vittorio Klostermann, 2002.
Hsieh, Pasha L. 'The Discipline of International Law in Republican China and Contemporary Taiwan', *Washington University Global Studies Law Review* 14(1) (2015), 87–129.
Hübner, Peter, and Christa Hübner. *Sozialismus als soziale Frage: Sozialpolitik in der DDR und Polen 1968–1976*. Cologne: Böhlau, 2008.
Hübsch, Reinhard (ed.). *'Hört die Signale!' Die Deutschlandpolitik der KPD/SED und SPD 1945–1970*. Berlin: Akademie Verlag, 2002.
Hüfner, Klaus. 'Allgemeinpolitische Rahmenbedingungen', in idem (ed.), *Kalter Krieg zwischen den deutschen UN-Gesellschaften 1952–1968: Die Auseinandersetzung in der Weltföderation der UN-Gesellschaften* (Berlin: Frank & Timme, 2017), 11–26.
———. 'Die deutsche Gesellschaft für die Vereinten Nationen (DGVN) in der WFUNA', in idem (ed.), *Kalter Krieg zwischen den deutschen UN-Gesellschaften 1952–1968: Die Auseinandersetzung in der Weltföderation der UN-Gesellschaften* (Berlin: Frank & Timme, 2017), 37–88.
——— (ed.). *Kalter Krieg zwischen den deutschen UN-Gesellschaften 1952–1968: Die Auseinandersetzung in der Weltföderation der UN-Gesellschaften*. Berlin: Frank & Timme, 2017.
Hunt, Lynn. *Inventing Human Rights: A History*. New York: W.W. Norton, 2007.
———. 'Response to Viewpoint: The Long and the Short of the History of Human Rights', *Past and Present* 233(1) (2016), 323–31.
Iandolo, Alessandro. 'Imbalance of Power: The Soviet Union and the Congo Crisis, 1960–1961', *Journal of Cold War Studies* 16(2) (2014), 32–55.
Ihme-Tuchel, Beate. *Die DDR*. Darmstadt: WBG, 2002.
Jaeger, Alexandra. *Auf der Suche nach 'Verfassungsfeinden': Der Radikalenbeschluss in Hamburg, 1971–1987*. Göttingen: Wallstein, 2019.
Jarausch, Konrad H. 'Die Postnationale Nation: Zum Identitätswandel der Deutschen 1945–1995', *Historicum* (Spring 1995), 30–35.
——— (ed.). *After Unity: Reconfiguring German Identities*. New York: Berghahn Books, 1997.

———. *After Hitler: Recivilizing Germans, 1945–1995*. Oxford: Oxford University Press, 2008.
——— (ed.). *Das Ende der Zuversicht? Die siebziger Jahre als Geschichte*. Göttingen: Vandenhoeck & Ruprecht, 2008.
———. 'Divided, Yet Reunited – The Challenge of Integrating German Post-War Histories', http://h-net.msu.edu/cgi-bin/logbrowse.pl?trx=vx&list=h-diplo&month=1102&week=a&msg=NKgozJwMKmO%2BdgxxrEQNdw&user=&pw= [last access: 5 July 2011].
Jarausch, Konrad H., and Michael Geyer. *Shattered Past: Reconstructing German Histories*. Princeton, NJ: Princeton University Press, 2003.
Jarausch, Konrad H., and Hannes Siegrist (eds). *Amerikanisierung und Sowjetisierung in Deutschland 1945–1970* (Frankfurt/M.: Campus, 1997).
Jasch, Hans-Christian. 'Civil Service Lawyers and the Holocaust: The Case of Wilhelm Stuckart', in Alan Steinweis and Robert Rachlin (eds), *The Law in Nazi Germany: Ideology, Opportunism and the Perversion of Justice* (New York: Berghahn Books, 2013), 37–61.
Jaschke, Hans Gerd. *Streitbare Demokratie und Innere Sicherheit: Grundlagen, Praxis und Kritik*. Opladen: Westdeutscher Verlag, 1991.
Jensen, Steven L.B. *The Making of International Human Rights: The 1960s, Decolonization, and the Reconstruction of Global Values*. Cambridge: Cambridge University Press, 2016.
Jetzlsperger, Christian. 'Die Emanzipation der Entwicklungspolitik von der Hallstein-Doktrin: Die Krise der deutschen Nahostpolitik von 1965, die Entwicklungspolitik und der Ost-West-Konflikt', *Historisches Jahrbuch* 121 (2001), 320–66.
Johnson, Jason B. *Divided Village: The Cold War in the German Borderlands*. London: Routledge, 2017.
Johst, David. *Begrenzung des Rechtsgehorsams: Die Debatte um Widerstand und Widerstandsrechts in Westdeutschland, 1945–1968*. Tübingen: Mohr & Siebeck, 2016.
Joseph, Detlef. 'Der "DDR-Unrechtsstaat" und die Vergangenheitsbewältigung', in Gregor Gysi, Uwe-Jens Heuer and Michael Schumann (eds), *Zweigeteilt: Über den Umgang mit der SED-Vergangenheit* (Hamburg: VSA-Verlag, 1992), 95–119.
Kailitz, Steffen (ed.). *Die Gegenwart der Vergangenheit: Der 'Historikerstreit' und die deutsche Geschichtspolitik*. Wiesbaden: VS Verlag für Sozialwissenschaften, 2008.
Kaiser, Anna-Bettina. *Der Parteienstaat: Zum Staatsverständnis von Gerhard Leibholz*. Baden-Baden: Nomos, 2013.
Kaschuba, Wolfgang. 'Deutsche Wir-Bilder nach 1945: Ethnischer Patriotismus als kollektives Gedächtnis', in Jörg Baberowski, Hartmut Kaelble and Jörg Schriewer (eds), *Selbstbilder und Fremdbilder: Repräsentation sozialer Ordnungen im Wandel* (Frankfurt/M.: Campus, 2008), 295–329.
Kersting, Franz-Werner. 'Helmut Schelskys "Skeptische Generation" von 1957: Zur Publikations- und Wirkungsgeschichte eines Standardwerkes', *Vierteljahrsschrift für Zeitgeschichte* 50 (2002), 465–95.
Keys, Barbara J. *Reclaiming American Virtue: The Human Rights Revolution of the 1970s*. Cambridge, MA: Harvard University Press, 2014.

Kier, Herfrid. 'Die "Affäre Wengler": Ein Beitrag zur Geschichte des Völkerrechtsinstitutes der Kaiser-Wilhelm-Gesellschaft zur Zeit des Nationalsozialismus', *Jahrbuch der Juristischen Zeitgeschichte* 14 (2013), 168–211.

Kilian, Werner. *Die Hallstein-Doktrin: Der diplomatische Krieg zwischen der BRD und der DDR 1955–1973. Aus den Akten der beiden deutschen Außenministerien*. Berlin: Duncker & Humblot, 2001.

Kim, Kyong Ju. *The Development of Modern South Korea: State Formation, Capitalist Development and National Identity*. London: Routledge, 2006.

Kinkela, Claudia. *Die Rehabilitierung des Bürgerlichen im Werk Dolf Sternbergers*. Würzburg: Königshausen & Neumann, 2001.

Kinsbury, Benedict. 'Legal Positivism as Normative Politics: International Society, Balance of Power and Lassa Oppenheim's Positive International Law', *European Journal of International Law* 13 (2002), 401–36.

Kleßmann, Christoph. *Die doppelte Staatsgründung: Deutsche Geschichte 1945–1955*. Bonn: bpb, 1984.

———. *Zwei Staaten, eine Nation: Deutsche Geschichte 1955–1970*. Bonn: bpb, 1988.

———. 'Verflechtung und Abgrenzung: Aspekte der geteilten und zusammengehörigen deutschen Nachkriegsgeschichte', *Aus Politik und Zeitgeschichte* 29/30 (1993), 30–41.

———. 'Der schwierige gesamtdeutsche Umgang mit der DDR Geschichte', *Aus Politik und Zeitgeschichte* 30/31 (2001), 3–5.

———. 'Spaltung und Verflechtung: Ein Konzept zur integrierten Nachkriegsgeschichte 1945 bis 1990', in Christoph Kleßmann and Peter Lautzas (eds), *Teilung und Integration: Die doppelte deutsche Nachkriegsgeschichte als wissenschaftliches und didaktisches Problem* (Frankfurt/M: Wochenschau-Verlag, 2006), 26–37.

Klusmeyer, Douglas B., and Demetrios G. Papademetriou. *Immigration Policy in the Federal Republic of Germany: Negotiating Membership and Remaking the Nation*. New York: Berghahn Books, 2009.

Knabe, Bernd. *Zur Praxis des politischen Strafrechts in der Honecker-Zeit: Fundstücke zu 27 Fällen von Hohenschönhausener Häftlingen*. Baden-Baden: Nomos, 2016.

Knoch, Habbo (ed.). *Bürgersinn mit Weltgefühl: Politische Moral und solidarischer Protest in den sechziger und siebziger Jahren*. Göttingen: Wallstein, 2007.

———. '"Mündige Bürger", oder: Der kurze Frühling einer partizipatorischen Vision. Einleitung', in idem (ed.), *Bürgersinn mit Weltgefühl: Politische Moral und solidarischer Protest in den sechziger und siebziger Jahren* (Göttingen: Wallstein, 2007), 9–56.

Koch, Alexander. *Der Häftlingsfreikauf: Eine deutsch-deutsche Beziehungsgeschichte*. Munich: Allitera, 2014.

Koch, Lars (ed.). *Modernisierung als Amerikanisierung? Entwicklungslinien der westdeutschen Kultur 1945–1960*. Bielefeld: transcript, 2015.

Koischwitz, Svea. *Der Bund Freiheit der Wissenschaften in den Jahren 1970–1976: Ein Interessenverband zwischen Studentenbewegung und Hochschulreform*. Cologne: Böhlau, 2017.

Kopeček, Michal. 'The Socialist Conception of Human Rights and Its Dissident Critique', *East Central Europe* 46(2–3) (2019), 261–89.

Koselleck, Reinhard. *Begriffsgeschichten: Studien zur Semantik und Pragmatik der politischen und sozialen Sprachen. Mit zwei Beiträgen von Ulrike Spree und Willibald Steinmetz sowie einem Nachwort zu Einleitungsfragmenten Reinhart Kosellecks von Carsten Dutt.* Frankfurt/M.: Suhrkamp, 2006.

Koskenniemi, Martti. *The Gentle Civilizer of Nations: The Rise and Fall of International Law 1870–1960.* Cambridge: Cambridge University Press, 2001.

Kossert, Andreas. *Kalte Heimat: Die Geschichte der deutschen Vertriebenen nach 1945.* Bonn: bpb, 2008.

Kössler, Till. *Abschied von der Revolution: Kommunisten und Gesellschaft in Westdeutschland, 1945–1968.* Düsseldorf: Droste, 2005.

Kostal, Rande W. 'The Alchemy of Occupation: Karl Loewenstein and the Legal Reconstruction of Nazi Germany, 1945–1946', *Law and History Review* 1 (2011), 1–52.

Kott, Sandrine. 'Cold War Internationalism', in Glenda Sluga and Patricia Clavin (eds), *Internationalisms: A Twentieth-Century History* (Cambridge: Cambridge University Press, 2017), 340–62.

Kraushaar, Wolfgang (ed.). *Die RAF und der linke Terrorismus.* 2 vols. Hamburg: Hamburger Edition, 2006.

Kretschmann, Carsten. *Zwischen Spaltung und Gemeinsamkeit: Kultur im geteilten Deutschland.* Berlin: be.bra, 2012.

Kronenberg, Volker. *Patriotismus in Deutschland: Perspektiven für eine weltoffene Nation.* Wiesbaden: Springer, 2005.

——— (ed.). *Zeitgeschichte, Wissenschaft und Politik: Der 'Historikerstreit' 20 Jahre danach.* Wiesbaden: VS Verlag für Sozialwissenschaften, 2008.

Krönig, Waldemar, and Klaus-Dieter Müller. *Anpassung, Widerstand, Verfolgung: Hochschule und Studenten in der SBZ und DDR 1945–1961.* Cologne: Verlag Wissenschaft & Politik, 1994.

Kutscher, Hauke-Hendrik. *Politisierung oder Verrechtlichung? Der Streit um die Verfassungsgerichtsbarkeit in Deutschland (1921–1958).* Frankfurt/M.: Campus, 2016.

Kvistad, Gregg O. 'Radicals and the State: The Political Demands on West German Civil Servants', *Comparative Political Studies* 21(1) (1988), 95–125.

van Laak, Dirk. *Gespräche in der Sicherheit des Schweigens: Carl Schmitt in der politischen Geistesgeschichte der frühen Bundesrepublik.* Berlin: Akademie-Verlag, 1993.

———. 'From Conservative Revolution to Technocratic Conservatism', in Jan-Werner Müller (ed.), *German Ideologies: Studies in the Political Thought and Culture of the Bonn Republic* (London: Palgrave Macmillan, 2003), 147–60.

Langguth, Gerd (ed.). *Die Intellektuellen und die nationale Frage.* Frankfurt/M.: Campus, 1997.

Large, David Clay. *Germans to the Front: West German Rearmament in the Adenauer Era.* Chapel Hill: University of North Carolina Press, 1996.

Lee, Christopher J. (ed.). *Making a World after Empire: The Bandung Moment and Its Political Afterlives.* Athens, OH: Ohio University Press, 2010.

Lee, Dong-Ki. *Option oder Illusion? Die Idee einer nationalen Konföderation im geteilten Deutschland 1949–1990.* Berlin: Ch. Links, 2010.

Leibholz, Gerhard, and Hermann von Mangoldt (eds). *Jahrbuch des Öffentlichen Rechts der Gegenwart, Bd. 1. Bearbeitet von Klaus-Berto v. Doemming, Rudolf Werner Füsslein, Werner Matz.* Tübingen: Mohr-Siebeck, 1951.

Lemke, Michael. 'Die Außenbeziehungen der DDR (1949–1966): Prinzipien, Grundlagen, Zäsuren und Handlungsspielräume', in Ulrich Pfeil (ed.), *Die DDR und der Westen: Transnationale Beziehungen 1949–1989* (Berlin: Ch. Links, 2001), 63–80.

Lindenberger, Thomas. 'Tacit Minimal Consensus: The Always Precarious East German Dictatorship', in Paul Corner (ed.), *Popular Opinion in Totalitarian Regimes: Fascism, Nazism, Communism* (Oxford: Oxford University Press, 2009), 208–22.

von Lingen, Kerstin. 'Defining Crimes against Humanity: The Contribution of the United Nations War Crimes Commission to International Criminal Law, 1944–1947', in Morten Bergsmo, Wui Ling Cheah and Ping Yi (eds), *Historical Origins of International Criminal Law* (Brussels: Torksel Opsahl, 2014), 475–506.

Linke, Angelika, and Jakob Tanner (eds). *Attraktion und Abwehr: Die Amerikanisierung der Alltagskultur in Europa*. Cologne: Böhlau, 2006.

Liu, Lydia H. 'Shadows of Universalism: The Untold Story of Human Rights around 1948', *Critical Inquiry* 40(4) (2014), 385–417.

Löhnig, Martin. 'Alternative Legal Publicism? Four Legal Publications from the Long 1970s and Their Reception in Legal Studies and Legal Practice', *Moving the Social: Journal of Social History and the History of Social Movements* 60 (2018), 95–120.

Lohr, Eric. *Russian Citizenship: From Empire to Soviet Union*. Cambridge, MA: Harvard University Press, 2012.

Lorenz, Sophie. '"Heldin des anderen Amerika": Die DDR-Solidaritätsbewegung für Angela Davis, 1970–1973', *Zeithistorische Forschungen* 10(1) (2013), 38–60.

Loth, Wilfried. 'Die Deutschen und die deutsche Frage: Überlegungen zur Dekomposition der deutschen Nation', in idem (ed.), *Die deutsche Frage in der Nachkriegszeit* (Berlin: Akademieverlag, 1994), 214–31.

Low Choo Chin. 'The 1963 Strasbourg Convention on Single Nationality Movement: The German Experience', *Journal of European History of Law* 2 (2014), 41–50.

Lüdtke, Alf, Inge Marssolek and Adelheid von Saldern (eds). *Amerikanisierung: Traum und Alptraum im Deutschland des 20. Jahrhunderts*. Stuttgart: Steiner, 1996.

Maier, Charles S. *The Unmasterable Past: History, Holocaust, and German National Identity*. Cambridge, MA: Harvard University Press, 1988.

———. *Once within Borders: Territories of Power, Wealth and Belonging since 1500*. Cambridge, MA: Harvard University Press, 2016.

Major, Patrick. 'Innenpolitische Aspekte der zweiten Berlinkrise (1958–1961)', in Hans-Hermann Hertle, Konrad H. Jarausch and Christoph Kleßmann (eds), *Mauerbau und Mauerfall: Ursachen, Verlauf, Auswirkungen* (Berlin: Ch. Links, 2002), 97–110.

———. *Behind the Berlin Wall: East Germany and the Frontiers of Power*. Oxford: Oxford University Press, 2009.

Major, Patrick, and Rana Mitter (eds). *Across the Blocs: Cold War Cultural and Social History*. London: Frank Cass, 2004.

———. 'East is East and West is West? Towards A Comparative Socio-Cultural History of the Cold War', in idem (eds), *Across the Blocs: Cold War Cultural and Social History* (London: Frank Cass, 2004), 1–22.

Manela, Erez. *The Wilsonian Moment: Self-Determination and the International Origins of Anticolonial Nationalism*. Oxford: Oxford University Press, 2007.
Markovits, Inga. *Die Abwicklung: Ein Tagebuch zum Ende der DDR-Justiz*. Munich: C.H. Beck, 1993.
———. 'Rechts-Geschichte: Ein DDR-Zivilprozeß aus den 1980er Jahren', in Alf Lüdtke and Peter Becker (eds), *Akten. Eingaben. Schaufenster. Die DDR und ihre Texte. Erkundungen zu Herrschaft und Alltag* (Berlin: Akademie Verlag, 1997), 259–78.
———. *Justice in Lüritz: Experiencing Socialist Law in East Germany*. Princeton, NJ: Princeton University Press, 2010.
Marxen, Klaus, and Annette Weinke (eds). *Inszenierungen des Rechts: Schauprozesse, Medienprozesse und Prozessfilme in der DDR*. Berlin: Berliner Wissenschaftsverlag, 2006.
Mazower, Mark. 'The End of Civilisation and the Rise of Human Rights: The Mid-Twentieth-Century Disjuncture', in Stefan-Ludwig Hoffmann (ed.), *Human Rights in the Twentieth Century* (Cambridge: Cambridge University Press, 2011), 29–44.
———. *Governing the World: The History of an Idea*. London: Allen Lane, 2012.
———. *No Enchanted Palace: The End of Empire and the Ideological Origins of the United Nations*. Princeton, NJ: Princeton University Press, 2013.
Meador, Daniel John. *Impressions of Law in East Germany: Legal Education and Legal System in the German Democratic Republic*. Charlottesville: University of Virginia Press, 1986.
Meining, Stefan. 'Zwischen Nichtbeziehung, Feindschaft und später Annäherung: die Deutsche Demokratische Republik und Israel', in Olaf Glöckner and Julius H. Schoeps (eds), *Deutschland, die Juden und der Staat Israel: Eine politische Bestandsaufnahme* (Hildesheim: Georg Olms Verlag, 2016), 176–91.
Menzel, Jörg. 'Vergangenheitsbewältigung in der frühen Judikatur des Bundesverfassungsgerichts: Beamten- und Gestapo-Urteil', in Thomas Henne and Arne Riedlinger (eds), *Das Lüth-Urteil aus (rechts-)historischer Sicht: Die Konflikte um Veit Harlan und die Grundrechtsjudikatur des Bundesverfassungsgerichts* (Berlin: Berliner Wissenschaftsverlag, 2005), 225–35.
Metzler, Gabriele. 'Staatsversagen und Unregierbarkeit in den siebziger Jahren?', in Konrad H. Jarausch (ed.), *Das Ende der Zuversicht? Die siebziger Jahre als Geschichte* (Göttingen: Vandenhoeck & Ruprecht, 2008), 243–60.
Meuschel, Sigrid. 'Legitimationsstrategien in der DDR und der Bundesrepublik', in Christoph Kleßmann, Hans Misselwitz and Günter Wichert (eds), *Deutsche Vergangenheiten – eine gemeinsame Herausforderung: Der schwierige Umgang mit der doppelten Nachkriegsgeschichte* (Berlin: Ch. Links, 1999), 115–27.
Mikkonen, Simo, and Pia Koivunen (eds). *Beyond the Divide: Entangled Histories of the Cold War*. New York: Berghahn Books, 2015.
Millington, Richard. 'State Power and "Everyday Criminality" in the German Democratic Republic, 1961–1989', *German History* 38(3) (2020), 440–60.
von Miquel, Marc. *Ahnden oder amnestieren? Westdeutsche Justiz und Vergangenheitsbewältigung in den sechziger Jahren*. Göttingen: Wallstein, 2004.
Mohnhaupt, Heinz. 'Europäische Rechtsgeschichte als Zeitgeschichte: Norm und sozialistische Gesetzlichkeit als Forschungsgegenstand', in Gerd Bender

and Ulrich Falk (eds), *Recht im Sozialismus: Analysen zur Normendurchsetzung in osteuropäischen Nachkriegsgesellschaften. Band 3: Sozialistische Gesetzlichkeit* (Frankfurt/M.: V. Klostermann, 1999), 197–228.

Möller, Frank, and Ulrich Mählert (eds). *Abgrenzung und Verflechtung: Das geteilte Deutschland in der zeithistorischen Debatte*. Berlin: Metropol, 2008.

Möller, Horst. '1949 – Zwei Staaten, eine Nation? Zum nationalen Selbstverständnis in den Verfassungen der Bundesrepublik Deutschland und der DDR', in Udo Wengst and Hermann Wentker (eds), *Das doppelte Deutschland: 40 Jahre Systemkonkurrenz* (Berlin: Ch. Links, 2008), 15–33.

———. 'Demokratie und Diktatur', *Aus Politik und Zeitgeschichte* 3 (2007), 3–7.

Möllers, Christoph. 'Pouvoir Constituant-Constitution-Constitutionalism', in Armin von Bogdandy and Jürgen Bast (eds), *Principles of European Constitutional Law* (Oxford/Munich: Hart Publishing/C.H. Beck, 2009), 196–204.

Mollnau, Karl A. 'Sozialistische Gesetzlichkeit in der DDR: Theoretische Grundlagen und Praxis', in Gerd Bender and Ulrich Falk (eds), *Recht im Sozialismus: Analysen zur Normendurchsetzung in osteuropäischen Nachkriegsgesellschaften. Band 3: Sozialistische Gesetzlichkeit* (Frankfurt/M.: V. Klostermann, 1999), 59–196.

———. 'Die staatsanwaltliche Gesetzlichkeitsaufsicht in der DDR als gescheiterter Versuch eines sowjetischen Rechtstransfers', in Gerd Bender and Ulrich Falk (eds), *Recht im Sozialismus: Analysen zur Normendurchsetzung in osteuropäischen Nachkriegsgesellschaften. Band 3: Sozialistische Gesetzlichkeit* (Frankfurt/M.: V. Klostermann, 1999), 241–78.

——— (ed.). *Deutsche Demokratische Republik (1958–1989): Recht und Juristen im Spiegel der Beschlüsse des Politbüros und Sekretariats des Zentralkomitees der SED, 1. Halbband*. Frankfurt/M.: Vittorio Klostermann, 2003.

——— (ed.). *Deutsche Demokratische Republik (1958–1989): Dokumente, 2. Halbband*. Frankfurt/M.: Vittorio Klostermann, 2004.

Morgan, Michael Cotey. *The Final Act: The Helsinki Accords and the Transformation of the Cold War*. Princeton, NJ: Princeton University Press, 2018.

Moses, A. Dirk. *German Intellectuals and the Nazi Past*. Cambridge: Cambridge University Press, 2009.

———. 'Cutting Out the Ulcer and Washing Away the Incubus of the Past: Genocide Prevention through Population Transfer', in Roland Burke, Marco Duranti and A. Dirk Moses (eds), *Decolonization, Self-Determination, and the Rise of Global Human Rights Politics* (Cambridge: Cambridge University Press, 2020), 153–78.

Moyal, Dina. 'Did Law Matter? Law, State, and Individual in the USSR 1953–1982'. PhD diss., Stanford University, 2010.

Moyn, Samuel. *The Last Utopia: Human Rights in History*. Cambridge, MA: Harvard University Press, 2010.

———. *Christian Human Rights*. Philadelphia: University of Pennsylvania Press, 2015.

———. 'Response to Viewpoint: The End of Human Rights History', *Past and Present* 233(1) (2016), 307–22.

———. *Not Enough: Human Rights in an Unequal World*. Cambridge, MA: Belknap Press, 2018.

Moyn, Samuel, and Andrew Sartori. 'Approaches to Global Intellectual History', in idem (eds), *Global Intellectual History* (New York: Columbia University Press, 2013), 3–30.
Mühle, Susanne. *Auftrag: Menschenraub. Entführungen von Westberlinern und Bundesbürgern durch das Ministerium für Staatssicherheit der DDR*. Göttingen: Vandenhoeck & Ruprecht, 2015.
Müller, Ingo. *Furchtbare Juristen: Die unbewältigte Vergangenheit unserer Justiz*. Berlin: Kindler, 1987.
———. 'Die DDR – ein Unrechtsstaat?', *Neue Justiz* 46 (1992), 281–83.
Müller, Jan-Werner. *Another Country: German Intellectuals, Unification and National Identity*. New Haven, CT: Yale University Press 2000.
——— (ed.). *Memory and Power in Post-War Europe: Studies in the Presence of the Past*. Cambridge: Cambridge University Press, 2002.
———. *A Dangerous Mind: Carl Schmitt in Post-War European Thought*. Yale, CT: Yale University Press, 2003.
———. 'From National Identity to National Interest: The Rise (and Fall) of Germany's New Right', in idem (ed.), *German Ideologies since 1945: Studies in the Political Thought and Culture of the Bonn Republic* (London: Routledge, 2003), 185–205.
——— (ed.). *German Ideologies since 1945: Studies in the Political Thought and Culture of the Bonn Republic*. London: Routledge, 2003.
———. *Verfassungspatriotismus*. Berlin: Suhrkamp, 2010.
Müller, Mathias. *Die SPD und die Vertriebenenverbände 1949–1977: Eintracht, Entfremdung, Zwietracht*. Berlin: LIT-Verlag, 2012.
von Münch, Ingo. *Die deutsche Staatsangehörigkeit: Vergangenheit – Gegenwart – Zukunft*. Berlin: de Gruyter, 2007.
Münkler, Herfried, and Jens Hacke. 'Politische Mythologisierungsprozesse in der Bundesrepublik: Entwicklungen und Tendenzen', in idem (eds), *Wege in die neue Bundesrepublik: Politische Mythen und kollektive Selbstbilder nach 1989* (Frankfurt/M.: Campus, 2009), 15–31.
Nachum, Iris, and Sagi Schaefer. 'The Semantics of Political Integration: Public Debates about the Term "Expellee" in Post-War Western Germany', *Contemporary European History* 27(1) (2018), 42–58.
Nathans, Benjamin. 'The Dictatorship of Reason: Aleksandr Vol'pin and the Idea of Rights under "Developed Socialism"', *Slavic Review* 66(4) (2007), 630–63.
———. 'Soviet Rights-Talk in the Post-Stalin Era', in Stefan-Ludwig Hoffmann (ed.), *Human Rights in the Twentieth Century* (Cambridge: Cambridge University Press, 2011), 166–90.
Neubert, Ehrhart. *Geschichte der Opposition in der DDR 1949–1989*. Berlin: Ch. Links, 1998.
Newton, Scott. *Law and the Making of the Soviet World: The Red Demiurge*. London: Routledge, 2015.
Nolte, Paul. *Die Ordnung der deutschen Gesellschaft: Selbstentwurf und Selbstbeschreibung im 20. Jahrhundert*. Munich: Beck, 2000.
Normand, Roger, and Sarah Zaidi. *Human Rights at the UN: The Political History of Universal Justice*. Bloomington: Indiana University Press, 2008.

O'Malley, Alanna. *The Diplomacy of Decolonization: America, Britain and the United Nations during the Congo Crisis 1960–64*. Manchester: Manchester University Press, 2018.

Olick, Jeffrey K. *In the House of the Hangman: The Agonies of German Defeat, 1943–1949*. Chicago: Chicago University Press, 2005.

Osiander, Andreas. 'Sovereignty, International Relations, and the Westphalian Myth', *International Organization* 55(2) (2001), 251–87.

Pahuja, Sundhya. *Decolonising International Law: Development, Economic Growth and the Politics of Universality*. Cambridge: Cambridge University Press, 2011.

Palmowski, Jan. 'Citizenship, Identity, and Community in the German Democratic Republic', in Geoff Eley and Jan Palmowski (eds), *Citizenship and National Identity in Twentieth-Century Germany* (Stanford, CA: Stanford University Press, 2008), 73–91.

——. *Inventing a Socialist Nation: Heimat and the Politics of Everyday Life in the GDR 1945–1990*. Cambridge: Cambridge University Press, 2009.

Panagiotidis, Jannis. 'The Oberkreisdirektor Decides Who Is German: Jewish Immigration, German Bureaucracy, and the Negotiation of National Belonging', *Geschichte und Gesellschaft* 38 (2013), 503–33.

——. 'Germanizing Germans: Co-ethnic Immigration and Name Change in West Germany, 1953–93', *Journal of Contemporary History* 50(4) (2015), 854–74.

Pannen, Ute. 'Bundesbilder: Debatten um die künstlerische Ausgestaltung des Reichstagsgebäudes und das Selbstbild der Berliner Republik', in Herfried Münkler and Jens Hacke (eds), *Wege in die neue Bundesrepublik: Politische Mythen und kollektive Selbstbilder nach 1989* (Frankfurt/M.: Campus, 2009), 171–91.

Paulmann, Johannes. 'Auswärtige Repräsentation nach 1945: Zur Geschichte der deutschen Selbstdarstellung im Ausland', in idem (ed.), *Auswärtige Repräsentationen: Deutsche Kulturdiplomatie nach 1945* (Cologne: Böhlau, 2005), 1–32.

Pedersen, Susan. *The Guardians: The League of Nations and the Crisis of Empire*. Oxford: Oxford University Press, 2015.

Pekelder, Jacco. 'Towards Another Concept of the State: Historiography of the 1970s in the USA and Western Europe', in Cordia Baumann, Sebastian Gehrig and Nicolas Büchse (eds), *Linksalternative Milieus und Neue Soziale Bewegungen in den 1970er Jahren* (Heidelberg: Universitätsverlag Winter, 2011), 61–83.

Pells, Richard. *Not Like Us: How Europeans Have Loved, Hated, and Transformed American Culture since World War II*. New York: Basic Books, 1997.

Perels, Joachim. *Das juristische Erbe des 'Dritten Reiches': Beschädigungen der demokratischen Rechtsordnung*. Frankfurt/M.: Campus, 1999.

Perry, Elizabeth J. 'Chinese Conceptions of "Rights": From Mencius to Mao – and Now', *Perspectives on Politics* 6(1) (2008), 37–50.

Peters, Butz. *Tödlicher Irrtum: Die Geschichte der RAF*. Berlin: Argon, 2004.

Pfeil, Ulrich (ed.). *Die DDR und der Westen: Transnationale Beziehungen 1949–1989*. Berlin: Ch. Links, 2001.

Port, Andrew. *Conflict and Stability in the German Democratic Republic*. Cambridge: Cambridge University Press, 2007.

Priemel, Kim-Christian. *The Betrayal: The Nuremberg Trials and German Divergence*. Oxford: Oxford University Press, 2016.

Pugach, Sara. 'African Students and the Politics of Race and Gender in the German Democratic Republic', in Quinn Slobodian (ed.), *Comrades of Color: East Germany in the Cold War World* (New York: Berghahn Books, 2015), 131–56.
Pula, Besnik. *Globalization Under and After Socialism. The Evolution of Transnational Capital in Central and Eastern Europe*. Stanford, CA: Stanford University Press, 2018.
Quigley, John. *Soviet Legal Innovation and the Law of the Western World*. Cambridge: Cambridge University Press, 2007.
Radkau, Joachim. *Theodor Heuss*. Darmstadt: WBG, 2013.
Rajagopal, Balakrishnan. *International Law from Below: Development, Social Movements and Third World Resistance*. Cambridge: Cambridge University Press, 2003.
Raphael, Lutz, and Anselm Doering-Manteuffel. *Nach dem Boom: Perspektiven auf die Zeitgeschichte seit 1970*. Göttingen: Vandenhoeck & Ruprecht, 2008.
Raschka, Johannes. *Zwischen Überwachung und Repression: Politische Verfolgung in der DDR 1971–1989*. Opladen: Leske+Budrich, 2001.
Reichhelm, Nils. *Die marxistisch-leninistische Staats- und Rechtstheorie Karl Polaks*. Frankfurt/M.: Peter Lang, 2003.
Rennig, Christoph, and Dieter Strempel. *Justiz im Umbruch: Rechtstatsächliche Studien zum Aufbau der Rechtspflege in den neuen Bundesländern*. Cologne: Bundesanzeiger, 1996.
Requate, Jörg. 'Demokratisierung der Justiz? Rechtsstaatlichkeit im Zeichen der Provokation', in Habbo Knoch (ed.), *Bürgersinn mit Weltgefühl: Politische Moral und solidarischer Protest in den sechziger und siebziger Jahren* (Göttingen: Wallstein, 2006), 181–202.
———. *Der Kampf um die Demokratisierung der Justiz: Richter, Politik und Öffentlichkeit in der Bundesrepublik*. Frankfurt/M.: Campus, 2008.
Richardson-Little, Ned. '"Erkämpft das Menschenrecht": Sozialismus und Menschenrechte in der DDR', in Jan Eckel and Samuel Moyn (eds), *Moral für die Welt? Menschenrechtspolitik in den 1970er Jahren* (Göttingen: Vandenhoeck & Ruprecht, 2012), 120–43.
———. 'The Failure of the Socialist Declaration of Human Rights', *East Central Europe* 46(2–3) (2019), 318–41.
———. *The Human Rights Dictatorship: Socialism, Global Solidarity, and Revolution in East Germany*. Cambridge: Cambridge University Press, 2020.
Rigoll, Dominik. *Staatsschutz in Westdeutschland: von der Entnazifizierung zur Extremistenabwehr*. Göttingen: Wallstein, 2013.
Rödder, Andreas. *Wertewandel und Postmoderne: Gesellschaft und Kultur der Bundesrepublik Deutschland 1965–1990*. Stuttgart: Stiftung Bundespräsident-Theodor-Heuss-Haus, 2004.
———. *Deutschland einig Vaterland: Die Geschichte der Wiedervereinigung*. Munich: Beck, 2009.
von Roenne, Hans Hubert. *Politisch untragbar? Die Überprüfung von Richtern und Staatsanwälten der DDR im Zuge der Vereinigung Deutschlands*. Berlin: Akademie-Verlag, 1997.
Rojahn, Gunther. 'Elfes – mehr als ein Urteil: Aufladung und Entladung eines Politikums'. PhD diss., Free University Berlin, 2009.

Romano, Angela. *From Détente in Europe to European Détente: How the West Shaped the CSCE*. Frankfurt/M.: Peter-Lang, 2009.

Rosenfeld, Gavriel David. *The Fourth Reich: The Spectre of Nazism from World War II to the Present*. Cambridge: Cambridge University Press, 2019.

Roth, Florian. *Die Idee der Nation im politischen Diskurs: Die Bundesrepublik Deutschland zwischen Neuer Ostpolitik und Wiedervereinigung (1969–1990)*. Baden-Baden: Nomos, 1995.

Rottleuthner, Hubert. 'Das Ende der Fassadenforschung: Recht in der DDR', *Zeitschrift für Rechtssoziologie* 16 (1995), 30–64.

———. *Karrieren und Kontinuitäten deutscher Justizjuristen vor und nach 1945*. Berlin: Berliner Wissenschaftsverlag, 2010.

Rückert, Joachim. 'Die Beseitigung des Deutschen Reiches – die geschichtliche und rechtsgeschichtliche Dimension einer Schwebelage', in Anselm Doering-Manteuffel (ed.), *Strukturmerkmale der deutschen Geschichte des 20. Jahrhunderts* (Munich: Oldenbourg, 2006), 65–94.

Ruggenthaler, Peter. *The Concept of Neutrality in Stalin's Foreign Policy, 1945–1953*. Lanham, MD: Lexington Books, 2015.

Rürup, Miriam. 'Legal Expertise and Biographical Experience', *Geschichte und Gesellschaft* 43(3) (2017), 438–65.

Salzborn, Samuel. '"Volksgruppenrecht": Zum Transfer(versuch) eines politischen Paradigmas in das europäische Minderheitenrecht', in Vanessa Duss, Nikolaus Linder, Katrin Kastl, Christina Börner, Fabienne Hirt and Felix Züsli (eds), *Rechtstransfer in der Geschichte: Legal Transfer in History* (Munich: Martin Medienbauer Verlag, 2006), 44–59.

Sanchez-Sibóny, Oscar. *Red Globalization: The Political Economy of the Soviet Cold War from Stalin to Khrushchev*. Cambridge: Cambridge University Press, 2014.

Sargent, Daniel. 'Diasporic Citizens: Germans Abroad in the Framing of German Citizenship Law', in K. Molly O'Donnell, Renate Bridenthal and Nancy Reagin (eds), *The Heimat Abroad: The Boundaries of Germanness* (Ann Arbor: University of Michigan Press, 2007), 17–39.

Sarotte, M.E. *Dealing with the Devil: East Germany, Détente, and Ostpolitik, 1969–1973*. Chapel Hill: University of North Carolina Press, 2001.

Saupe, Achim. 'Von "Ruhe und Ordnung" zur "inneren Sicherheit": Eine Historisierung gesellschaftlicher Dispositive', *Zeithistorische Forschungen* 7(2) (2010), 170–87.

Schaefer, Bernd. 'Ostpolitik, "Fernostpolitik," and Sino-Soviet Rivalry: China and the Two Germanys', in Carol Fink and Bernd Schaefer (eds), *Ostpolitik 1969–1974: European and Global Responses* (Cambridge: Cambridge University Press, 2009), 129–47.

Schaefer, Sagi. *States of Division: Border and Boundary Formation in Rural Cold War Germany*. Oxford: Oxford University Press, 2014.

Scheibe, Moritz. 'Auf der Suche nach der demokratischen Gesellschaft', in Ulrich Herbert (ed.), *Wandlungsprozesse in Westdeutschland: Belastung – Integration – Liberalisierung 1945–1980* (Göttingen: Wallstein, 2002), 245–77.

Schildt, Axel. 'Nachkriegszeit: Möglichkeiten und Probleme der westdeutschen Geschichte nach dem Zweiten Weltkrieg und ihrer Einordnung in die westdeutsche Geschichte des 20. Jahrhunderts', *Geschichte in Wissenschaft und Unterricht* 44 (1993), 567–84.

———. *Zwischen Abendland und Amerika: Studien zur westdeutschen Ideenlandschaft der 50er Jahre.* Munich: Oldenbourg, 1999.

———. '"Die Kräfte der Gegenreform sind auf breiter Front angetreten." Zur konservativen Tendenzwende in den Siebzigerjahren', *Archiv für Sozialgeschichte* 44 (2004), 449–80.

Schlak, Stephan. *Wilhelm Hennis: Szenen einer Ideengeschichte der Bundesrepublik.* Munich: C.H. Beck, 2008.

Schmoeckel, Mathias. 'The Story of Success: Lassa Oppenheim and his "International Law"', in Michael Stolleis and Yanagihara Masaharu (eds), *East Asian and European Perspectives on International Law* (Baden-Baden: Nomos, 2004), 57–134.

Schneider, Ute. 'Kommentar zu Frieder Günther', in Joachim Rückert and Lutz Raphael (eds), *Autonomie des Rechts nach 1945* (Tübingen: Mohr Siebeck, 2020), 89–100.

Scholtyseck, Joachim. *Die Außenpolitik der DDR.* Munich: Oldenbourg, 2003.

———. 'Im Schatten der Hallstein-Doktrin: Die globale Konkurrenz zwischen der Bundesrepublik und der DDR', in Eckart Conze (ed.), *Herausforderung des Globalen in der Ära Adenauer* (Bonn: Bouvier, 2010), 79–97.

Schöneburg, Volkmar. 'Recht im nazifaschistischen und im "realsozialistischen" deutschen Staat – Diskontinuitäten und Kontinuitäten', *Neue Justiz* 2 (1992), 49–54.

Schröder, Rainer. *Zivilrechtskultur der DDR. Vol. 1.* Berlin: Dunker & Humblot, 1999.

Schröder, Steffen. 'Die Juristenausbildung in der DDR', in Gerd Bender and Ulrich Falk (eds), *Recht im Sozialismus: Analysen zur Normendurchsetzung in osteuropäischen Nachkriegsgesellschaften. Band 2: Justizpolitik* (Frankfurt/M.: V. Klostermann, 1999), 441–86.

Schröter, Anja. *Ostdeutsche Ehen vor Gericht: Scheidungspraxis im Umbruch 1980–2000.* Berlin: Ch. Links, 2018.

Schulze-Wessel, Julia. 'Macht und Ohnmacht der DDR-Verfassung', in André Brodocz et al. (eds), *Institutionelle Macht: Genese – Verstetigung – Verlust* (Cologne: Böhlau, 2005), 439–52.

Senders, Stefan. '*Jus Sanguinis* or *Jus Mimesis*? Rethinking "Ethnic German" Repatriation', in David Rock and Stefan Wolff (eds), *Coming Home to Germany? The Integration of Ethnic Germans from Central and Eastern Europe in the Federal Republic since 1945* (New York: Berghahn Books, 2002), 87–101.

Sendler, Horst. 'Die DDR – ein Unrechtsstaat – ja oder nein?', *Zeitschrift für Rechtspolitik* 26 (1993), 1–5.

Sheehan, James J. 'The Problem of Sovereignty in European History', *American Historical Review* 111(1) (2006), 1–15.

Sheffer, Edith. *Burned Bridge: How East and West Germans Made the Iron Curtain.* Oxford: Oxford University Press, 2011.

Siegelberg, Mira. *Statelessness: A Modern History.* Cambridge, MA: Harvard University Press, 2020.

Sieveking, Klaus. *Die Entwicklung des sozialistischen Rechtsstaatsbegriffs in der DDR: Eine Studie zur Auseinandersetzung mit dem Rechtsstaat in der SBZ-DDR zwischen 1945 und 1968.* Baden-Baden: Nomos, 1975.

Silomon, Anke. *'Schwerter zu Pflugscharen' und die DDR: Die Friedensarbeit der evangelischen Kirchen in der DDR im Rahmen der Friedensdekaden 1980 bis 1982.* Göttingen: Vandenhoeck & Ruprecht, 1999.

Slaughter, Joseph R. 'Hijacking Human Rights: Neoliberalism, the New Historiography, and the End of the Third World', *Human Rights Quarterly* 40(4) (2018), 735–75.

Slobodian, Quinn. *Globalists: The End of Empire and the Birth of Neoliberalism.* Cambridge, MA: Harvard University Press, 2018.

Smith, Arthur Lee. *Kidnap City: Cold War Berlin.* Westport, CT: Greenwood Press, 2002.

Snyder, Sarah B. *Human Rights Activism and the End of the Cold War: A Transnational History of the Helsinki Network.* Cambridge: Cambridge University Press, 2011.

Sperlich, Peter W. *The East German Social Courts: Law and Popular Justice in a Marxist-Leninist Society.* London: Praeger, 2007.

Spilker, Dirk. *The East German Leadership and German Division: Patriotism and Propaganda, 1945–1953.* Oxford: Clarendon Press, 2006.

Steber, Martina. *Die Hüter der Begriffe: Politische Sprache des Konservativen in Großbritannien und der Bundesrepublik Deutschland 1945–1980.* Berlin: de Gruyter, 2017.

Stein, Mathias. *Der Konflikt um die Alleinvertretung und Anerkennung in der UNO: Die deutsch-deutschen Beziehungen zu den Vereinten Nationen von 1949 bis 1973.* Göttingen: V&R unipress, 2011.

Steinmetz, Willibald. 'New Perspectives on the Study of Language and Power in the Short Twentieth Century', in idem (ed.), *Political Languages in the Age of Extremes* (Oxford: Oxford University Press, 2012), 3–51.

Stephan, Alexander, and Jochen Vogt (eds). *America on My Mind: Zur Amerikanisierung der deutschen Kultur seit 1945.* Paderborn: W. Fink, 2006.

Stevens, Simon. 'Bloke Modisane in East Germany', in Quinn Slobodian (ed.), *Comrades of Color: East Germany in the Cold War World* (New York: Berghahn Books, 2015), 121–30.

Stirk, Peter M. 'The Westphalian Model and Sovereign Equality', *Review of International Studies* 38 (2012), 641–60.

Stockmann, Klaus. *Geheime Solidarität: Militärbeziehungen und Militärhilfen der DDR in die 'Dritte Welt'.* Berlin: Ch. Links, 2010.

Stolleis, Michael. *The Law under the Swastika: Studies on Legal History in Nazi Germany.* Chicago: University of Chicago Press, 1998.

———. *Sozialistische Gesetzlichkeit: Staats- und Verwaltungsrechtswissenschaft in der DDR.* Munich: C.H. Beck, 2009.

——— (ed.). *Herzkammern der Republik: Die Deutschen und das Bundesverfassungsgericht.* Munich: C.H. Beck, 2011.

———. *Geschichte des Öffentlichen Rechts in Deutschland. Vierter Band 1945–1990* (Munich: Beck, 2012).

———. *Geschichte des Öffentlichen Rechts in Deutschland. Dritter Band 1914–1945* (Munich: Beck, 2017).

Strote, Noah Benezra. *Lions and Lambs: Conflict in Weimar and the Creation of Post-Nazi Germany*. New Haven, CT: Yale University Press, 2017.

Teschke, Benno. *The Myth of 1648: Class, Geopolitics and the Making of Modern International Relations*. London: Verso, 2003.

Ther, Phillipp. 'Expellee Policy in the Soviet-Occupied Zone and GDR, 1945–1953', in David Rock and Stefan Wolff (eds), *Coming Home to Germany? The Integration of Ethnic Germans from Central and Eastern Europe in the Federal Republic since 1945* (New York: Berghahn Books, 2002), 56–76.

———. *Die neue Ordnung auf dem alten Kontinent: Eine Geschichte des neoliberalen Europa*. Berlin: Suhrkamp, 2016.

Thomas, Daniel C. *The Helsinki Effect: International Norms, Human Rights, and the Demise of Communism*. Princeton, NJ: Princeton University Press, 2001.

Thomas, Merrilyn. '"Aggression in Felt Slippers": Normalisation and the Ideological Struggle in the Context of Détente and *Ostpolitik*', in Mary Fulbrook (ed.), *Power and Society in the GDR, 1961–1979: The 'Normalisation of Rule'?* (New York: Berghahn Books, 2008), 33–51.

Thompson, Andrew S. 'Tehran 1968 and Reform of the UN Human Rights System', *Journal of Human Rights* 14(1) (2015), 84–100.

Thornhill, Chris. *A Sociology of Constitutions: Constitutions and State Legitimacy in Historical-Sociological Perspective*. Cambridge: Cambridge University Press, 2011.

Thoß, Bruno. 'Die Lösung der Saarfrage 1954/55', *Vierteljahrshefte für Zeitgeschichte* 38(2) (1990), 225–88.

Troche, Alexander. *Ulbricht und die Dritte Welt, Ost-Berlins 'Kampf' gegen die Bonner 'Alleinvertretungsanmaßung'*. Erlangen: Palm und Enke, 1996.

Uelzmann, Jan. 'Building Domestic Support for West Germany's Integration into NATO, 1953–1955', *Journal of Cold War Studies* 2 (2020), 133–62.

Ullrich, Sebastian. *Der Weimar-Komplex: Das Scheitern der ersten deutschen Demokratie und die politische Kultur der Bundesrepublik*. Göttingen: Wallstein, 2009.

Verheyen, Dirk. *The German Question: A Cultural, Historical, and Geopolitical Exploration*. Boulder, CO: Westview Press, 1999.

Völter, Bettina. *Judentum und Kommunismus: Deutsche Familiengeschichten in drei Generationen*. Wiesbaden: Leske+Buderich, 2003.

Vorländer, Hans (ed.). *Die Deutungsmacht der Verfassungsgerichtsbarkeit*. Wiesbaden: Springer-Verlag, 2006.

———. 'Die Deutungsmacht des Bundesverfassungsgerichts', in Robert Chr. van Ooyen and Martin H.W. Möllers (eds), *Das Bundesverfassungsgericht im politischen System* (Wiesbaden: Springer, 2006), 189–99.

Vowinckel, Annette, Marcus M. Payk and Thomas Lindenberger (eds). *Cold War Cultures: Perspectives on Eastern and Western European Societies*. New York: Berghahn Books, 2012.

Wagner, Heike. *Hilde Benjamin und die Stalinisierung der DDR-Justiz*. Aachen: Shaker Verlag, 1999.

Waltz, Susan. 'Universalising Human Rights: The Role of Small States in the

Construction of the Universal Declaration of Human Rights', *Human Rights Quarterly* 23(1) (2001), 44–72.

Wassermann, Hendrik. 'Jurist im Porträt: Otto Kunze (1904–1982) spiritus rector der Rechtspolitischen Kongresse der SPD', *Recht und Politik* 51(2) (2015), 116–17.

Weckel, Ulrike, and Edgar Wolfrum (eds). *'Bestien' und 'Befehlsempfänger': Frauen und Männer in NS-Prozessen nach 1945*. Göttingen: Vandenhoeck & Ruprecht, 2003.

Wehler, Hans-Ulrich. *Deutsche Gesellschaftsgeschichte. Fünfter Band: Bundesrepublik und DDR 1949–1990*. Munich: Beck, 2008.

Wehrs, Nikolai. *Protest der Professoren: Der Bund Freiheit der Wissenschaften in den 1970er Jahren*. Göttingen: Wallstein, 2014.

Weinhauer, Klaus, Heinz-Gerhard Haupt and Jörg Requate (eds). *Terrorismus in der Bundesrepublik*. Frankfurt/M.: Campus, 2006.

Weinke, Annette. 'Die DDR Justiz in der Wende 1989/90', in Günther Heydemann, Gunther Mai and Werner Müller (eds), *Revolution und Transformation in der DDR 1989/90* (Berlin: Duncker & Humblot, 1999), 571–93.

———. *Die Verfolgung von NS-Tätern im geteilten Deutschland: Vergangenheitsbewältigungen 1949–1969 oder eine deutsch-deutsche Beziehungsgeschichte im Kalten Krieg*. Paderborn: Schöningh, 2002.

———. *Gewalt, Geschichte, Gerechtigkeit: Transnationale Debatten über deutsche Staatsverbrechen im 20. Jahrhundert*. Göttingen: Wallstein, 2016.

Weinke, Annette, and Norbert Frei (eds). *Towards a New Moral Order? Menschenrechte und Völkerrecht seit 1945*. Göttingen: Wallstein, 2013.

Weisbrod, Bernd. 'Generation und Generationalität in der neueren Geschichtsschreibung', *Aus Politik und Zeitgeschichte* 8 (2005), 3–9.

Weitz, Eric D. 'Self-Determination: How a German Enlightenment Idea Became the Slogan of National Liberation and a Human Right', *American Historical Review* 120(2) (2015), 489–96.

———. *A World Divided: The Global Struggle for Human Rights in the Age of Nation-States*. Princeton, NJ: Princeton University Press, 2019.

Welsh, Helga A., Andreas Pickel and Dorothy Rosenberg. 'East and West German Identities: United or Divided?', in Konrad H. Jarausch (ed.), *After Unity: Reconfiguring German Identities* (New York: Berghahn Books, 1997), 103–36.

Wengst, Udo, and Hermann Wentker. 'Einleitung', in idem (eds), *Das doppelte Deutschland: 40 Jahre Systemkonkurrenz* (Berlin: Ch. Links, 2008), 7–14.

Wentker, Hermann. *Außenpolitik in engen Grenzen: Die DDR im internationalen System 1949–1989*. Munich: Oldenbourg, 2007.

Werkentin, Falco. *Politische Strafjustiz in der Ära Ulbricht: Vom bekennenden Terror zur verdeckten Repression*. Berlin: Ch. Links, 1997.

Wertheim, Stephan. 'The League of Nations: A Retreat from International Law?', *Journal of Global History* 7 (2012), 210–32.

Wesel, Uwe. *Der Gang nach Karlsruhe: Das Bundesverfassungsgericht in der Geschichte der Bundesrepublik*. Munich: Blessing, 2004.

Westad, Odd Arne (ed.). *Reviewing the Cold War: Approaches, Interpretations, Theory*. London: Frank Cass, 2000.

———. *The Global Cold War: Third World Interventions and the Making of Our Times.* Cambridge: Cambridge University Press, 2007.
Westen, Klaus. 'Das Menschenbild der ZGB der DDR', in Jörn Eckert and Hans Hattenhauer (eds), *Das Zivilgesetzbuch der DDR vom 19. Juni 1975* (Goldbach: Keip, 1995), 94–106.
Wettengel, Michael. '"Politik mit dem Kopf unter dem Arm." Zukunftserwartungen der Abgeordneten des Parlamentarischen Rates während der Beratungen über das Grundgesetz 1948/49', in Henning Albrecht et al. (eds), *Politische Gesellschaftsgeschichte im 19. und 20. Jahrhundert: Festgabe für Barbara Vogel* (Hamburg: Krämer, 2006), 42–62.
Wettig, Gerhard. 'Die Sowjetische Besatzungsmacht und der politische Handlungsspielraum in der SBZ (1945–1949)', in Ulrich Pfeil (ed.), *Die DDR und der Westen: Transnationale Beziehungen 1949–1989* (Berlin: Ch. Links, 2001), 39–62.
———. *Stalin and the Cold War in Europe: The Emergence and Development of the East-West Conflict 1939–1953.* Lanham, MD: Rowman & Littlefield, 2008.
Wheatley, Natasha. 'Mandatory Interpretations: Legal Hermeneutics and the New International Order in Arab and Jewish Petitions to the League of Nations', *Past and Present* 227 (2015), 205–48.
———. 'New Subjects in International Law and Order', in Glenda Sluga and Patricia Clavin (eds), *Internationalisms: A Twentieth Century History* (Cambridge: Cambridge University Press, 2017), 265–86.
———. 'Spectral Legal Personality in Interwar International Law: On New Ways of Not Being a State', *Law and History Review* 35(3) (2017), 753–87.
Wildenthal, Lora. *The Language of Human Rights in West Germany.* Philadelphia: University of Pennsylvania Press, 2013.
Wilkins, Dirk (ed.). *'Reichsbürger' – Ein Handbuch.* Potsdam: Demos – Brandenburgisches Institut für Gemeinwesenberatung, 2015.
Winkler, Heinrich-August. *Der lange Weg nach Westen. Band 2: Vom 'Dritten Reich' bis zur Wiedervereinigung.* Munich: C.H. Beck, 2000.
Winrow, Gareth M. *The Foreign Policy of the GDR in Africa.* Cambridge: Cambridge University Press, 2009.
Winter, Jay, and Antoine Prost. *Rene Cassin and Human Rights: From the Great War to the Universal Declaration.* Cambridge: Cambridge University Press, 2013.
Wirsching, Andreas. *Abschied vom Provisorium: Die Geschichte der Bundesrepublik 1982–1989/90.* Munich: Deutsche Verlagsanstalt, 2006.
———. '1989: Die Mauer fällt. Das Ende des doppelten Deutschlands', in Udo Wengst and Hermann Wentker (eds), *Das doppelte Deutschland: 40 Jahre Systemkonkurrenz* (Berlin: Ch. Links, 2008), 357–74.
Wölbern, Jan Phillipp. 'Die Entstehung des "Häftlingsfreikaufs" aus der DDR, 1962–1964', *Deutschland Archiv* 41(5) (2008), 856–67.
———. *Der Häftlingsfreikauf aus der DDR 1962/63–1989: Zwischen Menschenhandel und humanitären Aktionen.* Göttingen: Vandenhoeck & Ruprecht, 2014.
Wolf, Gerhard. *Ideologie und Herrschaftsrationalität: Nationalsozialistische Germanisierungspolitik in Polen.* Hamburg: Hamburger Edition, 2012.
Wolfrum, Edgar. *Geschichtspolitik in der Bundesrepublik Deutschland: Der Weg zur bundesrepublikanischen Erinnerung 1948–1990.* Darmstadt: Wissenschaftliche Buchgesellschaft, 1999.

———. *Die geglückte Demokratie: Geschichte der Bundesrepublik Deutschland von ihren Anfängen bis zur Gegenwart*. Stuttgart: Klett-Cotta, 2006.

———. 'Epilog oder Epoche? (Rück-)Blick der deutschen Geschichtswissenschaft vom Zeitalter der Zweistaatlichkeit bis zur Gegenwart', in Herfried Münkler and Jens Hacke (eds), *Wege in die neue Bundesrepublik: Politische Mythen und kollektive Selbstbilder nach 1989* (Frankfurt/M.: Campus, 2009), 33–63.

Zürn, Michael, and Nicole Deitelhoff. 'Internationalization and the State: Sovereignty as the External Side of Modern Statehood', in *The Oxford Handbook of Transformations of the State* (Oxford: Oxford University Press, 2015), 193–217.

Index

Academy for State and Legal Sciences, Babelsberg, 89–96, 205–6
Adenauer, Konrad, 1, 2, 3, 45, 46
Adenauer government, 43–44, 55–59
Africa, 106, 267–68; GDR and, 24n63; human rights in, 110–14, 123–24, 138n43; Third World liberation and, 110–14
Ago, Robert, 113
air crash, 142–43
Alleinvertretungsanspruch, 172
Allied Control Council, 34
Allied occupation, 1–2, 266
Allied Travel Office (ATO), 145–46, 160–61
Allies, 3–4, 5, 189–92, 260; citizenship and, 65n84, 74–75, 145–49, 166–72; Eastern bloc and, 106–7; law and, 7–8; Nazis and, 7–8, 34; postwar settlement and, 32–34, 36; West German Parliamentary Council and, 22n28
Altehenger, Jennifer, 25n71
Amnesty International, 25n77
Anghie, Antony, 24n67
Annäherungstheorie (proximity theory), 50
Anschluss, 76, 79
anti-colonialism, 9, 12, 23n60, 98, 137n7, 190
anti-communism, 46, 57, 67n135
anti-fascism, 3–4, 110–11, 113
anti-racism, 110–14, 117–19
antisemitism, 40, 85, 110
Antoniolli, Walter, 197
apartheid, 25n72, 111–14, 138n30
Apel, Hans, 250
Arbeitsgemeinschaft der öffentlichrechtlichen Rundfunkanstalten der Bundesrepublik Deutschland (ARD), 30–32
Arbeitsgemeinschaft Sozialdemokratischer Juristinnen und Juristen (ASJ, Working Group of Social Democratic Jurists), 236–37, 247–48
architecture, 29, 30
ARD. *See Arbeitsgemeinschaft der öffentlichrechtlichen Rundfunkanstalten der Bundesrepublik Deutschland*
Arendt, Hannah, 20n11
Arndt, Adolf, 44–46
ASJ. *See Arbeitsgemeinschaft Sozialdemokratischer Juristinnen und Juristen*
ATO. *See* Allied Travel Office
Aussiedler, 73
Austria, 3, 76, 79, 199–200, 234, 248
Austrian citizenship, 71, 76–80
Axen, Hermann, 127, 131

Babelsberg, 109–10, 114
BACDJ. *See Bundesarbeitskreis Christlich Demokratischer Juristen*
Baden-Baden, 197–98
Baden-Württemberg, 241
Bad Homburg, 71–72
Bahlmann, Kai, 168–69
Bahr, Egon, 105–6, 163
Basic Law, 7, 22n28, 242–48, 250–51; on citizenship, 49–52, 165–67, 172–74; drafting of, 37–38, 63n18, 63n24; KPD and, 55–60, 61; legal disputes over, 43–45, 187–95; preface of, 63n24; socialism and, 41–42, 93
basic rights, 15–16, 116–17, 248–51
Basic Treaty, 163–64, 165, 169, 172, 174, 178n112, 239–40; international law and, 187–94, 197–201
Bauer, Otto, 10
Baumgarten, Arthur, 89, 91, 109

Index

Bavaria, 48–49, 65n75, 85, 189–90, 193–94, 242
Benda, Ernst, 160, 171, 196–97, 200–201, 238–39, 242–43
Bender, Traugott, 241
Benjamin, Hilde, 8, 89, 95
Berlin Declaration, 1945, 33
Berlin Wall, 69, 86, 95, 111, 221, 236; citizenship and, 147–48, 155–56; legal division of people and, 10–12; legal identity clashes and, 96–98; self-determination and, 10–11
Berutowicz, Wlodzimierz, 227
Betts, Paul, 24n68, 25n74
BGH. *See Bundesgerichtshof*
Biafran War, 131
Bitburger Gespräche (Bitburg Talks), 239–40
Blumenwitz, Dieter, 244–45
Böckenförde, Ernst-Wolfgang, 248
Bonifacio, Francesco Paolo, 197
Bonn government, 3–5, 7, 9; citizenship and, 143–45, 148–49, 151–52, 157–65; GDR and legal disputes with, 43–47, 61–62, 229–30; German sovereignty and, 32–33, 60–61; KPD and, 52–60, 61; Law on Temporary Exemption from German Jurisdiction and, 117–18; Saar citizenship and, 49–51; SED and first major legal dispute with, 52–60; self-determination and, 81–83; in transition from Third Reich, 38–43; wartime rights and, 71–76
border control, 187–92, 201, 251, 261
bourgeois law, legal tradition and, 68, 87–92, 93, 95, 111, 226, 231, 247
Brandt, Willy, 12, 13, 16, 105–6, 122, 163, 207–8, 237, 240, 244
Brandweiner, Heinrich, 109
Braun, Sigismund von, 123–24
Brox, Hans, 196–97
Brubaker, Rogers, 70
Brückmann case, 167–72
Büchner-Uhder, Willi, 116–17
Buck, Bernhard, 92–93
Bulgaria, 204, 234
Bundesarbeitskreis Christlich Demokratischer Juristen (BACDJ, Federal Association of Christian Democratic Lawyers), 236–37, 240, 242, 244, 247
Bundesbürger, 221
Bundesgerichtshof (BGH, Federal Court of Justice), 57
Büttner, Horst, 89

Caldwell, Peter C., 88–89, 237
Canada, 142–43
capitalism, 95, 109, 204, 231, 235
Carter, Jimmy, 240
Catholic Church, 66n96
CCP. *See* Chinese Communist Party
CDU. *See Christlich Demokratische Union Deutschlands*
Charter 77, 25n72
China, 12, 33, 124, 267; PRC, 13, 24n65, 25n74, 110, 119, 126, 129–30, 133–34, 203, 269, 274n41; UN membership and, 110, 112, 119, 126–34, 140n109
Chinese Communist Party (CCP), 110
Christlich Demokratische Union Deutschlands (CDU), 228–29, 240–41, 243
CIC. *See* Counterintelligence Corps
citizenship, 4, 21n24, 101n77; administrative authority and, 84–87, 154–57; Allies and, 65n84, 74–75, 145–49, 166–72; Austrians and, 71, 76–80; Basic Law on, 49–52, 165–67, 172–74; Berlin Wall and, 147–48, 155–56; Bonn government and, 143–45, 148–49, 151–52, 157–65; Brückmann case and, 167–72; of children, 156, 160, 164–65; Cold War politics and, 75–76, 79–80, 142–43, 153–55; communism and, 72; criminality and, 152, 154, 157–62, 173–74, 222; in Czechoslovakia, 77–78; decolonization and, 143; denazification and, 65n84; double, 161–62, 164–65; Eastern legal reform and, 153–57; ethnicity and, 81–83, 85–86, 159, 270; Federal Administrative Court on, 76–80; foreign policy and, 142–43, 149–52, 155–56, 160–62, 164–66; FRG and, 11 12, 72–74, 84–86, 150–66; GDR and, 11–12, 14–15, 70–75, 84–86, 142–74, 175n25, 189, 246–47, 260–66; German sovereignty and, 69–70, 143, 151–52, 166–74; homeland and, 78–79; international law and, 154–66; Law for the Protection of Citizenship and Human Rights of Citizens and, 117–18; Law for the Regulation of Questions of Citizenship and, 78–79; legal elite on, 145–53; modernization and, 159–60, 164–66; *mündige Bürger* and, 16, 265–66; propaganda on, 74, 148–49; Saar, 47–52, 65n80, 65n84; SED and, 14–15, 143–52, 157–58, 174; in Soviet Union, 23n55; under Third Reich, 65n80, 69, 70–71,

74–75, 77–79, 86, 97, 150, 156; in US, 268–69; wartime rights and, 70–76. *See also* naturalization
Citizenship Law, 11, 164–65
Civil Code, 21n24
civil law, 18n5
civil rights, 23n61, 211, 246, 248, 263
civil unrest, 53, 226–28, 248
Cold War, 2, 29–30, 251, 259–60; Cuban Missile Crisis and, 153; German unification and, 55, 269–72; human rights and, 24n68, 26n80, 248–49; legal legacies in unified Germany, 269–72; new alliances of, 34; rights and, 4, 5; World War II and, 6–8
Cold War politics, 185–86, 234; citizenship and, 75–76, 79–80, 142–43, 153–55; international law and, 198, 248–49, 261–69; law and, 4, 5–8, 18n5, 37–38, 46, 88–92, 95; Ostpolitik and, 105–6; UN membership and, 115, 118–24, 266
Cologne district court, 67n135
colonialism, 76, 141n145; postcolonialism and, 267, 273n28. *See also* anti-colonialism; decolonization; imperialism
colonial peoples, 108, 135, 190
communism, 10, 33, 72, 110, 209–10; KPD and, 52–60, 61
Communist Party of Germany. *See Kommunistische Partei Deutschlands*
Constitution: of GDR, 19n7, 37–38, 39, 88, 202, 220–28, 253n14; Stalin, 88–89; Weimar, 6
constitutionalism, 10, 15, 17, 203, 220–28, 232, 235, 244, 253n14
constitutional patriotism (*Verfassungspatriotismus*), 16, 221, 248–51
continuity theory (*Kontinuitätstheorie*), 52
Corves, Erich, 154
Counterintelligence Corps (CIC), 238
Cremer, Fritz, 183, 184, 215n1
Crimea, 269
crime prevention, 204, 225–28, 242
Criminal Code, 21n24, 222, 225
criminality, 8, 204, 225–26; citizenship and, 152, 154, 157–62, 173–74, 222; emigration and, 146
Cuban Missile Crisis, 153
cultural memory politics, 245
Czechoslovakia, 77–78, 142

DDR-Bürger, 143–44, 147–48, 156
DDR-Staatsbürgerschaft, 11, 143–44, 147–48, 150, 165, 265
Decker, Günter, 81–84, 98
decolonization, 32, 262; citizenship and, 143; human rights and, 9, 135–36; international law and, 52, 185–86, 202; self-determination and, 83–84, 98; sovereignty and, 9, 24n67, 95, 135, 137n16
Dehler, Thomas, 45, 46
denazification, 7, 33, 65n35, 65n84
Department of Justice, US (DOJ), 46
Derlig, Annemarie, 157–58
Deutsches Büro für Friedensfragen (German Office for Questions of Peace), 65n84
deutsche Staatsangehörigkeit, 144, 154–56
Dickel, Friedrich, 152
Diestelkamp, Bernhard, 20n14, 36
discrimination, 40, 86, 110–14, 117–19, 209–10, 251
District Court, 17, 49–50, 67n135, 242
'Divided Germany' (Henselmann), 29, 30, 31
divided nations: global conflicts and, 266–69; legal division of people, 10–16; sovereignty of, 107–8, 122–26, 129–34, 259–63
Dlugosch, Erna, 84–85
Döblitz, Karl, 205–6
DOJ. *See* Department of Justice, US
domestic legality, 117–18, 228–33
domestic sovereignty, 96. *See also* German sovereignty
Dönitz, Karl, 40–41
Dorls, Fritz, 40
Drath, Martin, 60

Eastern bloc, 3–5; administrative authority in, 84–87; Allies and, 106–7; fact-finding missions by, 201–6; international law and, 33; Law on Temporary Exemption from German Jurisdiction and, 117–18; naturalization in, 86; socialism and, 11. *See also specific topics*
East German Committee for the Protection of Human Rights, 114
East German League for the United Nations, 110
economic rights, 96, 127–28, 226, 233–36
ECSC. *See* European Coal and Steel Community

EDC. *See* European Defence Community
EEC. *See* European Economic Community
effectiveness principle, 91–92
Ehmke, Horst, 46, 237
elections, 35, 38, 238–39, 241
Elfes, Wilhelm, 146, 175n21
Emergency Laws, 238–39
emigration, 109, 146, 215n1, 251
Entwicklungsgesetzmäßigkeit, 68
ethnicity, 81–83, 85–86, 159, 190–91, 270
EU. *See* European Union
European Coal and Steel Community (ECSC), 44
European Convention on Human Rights, 24n68
European Defence Community (EDC), 43–47
European Economic Community (EEC), 215, 226
European Union (EU), 269
exiles, 74–75
extraterritorial rights, 86, 167

fact-finding missions, 201–6
Family Code, 21n24
FAZ. *See Frankfurter Allgemeine Zeitung*
Federal Administrative Court, 76–80
Federal Association of Christian Democratic Lawyers. *See Bundesarbeitskreis Christlich Demokratischer Juristen*
Federal Constitutional Court: Basic Treaty trial and, 187–95; Brückmann case and, 167–72; German sovereignty and, 43–47; high court networks and, 195–201; Karl Loewenstein Papers, 65n75; Karlsruhe court and, 196–201, 244–45; KPD trial and, 52–60; Saarland trial and, 43–52; SRP trial and, 40–43. *See also* judiciary
Federal Court of Justice. *See Bundesgerichtshof*
Federal Law on Expellees and Exiles, 74
Federal Republic of Germany (FRG), 1, 3–5, 20n14, 68–70, 112, 190–91, 260–62, 265, 271; Basic Law and, 193–95, 251; bourgeois, socialism, and, 87–92; citizenship and, 11–12, 72–74, 84–86, 150–66; German Reich and, 38–47; human rights and, 25n77, 209, 228; KPD and, 52–60, 61; legal identity in, 221–22; legalist language and, 7–8; NATO and, 43; Nazi Party and judiciary of, 22n29; radicalization and, 87–92, 193–94; Saar

citizenship and, 47–52; wartime rights and, 73
Fichte, Johann Gottlieb, 10
First World War, 10, 76
Fischer, Oskar, 210, 230–31
Florin, Peter, 183
Fluchthilfe, 173
Foreign Office, 72–74, 150–56, 164–71, 222–23
foreign policy, 24n63, 111–13, 123; citizenship and, 142–43, 149–52, 155–56, 160–62, 164–66. *See also* international law; United Nations
formierte Gesellschaft, 116
Forsthoff, Ernst, 243, 256n125
France, 43, 47–51, 115
Francois-Poncet, André, 1
Frankfurter Allgemeine Zeitung (FAZ), 149, 151, 255n91
freedom, 237, 239–43, 247
freiheitlich-demokratische Grundordnung (free and democratic basic political order), 41–42
FRG. *See* Federal Republic of Germany
Friedrich, Carl J., 37, 62n13
Fruhtrunk, Günter, 183
Führerprinzip, 42

GDR. *See* German Democratic Republic
Geiger, Willi, 244
gender equality, 164
General Assembly, UN, 23n62, 124, 136, 183
General Treaty, 199–200
Genscher, Hans-Dietrich, 165–66
Gerber, Friedrich, 6
Gerhardt, Rudolf, 255n91
German Autumn, 244, 249–50
German Democratic Republic (GDR), 1–5, 68–70; administrative authority disputes and, 84–87; Africa and, 24n63; Bonn government and legal disputes with, 43–47, 61–62, 229–30; bourgeois, socialism, and, 87–92; breaking down invisible Western wall against, 145–49; citizenship and, 11–12, 14–15, 70–75, 84–86, 142–74, 175n25, 189, 246–47, 260–66; Constitution of, 19n7, 37–38, 39, 88, 202, 220–28, 253n14; domestic human rights and, 228–33; economic regulations and, 226, 233–36; formation of, 8; German Reich and, 38–47; independent GDR sovereignty and socialist law, 92–96; KPD and, 52–60,

61; naturalization, 85–86; radicalization and, 193–95; *Rechtsstaat* in crisis and, 240–48; UN membership for, 105–36, 207–14; wartime rights and, 70–76. *See also specific topics*

German-German border: border control and, 187–92, 201, 251, 261; deaths, 18n3; formation and postwar history of, 20n18. *See also* Berlin Wall

German-German relations, 12, 122, 163; fact-finding missions and, 201–6; first major battle and, 52–60; high court networks and, 195–201; historiography on, 105–8; international law and, 195–214; national division and, 186–215. *See also specific topics*

German Office for Questions of Peace (*Deutsches Büro für Friedensfragen*), 65n84

German Reich, 10–16, 29–32, 90–92, 201; end of German sovereignty and, 43–47; FRG and, 38–47; GDR and, 38–47; international law and, 32–36; legal continuity and Nazi past, 38–43; managing transitions and legal status of, 34–36; *Reichsraum* and, 38, 40; setbacks of claiming continuity with, 47–52; settling into frameworks of continuity with, 60–61; SRP and, 38–43; unheeded warnings to continuity with, 36–38; wartime rights and, 70–76. *See also specific topics*

German Society for International Law, 34

German sovereignty, 1–3, 259–72; under Bonn government, 3, 7; Bonn government and, 32–33, 60–61; citizenship and, 69–70, 143, 151–52, 166–74; contesting, 8–10; Federal Constitutional Court and, 43–47; first major battle over, 52–60; German Reich and end of, 43–47; Hallstein Doctrine and, 128–29; human rights and, 190–93; independent GDR sovereignty and socialist law, 92–96; legal continuity and, 38–43; legal elite and, 90–96; legal positivism and, 68–69; managing transitions in, 34–36; Ostpolitik and, 12–17, 144–45, 194–96, 236–39, 243–44; state legitimacy and, 207–14; UN on, 8–10, 12–13, 110–11, 119, 129–36; World War II and, 6–7. *See also specific topics*

German unification, 2–3, 37–38, 55–56, 269–72

Gesamtdeutschland, 37, 246
gifts, 183–85
Gliedstaaten, 193
globalization, 215n8
global rights, 5
Global South, 15, 112, 229, 251, 267–68
Globke, Hans, 57
Goldberg, Arthur, 122–23
Goppel, Alfons, 189
Gorbachev, Mikhail, 233, 234
Gosewinkel, Dieter, 11, 70
Graefrath, Bernard, 209–10
Grigoleit, Klaus Joachim, 187
Gross, Leo, 9

Habermas, Jürgen, 16, 250–51
Hacker, Jens, 63n33, 245–47
Hager, Kurt, 95, 233
Hague Academy for International Law, 205–6
Hague Convention, 150
Hallstein Doctrine, 62, 128–29
Hammarskjöld, Dag, 105, 113, 123, 127
Hänsel, Erich, 205
Härle, Elfried, 109
Häusler, Gerhard, 204
Havel, Vaclav, 25n72
Heimatvertriebene, 74
Heinemann, Gustav, 154, 238–39, 241
Heller, Hermann, 6
Helsinki Accords, 14–15, 186, 201, 211–13, 228, 231, 246, 248, 261–62
Hennis, Wilhelm, 238–39
Henselmann, Josef, 29, 30, 31, 60
Herrmann, Joachim, 222
Herzog, Roman, 242–43
Hesse, Konrad, 249–50
Heusinger, Hans-Joachim, 212
Heuss, Theodor, 30, 108
high court networks, 195–201
Higher State Court, 48, 59, 77, 167
Hill, Hermann, 247
Hillermeier, Karl, 242
Himmler, Heinrich, 75–76
Hirsch, Martin, 174, 239, 244, 247
Historikerstreit, 250–51
Hitler, Adolph, 40–41, 239
Holocaust, 34, 259
Homeland (*Heimat*), 40, 78–84
Honecker, Erich, 203, 220–21, 223–24, 233
human rights, 4, 5, 20n11, 216nn7–8, 216n10; activism, 25n77, 53–54, 114–16, 186, 209,

263; in Africa, 110–14, 123–24, 138n43; basic rights and, 15–16, 116–17, 248–51; Basic Treaty and, 189–91; Cold War and, 24n68, 26n80, 248–49; constitutionalism and, 220–28; convention, 115, 161, 206, 211, 216n8, 225, 229–30; covenant, 115, 118, 120–21, 135, 191, 202, 206, 211, 225, 231–32, 246, 251; decolonization and, 9, 135–36; domestic realities of, 228–33; economic rights and, 233–36; ethnicity and, 190–91; European Convention on Human Rights and, 24n68; FRG and, 25n77, 209, 228; German sovereignty and, 190–93; homeland as, 40, 80–84; international law and, 187–94, 206–14, 231–32, 248–52; legalist language and, 14–15, 115–18; revolution of, 24n68; self-determination and, 10, 12–15, 81–84, 98, 107, 114–18, 135–36, 143, 190, 264; Socialist Declaration of Human Rights and, 232–33; in Soviet Union, 25n70, 105, 118–19, 223; Third World liberation and, 124–25; UN and, 32–33, 206–14, 229–30; Universal Declaration of Human Rights and, 24n68, 36; UN membership and, 114–18, 124–26, 135–36, 140n101

ICJ. See International Commission of Jurists
identity: legal, 96–98, 214–15, 221–22, 231, 250, 261–62; national, 70, 149, 221, 245–47, 250–51, 262
identity theory (*Identitätstheorie*), 245–46
ideology: architecture and, 29; international law and, 22n39, 186, 267–68; of law, 1–2, 3, 5
immigration, 85, 109, 146, 164, 215n1, 241, 251, 270
imperialism, 94–95, 153, 209–10, 268
imperial legal doctrine, 68
India, 267
internal security, 225, 242, 247
International Commission of Jurists (ICJ), 53–54
international law: Basic Treaty and, 187–94, 197–201; citizenship and, 154–66; Cold War politics and, 198, 248–49, 261–69; colonialism and, 141n145; debates, 14–16; decolonization and, 52, 185–86, 202; Eastern bloc and, 33; German-German relations and, 195–214; German Reich and, 32–36; German Society for International Law and, 34; human rights and, 187–94, 206–14, 231–32, 248–52; ideology and, 22n39, 186, 267–68; Ostpolitik and, 244–46; politics of, 97–98; self-determination and, 95; separated legal identities and, 214–15; socialism and, 202–5; on sovereignty, 8–10, 21n22, 23n46, 23n62, 24n67, 60–61, 106–8, 117–18, 121–22; UN and, 8–10, 12–13, 23n62, 108–14, 121–26, 195–214, 267–69; World War II and, 23n62
international sovereignty, 96, 117–18, 121–22, 152
Investigation Committee of Free Jurists. See *Untersuchungsausschuß Freiheitlicher Juristen*
Iron Curtain, 53, 105–6, 151–52, 154, 186, 252, 262

Jaeger, Renate, 247
Jahn, Gerhard, 168, 190, 197
Jaurès, Jean, 10
Jellinek, Georg, 6–7, 21n22, 34, 49, 52, 61, 259
Journal for Legal Politics (*Zeitschrift für Rechtspolitik*), 236–40
Jovanovic, Blazo, 197
judiciary, 7, 192–95, 244, 247–50; cleansing of judicial elites, 8, 22n33; Federal Constitutional Court and, 40–47; high court networks and, 195–201; Nazi Party and, 22n29

Kaiser, Jakob, 73, 84
Kant, Immanuel, 10
Karlsruhe court, 196–201, 244–45 See also Federal Constitutional Court
Kaul, Friedrich, 54, 57–60
Keller, Rupprecht von, 121–22
Kelsen, Hans, 6, 21n22, 33–36
Kennan, George, 263
Kerimov, Dzhangir A., 90
Kern, Karl-Hans, 208–9
Kiesinger, Kurt Georg, 122, 153
Kleberg, Ernst-August, 71–73
Klenner, Hermann, 114–17
Kohl, Helmut, 242–43, 250
Kommunistische Partei Deutschlands (KPD, Communist Party of Germany), 52–60, 61, 67n135, 90
Königstein Circle, 71–73
Kontinutitätstheorie (continuity theory), 52
Korber, Horst, 168

Korea, 12, 129, 131, 136, 267
Korean War, 105
Korinek, Karl, 248–49
Korovin, Evgeny A., 10
KPD. *See* Kommunistische Partei Deutschlands
Kraus, Herbert, 82, 100n59
Krenz, Egon, 232
Kriele, Martin, 191–92
Kröger, Herbert, 54, 109
Küffner, Hanns, 58–59
Kunze, Otto, 237
Kusnezov, W. W., 227

Laband, Paul, 6
Lafontaine, Oskar, 270
Lassalle, Ferdinand, 10
Laun, Rudolf, 80–81
law. *See specific topics*
Law for the Protection of Citizenship and Human Rights of Citizens, 117–18
Law for the Regulation of Questions of Citizenship, 78–79
Law in Our Time (*Recht in unserer Zeit*) (Mollnau, Schöneburg, Weichelt), 224–25
Law on the Temporary Exemption from German Jurisdiction, 117–18
lawyers' associations, 247
League of Nations, 7, 12, 23n61, 76, 110, 219n109, 267
legal codes, 7–8, 15–16, 21n24, 92, 95–96, 225–26
legal doctrine, 7, 68, 96–98, 118, 134, 144, 191–92, 259–60
legal education, 14–15, 202–6, 224–27, 240–42
legal elite, 90–92, 191–93, 202; on citizenship, 145–53; on independent GDR sovereignty and socialist law, 92–96; legal identity and, 87–98; national division and, 96–98. *See also* judiciary
legal exceptionalism, 13, 134–36
legal identity: in FRG, 221–22; legal elite and, 87–98; national division and, 96–98, 261–62; separation of, 214–15; socialist constitutionalism and, 222–28
legalist language, 5, 7–8, 11, 14–15, 25n72, 36, 115–18
legal positivism, 68–69
legal revanchism, 80–84, 115–18, 167, 172
legal spheres, 52, 59, 69, 92–93, 186–87, 192, 203–6, 228, 238, 252, 262, 268; in division of people, 10–16

legal tradition, 7–10, 68–76, 87–92, 97–98, 190, 201–2, 226, 262
legal universes, 14–16, 105–6
Leibholz, Gerhard, 45–46
Lekschas, John, 226
Lenin, Vladimir, 22n45, 94, 106–7. *See also* Marxist-Leninist ideology
Leverenz, Bernhard, 192–93
Lex, Ritter von, 56
Liang, Yuen-li, 112–13
Lie, Trygve, 108
Linse, Walter, 53–54, 66n107
Liu, Lydia, 137n13
Loewenstein, Karl, 6, 46, 65n75
Lopatka, Adam, 234
Lorenz, Peter, 241
Löwenthal, Richard, 239
Lücke, Paul, 160
Luhmann, Nikolas, 240

Makarov, Alexander, 77, 79, 164–65
Malik, Yakov A., 127–28, 132
Mangoldt, Hermann von, 50–51
Mann, Francis A., 34
Maron, Karl, 175n25
Marx, Karl, 10, 235
Marxist-Leninist ideology, 10–11, 95
Maunz, Theodor, 193–94, 217n41
McCarthy, Joseph, 46
McNulty, Anthony B., 171
media, 29, 30–32, 57, 149, 151, 157–58, 187–88, 192–93, 200–201, 225. *See also Der Spiegel, Frankfurter Allgemeine Zeitung*
Melsheimer, Ernst, 89
militant democracy. *See streitbare Demokratie*
Ministry for Foreign Affairs, 203–4, 207, 210–11
Ministry for All-German Affairs, 81–84, 149, 152
Ministry of Justice, 49–51, 146, 154, 159–60, 198, 203–7, 211, 240; socialist constitutionalism and, 222–25
Ministry of the Interior, 71–74, 84–86, 155, 159–62, 165–66
modernization, 159–60, 164–66, 187
Moldt, Ewald, 210–12
Mollnau, Karl A., 68, 224–25
Moyn, Samuel, 24n68
Müller, Josef, 77–78
mündige Bürger, 16, 265–66

Nathan, Hans, 88–89

Nathans, Benjamin, 25n70
national division: German-German relations and, 186–215; imperialism and, 94–95; law during, 3–16; legal identity and, 96–98, 261–62
national identity, 70, 149, 221, 245–47, 250–51, 262
national self-determination, 4
national self-interest, 263–66
National Socialism, 38, 41–42. *See also* Nazi Party; Nazi rule; Nazis; Third Reich
NATO, 43, 145–46, 160–61
naturalization, 11–12, 72, 158–60; forced, 173–74; GDR, 85–86; under Third Reich, 74–75, 78–79
natural law, 6–7, 10, 115, 263–64
Nawiasky, Hans, 6, 34, 63n18
Nazi Party, 6–7, 22n29, 239; *Reichskonkordat* and, 66n96; SRP and, 38–43
Nazi rule, 3–4, 11
Nazis, 5, 110–11, 259; Allies and, 7–8, 34; denazification and, 7, 33, 65n35, 65n84; kidnappings of, 23n57; legal continuity and past of, 38–43; neo-Nazism and, 209; pension claims and, 64n46; prosecution of, 57–58
Nazi victim claims, 22n35, 63n32
neo-Nazism, 209
Nestler, Paolo, 183, 185
New International Economic Order (NIEO), 268
Nixon administration, 131
nuclear weapons, 214
Nuremberg Laws, 40–41, 75, 97, 266

Occupation Statute, 1, 38
October Revolution, 23n55, 106
Oppenheim, Lassa, 10, 23n46
Ostpolitik, 23n58, 24n65, 119, 135, 155, 173, 187, 203; German sovereignty and, 12–17, 144–45, 194–96, 236–39, 243–44; high court networks and, 195–96; history of, 105–6, 122; international law and, 244–46

Palestine, 267
Palmowski, Jan, 108
Parliamentary Council, 16, 22n28, 36–37, 43, 50, 60, 63n18, 117, 165, 228
partition, 267, 273n28
party politics, 236–37
Pashukanis, Evgeny, 10

patriotism, 16, 221, 248–51
peace rallies, 53
Peace Treaties of 1648, 9
Peck, Joachim, 90–91
pension claims, 64n46
People's Republic of China (PRC), 13, 24n65, 25n74, 110, 119, 126, 129–30, 133–34, 203, 269, 274n41
Perry, Elizabeth, 25n74
Pieck, Wilhelm, 38, 108
Polak, Karl, 36, 68, 88–90, 94–95, 101n82, 102n122, 106, 137n8
Poland, 29, 175n25, 194–95, 226–28, 234–35
political cleansing, 8, 22n33, 61
political magazines, 187, 188. *See also Der Spiegel*
political rights, 15, 120, 124–25, 211, 229–30, 251
politics, 1, 3, 236–37; cultural memory, 245; of international law, 97–98; of law, 14–16, 96–98, 198–205, 212, 228, 231, 239–41, 248–49, 266–69; of sovereignty, 132, 188, 262, 264. *See also specific topics*
Poppe, Eberhard, 233
Posser, Diether, 247
postcolonialism, 267, 273n28
Potsdam Agreement, 3–4, 33, 38
PRC. *See* People's Republic of China
prisoners of war (POWs), 34
propaganda, 207; on citizenship, 74, 148–49; Cold War, 234; law and, 25n71, 57–58, 91–92, 95, 232
protest movements, 53, 248
provisional state, 37–38, 55–56, 130–31, 135
proximity theory (*Annäherungstheorie*), 50
public security, 227, 242, 244

The Quiet Room, 183, 185

racism, 110–14, 117–19, 138n30, 209–10, 251
radicalization, 72–74, 193–95
RAF. *See* Rote Armee Fraktion
Ranke, Hans, 95, 211
Reagan, Ronald, 232
Recht in unserer Zeit. See Law in Our Time
Rechtsstaat, 2–3, 57, 240–48
reconstruction, 1, 7, 36, 156, 266
Red Army Faction. *See* Rote Armee Fraktion
refugees, 74–75
Reichsbürger, 201, 271
Reichskonkordat, 66n96
Reichsraum, 38, 40

Reimann, Max, 55–56
Remer, Otto Ernst, 40
Renger, Annemarie, 207–8, 219n109
Research Centre for Self-Determination and Nationality Politics, 69, 81
revolutionary legality, 8
Richterstaaten, 200
Riege, Gerhard, 148, 156
rights: civil, 23n61, 211, 246, 248, 263; Cold War and, 4, 5; economic, 96, 127–28, 226, 233–36; extraterritorial, 86, 167; global, 5; history of, 5–6; to homeland (*Heimat*), 78–84; law and, 5, 14–16; political, 15, 120, 124–25, 211, 229–30, 251; SED and, 14–15; separated legal universes and rights universes, 14–16; social, 248; socialism and, 14–15, 25n74, 96, 107–8, 114–21; in US, 115; wartime, 70–76. *See also citizenship*; human rights
Rinck, Hans-Justus, 199
The Rising Man sculpture (Cremer), 183, 184, 215n1
Ritterspach, Theodor, 196–97
Rote Armee Fraktion (RAF, Red Army Faction), 241
rule of law, 2–3
rules consciousness, 15, 225, 265–66, 273n22
Rummel, Alois, 250
Rupp, Hans Georg, 196–97, 199, 244
Russia. *See* Soviet Union

Saar citizenship, 47–52, 65n80, 65n84
Saar Statute, 47, 50–51, 189–90
Sanchez-Sibony, Oscar, 255n86
Sarge, Günter, 234–35
Schätzel, Walter, 74–76
Scheel, Walter, 198–99
Schelsky, Helmut, 239–40
Schenck, Guntram von, 171
Scheuner, Ulrich, 44, 85–87
Schiffer, Eckart, 161–62
Schmid, Carlo, 37
Schmitt, Carl, 6
Schnekenburger, Hubert, 151–52
Schnippenköter, Swidbert, 128
Schöneburg, Karl-Heinz, 224–25
Schönfeld, Peter, 166
Schumacher, Kurt, 37
Schwarzer, Herbert, 187
Second World War, 6–8, 23n62, 32–34, 36, 114–15

SED. *See* Sozialistische Einheitspartei Deutschlands
Seebohm, Hans-Christoph, 50–51
Seidl, Alfred, 241
self-determination, 4, 246; anti-colonialism and, 23n60, 190; Berlin Wall and, 10–11; decolonization and, 83–84, 98; ethnicity and, 81–83; homeland and, 80–84; human rights and, 10, 12–15, 81–84, 98, 107, 114–18, 135–36, 143, 190, 264; international law and, 95; Saar citizenship and, 51; socialism and, 10–12, 107–8; Soviet Union and, 137n7; UN membership and, 114–18, 135–36. *See also* national self-determination
Seuffert, Walter, 168, 171–73, 190, 193–94, 196–97, 244
Simon, Helmut, 199
Sixth Criminal Senate, Federal Court of Justice (BGH), 57
Smirnov, Leo, 205
social citizenship, 15
Social Democratic Legal Politics (memorandum), 243
Social Democratic Party. *See Sozialdemokratische Partei Deutschlands*
socialism, 3–6; Basic Law and, 41–42, 93; bourgeois and, 87–92; Eastern bloc and, 11; economic rights and, 96; independent GDR sovereignty and socialist law, 92–96; international law and, 202–5; law propaganda and, 25n71; National, 38, 41–42; rights and, 14–15, 25n74, 96, 107–8, 114–21; self-determination and, 10–12, 107–8; SRP and, 38–43; UN membership rules and, 109–10, 118–26. *See also* Sozialistische Einheitspartei Deutschlands
socialist constitutionalism, 10, 15, 17, 203, 220–28, 232, 235
Socialist Declaration of Human Rights, 232–33
Socialist International, 10
socialist law, 14–15, 68–70, 137n8, 150, 201–5, 224, 226, 235–36, 263–66; GDR sovereignty and, 92–98; scholarly disputes, 88–92; Yugoslavia and, 196. *See also specific topics*
socialist legality, 3–7, 25n72, 221, 251–52, 261; domestic human rights and, 228–33; economic regulations and, 233–36;

legal division and, 10–13; separated rights universes and, 14–16; socialist constitutionalism and, 222–26. *See also specific topics*
Socialist Reich's Party. *See* Sozialistische Reichspartei
Socialist Unity Party. *See* Sozialistische Einheitspartei Deutschlands
social rights, 248
Solidarność movement, 226, 227–28
Sorgenicht, Klaus, 222
sovereignty, 4; anti-colonialism and, 9, 98; decolonization and, 9, 24n67, 95, 135, 137n16; of divided nations, 107–8, 122–26, 129–34, 259–63; domestic, 96; international, 96, 117–18, 121–22, 152; international law on, 8–10, 21n22, 23n46, 23n62, 24n67, 60–61, 106–8, 117–18, 121–22; Jellinek's three components of, 61; Oppenheim on, 23n46; politics of, 132, 188, 262, 264; World War II and, 6–7, 23n62. *See also* German sovereignty
sovereignty doctrine, 106–7
Soviet bloc, 43
Soviet High Court, 227
Soviet Institute of State and Law, 10
Soviet legal traditions, 69, 88–89, 138n25, 223
Soviet Occupation Zone, 1, 128
Soviet Union, 8, 171, 227, 255n86, 269–70; anti-colonialism and, 137n7; citizenship in, 23n55; human rights in, 25n70, 105, 118–19, 223; October Revolution and, 23n55; SED and, 43; self-determination and, 137n7; UN and, 23n62, 127–28, 205–6
Sozialdemokratische Partei Deutschlands (SPD, Social Democratic Party), 44, 236–37, 270
Sozialistische Einheitspartei Deutschlands (SED, Socialist Unity Party), 8, 9, 11, 23n57, 33, 261–62; Basic Law and, 37; bourgeois and, 87–88, 91–92; citizenship and, 14–15, 143–52, 157–58, 174; constitutionalism and, 220–28; domestic human rights and, 232–33; KPD and, 52–60, 61; legal status and, 36, 61; Nazi victim claims and, 22n35, 63n32; political cleansing within, 61; rights and, 14–15; socialist law and, 93–94; Soviet Union and, 43; UN membership and, 105–14, 122, 127, 129–31, 205, 207, 211

Sozialistische Reichspartei (SRP, Socialist Reich's Party), 241; German Reich and, 38–43; trial against, 40–43
Spätaussiedler, 73
SPD. *See Sozialdemokratische Partei Deutschlands*
Der Spiegel, Frankfurter Allgemeine Zeitung, 120, 131, 157, 187–88, 200
SRP. *See* Sozialistische Reichspartei
Staat, 6, 61
Staatsangehörigkeit, 11, 148, 265
Staatsbürgerschaft, 11, 143–44, 147–48, 150, 165, 265
Staatsgebiet, 6, 61
Staatsgerichtshof, 80
Staatsrecht, 6–7, 10, 33–37, 70, 89, 98, 190–91, 193, 195–96, 259–60
Staatsrechtslehre, 33–34
Staatsvolk, 6, 49, 61, 150, 260–61
Stalin, Joseph, 55
Stalin Constitution, 88–89
Stanovnik, Janez, 128
Stasi, 2–3
state-society relations, 15–16, 243, 265
state succession, 36, 91, 113, 191–92
Stavropoulos, Konstantinos A., 12–13, 119, 127–29, 132
Stein, Erwin, 57
Steinberger, Helmut, 244
Steinbuch, Karl, 239
Steiniger, Peter Alfons, 36, 38, 88–89, 95, 98, 110–11, 116, 212–14
Sternberger, Dolf, 221
Stibi, Georg, 111–12, 120
Stockholm Peace Appeal, 214, 234
Stoph, Willy, 162
Strasbourg Declaration, 251
Strauß, Franz-Josef, 242–43
streitbare Demokratie, 58
Stuckart, Wilhelm, 40–41
successor state, 61, 92, 118
Suhr, Dieter, 247
symbolic politics, 1, 3

Taiwan, 13, 122–23, 126, 133, 269
Tarchov, V. A., 88
television, 187, 225
Teltschik, Horst, 228
Temporary Travel Documents (TTDs), 145
Tenbruck, Friedrich, 243
Terebilov, Vladimir, 205, 234

territorial expansion and dispute, 3–4
territorial integrity, 90–91, 118, 136, 190, 201, 213–14, 231, 261–62, 268
territory zones, 38, 39; border control and, 187–92, 201, 251, 261
terrorism, 240–42, 247, 248
Thant, 112–13, 116, 119–20, 125, 131–34, 137n16
Ther, Phillip, 274n43
Third Criminal Senate, Federal Court of Justice (BGH), 57
Third Reich, 1–4, 7, 8, 18n5, 41, 259–60; Bonn government transitions from, 38–43; citizenship under, 65n80, 69, 70–71, 74–75, 77–79, 86, 97, 150, 156; naturalization under, 74–75, 78–79; *Reichskonkordat* and, 66n96; wartime rights and, 70–76
Third World, 52
Third World liberation, 9–10, 83–84, 106–7, 111–14, 124–25, 140n101, 262
Thomas, Daniel C., 212
Tilmann, Winfried, 240, 247
Toeplitz, Heinrich, 87, 89, 146, 205, 209–10, 227–28, 230–31, 233–34
Träger, Ernst, 244
travel visas, 160–61
treason, 158
TTDs. *See* Temporary Travel Documents
Tunkin, Grigory, 205–6
two-state theory, 94
Tyrol *Optanten*, 165–66

UDHR. *See* Universal Declaration of Human Rights
UFJ. *See* Untersuchungsausschuß Freiheitlicher Juristen
Ukraine, 269
Ulbricht, Walter, 43, 69, 92–94, 98, 99n8, 101n82, 102n122, 105–7, 126, 222–23
UNIDO. *See* United Nations Industrial Development Organization
United Nations (UN), 7, 140n110; Charter, 213; General Assembly, 23n62, 124, 136, 183; on German sovereignty, 8–10, 12–13, 110–11, 119, 129–36; gifts to, 183; human rights and, 32–33, 206–14, 229–30; international law and, 8–10, 12–13, 23n62, 108–14, 121–26, 195–214, 267–69; International Year Against Racism and Racial Discrimination, 209–10; procedural rules of, 121–26

United Nations Industrial Development Organization (UNIDO), 131
United Nations (UN) membership: China and, 110, 112, 119, 126–34, 140n109; Cold War politics and, 115, 118–24, 266; double standards and, 126–34; GDR and, 105–36, 207–14; human rights and, 114–18, 124–26, 135–36, 140n101; importance of, 108–11; legal exceptionalism and, 134–36; SED and, 105–14, 122, 127, 129–31, 205, 207, 211; self-determination and, 114–18, 135–36; socialism and rules of, 109–10, 118–26; Third World liberation and, 107, 111–14, 140n101
United States (US), 22n45, 232, 238, 240; China and, 133–34; citizenship in, 268–69; DOJ, 46; on German citizenship, 74–75; Nixon administration and, 131; rights in, 115; Vietnam and, 133
Universal Declaration of Human Rights (UDHR), 24n68, 36
universalism of law, 261, 265–66
universality principle, 120, 127, 214
Unrechtsstaat (unlawful state), 2–3, 18n5
Untersuchungsausschuß Freiheitlicher Juristen (UfJ, Investigation Committee of Free Jurists), 53–54, 148
US. *See* United States

Verrechtlichung von Politik, 5
Versailles Treaty, 20n14
Vietnam, 12, 122–23, 129, 131, 133, 267, 269
Vogel, Hans-Jochen, 168
Volksdeutsche, 74–76, 78–79, 85
Volkszugehörigkeit, 78–79, 162, 268
voting, 72, 151
Vyshinsky, Andrey, 10, 88–89, 97

Wannsee Conference, 40–41
Warsaw Pact, 226, 234
wartime rights, 70–76
Wassermann, Rudolf, 247
Weather Forecast map, 31, 32, 187
Wehner, Herbert, 122, 159–60
Wehrverfassung, 43
Weichelt, Wolfgang, 224–25, 235
Weimar Constitution, 6
Weimar Republic, 6–7, 70, 239
Weitz, Eric D., 4, 20n11
Wengler, Wilhelm, 190–91, 216n25

Western bloc, 3–5, 26n81; legal revanchism and, 80–84; wartime rights resurrected by, 70–76. *See also specific topics*
Westernized civilization, 109, 115, 137n13
West German army, 43–44
West German Parliamentary Council, 16, 22n28, 36–37, 43, 50, 60, 63n18, 117, 165, 228
Westphalian myth, 9, 264
WFUNA. *See* World Federation of United Nations Associations
White Books, 228
WHO. *See* World Health Organization
Wildenthal, Lora, 25n77, 80
Wilson, Woodrow, 22n45
Winters, Peter Jochen, 157
Wintrich, Josef, 48–49, 56, 58
Winzer, Otto, 119, 125–26, 132, 212
Wirsing, Giselher, 157
Wolff, Friedrich, 209–10

women, 164
Working Group of Social Democratic Jurists. *See Arbeitsgemeinschaft Sozialdemokratischer Juristinnen und Juristen*
World Fair, Brussels, 29, 30
World Federation of United Nations Associations (WFUNA), 120, 207–8
World Health Organization (WHO), 120, 122

Year of Human Rights, 118, 123–25
Yugoslavia, 196

Zeidler, Wolfgang, 244, 248
Zeitschrift für Rechtspolitik (Journal for Legal Politics), 236–40
Ziegler, Walter, 205
Zweistaatlichkeit (two-state theory), 94

www.ingramcontent.com/pod-product-compliance
Lightning Source LLC
Chambersburg PA
CBHW071148070526
44584CB00019B/2708